AMERICAN RIPPER

The Enigma Of America's Serial Killer Cop

PATRICK KENDRICK

International Standard Book Number 13: 978-1-60452-163-4
International Standard Book Number 10: 1-60452-163-5
Library of Congress Control Number: 2020939189

BluewaterPress LLC
2922 Bella Flore Ter
New Smyrna Beach FL 32168

Softback or hardback copy version of this book may be purchased online at www.bluewaterpress.com.

Caution: this book contains depictions of graphic crime scenes. It is not recommended for young readers.

It's a terrible, an inexorable, law that one cannot deny the humanity of another without diminishing one's own; in the face of one's victim, one sees oneself.

—James Baldwin

Acknowledgments

This is a true story. The truth of this story, and the subsequent recording of its facts, could not have been presented without obtaining the aid of many dozens of persons. These people, for the most part, worked without financial gain, or for any other reason, other than being concerned enough to help see that the truth would be told. Not all of the hundreds of people who helped (mostly in supplying information relevant to this case) can be personally thanked by listing their names. This is particularly true of all the police and sheriff departments, without whom I could not have written this book. However, I will try to thank all of those people, without whom the book would not have been just difficult, it would have been impossible. Many of these people are now retired and some have died but their contributions must still be recognized.

I would like to thank, first of all, State Attorney Robert Stone, 19th Judicial Circuit, and his assistants, for all the many years it took to write this book. A special thanks to Marjorie Gorday and Nora Walthers. I would also like to thank Elton Schwarz, Public Defender, 19th Judicial Circuit, and his assistants. I would like to express my gratitude to almost all of the police and sheriff departments in the following counties in the state of Florida: Martin, St. Lucie, Palm Beach, Broward, Monroe, and Miami-Dade, but in particular; Capt. Patrick Duvall and the St. Lucie County Sheriff Department, Capt. David Yurchuk and the Broward County Sheriff Department. Capt. Ben Butler of the Plantation Police Department. J.J. Slattery, Tom Neighbors, and Sgt. Steve Newell of the Palm Beach County Sheriff Department. Helen Horn and Ruth McDougall at the Ft. Lauderdale Police Department, Lt. Mark Schneider,

Lake Park Police Department, and Lt. James Norman, Monroe County Sheriff's Department.

I would also like to give special thanks to the medical people involved, including: Dr. Joseph Davis, Miami Medical Examiner, Dr. Richard Souviron of Coral Gables for his forensic dental expertise, Debra Patterson, a psychologist and friend whose contributions were most helpful with this book.

A very big thank you to Gerald Arenberg of Police Times Magazine for his help in obtaining my investigative journalist credentials, and his personal support many years ago.

I would also like to thank the Palm Beach Post-Times, especially Randy Schultz, editor, for allowing excerpts from stories printed in that newspaper in May of 1973, and July of 1985. A special thanks to Bill Clarke and Dick Donovan and especially Miss Jayne Ellison, a distinguished reporter whom I look up to with great respect. Also, thanks to the late author, John D. MacDonald for his advice on the publishing business, and to author Harry Crews, whose insights and opinions about the case were helpful. Thanks to authors Rex Burns and Tim Cahill, and especially to Elaine Viets, without whom I may have given up on this project. Thank you to authors, Carla Norton and Harriet J. Ottenheimer, for looking at my manuscript and providing your thoughts and blurbs.

My thanks to the legal people involved, including: Michael Tarkoff, attorney, and Sandy Brown for her advice and knowledge, and a most special thanks to Livvie, paralegal and my sister, for her wonderful clerical assistance over the years. Thank you, Christine Wilburn, my attorney that stuck with me for years.

Thank you to my wife, Lisa, for allowing me to break my promise and publish this story, and to Joseph Clark at BluewaterPress LLC for publishing it.

A very special thanks to the families of the victims, who allowed me into their homes and lives and shared their tragedies with me. God bless you all.

A Bell Tolls

A bell tolls
The grey mist
Sneaks across
A cold dead fi eld
Into the forest of
Bewilderment
A real dream
Dies
Despairs
Icy fingers
Crawl across the
Dead body of Hope.
I asked
Little,
I gave
Everything
I am left with
Nothing.

~ Gerard John Schaefer,
the murderer

Day of Sorrow

It's only been a couple days
but it seems like twenty years.
Although he cannot hear me now,
I still shed many tears.
It seems as though when I look back
his face is what I see
and I softly call his name
He even answers me.
The sun will shine for me no more
My life is fi lled with gloom.
And when most people have their spring,
For me the fl owers won't bloom.
My future seems so awfully dark
'cause I am all alone.
To say, "farewell" I took some fl owers
And placed them on his tombstone.

~Susan Kay Place,
one of the victims.

Contents

Other books by Patrick Kendrick

Acoustic Shadows

Extended Family

The Savants

Papa's Problem

visit Patrick Kendrick's website at:

www.talesofpatrickkendrick.com

Chapter 1

The Abduction

I heard a slight groan, and I knew that it was the groan of mortal terror.

From *The Tell-Tale Heart,* by Edgar Allan Poe

July 21, 1972

At the end of a warm and brilliant day, Nancy Ellen Trotter, 18, and Paula Sue Wells, 17, trudged their way along highway A1A trying to hitch a ride. They'd been enjoying the Florida sun on the welcoming shores of Jensen Beach and now they faced the task of getting home. Home being a temporary place in Stuart, a then small town with a populace of about five thousand, that lay a short distance to the south of Jensen Beach. The girls walked slowly, occasionally extending a thumb when a car would go by. They were sunburned and tired, but pleasantly gratified as only a day at the beach can gratify two young girls, with adventure in their hearts.

Nancy and "Sue," as her friends called her, had only known each other a short while. They'd met while both were hitchhiking to Chicago. They quickly became friends and decided to abandon the Chicago trip and "thumb to Florida to get a suntan." The girls were similar in height and build, beyond that they were complete opposites. Nancy was fair-skinned, with long straight blonde hair that ran down almost as far as her elbows. Sue was darker, her hair short, wavy and almost black. Both girls were attractive, especially so in their bikinis, but they wore loose-fitting clothes over their swimsuits, an example of the modesty with which they were raised. The two of them came from equally small towns: Nancy from Farmington, Michigan, and Sue from Garland, Texas. Small towns like these seem to instill in their young a good sense of morals, even if in so doing they also instill an almost unbearable and universal curiosity that eventually compels girls like Nancy and Sue to wander out and find answers to questions a small town cannot answer.

The girls barely heard the sheriff's car as it idled up next to them and stopped. The squawk and fuzz of the radio brought their attention around to the patrol car. A Martin County Sheriff's Deputy stared out at them from behind the green-tinted window glass.

On the side of most sheriffs' and police cars are the words: "To Serve, To Protect," usually above and below the star-shaped insignia on the car door. Sometimes the words are stamped into their badges or delicately engraved on plaques or whatnots around the department's offices. Regardless of where the words are found, or if they are found, they are always implied. The words symbolize the whole meaning of law enforcement in general. They are the servants of the public, the protectors of the people. When you are in distress, the sheriff is a welcome sight. They make you feel safe.

"You girls know it's illegal to hitchhike?" the deputy asked as he stepped out of the car.

The girls looked nervously at each other and shrugged their shoulders. They shook their heads, indicating that they did not know it was illegal to hitchhike in that area.

The patrolman's attitude seemed to ease up a little and he slid back behind the wheel of the car. Nancy and Sue suspected they might be in some sort of trouble, so they did not move. They heard the deputy call into his station. They did not know to whom he was speaking, but heard him say, "I've got two girls here...requesting permission to take them home." A moment later, the deputy got out of the car, came around and opened the back door for the girls.

"It's okay," he said. "I'm going to give you a ride home."

The girls were somewhat relieved as they climbed into the back seat. It was a hot, searing Friday afternoon, certainly too warm to walk all the way to Stuart. It was July, and July in Florida is only slightly cooler than August, which is like saying the fire is cooler than the proverbial frying pan. The girls would appreciate an air-conditioned ride home. They could find no reason to complain about a gallant deputy chauffeuring them to their door. And he was more than hospitable now, in fact at one point, telling stories of his own hitchhiking experiences throughout Europe and the US. Joking about how sometimes you could never get a ride, and then one lone car would pick you up and just take you forever.

The deputy was Gerard John Schaefer, 26, a former patrolman with the Wilton Manor Police Department in Broward County, Florida. He displayed an encompassing, outgoing manner and would later be described by one person, as "a good guy who looked like Hoss of the Cartwrights on Bonanza." He began work with the Martin County Sheriff's Department and was on the job barely more than a month when he picked up Nancy Trotter and Sue Wells. He had not passed his probationary period, lasting less than a year, at Wilton Manor Police Department, but found work easily enough with the Sheriff's Department. Later, it would be discovered that he'd forged a letter of recommendation from Wilton Manor.

The letter, filled with high praise and glowing accolades for the young patrolman, would be instrumental in obtaining the deputy position for him. Schaefer did not introduce himself but was pleasant enough, even friendly. He asked the girls if they'd like to meet him in the morning, and he could give them a ride to the beach. The girls, having no other form of transportation, and feeling confident in having befriended the Good Samaritan deputy, agreed. They would meet the following morning, Saturday, at the band shell on East Ocean Boulevard. The girls thanked him for the ride home and waved good-bye. They felt good about not having to hitchhike to the beach the next day. They would get an early start and spend the day working on their suntans.

Saturday morning, July 22nd, 1972, and all across America people awoke, then laid back down in their beds with the satisfying realization that it was not a workday. Some rolled out of bed with startling, pounding hangovers that came from Friday night, payday. The coyote chased the roadrunner, forever in vain, across animated landscapes on flickering TV screens, while Ronald McDonald and the Hamburglar oversold their fast food and change-back-from-a-buck jargon.

Sue Wells and Nancy Trotter stood near the gleaming band shell, not far from the city of Stuart's courthouse, and felt the bristling heat of a new Florida day begin to caress their shoulders. They waited patiently for their ride, occasionally shuffling a stone underfoot and engaging in sleepy, insignificant conversation. They wondered if perhaps the deputy would not show. After all, he was a cop. Surely, he had more important business to attend to, or a family to occupy his Saturday. They did not have to wonder very long.

A "light blue car with white interior and bucket seats," pulled up near them: the driver was Gerard Schaefer.

"He picked us up between 9:15 and 9:30, but he was in plain clothes and in his own car," Nancy would later relate. "He told us they switched him to be a plainclothes cop today and that (on those days) "he just does observations."

"He started driving toward Jensen Beach, and he asked us if we wanted to see an old Spanish fort that was on the river. We said okay."

Then, as Schaefer drove along A1A, Nancy in the front seat, Sue in the back, the following scene began to take place.

Schaefer pulled off the paved road onto a predetermined dirt road that led back into a wooded area on Hutchinson Island, a long narrow strip of land that runs from Martin to St. Lucie County. It runs parallel with the coasts of Stuart and Jensen Beach and farther to the north into Lucie County. Indian River separates the island from the coast on the west side and the Atlantic Ocean stretches out along the east side. In 1972, before the many massive condominium high-rises sprang up out of the brine-soaked mud, it was a relatively deserted island. The only inhabitants were the few people who could afford the luxury of owning secluded beach houses on the ocean side. The west side of the island was virtually uninhabited as well as densely covered with thick underbrush.

Schaefer wove through the underbrush and parked his car near a dilapidated shed. The shed was held together with barely more than a few rusty nails and the fact that the wind could not readily get to it through the thick foliage. The girls got out, feigning interest. It was somewhat of a letdown compared to the "Spanish fort" they were anticipating. It was actually just an old storage shed. Inside were some soggy, black with wet-rot boards, and some equally decayed fruit baskets. The smell of damp fungus was sharp to dry nostrils, and animals and adolescents had stained the dark corners with urine. Now and again, something black and wet looking would slither or hop through the grass that grew between the floorboards.

Schaefer pointed out along the river, and with a sweeping gesture of his hand, explained how and where old Spanish boats used to come in to dock, his thick fingers pointing to places along the reed-covered bank. The girls grew impatient, after all, they were missing out on the beach, but they continued to be polite and soon they were back in the car and ready to leave. Then, the hospitable deputy's attitude began to change. He became very cold, he seemed distracted, and began to ask questions. Questions that were unexpected and totally inconsistent with the courteous behavior of the deputy up to now. His movements became more mechanical, as if his actions were becoming a step-by-step process. As if what he was about to do was well thought-out in advance. His large once-rounded shoulders seemed to draw back tensely, his mouth was an angry slit in his face. He was becoming excited.

Schaefer's own writings perhaps best describe what he felt and undoubtedly what he intended to do. The following is an excerpt from his writings that would later be seized in a search of his belongings: (Note: We have used his spelling and punctuation.)

"In order to remain unapprehended the perpetrator of an execution style murder such as I have planned must take precautions. One must think out well in advance a crime of this nature in order for it to work.

"We will need an isolated area, assessable by car and a short hike, away from any police patrols or parking lovers. The execution site must be carefully arranged for a speedy execution once the victim has arrived. Ideally would be 2 saw horses with 2 X 4 between them. A noose attached to the overhanging limb of a tree and another rope to pull away the 2 X 4 preferably by car. A grave must be prepared in advance away from the place of execution.

"The victim could be anyone of the many women who flock to Miami & Ft. Lauderdale during the winter months. Even 2 victims would not be difficult to dispose of since women are less wary when traveling in pairs. In any case it may be more preferable to bind & gag the victims before transporting them to the place of execution. Then again depending on what torture or defilement is planned for them other items may be useful.

Bars of soap & water. These are useful if you would want to wash a woman before her execution. Induce her to urinate and then wash her. *Soap* provides an excellant lubricant for anal intercourse. *Beer* is useful to induce urination make the victim groggy and more cooperative. *ap* can also be forced into the rectum to induce fecation when the victim has no particular desire to relieve her bowels. Possibly she may want to defecate since people generally have a desire to do this when they are scared. A *douch bag* may be helpful in degrading her further and is also useful for a soapsuds enema which would be a great indignity, especially if one victim was made to urinate or defecate on the other. This would be a gross indignity.

Nylon stockings are useful to tie the hands and feet of the victim. The victim should be made to strip to at least her underwear. If stripped completely nude an attempt can be made to excite her sexually. The effect would be especially interesting if the victim had her neck in the noose and hands tied behind her back. A white *pillow case* should be placed over her head and her mouth *gaged.* Her panties should be pulled down enough to expose the genitles and clitorial stimulation applied. During the height of her excitement, the support would be pulled away and she would dangle by her neck. She may be revived before death if desireable and subjected to further indecencies. After death has occured the corpse should be violated if not violated already. The body should be possibly mutliated and carried to the grave and buried. All idenity papers should be destroyed and the place of execution dismantled."

Schaefer interrogated Nancy and Sue. "Do you know of a place called the Halfway House?"

"Yes," they replied. "There's just a bunch of Jesus freaks there. We're staying with one of the girls who works there. She also works at McDonald's."

"Are there drugs there?"

"No, no," said the girls, exasperated. "You're wasting your time if you think there are."

"Where are the drugs in Stuart?"

"We don't know," said Nancy. "This is only our second day down here." She thought surely the explanation would convince Schaefer to discontinue his questioning. What could they know in two days?

The girls threw furtive glances at each other and snickered a bit. This guy couldn't be serious. They giggled and finally laughed aloud.

Schaefer did not laugh with them.

"I could dig a hole and bury you," he told them. However, the girls were not yet frightened. He was joking, wasn't he?

"There is no crime without a body," he continued.

It was very hot now, sitting in the little car with the windows rolled up. The air was almost sparse, the close atmosphere stifling and claustrophobic. The three occupants of the car perspired profusely. Sweat crept through the girls' scalps like spider's feet. Their hair and clothes were damp, the swimsuits underneath, soaked. Their nostrils flared as the air grew more stale.

"Look," said Nancy. "Can we just get out of here? We want to get to the beach."

There was more silence, and more sweat. Then Schaefer became motivated, back in control. His face took on a look of resolution. He had a plan.

"I'm afraid I'm going to have to put you under arrest," he told them. "As runaways. Nancy, dump your purse on the seat."

Nancy reluctantly complied. Schaefer fingered through the emptied contents. "Now get out of the car," he said to Nancy. Schaefer got out of the car, Nancy hesitated, so he went to her side and roughly pulled her out. Once outside the car Schaefer handcuffed her and pushed her back into the car. He did the same to Sue.

"Have you ever heard of 'white slavery'?" he asked as he got back into the car. He told them about people who still "buy" people today as they did in early American history. They use them for whatever they want. For mates. For pleasure. For porno movies. For killing. There are rich sheiks who'll pay handsome wages for young white girls.

"Would your parents pay ransom for you?" he asked grinning at them. He was obviously enjoying himself.

Sue, angered, mustered her courage and blurted out, "Well, go get your sheik and sell us!" Then the girls hushed. They were sweaty and hot, and bound against their wills. They fought back by refusing to talk to him. Oddly, they were not as much afraid as they were disgusted and feeling foolish for getting into this mess. Now, they would probably go to jail, and for what? Then they'd have to call their parents and go through all means of legal hassles.

Meanwhile, angered by the girls' silence, Schaefer began to seethe. He sat for a moment gripping the car's steering wheel, hands twisting, knuckles stretching against skin. Suddenly, he burst from the car. He walked quickly around to the trunk, opened it and withdrew a length of thick sisal rope and some sheets. He opened the doors of the car and made the girls get out. He put gags, torn from the sheets, over their mouths.

"If one of you tries to get away," he said, "I'll kill the one I have. Then, I'll come and catch and kill the other."

In Nancy's words: "He took Sue out in a field. He had my blanket (which she'd brought to lie on at the beach) and he put it on the ground. He made her sit on it, and he tied her legs together. And then he made another loop around her shoulders so that she was tied hand and foot, handcuffed and gagged. I was scared then ... I could have run away, but I couldn't because he had Sue there."

"Go ahead and try to get away," he told Sue. "I'll have Nancy and if you get away, I'll kill her. Then I'll come and kill you."

He took Nancy down to the river, through the thick growth of trees. The river was Indian River, a massive leg of brown-green, brine-water that separates Hutchinson Island from the mainland of Florida. There were small islands of trees jutting out of the damp ground. He took Nancy to one of these. The tree trunks were subject to the fluctuating tide of Indian River. At low tide, the large roots, some eight to twelve-inches thick, were exposed above the muddy earth.

Some of them were exposed to the point of sticking out of the ground almost a foot high. He made Nancy get up onto one of these roots, so she would have been as much as eighteen to twenty-four inches off the ground. He made a noose and slid it over Nancy's head and tightened it around her throat.

"That's when I started crying," she said. "Then he put the rope over a branch above me, and then tied it onto another branch. The rope went up and down and then hooked onto another piece of branch. Then he told me not to get away. If I had fallen off of those roots I would have hung."

While Nancy stood there tottering on the slippery root, she sobbed. The hard, rough root hurt her feet; the scratchy sisal rope raked the soft skin of her neck, and seemed to grow tighter with each move she made.

Schaefer watched her a while, pleased with his work. Toying with her, he reached back and pinched her buttocks. She looked at him disgusted. He laughed.

"I could rape you right now, right here, if I wanted to."

Nancy's heart pounded in her throat, pounded against the tightening rope, pounded so hard she was sure he could hear it. Suddenly, he turned and left her there, apparently remembering Sue.

As soon as Schaefer was out of sight, Nancy began to try to break free. She could turn her head enough to see the knots of the noose. She worked the gag from her mouth and began to chew on the knot. The rope left little coarse hairs in her mouth which ground into her gums as she chewed, and it tasted like car oil. Her legs were also tightly bound with rope around her knees. She tried desperately to work her legs free but to no avail. The attempt seemed only to cut the blood flow to her feet, making them numb and, consequently, making it difficult to keep a firm footing on the root.

"I finally turned around and fell against the branch where the other end of the rope was tied on. The rope was looser from my chewing on it, and I could untie it with my hand behind my back.

"I undid the knot myself, and then I got all the ropes off. I didn't take very long, maybe ten or fifteen minutes. But I still had the handcuffs on . . ."

She picked up the ropes that moments before had held her captive. She ran, keeping low, back up to the "Spanish fort." She hid the ropes because earlier she noticed he'd taken most of the ropes out of his trunk. Without ropes, if she was captured again, at least he could not hang her.

"I felt like I was in a movie. I sneaked back behind the Spanish fort and peeked out the other side, and saw his car was still there."

Nancy reasoned that the best thing for her to do would be to try to get away and get help. She could not be of any help to Sue in her present condition, and even if she wasn't handcuffed, Schaefer could undoubtedly overpower her. Besides, she did not know where he'd taken Sue, or if she were even still alive.

She scrambled through the brush as quietly as humanly possible, and back to the river. She waded in up to her knees. The water was sickly warm. The river bottom was silty mud filled with sharp little shells. With every step she took, her feet sank deep into the mud, and the broken shells were like tiny razors. The water smelled stagnant. She crept along the shore in this manner, the river bottom sucking at her feet as if to eat them, her pace made slower by the fact that she was handcuffed, and so, off-balance. She thought she heard someone call her. She stopped and listened. There it was again. She crouched low, her long blonde hair dripping into the briny water. She peered into the bushes. It was Sue.

Nancy started toward her and stopped. It occurred to her that this might be a trick. Schaefer probably went back, found her gone, and was now forcing Sue to call her. Baiting her.

Setting a trap. He was certainly clever enough. With incredible effort, and battling her conscience, she decided to leave and go for help.

"I kept going," she said.

"As I was going through the water, I heard sounds like someone was behind me. I started running through the water 'cause I thought he was after me. At the first clearing, I ran up on land and there was this whole bunch of undergrowth. I crawled under there and just stayed in the bushes, being real quiet.

"I knew there were snakes in here, but I didn't see any. I did see every kind of spider. Every time a bird flew up or the wind blew through the trees, I kept thinking it was him.

"Then the place just got really bad with mosquitoes. I couldn't brush them off 'cause I was still handcuffed. After a half-hour or so, I couldn't take any more. I knew that the road out there was parallel with the river, so I started heading toward the road. I was walking over all these bushes because I didn't want to take a path. I thought, he could catch me on a path, but I could run through the jungle as fast as he could. I fell down once in a while. And then I got to a place where there were too many trees and vines. I couldn't go in that direction anymore, and I couldn't get around.

"I still thought he was behind me at that point. And if he was, I was just going to give up."

Exhausted, feet cut and bleeding, the handcuffs so tight her hands had swollen and become numb, and now, no place left to run. She had to go back to the river. After an eternity of shouldering back through the brush she came upon the river. She followed the river, knowing that if she kept on this course, eventually she would be able to look across and see the A1A highway.

"I finally got to a place where I could see the road on the other side, so I walked out into the river and just started swimming. I knew I could swim with my hands behind my back.

I'm a pretty good swimmer. You kind of kick while on your back and kind of do the side stroke without your hands. The river was pretty wide because the cars on the road seemed pretty small when I started swimming,"

She swam in this labored position, a slight current fatiguing her; the water, murky and dark and concealing God knows what. A jellyfish stung her once and then another one stung her a little further ahead. She thought she may have been into a whole school of them but could not recall if there were even such things as schools of jellyfish. Whether or not there were, the two stings she sustained were extremely painful, yet she could not stop. Several times she was sure she would drown. Eventually, she came close enough to shore to touch bottom. She pulled herself up, utterly drained, having no more energy to get out of the water. She stumbled toward the shore and, still knee-deep in the river, began screaming at cars passing on the road.

As she screamed, she cried. The ordeal had been almost more than she could bear. Now she had to get help for Sue, and cars kept going by. Except one.

A Martin County Sheriff's patrol car came to an abrupt stop dead ahead of her. The same kind that had picked her and Sue up only yesterday and taken them home. The same car that Schaefer would be driving . . .

Oh, God, she thought to herself as she fell to her knees, I'm going to die. She could fight no more. He has me now . . .

The door of the car opened. The Martin County Sheriff, Robert Lewis Crowder, stepped out. Crowder, a short stocky man with wide shoulders and an ever-youthful face, walked toward Nancy. His short stature was well-hidden by his well-pressed clothes and meticulous grooming. His stunning blue eyes conveyed friendship and warmth,

He had spotted Nancy about eighty to one hundred yards away from the road, still in the river. He remembers feeling "sick and disgusted about the incident," but extremely relieved to have found both girls relatively unharmed.

Coincidently, about an hour earlier, a truck driver had found Sue, shaken and handcuffed, and yelling for him to stop. She'd told the truck driver the story and they had called the Sheriff's Department and requested to speak to the head sheriff, not a deputy. However, Sheriff Crowder was already out searching for the girls.

Crowder had been at home, typically relaxing on a Saturday afternoon when he'd received a call from Deputy Schaefer. Schaefer seemed reluctant to come to the point. Puzzled, Crowder asked why he'd called him at home, on a Saturday. What was it that could not wait until Monday?

"I've done something foolish," Schaefer told him, childishly. "You're going to be mad at me."

Schaefer explained that he had picked up the girls hitchhiking, that he was demonstrating the pitfalls, the dangers, of hitchhiking. He'd gotten a little carried away. He'd meant no harm. He was only trying to teach them a lesson. He'd tied them up. Probably, they didn't understand. They've gotten away.

Crowder quickly called one of his most trusted men and good friend, Lt. Melvin Waldron. They immediately began a search for the girls. Crowder, without revealing the whole story, left orders at the station he should be contacted as soon as anyone heard anything from either Nancy Trotter or Paula Sue Wells.

When the call came in from the trucker, concerning Sue Wells, Crowder was notified first. He went to the spot where the driver was calling from. There he'd found Sue, in much the same condition as he'd later find Nancy. He wrapped her in a blanket and put her in the backseat of his car, after first removing her handcuffs.

Sue related the story to Crowder as he drove her back to the Sheriff's Department. She told him Nancy was probably still out there and she was handcuffed too. "The last time I saw her she was in the river. I think she got away."

Crowder was worried about Nancy, with good reason. "She could have stepped into a hole, or on a stingray." (A stingray is a native saltwater creature which lives slightly submerged in the mud of Florida river bottoms. They have long whip-like tails with sharp poisonous barbs which they will quickly sink into your leg if you step on them.) "She could have died . . . And, she could have run back into Schaefer."

Crowder sidestepped down the bank of the Indian River to help Nancy out of the water.

"Nancy?" he called.

She nodded her head feebly.

"We've been looking for you," he told her. "We found Sue about forty-five minutes ago. She's okay. She's down at the station."

Later, Nancy would tell one reporter, "The sheriff (Crowder) was really nice. He undid the hand cuffs, wrapped me in a blanket and put me in the back seat of his car. I asked, 'What's going on?' He said, 'Guess we had one bad apple in the bunch.'"

Robert Lewis Crowder was the youngest sheriff to ever serve office in Florida. Former Governor Reuben Askew appointed Crowder the position of Sheriff of Martin county when he was just twenty-six years old. Askew needed a man to fill the position when the previous sheriff, Roy C. Baker, was suspended on charges of "official misconduct." Crowder, an ambitious and politically motivated young man, was already a detective for the Stuart

Police Department. When the offer came for him to take the sheriff's position, he knew that Baker had been

Martin County's sheriff for almost twenty years. Nevertheless, he saw opportunity in the position and accepted willingly.

As acting sheriff, Crowder was concerned with the upcoming election: he wanted to keep his job. One of the platforms he maintained was "to slash the long working hours of his deputies by increasing the manpower of the department."

The department began to accept applications for more deputies. Gerard John Schaefer was one of the very first to apply, was hired by Crowder.

"He was a clean-cut man with a college degree who had already been certified by the Florida Police Standards Board," said Crowder. "He had a polite demeanor, he was intelligent and personable, not at all like a person who might become overly aggressive in performing his duties. He already had his police training and was ready to go to work that day. We made a police check on him and his record came back clean. We needed men, so I hired him."

Crowder, after questioning Nancy Trotter and Paula Sue Wells separately, found their accounts of the incident to be identical. He then told Schaefer to "consider yourself fired." He said, too, that at this point he "informally" asked Public Defender Elton H. Schwarz to request that Schaefer be given a psychiatric examination.

"It was my opinion then," said Crowder, "that the guy was really weird. Schwarz had a couple of teenage daughters and I told him this could have been one of his children. I asked him if he wanted to put a man like this back on the streets.

"The mental examination never developed," said Crowder. "I don't think anyone recognized the potential seriousness of what he (Schaefer) had done."

Crowder would remain bitter toward the "Monday morning quarterbacks" who criticized his hiring Schaefer. In September of 1972, he would defeat Roy C. Baker for his comeback-bid to the office in the primary election. However, a few months later, he would lose the general election, and consequently, the office to Republican nominee and former deputy under Baker, James D. Holt. Crowder would later find employment as a security supervisor for Ebasco Services Incorporated. He returned to law enforcement and was under sheriff of St. Lucie for eight years before running for Sheriff of Martin County, winning the position and holding it for over twenty years.

Perhaps, because of the political instability in the Martin County Sheriff Department that year, Schaefer's other hideous crimes would go undetected for almost eight months. He would not be suspected for any major felony for, as he'd said himself, "There is no crime without a body," and as yet, there were no bodies. But why, one must ask, was there not more intensive investigations into the dozens of missing young women and girls in that South Florida area? Why didn't anyone pursue a psychological evaluation of Schaefer? Surely a trained psychologist could have given authorities enough insight into Schaefer's character to reveal the fact that he was at least very disturbed mentally, that at least extensive observation was warranted.

Schaefer would eventually be charged and convicted for aggravated assault. He would be sentenced to six months in jail, but even though he was found guilty and sentenced, he would not

begin his prison term until January 15, 1973, nearly six months after the abduction of Nancy Trotter and Paula Sue Wells. If only someone could have kept him incarcerated from July 22, 1972, when the Trotter/Wells incident took place, a very minimum of four lives could have been spared, perhaps many, many more.

Whether it was because Schaefer was a "clean-cut man" with a "clean record," a law-abiding citizen, or indeed an upholder of the law itself, a deputy, he would be dealt with leniently. And in so doing he would be free at least those six long months to kill and kill again. But then, he'd been killing for some time, long before he'd made the mistake of letting Nancy and Sue escape, by carelessly leaving them tied in the woods for an hour.

In fact, were it not for the ingenuity and the incredible luck that these two girls had that day, they undoubtedly would have been murder victims as well. For these two girls, the episode with Schaefer would only last about three hours. But it would be an unforgettable and frightening memory that would surface as ghastly nightmares and leave them panting and clawing at sweat-dampened sheets in the middle of the night for years to come.

Perhaps it is "Monday-morning quarter-backing," but *if* someone would have just executed a simple search of Schaefer's personal possessions, as they would have with any citizen caught tying and almost hanging two girls, perhaps they would have found the following "story." A "story" among many such "stories" that brutally describes the heinous crimes that this man committed. The following excerpt, as well as many others, was composed by Schaefer, and indeed would later be used as evidence against him. But while his defense would argue it was merely a man acting out his frustrated fantasies on paper, it is more correct to know the stories for what they are: the diaries of a madman.

The following story is as it was found, including all misspelled words:

"She was expecting dinner but instead was driven down a deserted road. She was asked to get out of the car and submitted to a frisk search. Then the handcuffs were locked around her wrists and the blindfold placed over her eyes. She was then led away into the dark to the place of execution. She was assisted in mounting the laddar and sat down on the top of it. The hangmans noose was placed over her head after a pillow case was dropped over her face in a hood arrangement. She sat there very composed and ladylike while I adjusted the rope. She obviously had no inclination of what was about to happen. I told her some stories about Viet Nam and then told her I had to make a radio call. I warned her that if she made a sound that she would be hanged immediately. I went back to the car and had something to drink and then brought the car up. I got out and tied the rope to the bumper so that if I pulled away it would pull out the ladder from beneath her and she would be left hanging. I went back to see her and asked if she were comfortable. She replied that she was getting bored and would I please hurry up with whatever business I had to attend to. I said I would and before I went back to the car I made sure that the rope was tight around her neck. I wanted her to stand up but she was afraid so I let her sit. She sat there very ladylike in a black chiffon dress with her hair done up and black pantyhose and highheels. She was wearing perfume and was very sexy. I went back to the car and finished off the bottle of wine and then promply at 9PM I started the car and after allowing it to run for a few minute I threw it into reverse and backed up quickly. I turned off the car and got out straing to see if the branches were moving in the trees or if there were anyother sounds. There were none. After fifteen minutes which I judged to be a sufficient time

for her to die I went slowly forward into
the grave of trees where the execution site
was arranged. I was notheing more than a rope
with a hangmans noose over a limb dangling
above the ladder where she was to sit. I had
a light but I almost didn't want to see what I
was responsible for. I approached in the dark
and could make out her body turning slowly
suspended from the tree. I went forward and
turned the light. I was a little shocked. There
was a considerable amount of blood staining the
white pillowcase hood that was over her head.
The noose was pulled tight around her neck
and her head was tilted to one side because I
placed the noose beneath her left chin. When
I was withing a few feet of her body I could
see that where her feet had been tied tightly
that she had broken the bounds obviously in
her violent death theos. One of her shoes was
kicked off. I was probably shakeing as I slowly
ran my hand up under her dress just above her
knees and began to work it upward. I felt a big
hard growing in my pants as my hand traveled
up her legs still warm and very much alive to
me. The inside of her thigs were wet were she
had urinated in her panties. Her underpants
and pantyhose were soaked. She was wearing
her pantyhose over her panties that were white
nylon mesh and very skimpy. I lifted her dress
and her wet slip and pulled down the pantyhose
over the back of her backside just leaving her
panties. I slipped my fingers beneath the rim of
her panties down near the front of her cunt and
moved then slowly back toward her asshole fully
expecting and hoping to find a nice pile of shit.
My fingers found the hair of her ass and inched
toward her hole. Her hole was open and my finger
easily slipped into her hot rectum. There was a
small amound of execrement littering the crotch
of her panties and more clinging to the area
around her asshole but there was not nearly as
much as I hoped to find. I went back to the car
and stripped and then returned to the grove.
I then untied the rope and lowered her body
to the ground where I stripped off her dress

and slip and pulled down her panties and hose to around her ankles. I then drapped her body over a crate that I had brought along for that purpose and fucked her up her asshole. I shot off almost at once and then felt very sorry for her. Oh, before I took her body down I forced myself to lift up the pillowcase hood and look at her face. The face was swollen and a little mottled. The eyes were closed and swollen at the temples her mouth was open and her tongue was visible but not protruding much. I was sick at the sight but I left the hood off becuase of the blood which I didn't like. After a few minutes I got on her again and fucked her ass same more. It was still hot in there and I shot off quickly once again. Then I stripped her out and threw her cloths into a pile. I then carried her body over to where i had rigged up a toilet seat between two creats and I sat her limp body on it. I then went down beneath the seat dnd stared up at her cunt and asshole playing with them and fantasing that she was in the act of shitting or pissing. After a while I tired of this and left her body on the toilet seat and went back to the car where I think I slept. After a while I went back to her and for the first time noticed that she was getting cold on the out side but was still warm on the inside when I fucked her asshole again. This time I left her nude body sprawled out on the ground with her ass sticking upo in the air sort of like she was kneeling.

    "I went back to the car and went back to sleep again feeling sick to my stomack. Later I woke up again and got out and went to her and stuck my prick in her ass again. This time I noticed that not only was her body getting cold but it was also getting stiff too. I woke up cold and went to the car leaving her leying in the pine needles after humping her hiney and then passing out over her dead nude body, sometime before. The next time I woke up it was nearing daylite so I went and took her body which was becomming stiff down in the joints of the arms and the legs and dragged it over to the rope. I replaced the noose around her neck and hauled her up to see what she looked like in the grey daylite. She was too difficult to haul up very far so I took her down and hauled her up on a lower limb where i could support her body as I was pullit it up. For the first tirre after removing her handcuffs I noticed that her wrists were very bruised most likely from where she tried to get out of her perdicament just before she died. Earlier I had lain beneath her and looked up her dress with a flashlight but now with her hanging there nacked she was not to stimulating. I went to the car and got a womans slip and put it on her then as she was suspended from the rope I stood on a crate behind her and screwed her ass from behind but it was hard to keep her still on the end of the rope because she kept wanting to swing out. Her body was cold by this tine and it was exciting in another way being able to fuck her cold corpse. I got off in her ass once more and then since was getting lite I took her down and wrapped her up in a white sheet and took her to the car. I dumped her body in the trunk and picked up her things and wadded them up all except her panties, pantyhose and slip which were soaked with her piss. I wanted to save thses for souvineers. I drove to another deserted spot and took her corpse out of the trunk wrapped up in the sheet. I haf dragged and carried it about a good 200 yards into the bush along a dike. She was very heavy now and it was real work just to move her. When I got to where I decided I wanted to dump her corpose I opened the sheet and rolled her out now noticing that in the full daylight that she was still wearing one earing and a gold chain. Thses I took and threw into a canal. Her cloths I also threw into another canal and then I rolled her corpse down the side of the dike to a palmetto thicket. I the daylight her corpse was very cold stiff and grotesque. She had large bruises on her legs from where she probably kicked herself during her death theos. This together with the distorted face and her bruised wrists made her appear very unattractive. I propped her up as best I could and stuck it in her asshole again and then turned her over and for the first time really noticed her auburn V covering her cunt. I forced her stiff legs apart as best I could and screwed face to face which was not easy since she was very stiff and a littler tite from the rigor mortis, between her legs. I finally got my nuts off in her and then I was exausted for awile. I sat for awhile and then decided to dump her body in the canal. I pulled her body down to the wather and pushed her in head first. Her auburn haid swam around her as she began to slip beneath the hyanciths. Finally the water came up over her butt and went into her asshole. I let her feet go and she sank beneath the water. I went back to the execution sit e and cleaned up any traces of our having been there and then went to a rock pit where I dumped her pocketbook and the sheet and a few rags and things. Then I went to Lums and had lunch on hernoney and didn't enjoy it to much.

"About teo weeks later I was curious to wether she floated to the surface. I was horrified when I went to where she was dumped and saw her body swollen and bloated tight skinned floating there. She was face down and her hair was covering her shouders. Her ass was sticking way up in the air and I was looking right at what had been her cunt and asshole. The maggots had evidentily been at work on her because there was a big hole from her cunt to the top of the crak of her ass and she stunk to high heaven. She was putrid with all the flies buzzing and landing on her too. I poked her with a stick trying to get her down under the lilliys but ended up havin to pile lillys upon top of her to hide her corpse, whick was a funny redish color.

"Another few weeks and she was out from under the lillys again and I tried to sink her with a few blasts from a shotgun. I would almost puke when I got a wiff of her corpes. It was that bad. I would always go there and beat off toward her just out of range of the smell. Eventually she began to rot away and every now and then when I could stand then stink I would drag her out

and try to mash it with a stick. It seemed even
the maggots didn't want have anything to do
woit her after a certain point. Anyway finally I
managed to break up the body and make it sink.
I took the skull and let the ants eat her brains
out if she had any and then I pulled out all
the teeth and scatted than over the county. The
lower jaw I buried and the rest of her skull
with the face smashed in and the teeth out I
put in another canal some ten miles for the
rest of her body. All in all she is probably
scattered over some thiry square miles and I
hope that she will continue to remain among the
ranks of the missing even though there is no
possible connection between us."

This, written by a man whose job was to serve, to protect. A man who would later brag to this author about his intelligence, which was never evident to me. Clever and devious does not equal intelligence.

A few days after the Trotter/Wells abduction, on July 26th, Sheriff Robert Lewis Crowder held a news conference. Because of his short stature, he had to look up a bit to see into the faces of the many eager reporters who'd gathered to hear the story of a "deputy gone wrong." But Crowder was trying to keep his head up anyway. The incident with Schaefer could only, would only, reflect on the character of the man who was responsible for hiring him. Obviously embarrassed, but trying to maintain as much dignity as possible, he told reporters that Schaefer had been "fired on the spot." He'd then told Schaefer to "report to Lt. Waldron, who made out the arrest ticket on my instructions."

"His action is a great embarrassment to anyone in law enforcement. It could not be foreseen from contact with the man. He remained calm, claiming he had just overdone his job. "He said he was trying to impress on them (Trotter/Wells) the danger of young girls running around the country."

Crowder said Schaefer had told the girls it was illegal to hitchhike in Martin County. But that, "the only law against hitchhiking in Martin County is in the City of Stuart, and it is not enforced rigorously."

In November of 1972, Schaefer went to court charged with two counts of aggravated assault and two counts of false imprisonment. Nancy Ellen Trotter and Paula Sue Wells were in the courtroom. They'd found work in Stuart and maintained a temporary residence in order to stay for the trial.

Under his attorney's advice, Schaefer pleaded guilty to one charge of aggravated assault against Nancy Trotter. All other charges were dropped on the recommendation of Assistant State Attorney, Jim Midelis. Sentencing was set for December 22, 1972.

Martin County Circuit Court Judge D.C. Smith presided over the hearing in November and would sentence Schaefer as well. He listened to Schaefer's plea for probation. Schaefer pleaded that he had "a very promising job with a grocery firm," and that he and his wife had lost everything including "my job and my respect."

Smith told Schaefer, "I don't want to embarrass you. But I can't conceive how you were such an automatic jackass and a fool as you were. I think we all concur in that you were a thoughtless fool."

Schaefer was sentenced to one year in jail, with the understanding he could be out in six months, and then begin a three-year probationary period. If Martin County had a work release program, he would be considered for it. The jail term would not begin immediately. After listening to Schaefer's attorney, Judge D.C. Smith consented to let the defendant remain free until after the holidays.

Schaefer seemed content with the sentence. He would be allowed to leave the courtroom and spend the Christmas holidays at home with his family. A misled, slightly disturbed man would get a chance to relax, and enjoy the yule tidings and the coming of a new year. Perhaps a new year with a fresh start.

No one could have possibly imagined that day, three days before Christmas, that three months earlier on September 27, 1972, Gerard John Schaefer had murdered two girls. And, a few days before his incarceration would begin on January 15, 1973, he would murder two more.

As he left the courtroom that day, he told reporters: "I made a stupid mistake. There was no sex involved. No one was hurt."

Chapter 2

Patrolman Schaefer

True . . . nervous . . . very, very dreadfully nervous I had
been and am, but why will you say that I am mad?
From *The Tell Tale Heart,* by Edgar Allan Poe

Gerard John Schaefer was born on March 26, 1946 in Neenah, Wisconsin. Neenah is situated along the northwestern coast of Lake Winnebago, a lovely summer resort area where tourists come to swim and fish for bass, to canoe, and escape from city drudgery. The lake is a catch basin for the river that ebbs out of Green Bay, a southward pointing finger of Lake Michigan. Highway 41 is both vein and artery to the heart of Neenah and the surrounding area. People escaping from Milwaukee, for a weekend on the lake, take 41 north passing through Fond du Lac on the way where they can if they wish, visit the wonderfully restored Galloway House, or the nearby pioneer village.

Others escape, out of Green Bay, take 41 south to the lake. If they have time or the desire, they can stop in nearby Appleton, just north of Neenah, and learn the history of papermaking at the Dard Hunter Paper Museum. The paper industry was the lifeblood of this area. This is a quaint, beautiful area despite the nearby lake named after the *Butte Des Morts*, which translates to "Hill of the Dead."

Gerard was born to Doris and Gerard John Schaefer, Sr. He was a healthy, normal baby, the first of three; Sara Jean and brother Gary, respectively. Gerard, Sr., known as "Jerry" to family and friends, was a traveling salesman for Kimberly-Clark, which was headquartered near Neenah. Jerry enjoyed his position with the company, and the moving about, meeting new people seemed to agree with him, at least at first. Doris preferred that he be home more, help look after the children, but she understood the role of breadwinner, and only occasionally revealed the—at times—insurmountable distress of raising the children, practically alone.

Before Gerard, Jr., young "John" as he was called, could attend grade school, the Schaefer family moved to Nashville, Tennessee, where Jerry, Sr., had been transferred by Kimberly-Clark. Shortly thereafter, the family moved to Atlanta, Georgia. They lived there in the Peach State, at 3553 London Road for four years, until John was about fourteen. The children attended public schools and progressed as well as could be expected, considering their frequent moving about. Finally, in 1960, the Schaefers moved to Fort Lauderdale, Florida.

Though South Florida was now what they called home, Gerard, Sr. was never there much. His job kept him traveling, but when he could, he would take John hunting and fishing. He recalls that John was a "beautiful shot," and though he wished he could have spent more time with the children growing up, he felt that they received a normal education and upbringing. Jerry had already begun the drinking habit that would eventually lead to the disintegration of the family.

With his father absent much of the time, young Schaefer began to increasingly venture into the nearby woods to fish and hunt, often alone. He developed a fondness and a desire to be with nature that would lead some people to refer to him as an "outdoors man" and "nature lover." Florida is a labyrinth of waterways; brown-water canals brimming with "shell-crackers,' "crawdaddies," and "mud-puppies." A young man of fourteen can find adventure at every turn, and John did. Neighbors who knew the Schaefers when they moved to Fort Lauderdale, recall John with conflicting stories.

John Keefe was about fifteen years old when he met Gerard Schaefer. "I went fishing with him once in a while," Keefe quoted, though he also says he knew him "no more, no less" from other kids in the neighborhood. He also recalls: "He really liked to hunt and fish and I remember that he and his father used to fish together. I think they had a lot of the same interests." Keefe remembers that Schaefer "drank a little," and dated girls "no more than anyone else," and that "he was no different than any of the other boys. He didn't stand apart from the crowd, wasn't a braggart, didn't swear any more than the other boys, and never got into fights."

Peter Maddock, another neighborhood friend, recalls Schaefer as being "preoccupied with girls." Maddock has stated, "When we were playing baseball, Gerard was with a girl. He never was involved in athletics. The girls seemed to get in the way (of his playing sports). He seemed older (more mature and experienced) and was able to buy booze without trouble. He had the contacts, I guess.

"But he really liked the girls and I don't recall that he had any one steady girl. I remember once he kept a bunch of us enthralled most of the night talking about his adventures with girls. We were all young and inexperienced ... and very interested."

Gary Hainline, brother to Leigh Hainline Bonadies (who has been missing since September 8th, 1969) recalled when they were neighbors and said they were "pretty good friends" at one time. "He was a gun collector, took pride in his guns, but seemed to enjoy killing things. He enjoyed shooting things. Things you can't eat ... songbirds, land crabs, that sort of thing."

Schaefer grew out of the dirty-kneed youngster, who played on the banks of canals or was gone, sometimes for an entire day in the nearby woodlands. Now, he'd grown into a tall sports-minded youth, and a good student. He still enjoyed the outdoors immensely but, as with all young men in high school, other things were on his mind.

In a Palm Beach Post-Times article, written by Dick Donovan, dated May 20, 1973, several of Schaefer's high school acquaintances would clearly remember their classmate. These people were part of the graduating class of 1964 from St. Thomas Aquinas High School. There were one hundred and seventy-one students graduating that year. Only one of those students would be accused of being a homicidal killer.

Many of those students were like Don Schweiger, who did not remember Schaefer very well. "He was just a guy I saw from time to time in high school. There wasn't anything special or outstanding about him. And I really don't believe I ever got to know him."

This statement says nothing unusual about Schaefer, but considering the relatively small group of students attending the high school and the fact that Schweiger and Schaefer shared a science class, the statement does at least reflect the idea that Schaefer, though "popular" in school activities, was a face that could easily be lost in a crowd. He would have been considered completely "normal."

Girls, however, remember Schaefer a little differently. Eloise Loftis remembered him this way: "He was kinda weird! That's about all I can say about him. He was kinda out of it, never a part of the group. He was the last boy I would have dated. I didn't like him. I don't know why. He was just weird, that's all."

This statement conflicts with the high school's records that show Schaefer as having been on the Raiders football team during his sophomore and junior years, and a "leading linesman" during this time. He was also an excellent golfer, who undoubtedly could have made a career of the sport. His high school yearbook had listed Schaefer under "Our Best Love: Ventures (which) Brought A Glow." Beneath this heading the following information is given: (*NOTE: The numbers following the headings indicate Freshman year, number 1, through Senior year, number 4.)

John Schaefer: Perfect Attendance 2; Aquinews (the school paper) 3; Blessed Sacrament Society 1; Science Club; 1,2,3; Football 2, 3; Golf 1, 2, 3, 4; Intramurals 1, 2, 3, 4.

The photo accompanying this outstanding high school record is that of a happy, handsome young man in cap and gown. There are other pictures of the young Schaefer throughout the yearbook: the tall, svelte golfer leaning into the driving position, golf club pulled back over his shoulder, the sun glinting off his I.D. bracelet, his long-lashed eyes posed on the tee. Another picture, in prom attire; the thick-necked football player, beaming at us, a wide-faced Cheshire-cat smile placed solidly over a black tuxedo. His sun-lightened, short brown hair brushed casually to one side; thick, dark eyebrows dramatically arched over his hue-shifting "bluish-gray" eyes. If looks could kill, this attractive, outgoing high school student was definitely armed to the teeth.

Donna Waldron, another classmate, said that she and Schaefer were not close friends, but that she remembered that he wanted to be a forest ranger. This would be consistent with his later becoming a "guide" in the Everglades.

"I think he may have been a golfer," Waldron recalled, "but I can't remember for sure. He was a loner. Not part of any clique. He would do strange things. Like he would be sitting in class and all of a sudden, he would start talking to himself. I didn't like him, and I didn't like him dating one of my friends. But I expected them to get married."

Barbara Krolick remembers Schaefer as "never the kind of person I wanted to know. I can't remember him being friends with any of the guys. He was always on the outside looking in. As a matter of fact, the only thing I really remember is that I always had to tuck my skirt under my legs because John (Schaefer) would practically stand on his head to look up a girl's skirt."

Loftis remembered this peculiarity as well, she said, "Nowadays, when a guy does that, we just shrug it off. But when they do it in high school, wow! It's weird."

Krolick added, "I feel sorry for him, if he did the things they say he did. But I wasn't surprised when I heard about him being arrested. I don't know why, but I wasn't."

In June of 1964, Gerard John Schaefer graduated from St. Thomas Aquinas High School. It was during the following summer that Schaefer was to have been "self-employed" as a "hunting and fishing guide" in the Everglades, and a "coin dealer" though there are no records to substantiate those claims. Gerard was ambitious and intelligent and so, after enjoying a summer of fun and sun doing what most high school graduates do, he went back to school.

Schaefer enrolled at Broward Junior College (now Broward College) in the first semester of the 1964-1965 academic year. It was to be the beginning of a troublesome, and anguishing college career. He began his education as a social studies major. Later, he would change his inclination to the College of Education where he would endeavor to be a teacher, with a background in physical education. That is when many of his "problems" began to manifest themselves.

Initially, Schaefer's college career was like that of many freshmen students, bouncing inconsistently from such subjects such as General Zoology (from which he withdrew and later upon repeating the course, failed) to Golfing, at which he excelled. His other courses were mostly required subjects, and his grades tended to run about average.

In the first semester of the '65-'66 academic year, Schaefer began to have difficulties in school, perhaps because he'd taken an overload of subjects, with a possible cumulative total of 28.5 credits. He was taking eight different courses, out of which he would quickly withdraw from three: Scuba Diving, Women's Instructional Swimming, and again, General Zoology, leaving him still with 19.5 credits to try to achieve. (Throughout his stay at Broward College, Schaefer would continually take exaggerated overloads of credit hours, usually dropping or withdrawing from about one-third of those credits to enable him to successfully finish his other courses.) His remaining courses landed him C's and B's, except World Literature, which he failed, and Creative Writing, in which he received an A.

It is this last class that is most significant. Teaching the class was Harry Crews, author of "A Feast of Snakes," "Car," and several other critically acclaimed novels, as well as being a successful writer for several magazines, including *Playboy*. Crews says he remembers Schaefer being a student of his, "but not a particularly gifted one, either." At any rate, Crews did give Schaefer an A, and it was most likely this high grade that would compel Schaefer to begin thinking of himself as at least a "pretty fair writer." Up to that point he'd only received one other A, in Golfing.

Years later, Crews would consider writing a book on Schaefer's life but chose not to, stating "he (Schaefer) was so decidedly full of shit that anything he would tell you would be a lie anyway."

Schaefer enrolled in the second semester of the '65-'66 academic year, again taking an overload of 25 credit hours. He withdrew from all of them. He left school for a while and began again in the first semester of the '66-'67 academic year. Throughout this year, he traditionally maintained overloaded schedules, and withdrew accordingly. He did, however, finish his sophomore work at Broward, applied and was accepted at Florida Atlantic University in Boca Raton, where he began his studies in the winter quarter of 1968.

Schaefer's years at FAU were much more coherent, in that he did not withdraw from any classes, though he still took overloads of 18 and 20 credit hour semesters. His grades ran from average to above average. And he seemed, at least outwardly, to be adjusting well to his college schedule. In 1968, while attending FAU, Schaefer met, and would later marry, Martha Louise Fogg, or Marti as she was known to her friends. Marti was still attending classes at Broward College when the two of them met.

At first, Marti and Gerard seemed to be an ideal couple. Both were hardworking students, endeavoring to better themselves, and they both had an interest in creative writing. Both had some of their work published in a literary magazine, Pan Ku put out by Broward College. It was most likely this common interest that drew them together. This, and an interest in the sciences. Marti was a biology science major, and Gerard was now working toward a Bachelor of Arts degree "with a major in geography."

There was trouble, however. The marriage of the young students began to fall apart almost immediately. Marti would forever refuse to discuss exactly what caused the couple to separate, but Gerard would complain that their biggest problem was an "incompatible sex life." He would also state he told her "to put out or get out." Eventually, she chose the "get out" option.

Schaefer was now increasingly taking more science-related courses and, rather interestingly, more human behavior and psychology courses. Perhaps he was taking these courses to better understand himself and his now-failing marriage. While still a newlywed, Gerard penned a suicide note, which was found and delivered unto the hands of Dr. Raymond Killinger. Killinger referred Schaefer to Dr. R.R. McCormick, a "psychometrist" who studied Schaefer. McCormick sent back to Killinger the following psychological evaluation:

Dr. Raymond Killinger, the Psychiatrist for Florida Atlantic University referred John to the Florida Atlantic University Testing and Evaluation Center for psychological evaluation on an emergency basis. Telephone conversation with Dr. Killinger revealed that John has had incidents of acting out behavior involving the use of firearms and he did leave a suicide note. Dr. Killinger was interested in projective testing which would assess the extent of disorganization and support any consideration for urgent action requiring intervention in order to protect John or the community.

John reported to the Testing Center, as requested, on his own and rapport was quickly established with him. He appeared to be seeking assistance for his difficulty and had confidence in Dr. Killinger who had sent him for this testing.

Discussion:

> This examiner was able to hold John's attention and cooperation through approximately two and one-half hours of testing. Rapport was excellent and the testing results are prolific in psycho-dynamic information. These results are consistent and indicate that John is immature, has poor ego control, is aggressive and rebellious and primarily has an intense father conflict. In addition, his personality dynamics incline him to blame others for his own difficulties. He is extremely confused in terms of self-image and is alienated from himself and others.

However, he does have a capacity to relate to others and is approachable in a therapeutic relationship. At this point John's own resources are not sufficient for a solution to his problems and he is in need of supportive therapy which will ameliorate the severity of his symptoms.

This examiner does not find any indication of excessive depression which might indicate suicidal tendencies. It is felt that a characterlogical neurosis with a paranoid trait overlay are more descriptive of his personality structure. In addition, Bender-Gestalt revealed perseveration of the fundamental outstanding Gestalt principal by the use of the primitive loop as a unit symbol. This is indicative of decreased ego control and of impairment in reality testing which is often found among psychotics or individuals with intra-cranial pathology.

In the post-testing interview John was asked how he felt and he indicated that he felt fine now but that he would have times when everything feels unreal. "I feel fine but at times I feel different—like it isn't real, not like I black out, but things just go"—John motioned with his hands downward toward his head with fingers extended.

Recommendations:

It is felt that John's psychological disorganization is severe and his frustration level low with consequent inability to cope with normal stresses. It is suggested that the nature of his reported alteration of consciousness be further investigated through additional psychiatric and neurological evaluation.

It is suggested that an evaluative conference be held with all those who are involved in treating John, at which time information may be brought together and a consensus of opinion reached which will define treatment goals.

Killinger then sent Schaefer to the Henderson Clinic of Broward County where he began a program with a Dr. Charles W. Long, a psychiatrist who continued to see him until May of 1971, throughout his short-lived marriage which ended abruptly in 1970. Schaefer's divorce was as quiet and passionless as his marriage.

Schaefer made no more attempts on his own life, but his role in society, as far as functioning in a "normal" capacity was becoming questionable. In March, 1969, Schaefer first applied for a student teaching internship, which would begin the following academic year in September, 1969. He was accepted and allotted an internship which was to have run from September 23 through December 16, 1969, at Plantation High School, in the city of the same name. His college supervisor was Dr. Charles Bates and his supervising teacher at Plantation was Mr. Robert Dunn. The director of the internship program was Dr. Louis Camp.

Schaefer began the program, having listed his area of specialization as geography, though he was given social studies as his topic to teach. During the first month, his parents ended their twenty-two-year marriage, when Doris Schaefer was granted a divorce on grounds of "extreme cruelty, chronic drunkenness, and adultery." Gerard Schaefer, Sr. entered a hospital in Nashville, Tennessee, to "cope with his drinking."

Schaefer's first progress report as of October 13, 1969, written by Mr. Dunn, gave him an "About Average Chance," in all student teaching areas. The visiting professor, Dr. Bates, did not see things even that optimistically. On his report, under "Relates well with children," he wrote, "Can't Predict." Under "Relates well with faculty," Dr. Bates wrote: "Can't Predict." He wrote the same notation for "Ability to evaluate self" and "Has good rapport with cooperating teacher." There were no other recommendations at that time.

By November 7, things had taken a turn for the worse. This time Dr. Bates had left the progress report blank but noted "comments" were listed on the back of the report. The comments were: that in conference with Mr. Dunn, as well as other members of the school's faculty, "it was decided to withdraw Mr. Schaefer from the program."

Dr. Bates wrote:

Reasons:

```
     1. Putting on bulletin - 1st drawing -
   "veto the nonintercourse act."
```

2. Explains to class how he evaded the draft. (A check with the Fort Lauderdale Draft Board revealed that he was rejected for military service on not one, but four separate occasions. His classification was that of 1-Y. This classification is assigned to persons for "mental, morals, or physical" reasons. The classification later changed to 4-F, which means ''not eligible" after his twenty-sixth birthday.)

3. Lack of cooperation and not accepting advice from Mr. Dunn & Mr. Cox.

4. Phone calls from parents that he is not a proper influence on students.

5. When all this (was) pointed out, he returned & said he had the "right" to express his opinions.

6. Says he does not intend to teach.

7. (Says) George Washington smoked "pot."

That same day, Dr. Bates sent a letter to Schaefer asking him not to return to Plantation High School on Monday, November 10. Oddly, after such harsh criticism, Dr. Bates asked Schaefer to withdraw from student teaching, but to re-apply for September, 1970.

In March, 1970, Schaefer again applied for an internship. The following information was listed on his application:

Major: Geography,

Experience: Professional hunting & fishing guide - Broward Co. 1964-69. Professional trap & skeet shooter instructor, Broward & Dade (counties) 1967-69. Construction worker, Broward & Dade 1964-69, part-time.

(It is interesting to note that none of his former job experiences list names of supervisors, specific addresses, or any other pertinent information.)

Kinds of Work with Children and/or Young People: N.R.A. rifle & shotgun instructor, Broward Co., 1967-69. Entertainment- Sing Out America '66, National Cast, 1966, (for 8 mos.)

Indicate dates and schools of Teacher Aide Program: New River Junior High School, Fort Lauderdale, March - June '68, Sept.-

Dec.'68, Jan.-March, '69. (Note: There is no
mention of the aborted program at Plantation
High School.)

Most of the other information on this
application is accurate and verifiable, but
most fascinating is the following:
Personal Background Information:
Hobbies and Special Interests: hunting &
fishing, coin collecting, skin-diving, camping,
tennis, stamp collecting.
Reading: Historical novels, true-
life adventure.
School subject matter: Geography,
History, English.
Recreation: Golf, basketball, tennis.
Travels: Between 1966-1969 I have been in
46 states, Mexico, 7 Provinces of Canada, and
the Bahamas.
Community Activities: Umpire Little League
baseball, Boy Scouts.

This application was completed and turned in to the College of
Education, FAU, where Dr. Louis T. Camp was still departmental Chairman.
Once again, Gerard John Schaefer was accepted into the student teaching
program, despite his previous failure in that position. This time, however,
his supervising teacher was the astute Mr. Richard Goodhart, and his
college supervisor was the equally perceptive Mrs. Betty Morris. His new
assignment was to run from April 2, through June 10, 1970. The school
where he'd be teaching was Stranahan High School in Fort Lauderdale.
It was at Stranahan where he most likely first spotted a beautiful young
student named Susan Kay Place. She would become a most significant
factor in the strange case of Gerard Schaefer.

Schaefer's first progress report, completed by Mrs. Morris, showed
that he was already experiencing difficulties. Almost all categories of
achievement were marked with "Doubtful Success," and several notations
were made. "Very rigid and authoritative (attitude). Says he must spend too
much time reading. Does not accept criticism well. Student has been able
to work with only one class, very weak in planning... " Other comments
observe that Schaefer was either late to teacher meetings, or did not show
at all, and often ended classes early.

The next progress report was worse. Again, "Doubtful Success" was listed in most categories, and under "Demonstrates knowledge of subject matter," Mrs. Morris wrote, "No background in History"; a subject Schaefer was supposed to have known well. Other comments were: "Teaches only outline. Has not used time . . . to enrich class," and "leaves school early . . ."

The next report had the comment "Very, very limited" under "Knowledge of Subject." The "Doubtful Success" column was filled from top to bottom. This report was again filled with comments, including: ". . .Comments, Shut-up to students . . . lack of initiative, inadequate preparation, lack of punctuality . . . grave doubts concerning his suitability for teaching."

The next report was written in a hasty hand, probably while Mrs. Morris was still upset with her uncooperative student teacher. Quickly scrawled are comments such as: "Too defensive to evaluate," and "Student seems to have a severe inferiority complex, demonstrating the classic defense mechanism of superiority evidenced by authoritative, dictatorial approach."

Later discoveries would show that before Schaefer was accepted to teach at Stranahan, Boca Raton High School had refused to accept him, because of "attitude" problems. Finally, Mr. Goodhart wrote a letter voicing his concerns to Dr. Camp.

> Dear Dr. Camp:
> The following is a resume of the activities of *John Schaefer* as an intern at Stranahan High School from April 1 through May13, 1970.
> The first notification Stranahan H.S. had of Mr. Schaefer's assignment as a social studies intern teacher was the arrival of his college supervisor, Mrs. Betty Morris. After a good deal of inquiry, our principal determined that Mr. Schaefer had indeed been assigned to Stranahan. He arrived at approximately 1 PM. The principal and I, in conference, tried to determine where to place him; he remained outside the office waiting for an interview. I offered to accept him rather than disrupt another teacher's plans at such a late date. When we called Mr. Schaefer in to discuss his assignment (at approximately 2 PM) we found he had left.
> On the following day Mr. Schaefer arrived (unshaven) and explained that he had to quit his job and go to the doctor as reason for

leaving so abruptly. For the next few days
he observed my classes, he arrived late on
April 3 and 6 and left early on April 6. He
had been given the schoolteacher's handbook to
study when he arrived. This book contained the
teacher's duty hours. I doubt that he read it.

On April 7 he was assigned to prepare to
teach the Americanism vs. Communism unit to
one of my Modern European History classes.
He was given the texts used and was told
to work- up an outline unit for inspection
and criticism (he never did). He complained
that this "was not his field" that he was
a geography major. He admitted that he
had recently completed the "Communism vs.
Democracy" course at FAU.

On April 18 he was given the three Mod.
Eur. Hist. classes in order that he might
become acquainted with them. At this time, I
was under the impression that he had completed
almost all of his intern program at Plantation
H.S. but had dropped out due to philosophical
differences with the administration of that
school. I deliberately avoided contacting
Plantation at that time (I spoke to his
directing teacher and the Dept. Head about
Schaefer yesterday).

During the next two days he attended an
all-day seminar at FAU and observed. On April
14 he was assigned to teach the 3rd period
class the Am. Vs. Comm. unit. It was quickly
apparent that he was weak in his knowledge
of subject material and that his knowledge
of the techniques of teaching (even the most
rudimentary) was practically non-existent.

At this time (April 14) he was told in a
rather long discussion with me, that he would
have to prepare rather detailed lesson plans,
check the teacher's bulletin board and observe
my daily routine.

On April 15 he attempted a role-playing
assignment. It was not satisfactorily given
and caused much confusion. No lesson plan
was given to me. The class was fairly noisey
but sympathetic to his problems. He attempted

a lecture (In spite of a warning that he should not attempt to lecture with his almost nonexistent background in the subject.) He managed to impress the students with the fact that he didn't know much about communism and its background.

On April 16 (the day he had scheduled the role-playing,) he went to traffic court to fight a speeding ticket. (He says he won). In the afternoon he observed my class and others. On April 17 he again lectured, in a rather defensive, authoritarian manner. Most of the class ignored him. On April 20 he attempted to conduct his role-playing class. It was supposed to be a session between the Czar's secret police and representatives of the various factions in Russia around 1900. I taped the session, Mrs. Morris has the tape, it is almost unintelligable. For the last 1/2 of the period (since nothing much was happening) I suggested that he go over some questions I had assigned the class while he was absent. A student quickly put the questions on the board; he did not go over them. He showed so little vitality (according to my observation notes) was listless with occasional sparks of sarcasm (a problem we had discussed). He made little or no attempt to keep the class's interest.

On April 21 & 22 half of each class being tested was absent. I allowed him to take over all three classes and conduct an Earth Day/70 discussion. He used a tape of anti-pollution songs which I had made up and supplied. He had a lesson plan, but it was rather sketchy.

On April 23, he took over all classes (I had a meeting in Miami). Before I left, we discussed his making up a test. He was instructed to type it up and come into school on Friday (a teacher work day) and ditto it off. As president of the Florida Council for the Social Studies I had an all-day meeting in Miami. On Friday he apparently went fishing.

He arrived a little early on Monday, April 27 and ran off the test. As we were intending

to use the test 1st, 3rd, & 5th periods, we
had to use the first part of the period to
assemble the test and correct his mistakes.
Mrs. Morris has a copy of the test. In
analyzing the test with him I pointed out
evidence of prejudice in the wording of one
question. He seemed unaware of this despite
his problems at Plantation. We also discussed
another possibly unnecessarily controversial
question. Aside from numerous errors of
spelling and grammer the test was, in my
opinion, a fairly good one.

On April 28 he again arrived unshaven (this
was his appearance approximately 25% of the
time). He demonstrated poor class control and
generally gave a poor class performance. We
discussed his academic problem, I suggested
he use Geo-politics as the basis for a class
after he reminded me of his geographical
background. He was several minutes figuring out
what I was talking about.

We had had several sessions discussing
alternatives to lecturing, one of which he
used. On April 29 he did attempt a Socratic-
question discussion class but kept cutting the
students off when they attempted to answer. On
April 30 he essentially repeated his mistakes
of the past weeks. As students attempted
discussion, he cut them off despite repeated
counselling about this.

For the next several days he continued as
above. Mrs. Morris observed him on May 8 and
had a lengthy discussion with her followed by
one with me concerning his inadequacies. He
said he "had no idea" he was doing so poorly.
On May 4, however, I had requested that the
class he was teaching rate him and comment on
his teaching. The class consensus was that he
had poor class control and didn't hold their
attention. He had carefully read those rating
sheets on May 5.

On May 8, Mr. Schaefer was assigned the 1st
and 3rd period classes and told to prepare
lesson plans for the following Monday. On
Monday, May 11, his lesson plans for that day

were submitted, they were fair to adequate in my opinion. He snapped at the class and had a good deal of trouble getting them to respond to his "leading" questions. He did not accept or enlarge upon the answers he got. His lessons and preparation showed considerable improvement over his previous performance; to approximately the level of a second, or third week intern, in my judgment.

On May 12 he again lectured, this time using the blackboard and o/h projector. A rather pedestrian performance which Mrs. Morris observed. After school we had a two-hour discussion concerning his problem. I indicated that in light of his improved performance of the past two days the question in my mind was no longer "Why couldn't you get started?" but rather "Why had you taken so long to get started?" I suggested that he consider alternatives to teaching. He said he had no alternatives prepared. I promised to let him know my recommendations to you when I gave them.

My recommendations are as follows:

In my opinion John Schaefer has not and will not complete the intern program in a satisfactory manner. My judgment is based on the above observations taken from my daily log and on my personal contact with Mr. Schaefer.

Mr. Schaefer impresses me as a student who is both defensive, fearing failure, and at the same time unwilling to exert himself to keep from failing. Despite his protestation that he is concerned and wants to be a good and influential teacher, he gives me the impression of a person seeking a safe, secure, easy niche where he will be required to put out a minimum of effort. As mitigating factors, I believe his poor first experience in interning has made him overly defensive this time. Also, his personal problems with his home life may also have contributed to his unsatisfactory performance.

I would not advise anyone to hire Mr. Schaefer as a teacher. I do not think he

```
knows any Social Studies subject well enough
to teach it. I do not think that he has
an adequate knowledge of the rudiments of
teaching and I do not think his attitude is
that expected of a teacher.
     I request that you withdraw him from the
internship assignment at Stranahan High School
as soon as possible and in no case later than
Monday, May 18.
     I am concerned that Florida Atlantic
University would consider assigning a
student with Mr. Schaefer's inadequacies to
the intern program. I trust future interns
will be more adequately prepared and more
carefully screened.
                    Sincerely,
                    Richard Goodhart, Jr.
                    Social Studies Dept. Head
```

Dr. Camp read Goodhart's letter with great interest. The following day, in a letter, he thanked Goodhart and apologized for the "circumstances" concerning Schaefer. On May 19, 1970, Dr. Camp drafted a letter to the Wimberly Academic Affairs in charge of the College of Education, requesting that Gerard John Schaefer be withdrawn from student teaching.

* * *

At approximately this same time, May of 1970, Gerard Schaefer began to reveal a rather odd facet of his character. He seemed to have developed an interest, indeed, a growing obsession with capital punishment, in particular, hanging. The following letter, written on Florida Atlantic University letterhead, was sent to Candar Publishing, Valley Stream, New York. It was post-dated May 15, 1970, just two days after Goodhart had written Camp the letter asking for Schaefer's removal from student teaching, and probably the same day he was verbally informed by Camp that he was being withdrawn from the program. All spelling and grammatical mistakes are his.

```
Dear Sirs,
     While attending school this year in Kansas,
I was in charge of gathering data for a paper
one of the professors was doing on the evils
of capital punishment.
```

In Kansas the legal method of execution is hanging. To gather information on this subject I turned to English history since that method of execution has been practiced in that country until just recently. Arthur Koestler, in his book, "Reflections on Hanging" attempts to play on human emotion by describing the grossities and horrors of execution by hanging. Detailed descriptions of executions are apparently at a minimum in most libraries which does not help the research assistant at all.

In his book Koestler states, "Women are required to wear waterproof underwear on the morning of their execution."

That statement brought questions to mind that I have had little success in finding answers to. I thought that a magazine such as "Man's Action" might be able to aid me in finding the answers or refer me to material that would contain this information.

1. We know that hanging is a particularly degrading death and that the victim, either male or female, in addition to suffering bodily disfigurement will urinate and defecate due to the loss of control when the rope tightens and the social need for it. The question is: Why is it that a woman is required to wear waterproof underwear? Does a society that does not flinch at taking a human life become offended at the sight of urine dripping from a hanging corpse? Are men also required to wear similar underwear? If not, why not? Koestler makes no mention of this practice in regard to men. Are the procedures when hanging a man different than when hanging a woman? Are there any other regulations in regard to what a victim must wear? For instance, are women required to wear slacks instead of a skirt for purposes of modesty? Are victims encouraged to empty their bladder and bowels before their execution?

Due to the delicate and rather gruesome nature of these questions it is understandable

```
why information is not readily available.
However, a magazine with such a broad spectrum
as your own may be able to obtain this type
of information easier than myself. I will
appreciate any help you may be able to give in
answering these questions. I will be looking
forward to your reply and the next issue of
Man's Action.

            Sincerely yours,
            G. John Schaefer, Jr.
            Research Assistant
```

There are, of course, no records of Schaefer ever attending any schools in Kansas. Additionally, Florida Atlantic University has no records indicating that Schaefer worked as a "research assistant" for any class, or professor, even remotely interested in such a topic. Candar Publishing was a company who used to publish pulp men's adventure magazines, with a somewhat sexual slant, one such was *Man's Action*. They simply responded back: "Sorry, we can't help you with any information on this subject." Indeed, they could not. The content of their magazine was usually some bawdy party jokes and "true-life" adventure stories and had nothing to do with capital punishment.

The letter also demonstrates that Schaefer was quite capable, and likely, to use another person's letterhead to better qualify himself, or to seek information or approval by misrepresenting himself. Other letters were written, some to foreign countries, describing himself as a "research student in sociology," seeking information on "the subject of legal life-taking." Again, there were questions pertaining to the victims' "bodily excretions."

Just prior to this time, Schaefer was living in a rundown hovel, a rented house, located in the suburbs of Fort Lauderdale. His alienated wife, Marti, had already moved and left him and his dog to fend for themselves.

The young, rather eccentric, college student was now on his own, probably for the first time in his life. He was no longer the aspiring Arnold Palmer, the trim, athletic golfer of yesteryear. His once muscular chest was beginning to slide down into his waistline. He appeared bloated and he moved lethargically. His once sunny hair was dull and receding away from his forehead. The pressures of rejection, from the intern program and from a failed marriage, had taken their toll. Still, he was a big man, and not without a certain persuasive presence, an undeniable charisma. With a haircut and pressed outfit, he could still impress people, especially so with his college banter, though he often chose to dress in rumpled clothes and mumble when he talked. He was, if nothing else, a paradox. A man whose characteristics and even appearance, no two people would ever agree on. He was, as one person would describe him, a "human chameleon, in both mind and body."

The recent divorcee did not like living alone, and needing help to pay the bills, he soon found a roommate, an old high school friend, John Dolan.

The following is an excerpt from a conversation Dolan gave the police during the homicide investigation three years later. (NOTE: All questions are prefaced with an abbreviation, "Q." All of Dolan's answers are prefaced with an "A.")

Q: You knew John Schaefer? Gerard John Schaefer, Jr.

A: Right, right.

Q: How did you first happen to come about meeting him?

A: School. He went to Aquinas.

Q: That's where you went to high school?

A: Right.

Q: And you were in the same grade with John?

A: Right, right, right.

Q: Would you consider yourself, at that time, to have been fairly good friends with him?

A: I knew him. I knew him, and we did double on dates and things like that.

Q: Back in high school?

A: Yeah, right, right. I had other closer friends, you know.

Q: You didn't live in the same general area as John?

A: No, no.

Q: Do you recall names of any of the girls back in high school that John was dating?

A: Just that one, Kathy Brickson (phonetic).

Q: Kathy Brickson?

A: Yeah, that was the only one.

Q: Have you seen her at all since she has gotten married?

A: No, I hardly saw her in high school,

Q: You don't even know what her name is now, her married name?

A: No, no.

Q: We have been trying to locate her. We have had a little bit of difficulty on that. Did you keep in touch with John after you graduated from high school at all?

A: Ah, let me see. What happened after I graduated from high school? I went to junior college, and John was gone, you know, I don't know where he went, you know. I was going to junior college. Then I went into the service. I came back out in sixty-eight.

Q: When did you go in the service?

A: Sixty-five.

Q: Sixty-five?

A: Yeah.

Q: What branch did you go into?

A: Navy. I came out in sixty-eight.

Q: Whereabouts were you stationed?

A: I was stationed in San Diego and in Vietnam and in New London, Connecticut.

Q: About when were you stationed in San Diego?

A: The first year of my tour.

Q: You went to boot camp there?

A: No, I went to boot camp at Great Lakes.

Q: Then you transferred over to San Diego?

A: Right.

Q: Then you shipped out from there over to Vietnam?

A: Right.

Q: How long did you spend in Vietnam?

A: Eighteen months.

Q: And then you were transferred back to New London, Connecticut?

A: Right.

Q: And is that where you were discharged from?

A: Separated.

Q: What type of discharge did you receive?

A: Honorable.

Q: You completed your tour of duty?

A: Right.

Q: Your enlistment?

A: Right.

Q: What rank were you when you were discharged?

A: E-3.

Q: E-3, what was that the equivalent to?

A: PFC, I guess.

Q: Seaman First Class?

A: Yeah, right.

Q: Where did you go after you were discharged?

 A: Home.

Q: Back here to Lauderdale?

A: Yes.

Q: Did you continue going to college then or did you go to work or what?

A: I went to work for three months, and then I went back to college and got my AA degree and went up to Florida State.

Q: Your AA? That was at Broward Community College that you got your AA?

Q: Right.

A: When did you receive that?

Q: That was in the seventies, I guess.

A: You went to Florida State from there?

A: Yeah.

Q: And how long were you up at Florida State?

A: Two quarters.

Q: What were you studying up there?

A: Government.

Q: Did the transfer then bring you to Florida Atlantic

A: Well, I worked about a year in between.

Q: Whereabouts?

A: Sears.

Q: When you started up here at Florida Atlantic?

A: Yeah.

Q: When did you start at Florida Atlantic?

A: The fall quarter of 1971.

Q: Was John attending Florida Atlantic at the time you started back?

A: No, I don't think he was. I don't recall ever running into John. Let me see, let me think. No, I don't think he was. Not at all.

Q: Did you and John ever share an apartment at all?

A: Right, we had that over in (indistinguishable) Village or whatever you call it.

Q: In Fort Lauderdale? Okay, were you going to the school at that time or working or what?

A: I was working. I wasn't going to school.

Q: Whereabouts were you working at that time?

A: At Sears.

Q: That is when you were selling shoes there?

A: Yes.

Q: Okay, what was John doing at that time?

A: He was interning.

Q: That was when he was in the student intern program?

A: Yes.

Q: During that time did the two of you double date or have common friends at any time?

A: Yeah, we had some friends. You know, people that lived there. That place, you know, was the worst place I ever lived in my life, you know.

Q: What was wrong with it?

A: Everything was wrong. The ceiling went like this, the ceiling went like that, and the floor went like that, the plumbing didn't work sometimes.

Q: Was it an old building?

A: Really, really awful. His dog was drooling all over the place. The place smelled like a kennel. Man, it was just bad.

Q: How long did you live there?

A: Not too long. Three weeks—I really don't know. But I moved when I made up my mind to move. It was because I was completely disgusted, and I was a little bit scared. I really didn't know why I was scared, but I was scared.

Q: You don't have any reason as to why you were scared?

A: I don't know. John was just, you know, kind of getting a little bit weird. Somebody asked me about John after that, you know. Well, like say, I don't know. Maybe I said this to somebody, you know, that I thought John was a little bit weird. Like he told me like—after all this stuff came out in the papers, you know, like I had the feeling like that he was playing some kind of morbid joke on me, you know.

Q: You mean you felt that after the spring of '73? After he was charged with murder?

A: Right, yeah. Like, say for instance—I saw him when he came back from Europe. I had seen him a couple of times after I moved out of there. Mostly because I didn't have anything else to do. But, you know, those evenings I said, "Oh, what the hell, I'll go over to see what John is doing." I was always kind of scared of him. But when he came back from Europe, you know, like he had these pictures you know, and he showed me these pictures. They were just, you know, like normal tourist pictures, you know. And he says, "I got some more, you know, that I took." I said, "Oh yeah," you know, and I thought, you know, he had them hidden away because they was, you know, maybe he got into some kind of (indistinguishable).

Q: Where was he living at that time?

A: In his parent's house.

Q: When you had this conversation with him, was it back in his room?

A: Yeah, right.

Q: The back, north bedroom?

A: Yeah. And he says...

Q: Do you know about when this was?

A: This was when he returned from Europe, shortly after he returned from Europe.

Q: About what year was this?

A: 1969. Wait a minute, seventy. It must have been '70.

Q: It was before he was married to Marti? Or had he been married to Marti?

A: Oh, he had already been married to Marti.

Q: That was when he got divorced that he made the trip to Europe?

A: Yeah. He said he had some more pictures, you know, and I wanted to see them, you know, because I thought they would be, you know. He said, "Oh, you don't want to see those," you know.

Q: Did he tell you what they were like at all?

A: No. I said, "Well, what are they?" And he just laughed, you know. And on other occasions, you know, when we were rooming together, he'd say things to me. One time we got into an argument, and I never figured out what we were arguing about. He was just arguing with me, and told me that, you know, I was completely wrong and everything like that, you know.

Q: You don't have any idea what the argument was about?

A: No, I have no idea. As a matter of fact, it took me a while to catch on that we were in an argument and then by the time—I am trying to figure out what he is talking about, you know, and then the argument is over, and he said I am wrong. So, I didn't even know what the argument was about, you know. Like he told me, he liked to kill. And he said that one time he drank blood, you know. You know, I was struggling to figure out, you know, how a reasonable person would be drinking blood, you know. I figured it had something to do with some kind of...

Q: He likes to kill? Did he mention what he likes to kill?

A: No, no. I assume, you know, he was hunting, you know, and that's why that he was hunting because he liked to kill, you know. I figure if a person likes to kill, you know, about the best place to kill—I don't hunt.

I have no idea what goes on in a person's mind, you know, when they are out there or what even motivated them to go out hunting, you know. When he said he drank blood, you know, I was really . . . I am sitting there and I am thinking, you know, what kind of a thing is this, you know, and he is laughing, you know, because I am trying to say, you know, well, this is a reasonable person I am talking to now. How do I fit this in, you know? He's got a big joke out of it, you know.

Q: Would you say he was only kidding with you?

A: No.

Q: Did he ever show you these pictures?

A: No.

Q: Never showed them to you?

A: No.

Q: Did he ever talk to you about public hangings or anything that way that he might have brought up from time to time?

A: Hangings? Public executions? No, no, he never mentioned anything like that.

Q: Did you notice anything else unusual during the period of time that you were either staying with John or that you were visiting in his house or going out together or anything like that?

A: He had an exceptionally large amount of these skinning knives, you know. And I asked him why he had all those, and he laughed about that, too

Q: Did he say anything about it?

A: No. I really didn't, you know, John would get into these moods, you know, where he started talking, you know, and he would get real weird. I just didn't want to talk to him anymore, you know.

Q: Did he appear to be this way all the time, or did this appear to be something that would come on to him and all of a sudden, he would start talking about these things and then he would go back to the way he used to be?

A: There was no like—you mean, a big switch or anything like that? Like you could see?

Q: No, no there was nothing like that. It was like, you know, it seemed, you know, kind of a natural flow of conversation or something like that, you know, where he would get right into it. No, there was nothing like a big switch or anything like that.

In direct contradiction to Dolan's comments, are those of Betty Owens. Owens was a friend of Schaefer's when he attended Broward Junior

College. She worked as a staff advisor for the literary magazine the college published at the time Pan Ku, which is how the two came to know each other. She remembers nothing strange or eccentric about her college chum, and still considers him a friend whose companionship is sorely missed.

"I remember John as a very fine, intelligent boy . . . very sensitive with a personality very distinctly his own," Owens was quoted as saying. "He was quick to smile and laugh . . . a love everybody, kind, and quiet sort of a boy.

"Often, he would come into the office (of Pan Ku) and we would sit there, drinking coffee and chatting about various things. He was interesting to talk to, very sharp, with a keen intellect, and he had a way with prose. Very definitely, he had a keen intellect.

"I remember one time when he came into the office... it was just after his student teaching withdrawal at Plantation High School. John was very, very low. He wanted very much to be a teacher. While we were talking about his teaching trouble, some other people stopped by the office and the conversation changed and John began to laugh and joke. He really kept us in stitches for about an hour and a half. It was all John."

Owens said she remembered Schaefer seeing a psychiatrist, while he was still married to Marti. She did not know why he was getting treatment, nor did it reflect on their friendship. Whatever his problem was, she was sure it was minor and that he could deal with it.

"He wasn't ashamed about it. He didn't try to hide it from me...but I never tried to pry. But at times he would stop at the office on his way to one of his sessions with the psychiatrist and, if I was away, he'd leave me a note that said something like... 'On my way to the head shrink. Stopped by to say hello,' or something like that.

"I kept hoping things would work out for him . . . that he would find his place and wouldn't encounter anymore frustrations. He wanted to be a teacher and that was a frustration. I really liked him and if he walked through that door, even now, I would be very happy to see him again."

Understandably disillusioned with teaching, on September 1, 1970, Gerard Schaefer filled out an application for the City of Wilton Manor, a suburb of Fort Lauderdale. Position applied for: Police Officer. He'd seen the job opening while going through the employment ads in the Fort Lauderdale News.

He listed his address as "2716 SW 34th Avenue, Fort Lauderdale," stating he'd lived there "11 years." He also stated on the application that he was married. He did not mention ever living in the ramshackle home on 1810 SW 22nd Street, Fort Lauderdale, where he lived with John Dolan, and prior to that, with his wife, Marti. He also neglected to mention that she'd filed for divorce on May 15, 1970 while he was living on 22nd Street and that now, he was indeed divorced.

Under "previous government employment," Schaefer wrote: "Florida Atlantic University, 1968, Research Assistant." Any physical limitations? "Chronic Allergies." Under "Education," he wrote: "5 years college; Major—Education & Physiology." He left the questions about Military Service blank. He listed under "special skills:" "typewriter 30 words per minute" and "Airboat Operator."

The entire application for the job of police officer was two pages.

The most interesting section of this application was the "Employment Record." In this section the applicant is to start with the last employer and list all previous employers. Schaefer wrote that his last employer was a man named "J. Malm, of Marakesh." The mysterious Mr. "Josta" Malm would later be sought for questioning by the Broward County Sheriff's Department, and several other South Florida police agencies, as well as the international police agency, Interpol. He would not be found. But for now, Schaefer listed Malm's address as 21 Isle De France Blvd., Morocco, and said that he'd worked under Malm from June of 1970 through August of 1970. His salary for that period he left blank, but his job title was, "Buyer of Arab & Berger Crafts." His duties included: "Travelling the Atlas Mountains and the Sahara Desert by VW Bus, purchasing tribal goods to be sold in Europe." His reason for leaving was, "Returned to U.S."

From January of 1970, until April of the same year, Schaefer wrote that he'd worked for "Loxahatchee Recreational, Inc." His duties: "Assisting the running of the Fish Camp, selling licenses, and booking fishing parties."

He did not mention any student teaching jobs on the application at all. He did list that for $1.60 per hour, he worked as a research assistant, from January of '68 until April of '68. His employer was: "State of Florida," address: "Tallahassee."

His last employment reference was himself, as once again he listed his expertise as "Hunting & Fishing Guide -- Coin Dealer." He gave a beginning date of June, 1964, an ending date was simply filled in with a slash, indicating he'd never left that capacity.

One year after filling out this application, Gerard Schaefer, Jr, was hired as a police officer for the City of Wilton Manor.

With the new job came the demand for more education. Wilton Manor enrolled rookie cop, Gerard J. Schaefer, into the Broward County Police Academy, in September of 1971.

Schaefer was exultant. A new job and now back in school to learn a career. It was a new beginning. So enthusiastic was he, that he asked Teresa Dean to be his wife.

Teresa met Schaefer while she was working at the Econo-Way grocery store in Fort Lauderdale. She was a cashier there and was immediately stricken by the man with the sparkling eyes, and almost overwhelming charisma. He was working for the Wackenhut Corporation as a security guard and was most impressive in his neatly pressed uniform as he took his place in Teresa's check-out line. At six feet, one-inch, and two-hundred-and-five pounds, his presence could not go unnoticed.

The frail cashier trembled a little when the guard finally stepped up with his order. Her eyes were level with his massive chest, that was illuminated with sparkling buttons, his name tag, and a shining badge that reflected a distorted image of the shy grocery clerk. They began to see each other often; the strong outdoorsman showering his petite Econo-Way clerk with gifts on almost every date. She reciprocated by lending understanding and affection for her lumbering security guard. It was an odd match to be sure, but she was impressed with his worldliness, and he with her gentle beauty, and it is sometimes the widely contrasted individuals who make the best couple. He was not the most athletic, or ambitious, or even the most handsome fellow around, but compared to many of the long-haired, pot-smoking flower children of that time, he was a rock. He was, to the naive Teresa Dean, an object of profound security, a real man. He knew what he wanted, and so, when he secured the police officer job with Wilton Manor, and began what might have been a good, solid career; he asked for her hand in marriage and she accepted.

They were married in September of 1971, and like all newlyweds, lived in an unreal frame of mind, a happiness that seemingly would never end. Schaefer was busy with school, which did not allow the young couple to spend as much time together as they would have liked. However, when they could, they often took weekend excursions to settings of idyllic beauty, of which there are unlimited quantities in South Florida. One of their trips took them to Sanibel and Captiva Islands, off Fort Myers Beach. There, they watched the sun sink into the ocean as pelicans awkwardly dipped into the Gulf of Mexico for a quick fish dinner. The din of music drifted over to them from the popular old Bubble Room lounge. The white sand changed from hot, to warm, to cool and invited bare feet to run through it as dusk fell.

Then it was back to work, and school, and real life. They were happy, and nothing that anyone said could change that. He was as pleased as could be with his new bride. They were so much more compatible than he and Marti had been. Teresa was equally elated; Gerard was turning out to be a fine husband. Oh, sometimes he stayed away too long, hunting and fishing, but she understood that. She was not demanding. A man needs to do those things, have some time to himself, and frankly, almost anything he wanted to do was fine with her.

Not everyone felt the same way about Gerard as did Teresa.

Wilton Manor's Police Chief, Bernard Scott, the man who hired Schaefer and less than one year later would fire him, had a very different view of Gerard than did Teresa.

"He used poor judgment, did dumb things," said Scott. "If he was sent to control traffic at an accident, John would wander into a store and buy a bag of potato chips . . . dumb things like that."

In direct contradiction though, Scott awarded Schaefer a commendation for his traffic control work. An odd gesture for a man who would later comment, "I'd put my uniform back on and walk the streets myself before hiring him (Schaefer) back." Other fellow officers would be quoted as saying he was "a badge-happy cop," or "He would hardly get his patrol car out of the driveway without stopping a (traffic) violator."

Despite some favorable comments and the commendation, Scott did not believe Schaefer had what it took to be a good police officer. He called Schaefer into his office in April of 1972, planning to fire the inconsistent rookie. "But he (Schaefer) pleaded for another chance, almost with tears in his eyes, and was kept on the force."

"The next thing I knew," said Scott, "I had a call from a Fort Lauderdale police sergeant who said Schaefer had been called in for a job interview." During the interview, Schaefer started "bad-mouthing me (Scott) and my (Wilton Manor) department." Scott said that was the "final straw."

"When he reported for duty that day, I fired him on the spot."

A police cadet who attended Broward County Police Academy with Schaefer remembers him well. Thomas Stempkowski, an officer with the Oakland Park Police Department since September of 1971, recalled several details of Schaefer's character and revealed some rather fascinating information in the following conversation.

"Did you attend the Broward County Police Academy?"

"Yes, sir, I did."

"When was that?"

"Through September of 1971 and December of 1971."

"That was continuous?"

"Yes."

"While you were attending the academy, did you have occasion to meet John Schaefer, Gerard Schaefer?"

"Yes, sir."

"Rather than myself asking you a lot of specific questions, why don't you just relate how you came to meet him and what you do remember about him and then, if I have any specific questions, I will break in."

"Well, while in the police academy with him, the few occasions I had to talk to him, the thing that I remember most about is the fact he used to talk about sex quite a bit and used to become very detailed about relations he would have with his wife."

"Did he ever tell you his wife's name?"

"Not that I remember. He mentioned the fact that he had been married once before and divorced, but I don't remember the name or if he mentioned his wife's name to me."

"About how many people were there in your class?"

"I believe about thirty-two."

"Did you meet all of the people in the class?"

"Yes."

"Did you get to know them all?"

"I knew them all, some better than others."

"Would you say that you remember them all today?"

"Maybe not all the names but if I saw them, I would remember them."

"Is there anything that makes, other than what you have told us already, is there anything that makes Schaefer stick out in your mind more than any of the others?"

"Yes, because of what he was. He was with Wilton Manor. Occasionally, I would run into him while I was on patrol and that makes him stick out, plus the fact he would talk about a few things that some other men I knew didn't."

"Did he ever show you any pictures, talk to you about pictures?"

"Yes, sir. He showed me a picture once."

"How many pictures did he show you?"

"I only saw one."

"Can you tell us what that picture was, what it showed?"

"It was a photograph of a woman lying, I believe it was on a couch, and it appeared that she had been strangled and mutilated."

"How do you mean mutilated?"

"It looked—it has been a while since I saw it—it looked as though she had been cut on her body, strangled, possibly beaten around the face."

"Could you tell whether there was more than one what appeared to be cut marks on her body?"

"I can't remember right now. The photograph I saw wasn't what you would call a very good photograph. It was very poor resolution. It was like the film had been developed by an amateur, as though it might have been a contact print because of the size."

"Was this a black and white photograph?"

"Yes."

"Do you remember what size the photograph was?"

"It was, I would say, about maybe two inches by one and a half inches."

"Did he tell you where he got that photograph?"

"Yes. He told me a friend of his who was a detective on a police department from some northern jurisdiction out of state, I forget where, gave it to him and he said it was a photograph of a woman who had been murdered."

"He never told you who this person was that gave it to him?"

"No. He never mentioned the name. I believe he mentioned the jurisdiction, but I don't remember it at this time."

"You say you just saw one picture?"

"Yes, sir."

"Did he show you this picture on more than one occasion?"

"No, sir, just showed it to me once."

"Was there anybody else present when he showed you the picture?"

"I believe so, but I don't remember who."

"About how long had you known him at the police academy when he showed you this picture?"

"It is hard to say. I had known him for a while. I would say six weeks to two months."

"About how long had you known him when he started talking· about his sexual experiences with his wife?"

"Three or four weeks."

"Would you describe the relationship with him as close friendship?"

"No, sir, I wouldn't."

"Had you become fairly friendly at this time, though?"

"Just enough to talk to occasionally."

"When the conversation went to sexual experiences, was he usually the one that brought this up?"

"Yes."

"Was there ever anyone else present other than you and Schaefer when these conversations took place?"

"Yes, sir. I believe on one occasion Patrolman Upham was present, Rick Paduda, John Nelson, and a George Smith. They were all on the Oakland Park Police Department at one time."

"What was it he used to say about sexual relations with his wife?"

"He used to, like right after lunch, he would come in and mention the fact he had sneaked home and had relations with his wife or if I happened to pass to talk to him for a few minutes in the morning before class would start, he would start talking about relations with his wife."

"Can you be any more specific than that?"

"He would mention things such as cunnilingus, fellatio, anal intercourse."

"Did he seem to talk about one more than any of the others?"

"Not that I remember."

"Did he ever talk about sexual relations with anyone other than his wife?"

"I believe so, but he mentioned that, the way he mentioned it was that it had been prior to his marriage."

"Did he talk about different positions that they would use?"

"Yes, sir."

"Can you tell us what those were?"

"Well, he would mention positions they would use so that his wife, he could perform cunnilingus and she could perform fellatio at the same time."

"Any others?"

"Yes, sir, anal intercourse. He would mention a few things such as that, such as, at one point, I remember he mentioned about having his wife lean over a chair."

"Any others that you remember?"

"Not offhand, sir."

"And you say he talked about this on more than one occasion?"

"Yes, sir."

"Are you married?"

"Yes, sir."

"Does it seem unusual to you that he was talking about this in relation to his wife?"

"Yes, sir."

"Would it have seemed unusual if he was talking about this in relation to just a girl that he had known?"

"If he had just mentioned a fact maybe he was single and going to bed with somebody or made love with someone, I wouldn't have thought anything about it; but the number of times and the way he talked about it, I thought it was a little odd, but I didn't think too much about it."

"Did any of the other people who were taking part in these conversations volunteer any information about their sexual experience?"

"Not to my knowledge. Possibly on a few occasions, someone might mention something about prior to their marriage or, if they weren't married, maybe they had something to do with someone."

"Would he just come up and start talking about these things out of a clear blue sky?"

"Yes, sir. If, say, for instance, we were standing outside the police academy and if a girl walked by, he might make a comment and go off from there on his conversation."

"And I think you testified that he never mentioned having relations with any other women other than his wife, is that right?"

"He mentioned it, but like I say, the way he mentioned it, it was as though he were talking about a time that was prior to his marriage."

"Did he ever mention to you anything about when he was in Europe or Africa?"

"Yes, sir."

"Could you tell us what he said about that?"

"One day, we were practicing handcuffing and he mentioned he had an unusual set of handcuffs that I had never seen the brand before and they were somewhat odd-looking and we all asked him where he got them and he said they were taken off a man who had been publicly executed, and I believe he mentioned one of the North African countries." (These handcuffs would later become an important point of interest in the bewildering case of Gerard Schaefer.)

"Did he say that he had been there?"

"Yes, sir, he did."

"Did he say what he was doing there?"

"Yes. He mentioned that he had been a bodyguard or something for a jewelry salesman or a jewel merchant."

"Did he say when that was?"

"He never mentioned the time period. He just mentioned that he had spent some time in Europe."

"Did he ever mention any other unusual experiences other than being a bodyguard in Africa?"

"Well, he mentioned how he got the handcuffs that he cut them off the body of a dead person."

"Did he have a key for those handcuffs?"

"I never saw a key, whether or not he had a key."

"If he was using them, if you place handcuffs on a person, don't you need a key to get them off?"

"I never saw the key. He mentioned the fact he wanted to use them, and no one would volunteer to be his subject for that."

"Did he ever mention any other things that would be unusual other than taking the handcuffs off of a dead person and being a bodyguard in Africa, any other strange or unusual experiences?"

"Not that I can remember right now."

"Did he seem to have many friends in the class?"

"To be truthful, no. Everyone knew him, but no one seemed to be very close to him."

"Did he seem anxious to try to make friends with people or did he seem as though he were a loner?"

"It seemed as though he was kind of a loner."

"But he would often come up and join the group?"

"He would join groups to talk for a few minutes and then wander off again."

"Did you ever see him on any other occasions after you finished your work at the police academy?

"One occasion stands out when I was investigating a hit-and-run accident with injuries."

"I have here a statement or a copy of a statement which was signed by you made on April 6 of 1973. Is that the statement that you wrote?"

"Yes, sir. It is a copy of it."

"Is that in your handwriting?"

"Yes, sir."

"Would you read through that statement and tell us if there is anything in there that is incorrect or that you feel should be added to it at this time or changed in any way."

"A few things in here that have not been brought out, whether or not you want them brought out."

"Yes, I was going to get to those. That is why I wanted you to read that first. Would you say everything in here is accurate as you remember it?"

"As I remember it, yes, sir."

"There is this part in here that says, during one of the conversations we had, Schaefer made mention of the fact he had toured Europe or visited several bordellos."

"Yes, sir."

"And it says he would go into detail about the sex acts that he committed. Do you remember what the details was that he went into?"

"He mentioned that his favorite country was Sweden. And I asked him why and he said because of the bordellos. And he mentioned the fact that he visited them frequently and had women perform fellatio and anal intercourse."

"Were those the terms he used?"

"No, sir."

"What were the terms he used?"

"He mentioned terms such as blow job and cornhole, if I remember correctly."

"Did he describe anything other than going to these bordellos in Sweden, any other experiences in detail?"

"Not that I can think of offhand."

"And you said that you don't remember him ever mentioning his wife's name?"

"I only saw his wife, as I best remember, once at a party that we all attended. We were going to the academy at that time. He never introduced me to her. I think we just kind of passed."

"Did you have occasion to meet him any time after the academy other than when I think you discussed some accident you were investigating?"

"Yes. I was investigating a hit-and-run accident with injuries and a car that we were looking for had been found in Wilton Manor. I had gone over to check the damage of the vehicle to see if it could be the vehicle that we were looking for and, when I got on the scene, Schaefer was there. And I remember he walked up to me and said, 'Is this the asshole you are looking for?' And at this time, there was a large group of people standing around who were all civilians and some were young and I didn't even speak to him because I didn't feel the comment he made with civilians standing around was worth even answering."

"Was that the last contact you had with him? Did you report this to anyone, the language that he used?"

"Yes, sir."

"Who did you report it to?"

"A sergeant. I don't remember the sergeant's name. He was standing by. He looked at me and I looked at him and I said, 'Did you hear that?' and he said, 'yes.'"

"This was a sergeant from Wilton Manor?"

"Yes, sir. I may have, I think I saw him one other time. It was just passing. I nodded to him and waved, and he nodded to me and waved."

"Was he (Schaefer) a patrolman at that time?"

"Yes, sir."

* * *

Teresa Schaefer cleaned and pressed her husband's uniforms. She was a good wife, supportive, and proud of her husband's position as policeman for the city of Wilton Manor. She deftly worked the tip of the hot iron around the embroidered patch that symbolized the city's police department. She starched the collars and pleated the sleeves and the trousers, then carefully placed the outfits onto hangers. Before going on to the rest of the laundry, she made sure the uniforms were right. That self-imposed duty, borne out of love and care for her husband, included replacing the "silverware" onto the uniform's shirt. She performed that labor as lovingly as the rest, making sure each button and nametag were polished and shining. And the badge, the most important part of a policeman's uniform, the emblem that symbolized the law; it too, was made to sparkle and glow. She always took extra time to shine the badge before pinning it on the shirt. Her thin fingers handled it gingerly, with respect for what it was supposed to stand for.

She had no idea, as she fingered the delicately sculpted surface of the badge, that she was holding a weapon. A weapon as ominously lethal as the gun her husband wore on his side, even more so, for where a gun might frighten someone away, a badge, worn by a protector of the people, would invite people closer. It would envelope them with security; people trust the wearer of the badge, and so, easily drop their defenses when in the company of a law enforcement officer.

It is for that reason that this badge was so potently dangerous, so deadly. For on this man, Teresa Schaefer's loving husband, the badge was not a symbol of law and order. It was a cold metallic invitation to law . . . and murder.

Chapter 3:

Susan and Georgia

*And the silken, sad, uncertain rustling of each curtain
thrilled me . . . filled me with fantastic terrors never
felt before.*

From *The Raven,* by Edgar Allan Poe

In the fall of 1972, Fort Lauderdale prepared itself again for the onslaught of the coming tourist season. It was expected to be a mild winter, as usual, and all went as before. Merchants, closed for the slow, steaming summer, began to dust off counters and clean windows as they opened their shops. Kids were in school, had been for a month. Traffic was thick and getting busier. The ocean perpetually polished the shoreline of the "gold coast." People went about their business.

There was no cause for fear. The panic that invariably grips a city during a major crisis was not here. There was no crisis. There were no Son of Sams, no Boston Stranglers or Hillside Stranglers, no Zodiac killers. This was the problem. The newspapers were free of the sensationalistic exploitation pieces that usually herald the heinous deeds of a serial killer. People did not, in those days, run to their TV sets to flick on the breaking news about another maniac killer. There was not internet, which was a blessing and a curse. Information was not easily found nor shared.

There were no investigations being conducted, either. No heavy-browed, pipe-smoking chief of police holding press conferences daily to reassure frightened citizens. No city mayor vowing to capture a crazed criminal. There were no forewarnings.

There were, however, literally dozens of people "missing", from late 1969 through to the fall of 1972. Some men, but mostly women, young, twenty-five and younger, some only eight- and nine-year-old children, all gone without a trace. This is not to say their disappearances were not investigated. The Fort Lauderdale Police Department as well as investigators from surrounding towns and cities, often conducted intense searches. The Broward County Sheriff's Department, Oakland Park Police and Plantation Police Departments all carried out investigations as were warranted.

But, as Gerard Schaefer had pointed out "without a body, there is no crime." This again was the problem. Many of these people who were missing were already dead. Many still have not been found and never will be. Some have "turned up," even in more recent years, the bodies just now revealing themselves and hinting at one of the most bizarre crimes in American history.

Missing persons do not make big headlines. Unless it is a celebrity, or a politician, or the daughter of a rich businessman, no one notices. A few lines are reserved in the local newspaper, on page nine, just before the furniture sales ads.

In a city like Fort Lauderdale the missing are as newsworthy as the local surf report. Fort Lauderdale is a tourist city, and as such, people are less likely to have their roots there. Ask twenty people on the streets if they were born there and you'll get twenty negative answers. They are from Chicago, or Indianapolis, or Atlanta, or New York. They are not staying. They have a friend who lives there. They're on their way down to Key West or back up to Jacksonville.

They're temporarily the district sales manager for such and such company. They used to party here when they went to college. They are commuting, and so forth. So, if they end up missing it is not unusual. "Yeah, I think I remember her. Bonnie or Barbara, right? Lee or Linda? Had kinda green eyes, or were they brown? Didn't she have blonde hair?"

Consequently, the police have always had their work cut out for them in Fort Lauderdale. The problem was further complicated by a persistent lack of personnel. Law officers were in constant demand in Broward and Dade counties, and there was a drastic shortage of medical examiners. In fact, in September 1970, a Fort Lauderdale newspaper ran an article which told of the shortage. Dr. Paul Hughes, the county health director at that time, told a reporter that "many people have died without a diagnosis of cause of death because of the lack of medical examiners."

Things have come a long way since the early seventies in South Florida. Improvements in forensics and investigative techniques have been made, as well as a conscious effort to maintain and train well-stocked law enforcement agencies. Information is shared over databases and even in perfunctory searches on the net.

But things are still not good. The Adam Walsh murder, ten years after the events of Schaefer's case, is an example. More recently, Jayme Closs, the thirteen-year old girl who was kidnapped, her parents murdered, still took months to find, and that was only because she escaped. Some progress has been, and is being made, even now, but in the early seventies, you could get away with murder.

* * *

They met at the adult education center at 1441 South Federal Highway in Fort Lauderdale. People attended classes at the center for various reasons. Some wanted to finish up school, get a diploma. Some wanted to further their education, either for employment or their own fulfillment. Others just went to be doing something, while went to meet people.

It is impossible to say exactly what it is that initiates a meeting and perpetuates an instant friendship between people. They spot each other, look again and then when the first coffee break interrupts the class, one will offer a light for a cigarette or a friendly smile. Whatever sparks the initial meeting, call it chance, fate, or destiny, it happened one day to three very different people. For two of them the meeting would be a death sentence, as sure as shaking hands with the Grim Reaper himself.

For the other, it could be one more dive into the depravation of murder, not the first, nor the last. A criminal depravity unparalleled in Florida history, and yet undetected for years. A sickness for which there was no cure, because there were no symptoms, a sickness which could only be called evil incarnate.

Susan Place felt she had to go to the adult education center just to get her diploma. She'd gone to a local high school, Stranahan High, but found the students to be snobby and cool. Most everyone who met Susan liked her, but many people never got the chance. Though she loved people, she was somewhat introverted because of her epilepsy, and a slight paralysis of her left side. A lack of oxygen at birth had caused the paralysis, and though Susan tried not to let it bother her; most teenagers generally don't understand when a person is even mildly handicapped and treat them differently. To most high school kids, epilepsy is misunderstood as well, many believing the ailment is contagious or at least "very weird." In addition, Susan was new to the area. She'd grown up in Royal Oak, Michigan, a suburb of Detroit, and had left most of her friends there.

Susan was an interesting girl, and the friends she did make, though few, genuinely loved her. And she was a lovely girl. Her oval face complimented her long, thin features and high cheek bones. Her eyes were cerulean blue. Her hair, long, blonde and so shiny and straight it seemed tangle-proof until the wind would whisk its golden strands across her face and neck. Those who knew her well knew that Susan lived for music only, playing both piano and guitar, as well as singing. She and her older sister, Kristen, would spend hours together, playing their instruments and singing. They hoped one day to form a band. But there were problems.

Susan had not been very fortunate since moving to Oakland Park, a suburb of Fort Lauderdale. Besides the cool reception she'd received at Stranahan High, she'd run into other prejudicial treatment. One day she had called her mother crying and asked, "Why do I have to be an epileptic?" This was brought on by her having been fired from a local grocery store where she was working as a cashier. The store's manager told her that their insurance company had ordered her fired because she'd listed on her job application that she was epileptic. The general resentment and harsh treatment she'd met with, both at her job and school, prompted her decision to go to adult school. She could finish her education quicker and get on with her real interest, music.

Her father, a general contractor who'd gone to Florida for his health, and her mother, a comptroller for a furniture warehouse, were supportive of her decision. Mr. Place would even give her rides to the school, when at times she preferred not to take the bus. She was seventeen, and her parents felt she was certainly mature enough to make the decision as to where she chose to be educated. She had never been a troublesome girl and parents and daughter held a mutual respect and admiration for one another,

Susan had left home a couple of times, one time going as far as New York. However, she always returned home. Once she was gone ten days, but she called saying, "I know you'd be worried, Mother. I'm ready to come home." And she did.

Susan had recently made some purchases: a quality stereo system, complete with headphones, and a new guitar. Her parents helped with the purchases, an early and thoughtful treat for an upcoming, special birthday.

* * *

Georgia Jessup was one of those sensitive people who let the troubles of the whole world bear down upon them. Her mother would later tell reporters, "The world was her oyster and she wanted to change it. She just wasn't satisfied with the world. The war bothered her."

Indeed, the Vietnam War "bothered" many people. In relation, the people known as flower children, were apparent everywhere in the late sixties and early seventies. In some ways, Georgia was a flower child. She dressed in the puffy, loose-fitting blouses and jeans adorned with leather and cloth patches sewn on randomly. Like many of the beachcombers that wander "the strip" along Ft. Lauderdale beaches, she adopted a nickname. Hers was "Crystal." Crystal is a slang term for some powdered or flaked drugs, but Georgia was not a habitual abuser. It was not uncommon for high school students to smoke marijuana, and she did smoke pot occasionally, probably due to peer pressure, more so than actual desire. She was not into the hard drugs that are so readily available on the strip. The name Crystal seems to have come from her sparkling eyes and effervescent personality. That, and she did not care for her given name. It sounded "oldish."

Georgia was only sixteen, but she appeared more mature. Her body had developed at a young age, which did not go unnoticed at high school. Many young men found her attractive and she did not lack for want of dates. She was a young lady of high morals, though, and she kept the boys at arm's length while still enjoying their company. She was an active girl, her thick brown hair, tinted with highlights of red, would bounce upon her shoulders as she'd run out of the house ready to experience the day. Her mother described her as "a rose in bloom."

As a child, Georgia displayed the open friendliness that would make up her character for the rest of her short life. As she grew up, she remained trusting, perhaps overly so, believing people were basically good.

Georgia had many varied interests as most girls do when they are sixteen years old. She liked to write, but had interests in architecture, interior decorating, and of course, modeling, like many young women. She'd even had offers to pose for some photographers once. Her father did not like the idea and convinced her to give it up. He did not trust the photographers. "They were not from Sears," he'd said. Two of Georgia's most prevailing interests were that of reincarnation and extra sensory perception. She was investigating the feasibility of establishing a course that would deal with such subject matter. She believed she had lived before in previous incarnations and this would later be one of the primary reasons she was attracted to a man named "Jerry Shepherd." She thought she'd known him in another life.

Georgia was a good student, with a high B average in school. However, she dropped out so she could attend classes at the adult education center. Her father, George Jessup, believed that she "lost her place in school, probably from moving around so much."

George and Shirley Jessup, Georgia's mother, were divorced. The parents' separation was an amiable one, and both shared the task of raising the teenage girl. The parents stayed friends and often the one would stop by the other's house and have dinner and visit. Georgia stayed with her father while attending the "adult" classes because his apartment was not far from the educational center. The Jessup parent-daughter relationship was not as harmonious as with the Place family. Georgia was almost too independent for her age, a popular malady of all teenagers, perhaps more so in the early seventies. She wanted to be a "free spirit" and occasionally she would have to be reprimanded and reminded that she was not yet an adult. Sometimes she would hitchhike, a practice both parents loathed. But with George and Shirley Jessup both holding down jobs that consumed much of their time, parental control could only be administered part-time.

Georgia began to stay out later and roam farther. Finally, she began to run away. She was never gone long, and she was not malicious. She knew her mother was beside herself with grief whenever she'd leave home, so she would eventually call to tell where she was. The Jessups did not deal out corporal punishment, choosing instead to use restriction for Georgia's penance. Making her stay home would discipline her more than a beating, at least, George Jessup believed it would. But Georgia began to grow more distant, and run away more often, particularly after she met "Jerry Shepherd."

"Jerry Shepherd" was twenty-six, eleven years older than Georgia. He had met both Susan and Georgia at the Adult Education Center in downtown Fort Lauderdale. He told them he was from Colorado and was planning to return there after a trip to Mexico. He was an "outdoorsman," who spent much of his time in the wilderness when he was not attending classes at the University of Colorado. He was tall, well-traveled and a nature lover. To the girls he was a missing link. He was older, more experienced, yet nothing like a restrictive parent. And he was nothing like the young boys whom Georgia found immature, and Susan found cruel and distant. "Jerry" never noticed Susan's handicaps and he encouraged Georgia's "free-spirit" attitude.

Jerry Shepherd was not one to stay in one place very long. He would be leaving soon and both girls were invited to come along if they wished. The girls, at first, were reluctant. Susan had no real desire to go any place in particular, yet she wanted to escape for a while. Get away from the prejudice and cruelty she'd come to know. However, she did not want to hurt her parents. Georgia was hesitant because she was already on restriction, having run away about six days earlier. She had planned to go to Colorado to meet Jerry but was picked up by police in West Palm Beach, about fifty miles north of Fort Lauderdale. Susan had been with Georgia, not ready to commit herself to leaving home yet. It was Mrs. Place who came to pick the girls up. They were only gone a few hours. Ironically, during that time Shepherd went to Georgia's house. He politely introduced himself to Mr. Jessup and said he was looking for "Crystal," then he quickly changed her name to Georgia, when he read a look of discontent on Mr. Jessup's face. Mrs. Jessup was there, too, at the time. She did not see Shepherd clearly, but she heard his voice (at the front door in conversation with Mr. Jessup) and noted that he was "a big man."

Overall, the girls liked the idea of "taking off" and told him they would think about it. He was not pushy, in fact he was quite polite, but again and again he expounded on the beauty of the west, of nature, and of distant Mexico's antiquity and culture. He talked softly, with reassuring calmness, and persuasion. His experience had no end. His open-mindedness and worldly manner were very appealing to the girls. He'd done it all before. He was someone to be looked up to and admired.

Susan and Georgia were convinced, not wholeheartedly yet, especially Susan, but Georgia's recalcitrant behavior grew stronger. She wanted, now more than ever, to "fly the coup." There were still complications, though, and just a few days before September 27, 1972, she wrote the following letter to Jerry Shepherd. (NOTE: the spelling and punctuation errors are hers.)

```
Hi Jerry,
    How are you. I don't know if you will
receive this letter in time, (I hope ya'
do). I can't make it Wed. Sep. 27. As I'm
restricted. I can't go out anywhere. Because
```

I took off for Colorado Mon. got to West Palm
Beach by Wed. (Took so long because I went
from one party to another.) Got busted or you
could say caught. I was hitchhiking. Cops
stopped me. It was a total bummer. I'd love
to go to Mexico with ya'. But I don't have
a passport. My father was pretty mad at me.
But thats life. I'm in need of my freedom. I
really am. I just wish I could split. The only
way I could leave would be to leave in the
daytime while dads at work. (Excuse my sloppy
writing, when I'm stoned my hand gets shaky.)
I'm stoned again.

   Wow, you letter I that I read the first one
well I just read it today. My sister had it I
found it in her drawer. It was so descriptive.
It sounded so beautiful to live with *Nature*
like you were. To have the squarrels, birds
& all the animals as freinds. I could really
dig it. I could *really* find myself that way. I
wish I could see ya. I'd love to *travel* with
ya too. But no passport. Darn it. If I had a
passport I be floating in happiness, because
then I could go. Since I don't, I *could only*
travel in the U.S. I am very lonely where we
live because theres no one I can talk to.
I wish some of my friends would move over
to this neighborhood. You know something,
rememer you said when we met it was as if we
were old friends meeting again. Well it was
that way. Maybe you were a friend of mine in
a former life. It's not impossible ya' know. I
have a tent. I only wish I could use it. But
my dad would never agree to let me go camping
by myself. Oh well at least I can dream.
Please write to me.

               Peace & Happiness to you always
                                Love
                         Crystall

The letter reflects the nature of the girl, the naïveté not uncommon to
sixteen-year-old girls. It also indicates several interesting points listed in
the following.

One: Georgia spoke to Shepherd about "getting stoned," or smoking pot. This would indicate that either he smoked marijuana as well or at least condoned such behavior, with Georgia. (Such behavior would be inconsistent with Schaefer).

Two: Apparently, Shepherd had written Georgia at least twice, because she said she read his letter, "the first one."

Three: That Georgia wanted to "run away," but that in truth realized she could not, and was not planning to do so. She did indicate she would like to travel with Shepherd throughout the US but began the letter by saying that she could not leave on September 27, 1972.

These points may be insignificant, but further into the case they justify some thought. At any rate, on September 27, 1972, Georgia Jessup did leave her home. Apparently, she was not forced, as she and Jerry Shepherd would later show up at Susan Place's home, at which time, if she was being knowingly abducted, she would have shown some signs of resistance. She did not. She did take a blue suitcase, containing all her possessions, a few of her mother's possessions, and inadvertently, a dress belonging to her little sister. She wore a pair of blue jeans with sewn-on leather patches, one of which was an owl, another the Road Runner (from the popular cartoon show). She also wore her mother's blouse, a distinctive blue-and-white striped long-sleeved shirt and black spiked shoes. Presumably, the blouse, the high heels and the jewelry she was wearing (also some of which was her mother's) made her appear to be more mature, less adolescent. She would have wanted to look her best, appear womanly to a man clearly her senior. It is unknown how Shepherd convinced her to go with him, but it would not have been a difficult task. A young, enthusiastic girl, longing for unbiased freedom, would have been an easy target. And so it was.

Susan Place, too, would have been an easy target. Young also, but impressionable and more accurately, vulnerable. An escape, however temporary, perhaps would lend her the solace she needed to sustain herself. Susan did not plan to just "run off" this time. She had for weeks been dropping hints to her mother that she was considering a trip to Colorado. There would be no surprises as in the past. She respected her mother and knew she was respected in turn. She was, after all, nearly eighteen and quite grown up. In one week, on October 4th, 1972, Susan would have celebrated her eighteenth birthday. She would never make it.

* * *

On September 27, 1972, newspapers told us that: the US had proposed a "major shakeup" of the world's monetary system; Hubert Humphrey was lending his support to George McGovern, and the Senate had rejected an "end-war" amendment. But none of these things entered the mind of "Jerry Shepherd" that day.

Shepherd dressed methodically, with contained nervous anticipation, as though for a wedding. He was preparing himself for a mission. As he dressed, he glanced alternately between his full-length mirror and into his closet. He seethed as he peered into the closet. He wished his uniform were still in there. He would have liked to have worn it. Chances were he'd never get to wear another one like it, but who could say for sure? Perhaps, in another town, another state, someone would recognize his potential, let him be a cop again. He liked doing police work. Liked the authority, the prestige he felt when he put on the uniform, badge, and gun. But the uniform did not necessarily make the man. He knew that to be true and shrugged contentedly as he pulled on a pair of tan slacks and a rather gaudy and rumpled plaid shirt. The slacks were getting a bit tight, harder to fasten the snap. He sucked in his stomach and patted it as if to reassure himself that he was in tip-top shape. He topped off his attire with an old, comfortable, roll-up fishing cap and beamed at his own reflection.

No, the uniform would not be a problem. He could still carry out the deeds which he had charged unto himself. Deeds which made up his own brand of law and order. He believed he had the power to extricate decadence from this world, a task suited to a law officer. He was the "eliminator of wicked persons in society, especially immoral women." Indeed, that same evening he was setting out on one of his self-ordained missions, to meet with two questionable young women. He had quite a drive ahead of him that afternoon, so he finished dressing and took a last glance at his image in the mirror.

He was twenty-six, dark jowled, though clean-shaven. His hair, a light-brown mat combed casually to the side, and longer than when he had been with the sheriff's department a few months ago. His eyes were deep set, seemingly lacking in color, then suddenly sparkling with various hues, depending on the light and colors surrounding him. He would not have argued had someone described him as handsome. He enjoyed receiving compliments. He finished last-minute preparations and went out to his car. He placed a few items, instruments of justice, into the trunk of the blue-green Datsun. Then he went back into the house and kissed his wife good-bye.

Yes, he would have to teach these two girls the hazards of an indecent lifestyle. They would learn what it meant to be law-abiding and morally responsible. They would learn whether they wanted to or not. They would learn if he had to kill them.

* * *

Susan Place was excited about the coming evening. She dressed hurriedly, but carefully, and dabbed herself with hints of flower-scented perfume and just the right touches of eye shadow and mascara. She didn't want to look "whorey" as Georgia would have said. As she worked on her face in the mirror, she smiled approvingly. So, what if she did have epilepsy? She also had flawless skin, when most girls her age were plagued with pimples. And her figure, though petite and slight, was very much that of a young woman. She was thin, but graceful.

She pulled her mouth in, then pushed it out, then in and out again, an almost involuntary motion that all women perform after applying lipstick.

It was a particularly warm afternoon and dots of sweat the size of pinheads formed under the light peach fuzz that grew above her gem-colored lips.

She kept her eyes forward, looking at her mirror image as she turned her head from side to side. The sunlight filtered through her bedroom window, caught her wonderful pale hair and made it gleam like wheat-colored strands of glass. With her pink sleeveless shirt and hip-hugger pants she looked quite elegant. Only her two-toned, blue suede shoes revealed her still youthful character.

The following is an excerpt from a deposition of Mrs. Lucille K. Place, Susan's mother. The questions were asked by Mr. Lem Brumley, Chief Investigator for the State Attorney's office. Also present were: Jack Sewell, Investigator, State Attorney's office; Wayne Scambler, St. Lucie Sheriff's Department; and then Lieutenant (later Captain) David Yurchuk of the Broward County Sheriff's Department.

Q: I draw your attention now to the evening that your daughter disappeared. Do you, of your own knowledge, recall the date?
A: The 27th.
Q: Of?
A: September.

Q: What year was that?

A: 1972.

Q: I understand that that evening there was a man that came to the house there. Tell us about him.

A: About how he came to the house and everything you mean?

Q: Right.

A: My husband had gone out and I was in the backyard gardening and I said, "Lock the front door when you go because I won't hear anybody come in."

Q: You told your husband this?

A: Yes. He took the car and left. My car is usually sitting there and we both go in his car. Suddenly I saw the light go on in the bathroom and in Susan's room, so I came in, and Susan was sort of straightening her room and Georgia was sitting in the chair in her room and Gerald, as they introduced him to me, was filling the doorway. He was a big guy; he was sort of leaning in the doorway.

So, I said, "What's going on?"

Susan said, "I'm just cleaning up my room." But she had told me prior to this that she and Georgia had wanted to go to Colorado because one of their other friends had gone there and said it was so great. A lot of young people were going to Colorado. I sort of suspected she was preparing me for her to go to Colorado. She was letting me know ahead. I was kind of suspicious, I thought maybe tonight was the night they were preparing to go. They were standing in the doorway after they introduced me.

Q: How did the introduction come about?

A: I came around the corner and I said, "What's going on here?" Susan said, "I'm cleaning up my room. By the way, this is Jerry." I said, "How do you do?" And that was all there was to that.

He was so soft-spoken that I thought that's kind of odd for a young person. He just kept standing there. I went in the kitchen and I got to thinking about it, so I was going to go out there and get his license number just in case. I had an intuition something was going to happen; they were either going to leave or something. I went out and I took a piece of paper and I think the Oakland Park police have this paper.

Q: Did you give it to them?

A: Yes. They picked it up at our house and they wrote on it, whatever they have to do to it, and asked if I would recognize it in court and I said, "Yes, that's the original piece of paper I copied his license number down on."

I looked in his car and all there was in the back seat was a cooler, a Styrofoam cooler, white one with a top. I wrote down the make of the car, but I'm not too good at that. I went back in the house, Sue was still messing around in the room and she came out, she said, "Mother, I have something to tell you."

I said, "What do you have, a problem?"

She said, "No, not really."

"Are you sick?"

"No."

Then she started to cry. I said, "You're going away, aren't you?"

She said, "Yeah, just for a little while."

So, I knew this was the trip she and Georgia had planned, and this was the fellow that was going to take them. Sue told me a boy that lived in Colorado was going to school there, had a friend there they could stay with.

Q: You say you knew he was going to take them. How did you know this? Had Sue made reference to him before this?

A: Yes. She said he was a "good guy and looked like Hoss of the Cartwrights on Bonanza." As soon as I saw him, I knew immediately that was the fellow.

Q: How long had she known him?

A: This is the first time I seen him, and she only met him once before, I think, through Georgia. I guess Georgia had been corresponding with him, or something. I don't know.

Q: Okay.

A: Then she started to cry, and I said, "Why do you have to do this?" She said, "I'm kind of tired of Fort Lauderdale, I just want to get away for a little while."

So, I didn't say any more and she went back in the room. As she was going back, I said, "Why don't you let the kids go out on the porch and sit?" I thought maybe I could talk to her a little more sensibly without them being around. They went out and sat on the front porch. I couldn't get anywhere with her, finally I got a little provoked and said, "Sue, if you go this time, that's it." I walked away. Finally, she came in my bedroom and she asked me to come outside and talk to them, the two.

Q: Talk to who?

A: Jerry and Georgia, because she had told me that last time, she went away without letting me know, she said, "Mother, I'll never run away again." She said, "It upsets you too much." This time she was telling me she was going. And I went outside then with them and he was sitting by our front door and Georgia was sitting in the other chair, there was only two chairs, and I said, "Well, what's going on?" I said, "So, you want to go to Colorado," and Sue kind of—She didn't want me to say that, I don't think. She said, "When did I ever tell you that?" I guess she was covering up. These kids weren't supposed to know where she was headed. I said, "Well, maybe I was mistaken, but I thought you said that."

Then we sat silent for a few minutes, and then we argued back and forth about why she had to go away. She said, "Well, I'm just going away for a little while."

"How long is a little while?"

"Just a little while."

She couldn't name any definite time like a week or two weeks or anything. She said, "If you want, I'll write you every day. I was uptight and I said, "Don't bother." I thought maybe I could swing her my way and reconsider as a mother would.

Q: Sure.

A: You try to think an alternative, either you go, or you stay. I thought maybe I could swing her, but it didn't work.

Q: Did Jerry join in this conversation at all?

A: At times, yes.

Q: What was his attitude?

A: He was philosophical. Like a mother shouldn't do that to a daughter if she tells her she's going away, she couldn't come back. I said, "Right," to him. "Are you a psychiatrist?" He said, "No." He didn't raise his voice, he was real calm and very smug about the whole thing. He acted like—he sat there like this and all the while I was talking, he was just rubbing his finger inside his shoe, so that made me take note of his attire while he was sitting there.

Q: What was that?

A: He had on a canvas hat like a fisherman wears, flat on the top with a brim, stitched brim. He had on some sort of a plaid shirt with sleeves rolled up, in the blue tones, and he had tan pants. I don't know whether they were coarse or not, and these moccasins like Indians use. It seems like they had fringe. I wouldn't swear to it.

So, when I told Sue "Why do you have to go away?" he said...no. Excuse me. I asked, "Why do you have to go away?"

She said, "Well, I'm tired of these people in Fort Lauderdale and I want to make it over with my new friends."

I said, "Well, if you can't make friends here, how can you make friends someplace else?" That's what Jerry said, "Well, that's very true," and that's almost the end of his conversation.

Q: From the conversation that he or the words that he spoke, did he indicate that he was going to take them, that he was the one that was going to take them off, take them to Colorado?

A: No, not to Colorado.

Q: Take them wherever they were going?

A: What he said was—just before I went back in the house, he said—he looked at his wrist, he must have had a watch on, I didn't take that much notice, he said, "It's getting kind of late. We were just going to the beach and play guitar."

Prior to coming out on the porch, Susan had her guitar out and she was going to take it. I said, "No, you can't take your guitar." She was buying it on time, and we had to make the payments and she was getting kind of lax. I said, "You can't take the guitar, I'm going to steal it and you have to pay for it. When it is paid for, you do what you want." She didn't have her guitar out there or anything. When he said it was kind of late, I went back in the house and kind of looked at the time, it was around 8:30, quarter of 9:00, and I went back to the window and I looked and just as I looked, they were driving out the driveway. I didn't see them get in the car, but they drove out."

Mrs. Place stared after the blue-green Datsun as it puttered away from the house. She could see her daughter's hair, like corn-silk, flopped over the top of the seat, a glimpse of the side of her face. Her friend Georgia already making wide hand gestures and soundlessly joking. Susan had grown up so fast! Mrs. Place smiled to herself, she shouldn't worry so much about her. She watched the car until it was almost out of sight. She could not have seen into the trunk of the car, where lying across the spare tire and wheel jack, were an axe, a .22 caliber rifle and a heavy-bladed hunting knife. Placed there in the trunk, on top of everything else, where they could be grabbed quickly.

Mrs. Place could've sworn she saw her daughter look back at the house one last time. She would never again see her alive.

As the Florida sun slowly sank in the west, like a dying ember, it threw off a spray of blood-colored sky.

Chapter 4

Missing

"Deep into that darkness peering,
long I stood there wondering, fearing,
Doubting, dreaming dreams no mortal
ever dared to dream before."

From
The Raven, by Edgar Allan Poe

Susan Place cringed in a corner of an otherwise blank and empty room. As her mother approached her, she noticed how frightened her daughter was. Susan's eyes were wide and hysterical with fear. Her white-knuckled hand was clasped tightly over her mouth as if to hold back a scream that would have burst her mother's heart. Mrs. Place reached out toward her trembling daughter. Suddenly, Susan removed the hand which had been covering her mouth. The hand was dripping with blood. She stared blankly at her mother, as if to explain, but when she opened her mouth there was no sound and Mrs. Place could see that her daughter's teeth had been wrenched out. More blood spilled out of Susan's mouth onto her chin, but her mother could stand no more.

Mrs. Place woke up in a cold sweat, her pulse so rapid she thought she might be suffering a heart attack. She tried to gather her wits, but her mind swam incoherently. The dream had seemed so real. It would be the first of many such dreams. Always, after the dreams, the next day's newspaper would tell of another body found somewhere in Florida.

She had finally accepted the fact that her daughter had left home, possibly for good. Perhaps she'd found happiness in Colorado, or some place. But Mrs. Place could not accept the fact that Susan had not called her. Susan would have called if she were okay. Mrs. Place was sure of that. Still, she'd heard nothing from the police department, and she felt that no news was good news.

Finally, Sunday morning, after another night of horrid dreams, Mrs. Place woke up and thought, that's it. Susan had been gone four days: she would have called. There was no real reason for her not wanting to come home—they hadn't had a quarrel—and she had not taken any clothes, or personal belongings. It was just not like her. Worse yet, Susan had to take medication for her epilepsy and Mrs. Place found the pills still in Susan's drawer. She had even told Jerry Shepherd that Susan had to have her medication. Surely, he was responsible enough to see that she got it. Mrs. Place could take no more. She called a friend of Susan's, Jan Snyder, and asked if she'd heard anything. She was given the phone number of Shirley Jessup, whom up to now she'd never met.

Shirley Jessup told Lucille Place that her daughter had run away from home, too. She said she'd gone by her former husband's home for dinner the night of September 27th and she'd found a note which read, "I'm sorry, Mother and Dad. I love you both very much. I have to find my head." Mrs. Place gave Mrs. Jessup the tag number from Shepherd's car, then called the Oakland Park Police Department. She reported the tag number, type of car, time of departure and all pertinent information to a Detective Spire. In addition to that, she gave an accurate description of Jerry Shepherd. Spire said he'd take care of everything. When another week passed, and Mrs. Place still had heard nothing, she called Spire back and asked what he'd found out. She was told that, "that license plate is from Pinellas County." And, "These kids drive different cars and you don't know whose car it is." She would not receive any more information from the Oakland Park Police.

What happened was this: Either in writing down the tag number, one of the investigators left out a digit, or as is more commonly accepted, there was a "computer foul-up." At any rate, they found a car, but not the blue-green Datsun in which Susan had left. The most blatantly revealing fact here, though, is that the first two digits of the tag number were 42. Most people associated with tag identification should have known that at that time in Florida, a car with a tag number beginning with 42 meant that the car was registered in Martin County, not Pinellas. No one made that observation.

Mrs. Place felt that the police did not conduct an investigation, or at best performed a very minor one. Whether or not this is true is not the relevant issue here, but one can only wonder why it would take another six months before that car would be found. It would be found in Fort Lauderdale, in the driveway of the owner's mother's house. In plain sight.

Months passed and fall became winter, a seasonal change which is almost entirely indistinguishable in South Florida. The parents of both Susan and Georgia continued to worry. When they could, they asked around for their daughters and by now the Places and the Jessups talked regularly on the phone. They did some investigating on their own. Often, they would take long rides into other counties around the state hoping to see something, anything that might give them a clue to their daughters' whereabouts.

The mysterious blue-green Datsun had seemingly vanished "into thin air," and so had the uncanny "Jerry Shepherd," who police could find nothing on. There was a Jerry Shepherd in Fort Lauderdale, but he was not the man who'd come to the Place home the night of Susan's disappearance. After investigating the wrong Shepherd, the investigation either slowed or came to a creeping halt. There was no new information given to either the Places or the Jessups, and time was wearing on. The Places, who were spending an increasing amount of time driving and searching, asking around, were becoming discouraged. Every girl with long blonde hair jerked their attention toward her. Their hearts would leap, hopefully, only to sink into deeper despair when they discovered it was not their daughter.

Finally, by early 1973, Mrs. Place made a decision. It was a difficult decision, but it had to be made. Ordinarily, Lucille Place was not a pushy person. She would step aside, go quietly with the flow. She is a dignified woman. But over four months had come and gone since Susan's disappearance and the police still had no news for her. She wanted to know what had happened to her daughter.

The following is another conversation between Mrs. Place and Chief Investigator for the State Attorney, Lem Brumley.

A: Well, it was in February that I called up Spire and I said, "Send me copies of everything that you have, I'm going to be my own detective." I said, "You aren't doing anything. I'm going to do my own investigation." He said, "I'll be glad to." He sent me photocopies of all the information. He said there was some stuff I wouldn't be interested in that he didn't put in. I read it all over and I kept thinking about it and thinking about it. I said, "Something has to be done, they don't disappear into thin air." I said, "I know Sue would have called me at Christmas, at least." She wasn't that type of girl. She loved me very much.

Well, I kept praying as to where to find her. So, this one weekend I just—excuse me.

MR. BRUMLEY: Take a minute.

(Here Mrs. Place stopped to cry.)

MRS. PLACE: I thought maybe if she was dead that spiritually something would lead me to her. So, I said, "Ira, let's go take a ride up to Fort Pierce." So, we took the Turnpike up to Fort Pierce and coming back—

Q: Did you have in mind—

A: I was coming through Stuart, yes. I knew that address was there, 333 Martin Street, which Mrs. Jessup had gotten.

Q: That trip had a purpose?

A: It certainly did.

Q: As far as you were concerned, it had a purpose?

A: Yes. I don't know why it didn't have a purpose sooner, but it seemed like this is what I was meant to be doing.

So, coming through Stuart I started noticing all these 42 tags you know, the digit on the license plate. I said, "This can't be Pinellas County, this Datsun he was driving, not with 42 right here in Stuart," I said. He must have lived here. I had that address in my purse and we circled around and finally found our way. It was about two blocks, I guess, and I went up to the apartment at 333 Martin and I talked to the manager. He was very kind. Mr. Spencer, his name was. He invited me in and I said, "I'm having a problem, my daughter is missing and I have reason to believe that Gerald Schaefer, (Mrs. Place had gotten the correct name from Shirley Jessup, who'd identified the tag number through the Broward County Sheriff's Office.) who formerly 1ived here, has something to do with it." He said, "Oh, no, not him, again."

Q: How did you know his right name?

A: This is what Georgia's mother said he gave to Georgia. I never heard his last name.

Q: How did you have his right name at this time?

A: Well, from the license tag. Mrs. Jessup called the license bureau, I don't know, wherever you can get the tag identified, and found out it was registered to a Gerald Schaefer.

Q: Go ahead.

A: Mr. Spencer said that he (Schaefer) was, at the present time, in the Sheriff's Department Jail on an assault charge on teenagers. I nearly collapsed. So, he recommended that we go right over there, which we did. He did say that this man was a very strange person. He said, "Really weird."

He (Spencer) said, "Even one time while he was living there in the apartment, he drove up on the lawn with his police patrol car right up on the middle of the lawn in the apartment complex with the siren going and the lights." When he asked him to remove that car, he got very belligerent, but he did do it.

We went over to the Sheriff's Department and talked to—I forgot his name—Sergeant Scott. I think he was in charge of this other case. As long as Schaefer was in there, he was taking all the information. We went into his office and he immediately called the identification on that car again and got back exactly what I said.

We had described Schaefer to him and another officer in the Sheriff's Department and this other officer said, "That's Schaefer to a T," the way we described him, no mistaking. I had a picture of Susan with me and I gave it to Sergeant Scott, and he said, "You stay here. I'm going up to talk to Schaefer right now. So, he took the picture and went up there and he was gone about 20 minutes. He came back and he said, "Schaefer denies ever knowing this girl or ever seeing her." But," he said, "I know what he is, he's a compulsive liar." So that's as far as we got.

Q: Did he show you a photograph that day?

A: That's right. He brought down a negative type photo, it was one you had to hold up to the light to see, and I had no doubts that was him, and my husband said, "That's him," right off the bat.

Q: This was a negative, not a photograph?

A: It was a negative, a side view and a front view.

Q: Do you still have the photograph that you gave to Sergeant Scott?

A: I don't know if I have it still or not, or did I leave it with him? No, he has it. I don't have it with me. But I have another one just like it at home.

Q: You do?

A: Yes.

Q: Was it a good photograph?

A: It was a very good likeness of her.

Q: Mrs. Place, I'm going to hand you five photographs and I'd like for you to look at them and tell me if you see the man that was identified to you as Jerry on the evening on which your daughter disappeared.

A: This is him. This fellow looks a little bit like him, but that's the one, I can tell by the nose.

Q: You're absolutely sure?

A: Positive.

BRUMLEY: For the record, she identified a photograph of Gerald Schaefer, photo taken at Wilton Manor Police Department, September 16, 1970.

The photo was taken for Schaefer's employment as a police officer at that department.

(Note: Throughout this deposition the person referred to as "Gerald" was intended to be Gerard.)

Further statements, taken that same day, May 2nd, 1973, substantiate Mrs. Place's testimony. Mr. Place's statement describes both the man that left with his daughter, and the car in which they drove away.

BRUMLEY:

Q: Mr. Place, I want to ask you some questions about the disappearance of your daughter, Susan Place. Do you recall the date that she disappeared?

A: It was on the evening of the 27th. What day it was, I don't know.

Q: Okay. The 27th of what?

A: September.

Q: 1972?

A: Yes.

Q: On that evening, did you meet a man that you know as Jerry?

A: Yes.

Q: And since then has been identified to you as being Gerald Schaefer?

A: That's right.

Q: Tell us, if you will, exactly what happened and how you met him.

A: Well, I came home from shopping and I walked through the house and I see this man standing in the doorway of my daughter's bedroom. So, I went in the kitchen to put down the groceries and came back to see what was going on and I don't remember whether it was my wife or my daughter that introduced me to this man as Jerry.

Q: Okay. Did you shake hands with him?

A: And I shook hands with him, and I think I said, "Glad to know you," or "Pleased to meet you," or something like that.

Q: He remained at your home after that for a while?

A: Yes. They went out...

Q: An hour or...

A: I don't know. I imagine a half hour or something like that. Then the two girls and this Jerry went out on the front porch.

Q: And how long were they out there?

A: I really couldn't say how long they were out there. I mean, a half hour, forty-five minutes, something like that. I get on the phone talking to some of my customers and time just keeps going.

Q: Did they leave your house?

A: Yes, they left my house.

Q: And how were they traveling?

A: In a car.

Q: What kind of car?

A: Well, that '67 Datsun.

Q: What color was it?

A: Sort of turquoise, blue.

Q: How do you know that was the color of the car? Where was it?

A: It was parked in my driveway, in the south part of the circle.

Q: Have you seen the car since then?

A: No.

Q: Just a few minutes ago I showed you a series of six pictures and you've selected one of those photographs out and identified it as being the one of the person that was at your home that evening and identified as, or introduced to you, rather, as Jerry; is that correct?

A: That's right.

BRUMLEY: Just for the record it is a photograph of Gerald Schaefer taken at Wilton Manor Police Department, September 16, 1970.

Q: Mr. Schaefer, sometime in the later part of May, you and your wife took a trip north on US 1, more or less a pleasure ride; is that right?

A: Yes. We took a ride up there.

Q: Tell me exactly what happened there in regard to the 42 license plate that...

A: We took a drive on up, we took the Sunshine Parkway up to Fort Pierce, then we came back down to Federal Highway. We were riding along; the wife saw all these 42 tags. She said, "This can't be Pinellas, this has got to be where this license plate is from."

Q: You refer to Pinellas County. Why did she say...

A: That's what one of the detectives at Oakland Park said; that the computer said that that's where that tag number was from, the 42 D.

Q: This tag number we are referring to, how did you have the tag number?

A: Mrs. Place took it down that night, she wrote that number down in our driveway.

Q: That's the night your daughter disappeared?

A: That's right.

Q: This is the number off of the automobile that was driven by this Jerry?

A: That's right.

Q: Go on with the story.

A: So, they had the license number—she had the license number and then she called Miss Jessup and got the address. I think it was 333 Martin Avenue.

Q: That's in Stuart?

A: In Stuart. So, then we went over there, and we talked to the manager, she did, and he told her that he thought he had seen the last of Schaefer because he was locked up in the jail. So, we went up there and explained to them what he looked like and they said it was Schaefer.

Q: You went to the jail, you mean?

A: Yes, and then they brought—Sergeant Detective Scott came out and talked to us and identified this picture right there.

Q: In other words, Detective Scott showed you a photograph?

A: That's right.

Q: And you identified that photograph as the man that left, that took your daughter from home?

A: That's right.

Q: On the evening that your daughter disappeared, your wife mentioned to you some time that evening that she had written down the tag number of the car that belonged to this Jerry; is that right?

A: I'm positive of it, yes.

(Here Detective. Yurchuk joins the examination.)

Q: You went up there in the month of March?

A: Yes.

Q: Of '73?

A: Yes.

BRUMLEY: I said May. Let there be a correction on that.

YURCHUCK: Also, at the beginning, I think you called him Mr. Bales, it is Mr. Place.

MR. PLACE: He called me Mr. Schaefer.

YURCHUCK: Yes, but you're Mr. Place.

MR. PLACE: That is right.

Q: What was she wearing when she left, your daughter?

A: I really couldn't tell you the colors. She was wearing something without arms in it, one of these... I don't know what the hell you call them, and she had some hip-hugger slacks on; some of these short jobbies with the short parts, but I didn't pay that much attention to what she was wearing.

Q: Did this fellow say good-bye to you?

A: No.

Q: How long do you think you saw his face or was in close contact, visual contact, with him the entire time he was at your home?

A: He was right in the hallway at the time he looked around and there's a light above.

Q: You saw him a number of times?

A: I saw him right there, that's when I was introduced to him, and I saw him on the front porch, he was sitting on one of the chairs and I got a side glance right there as he looked around.

Q: How long did he stay at your house?

A: I would say he was probably in there at least 15, 20 minutes from the time I was there, and he was there when I got home. So, I really couldn't say other than that before they went out on the porch.

Q: Let me get this on the record. Within the past hour we have shown you a series or rather a collection of various items in the property room here in the Broward County Sheriff's office and I understand you did not recognize anything among those items as belonging to your daughter, other than the pair of shoes there that looked similar to the ones that she owns or has.

A: Well, they were Thom McAn and she had shoes just about like that.

Q: Only your daughter's was two-toned blue color?

A: Two-toned blue. Those looked like they had been of course they have been out in the weather a long time. Maybe if they were turned over there could be a dye there showing it.

Mrs. Place identified the shoes in question as positively as possible to the naked eye. The size of the shoes was later verified by lab technicians, and the fact that Mrs. Place recalled having purchased Thom McAn shoes in a size six and a half, allowed the shoes to be identified as belonging to Susan Place, and entered as evidence. Though the shoes were weather-beaten, and faded almost colorless, Mrs. Place still discerned that they were blue, and were indeed Susan's.

Shirley Jessup later talked to Lt. David Yurchuck of the Broward County Sheriff's Office, with Brumley. Her statement further incriminated Gerard Schaefer as having at least known her daughter, and mentioned of a brown suede purse, which would later cause some controversy in this case.

YURCHUCK questioning Mrs. Jessup:

Q: Ma'am, I'm going to ask you questions about your daughter, Georgia Jessup. When did she disappear from your home?

A: Well, it was September 27th, I believe.

Q: What year was that?

A: 1972.

Q: Do you recall what she took with her when she left the house?

A: Yes. She took about all her clothes in the suitcase because the suitcase was missing, blue suitcase. I don't know what all she took other than all her clothes, maybe some magazines or something.

Q: In other words, she took most of her belongings with her?

A: Yes, practically all she owned she took.

Q: And she was staying with your husband, who you are separated from?

A: Yes.

Q: What was that address?

A: I believe it was 1440 Miami Road, Fort Lauderdale, apartment six.

Q: During March of 1973, you received a tag number, or you had in your possession a tag number received from Mr. and Mrs. Place;

   is that correct?

A: It wasn't exactly that way. We had the tag number since October or September.

Q: What did you do with the tag number?

A: I gave it to the Sheriff's Department.

Q: What did they tell you?

A: They said they would take care of it.

Q: Did you then call the Sheriff's Department again, and get an address on that tag?

A: Yes, I did. I don't remember the exact date, though it was a few weeks later.

Q: What address did you get?

A: I think it was 333 Martin Street, Stuart.

Q: Do you recall the tag number in question?

A: 42Dl723, I believe.

Q: Do you know who that car came back registered to?

A: Yes, Gerald Schaefer.

Q: What did you then do with that information?

A: Well, I gave up—I believe I told the police about it—I'm trying—it's been so long ago, and I wanted to have him arrested and get an arrest warrant out for him because I figured he was 20, 21, and they told me there would be no point in arresting him, it was just two kids taking off.

Q: Did you ever see this man?

A: I saw him partially through the door.

Q: Could you identify him?

A: No, sir. I don't believe I could. His voice I heard...

Q: You eventually gave that information you received from the Sheriff's Department to Mr. and Mrs. Place; is that correct?

A: Yes.

Q: What did they do with it?

A: Well, they went for a drive one weekend, but I guess they were planning it lots of times and they went out to Stuart and they found out he was still living there and he was in jail and everything when this case blew up.

Q: I contacted you on about 11 April 1973 and I showed you a small suede-type purse. Had you seen that purse before?

A: Yes.

Q: Where did you see it?

A: My daughter's possession. She carried it with her all the time.

Q: And when did you last see her with that purse?

A: Probably about two days before she disappeared.

Q: You say she always carried this purse. Can you fully describe it for me?

A: Well, it was brown suede and it had fringe on one side of the top, it was a drawstring type bag.

Q: Have you ever held this purse?

A: Yes.

Q: And you saw it with her in her possession daily, almost?

A: Yes. I'd say that.

Q: Are you sure in your mind that that is the purse that belonged to your daughter?

A: Yes, I am.

Q: Today, being the 2nd of May, 1973, I again showed you some articles in the Broward Sheriff's evidence room. Can you tell me if you identified any of those articles as being those of your daughter's?

A: Yes, I did.

Q: And can you tell me of anything in particular, or describe anything that you did identify?

A: Well, I identified practically all the clothes and jewelry.

Q: Did some of them belong to you?

A: Yes, some of them belonged to me.

Q: And you were giving them away?

A: She borrowed them from me.

Q: So, you positively know they are yours or her clothing?

A: Yes.

Q: Which garment was yours, do you remember?

A: Yes, the blue-and-white long-sleeved blouse was mine.

Q: That was yours, personally, and you gave it to Georgia?

A: No. She borrowed it from me, you might say.

Q: And the articles of jewelry there, the earrings and so on, did you then also identify them?

A: Yes, I did.

Q: Are there any other articles that you saw in there among the jewelry that looks suspicious or might have been your daughter's?

A: You mean the other jewelry?

Q: Yes, that you were showed on the 11th of April.

A: Possibly that little doll. I don't know for sure.

Q: But you can't say for positive?

A: No, I can't say for positive about that; but I know she had things like the ones that they showed me. I couldn't say for sure.

Q: But what you are positive about is the small purse?

A: Yes.

Q: And the articles of clothing that you saw today?

A: Yes.

YURCHUCK: Any questions?

BRUMLEY:

Q: Mrs. Jessup, on the clothing, how can you identify those from others just like them?

A: The clothing?

Q: Yes.

A: Well, my daughter wears those type of britches, those type. That one blouse that was there that was mine, the blue-and-white one, I never saw another one like it. I remember where I bought it from and everything and the halter, that blue halter, I never seen another halter like that. My daughter bought it because it was different.

Q: Is that the one with the wire neck?

A: Right.

Q: How about the purple striped pants?

A: I believe, now that I recall those, I knew she bought those new, just before they disappeared.

Q: I noticed a bleached-out spot on the leg of those pants. I believe it was those. Do you recall that?

A: I tell you I didn't see those today. I couldn't hardly see from crying. I noticed a little, I guess, brownish or something in there. It looked like it belonged... a child's dress or something. It looked like it belonged to one of my little girls, that she had taken it by accident as she packed. I recognized that right off the bat.

Q: The article of clothing Lieutenant Yurchuck showed you in the paper bag that had patches on it...

A: I couldn't look at that, my stomach started to—I probably should have looked at it, but...

Q: Could you describe to me the clothing she was wearing when she disappeared?

A: I tell you I don't know because it was like she was staying with her father.

Q: And you didn't see her on the evening that she left?

A: No, I did not.

Q: Can you tell me if she had a pair of blue jeans with any type of sewed-on patches of animals or characters or...

A: Yes, she had a pair of blue jeans with the Road Runner on them and she had an owl on it, too.

Q: Owl?

A: A little owl. But I can't recall the size of the owl or the color or anything, but I remember an owl. It seems to me like it was red and gold, or something; but it's been so long.

Q: Your daughter's past, how old was she?

A: Sixteen.

Q: What was her birthday?

A: July 15.

Q: Of what year?

A: She was born in 1956.

Q: 1956. Was she going to school?

A: Yes, she was.

Q: What school was that?

A: It was the one on—I can't recall, it is the adult educational center on, I believe, Federal Highway near Davie Boulevard or 15th Street, downtown adult educational center they call it.

Q: Had she been in any kind of trouble before, been arrested or picked up?

A: Yes, she had. I believe it was June or July of 1972, her and a friend were caught shoplifting as I had to go talk to juvenile—that place over on 84. (Referring to the juvenile detention center.)

Q: Did she go to court?

A: No. They said that they didn't think it was necessary, just talked to her; it was the first time she had been in trouble.

Q: Had she run away from home before?

A: Yes, she did. I think the year 1971 she ran away from home for four days and then she run away...

Q: That time she come back on her own?

A: Yes, she did.

Q: She call you before she came home?

A: No. I don't think she did that time.

Q: Did she run away another time?

A: Yes, she run away, I believe, a week previous to her disappearance she ran away. I don't know, about the 20th, 21st of September of '72.

Q: Do you know where she was then? Did she ever tell you?

A: Supposedly she was picked up, her and Sue, in Palm Beach by the police. She was only gone like three or four hours. I didn't even call in, and she returned home.

Q: How did she return home?

A: I believe Mrs. Place drove her home. She picked up the girls in Palm Beach.

Q: On this man Schaefer, or you may know him by some other name, did she ever say anything to you, or do you know anything about him through your daughter?

A: Yes, she told me a little bit about him. She just said he was a very smart, intelligent man and she liked him very much and he was the intellectual type and he loved nature, stuff like that, and I believe she said that he was going to the University of Colorado.

Q: Did she tell you how old he was?

A: I believe she didn't outright tell me. She insinuated he was around 20 or 21 years old. I was telling her I thought that he way too old for her.

Q: Did she say anything else about him?

A: No, not too much.

Q: How long did she know him before she disappeared?

A: Well, I asked her, and she said that she had met him a long time ago and she was renewing her acquaintance with him; that she had not seen him for a long time. But I don't know if that's true or not because my daughter believed in reincarnation. I think she was referring to that she met him in a previous life or something. It sounds funny, but that's the way she was talking.

Q: This time that she met him, how long did she talk about him before she disappeared?

A: A few times. We had been gone—we were living in Chicago for about a month and a half and I don't recall her talking about him...

Q: Who's we, you and Georgia?

A: Georgia, and myself and another daughter. We had gone to Chicago in July and come back the latter part of August, 1972, gone about five or six weeks, and I don't recall her talking about him then, not until afterwards because she had lots of friends and everything and she was talking about other boyfriends.

Q: Sometime during the month of September, could you say it was two weeks or three weeks before she disappeared or a week before she told you about this man?

A: I'll tell you; I think it was about two to three weeks, I can't be sure on that. I know it was...

Q: But it was several days?

A: I know it was after we had come back from Chicago. We came back down here to Florida.

Q: Did you ever suspect that she was going off with him during the day or dating him at night or did you know that she was, if she was?

A: No. To tell you the truth, I don't know. She had been living with her father for a few weeks because of school. I guess school was about two blocks from his home, she used to go down the beach quite a bit.

Q: Which beach?

A: I guess near Las Olas, where all the kids hang out, the Strip, I guess they call it. I believe that's probably...but I know she had other friends. I can't be sure about it.

Q: On her other friends, do you know their names?

A: You mean boyfriends?

Q: Anyone who may know her. Let me put it this way: Anyone who may have been close enough to her to have seen her and Schaefer together.

A: Well, I know she used to hang out at Captain Kidd's; it's an eatery on the beach right around the corner from the Elbow Room on Las Olas. Someone over there may have seen them. (In fact, no one had, but further investigation and questioning at Captain Kidd's revealed Georgia had not stopped in on the night of September 27.)

Q: Do you know anyone, like a friend she took home or maybe she spent the night with or ran around with on a regular basis?

A: The only friend I know would be (Janice Sneider) that would know anything at all because her and Sue are Georgia's best friends.

Q: Do you know any boyfriends?

A: Mostly by their first names. There was one that she used to go with right before we went to Chicago and I guess she saw him right after. (The police questioned this boy and were satisfied with his statement and alibi and so did not include him as a suspect.) I know his name, but I can't think of it right now. My other daughter, she's in the other room, she knows his name. I can't even think of it right now.

Q: Did she go with him after she came back from Chicago?

A: I think she was with him a few times after that. I'll think of his name pretty soon. It just escaped me for a minute.

Q: Does your daughter have any name other than Georgia?

A: Yes, Crystal. Everyone knew her as Crystal.

Q: I understand that you have or did have a letter and you have turned it over to the police, the letter your daughter wrote to Jerry Sheppard.

A: Yes.

Q: Do you know for a fact that the name Jerry Sheppard was on the envelope?

A: Yes. I know for a fact. The envelope was misplaced because we're all in the process of moving, but I saw the name Jerry Sheppard and it was a box office number. I believe it was in Daytona Beach, to the best of my knowledge. (The name "Jerry" further substantiates Mrs. Place's statement, as that is how the man in question was introduced to her.)

Q: Did she ever mention Daytona Beach to you?

A: No, she didn't. She did not. This letter came back, it was returned to my former husband's address a few days after she had left. But I did see that name, Sheppard, and I know he was introduced...I didn't see him very good, but I heard him talking to my former husband when I was over at his house when he was looking for Georgia one time and he introduced himself as Jerry Sheppard.

Q: To your husband?

A: Yes. He was looking for Georgia at that time and ironically it was the night she had run off and was picked up in Palm Beach.

Q: How long before her disappearance was this?

A: I'd say approximately six days. I believe the police have the... Palm Beach police have the exact date. I think the 21st, approximately, of September.

Q: And he came to your husband's house?

A: Yes, he did.

Q: And you were there?

A: Yes.

Q: And exactly what did he say, if you can recall?

A: Well, I just heard him, the door was open, and I saw him partially and not enough to identify him; but I just saw he was a big man and that's all I could see.

Q: What did he say to your husband?

A: Well, he asked if Georgia—or—Crystal was there.

Q: Do you recall if he said Georgia or Crystal?

A: I think he said Crystal.

Q: What do you...?

A: I think he said Crystal and then he said "Georgia" after that, and then George was saying something, "Well, she's not here right now," and he went outside and closed the door and talked to him outside. But I remember seeing him partially and heard his voice.

On September 27th, 1972, Susan Place and Georgia Jessup met a terrible fate. An end so unspeakably horrible, for two young women whose only mistake was to be too trusting, too vulnerable. What exactly had happened to them, and why? Who was the man responsible? And why did it take six months for the parents, not the authorities to find a suspect? The answers began to reveal themselves, and in so doing opened an investigation that would involve hundreds of investigators in at least four different counties, as well as isolated states throughout the United States. The answers began to tell the tale of a crime unbelievable in its horror, and yet, the most incredible, undeniable fact in the case was that the crimes were being committed over at least a three-year period, and no one seemed to even notice.

Chapter 5

The Discovery

*If still you think me mad, you will think so no longer when
I describe the wise precautions I took for the concealment
of the body.*

From *The Tell-Tale Heart,* by Edgar Allan Poe

Spring had arrived. Again, in Florida, this is not a dramatic seasonal change. It is slightly warmer, a little brighter. Spring cleaning is due, but often is put off for a relaxing day at the beach, or a backyard barbecue. Flowers bloom, and so does hope.

Mrs. Place was full of hope as she and Mr. Place walked warily into the Martin County Jail. The couple had never had an occasion to see the inside of a jailhouse, and so were intimidated by the depressing atmosphere; the painted pallor, the clanging of iron bar doors, and the world-weary appearance of the policemen on duty.

After meeting Sergeant Scott and giving him a picture of Susan to show to Gerard Schaefer, they waited. They could barely contain their anxiety, their hope that possibly, just maybe, Schaefer could tell them where Susan was. Perhaps he knew where she was staying. They prayed that he was the right man, even though his name wasn't quite the same as Jerry Shepherd, perhaps they'd heard it wrong. When Sergeant Scott returned with the news that Schaefer had never met Susan, the Places were once again despondent. Could they at least see a picture of Schaefer? His description sounded very much like the man that had left with their daughter.

Scott did not have a photograph of Schaefer, but he did still have the negatives from the arrest record photographs. He gave one of these to the Places. Mrs. Place felt her heart would stop. Mr. Place felt anger. They both made a positive identification.

The man in the photo negative, Gerard John Schaefer, Jerry Shepherd, whoever he was, whatever he called himself, he was the man who left with Susan Place and Georgia Jessup on September 27th, 1972. The Places told Sgt. Scott this was the man. Scott told them that, though Schaefer swore he did not know Susan, he was also a compulsive liar, and with time, something would turn up. They could not have known at that time how close to the truth they were.

Frustrated and depressed, the Places returned home, once again empty-handed. They did not wait for the police again. Now that they had a positive lead, they decided to take action themselves. Perhaps some newspaper attention might help them. It was worth a try. They needed to find a reporter who might be interested in their story. They were given the name, Jayne Ellison.

Jayne Ellison looked like Aunt Bea from the old Andy Griffith Show. But her homebody, sweet aunt looks belie her true nature. When she takes an interest in a story, she jumps into it. She bathes in it. She eats it and sleeps it and attacks it with all the sweetness of a wet wolverine. She is retired now, but when she worked as a reporter, she and her investigating partner William Clarke, worked on only a few exclusive topics. They worked with the largest newspaper in Palm Beach County, the Palm Beach Post-Times. Primarily, Ellison and Clarke covered homicide cases, and medical stories, either large malpractice suits, or new discoveries in medicine. They did not cover missing persons' stories. Too often, the missing person turned out to be missing because they wanted to get away, change their lifestyle, or often as not had already returned home by the time the story hit the press. Missing persons, unless they were celebrities, did not make headlines, and no reporter desires to run copy next to the want ads. However, when the Places told Jayne Ellison their story, she could see their desperation, and she began to wonder how often did this type of thing happen in South Florida and why wasn't more being done about it?

Ellison recalls her first meeting with the Places:

"They came to me, you know. The Places came to me. And I said to myself well, missing girls, (must be) 500,000 a year. That was my reaction. Anyway, when they finally got the police to check on this license number, don't ask me how or why but somehow it (the tag number) was in a distant county. But it was an error. An absolute error.

"When they (the Places) thought they had traced this up to Martin County, nobody would listen. That was when they came to me. They said nobody would listen.

"I told them I didn't do missing persons stories. But then I began to work on it anyway. And I was sure that he (Gerard Schaefer) was right up there in Martin County Jail. Because I remembered the Trotter/Wells incident. And I couldn't understand why nobody was interested in this.

"I spent all week dogging this. Got a good description of the man who lived there (in Martin County) in that apartment, and it matched, orally, the description of the man that had taken their kids to the beach.

"Then came the grisly discovery."

Ellison told the Places she would investigate it, ask around a bit, and if nothing else, perhaps she could find out where the girls had gone. She would keep in touch, but she also warned them not to get their hopes up too much. She also put together a small article which she ran in the Palm Beach Post-Times titled: "Missing Girls' Mothers Continue Waiting, Hoping." The article told about the plight of the Places, but did not mention any suspects, because there were none. It went on to state that the girls had been missing since September 27th, 1972, and that the parents eagerly awaited hearing from them.

It also explained that the search for Susan Place and Georgia Jessup had dead-ended in Stuart, and that the Oakland Park Police Department was "frustrated" because "the girls were old enough to leave home and it is difficult for local police to trace, or justify, a search unless there are indications of foul play." Ellison also ominously added that though there was no evidence of foul play, "this is the third set of young girls missing from that area." A most intuitive observation on Ellison's part. There was a chance that a reader might know something, be able to lend some helpful information to the worried parents. There was a chance, just maybe, that the girls might even see the story, and call home. It was worth a try, so Ellison ran the story and, at least temporarily, dismissed the subject from her mind.

* * *

April Fool's Day, 1973

Sunday morning laid out a sweltering blanket of steam and heat, perhaps a premonition of the stifling hot summer to come. The heat was what was on Henderson Holley's mind as he smashed a beer can underfoot. The heat, and recyclable aluminum. He carried an old shovel handle with a nail taped onto the end of it. A "beer-can spear," he called it. He speared the flattened beer can and scraped it off into his collecting sack. It fell to the bottom and clattered amongst the other flattened cans.

Holley was sure that his son Jesse could find better things to do on a Sunday morning than search for scrap metal. But a recession is no picnic and oftentimes a couple hours of collecting aluminum cans would net a few dollars from the recycling plant to get through the week. Money was damned hard to come by in South Florida in '73, legally, anyway.

The Holleys had been salvaging in an area near the beach for a few hours. The earth in that area, just north of the Florida Power & Light nuclear power plant, has an odd odor. It is not the power plant that is situated on Hutchinson Island, which spreads out adjacent to Ft. Pierce, Florida, that emits the odoriferous air. It is the land here. The black and branchy soil contains equal amounts of sea spray and sea fossils combined in a hard, sandy composite. Prehistoric ocean creatures moaned out the last of their haunted wails into this soil and the land pushed its way into existence like a lesion on the skin of the earth. The soil reeks sharply of decay. It should for all purposes be an excellent planting soil, but the salt content kills the life-giving nutrients in it, and only the heartiest of foliage grow here.

Holley and his son spread out to cover more ground. Picnickers and litterers find ways of dispersing beer cans in the most unimaginable ways and places.

Henderson Holley wandered out, away from the dirt road that ran off A1A highway, due east to Old Beach Road which runs parallel to the Atlantic Ocean. Jesse moved eastwardly along the dirt road, toward the beach area as Henderson went south. Henderson went slowly, patches of sunlight splattered through the dense undergrowth and sparkled silver through his sandy gray, close-cropped hair. He walked, waddling duck-like to and fro, the spongy ground giving underfoot, a stocky, sun- browned leathery man. An odd-job handyman, looking for a few pieces of recyclable aluminum.A penny here, a penny there. He wasn't having a lot of luck that day, and the suffocating heat combined with the earth smell were almost unbearable to Henderson. He strolled lazily and farther from Jesse hoping to find at least a few more cans, or a puff of fresh air. He did not find either.

Holley spied what at first appeared to be a flattened out blue-and-white Busch beer can. He poked at it with his beer-can spear and noticed it was some sort of clothing. Kids, he thought, out here fooling around in the bushes and lost part of their clothes. He noticed then there were some other clothes, a black high heeled shoe, some white panties, a pink blouse, some other shoes, blue in color.

The clothes were filthy and stained. He thought, no wonder someone threw them away out here. It looked as though someone had been trying to clean up a spill of something with them. Brown bugs and grub worms scattered about the damp outline of where the clothes had been pressed into the ground. There was a large hole, and it appeared that someone must have begun to bury something there. Or, having buried it, had returned and dug it back up.

The stench had grown worse now, and Henderson thought, uh-huh, I'll bet it's the construction of that nuclear plant spilling poison into Blind Creek and killing the fish a few hundred feet south. He was kneeling and looked up to swat a thick horde of flies and mosquitoes away from his head. That's when he first noticed something. He did not know what it was at first. It appeared to be an odd angulation of branches coming from the base of a gnarled tree trunk. He approached it slowly, an animal instinct raising the hair on the back of his neck. What he found at once made his mind reel and darken, he became dizzy and sick at his stomach.

Tied to the base of the tree, carelessly hidden with palm fronds, was what was left of a human body. The head was missing. The torso bent forward and twisted back around as if the spine had been smashed or severed. There were scratches, possibly clawing marks, in the trunk of the tree near the hands, undoubtedly where the person had been tearing uselessly toward freedom. One arm had been removed, but the remaining hand still had a piece of cord, or rope, knotted around it.

Henderson Holley backed slowly away from the corpse. He felt he was going to be sick, and he wanted to call out to his son, but his voice would not come. As he backed away from the thing at the tree, he found something else, almost tripping over it. In the hole where he first saw some clothing, buried only with a thin layer of rain-washed soil, were a few more pieces of a body.

Looking about in horror, he began to find more parts of a second body. Again, the spine had been severed, but this time it was completely shorn in two.

Again, the corpse was headless. Henderson looked around him, awestruck. He felt as though he'd wandered into some unholy burial ground. He was afraid to move in any direction; he did not want to find more, or possibly step into another body. As he looked around, he noticed one of the bodies was still wearing a pair of pants. They were blue jeans, and on them, weathered but still recognizable were some emblem-type patches. One was an owl and the other was a cartoon character, the Road Runner.

Holley screamed to his son, "Jesse! Please! Come tell me what I've found!"

* * *

The two men sped down A1A Highway, braking suddenly to peer out the window in hope of spying a phone. Then they pressed on. There were no public phones on Hutchinson Island, not in that desolate beach area. The Holleys had no luck at the power plant, either. They slowed as they went by, but seeing no phone at the entrance, continued on. They decided to go to Calvin Wiggins' home. He was a city employee, maybe he'd know what to do. In truth, the men believed Wiggins worked with the police department, but Wiggins actually worked with Stuart Ambulance as an ambulance attendant. The Holleys knew they could at least find a phone at Wiggins' home, so without any more delays, that is where they went.

Wiggins is Henderson Holley's son-in-law. He talks with the typical drawl, native to the residents of the St. Lucie and Martin County area. Many families in this area migrated from other southern states; Tennessee, North Carolina, Alabama, Mississippi, and many from Georgia.

These people came to Florida, looking for work and a warm climate, but also wanting to avoid the more metropolitan areas such as Fort Lauderdale, Miami, and the Palm Beaches. These people settled in Ft. Pierce, Stuart, and Jupiter (pre-Burt Reynolds) and many are long-time residents who would live nowhere else, though they occasionally take seasonal hunting trips back up to the woods of Georgia. They are hard-working people, many of whom are now being pushed farther west, into Central Florida, where the land and the people are more like their Florida was in the 1950's and 60's. They are shy with strangers but friendly, and they seem to like to recollect and share stories of local history.

Wiggins recalls that the Holleys came to his house that April 1st, 1973. He was working around his house, yard work and Sunday chores, when they arrived. "They were pretty excited and wanted to use the phone. But they didn't know who they should call. They said they found some bodies on Hutchinson Island, but they weren't sure if it was the St. Lucie County side, or the Martin County side. So, we called both sheriff departments."

The Holleys also wanted to take Wiggins back to the scene with them to meet with the Sheriffs, and to "have a look." Wiggins was sickened by what he saw. "They were mostly in pieces and in pretty bad shape. They'd been there a while." The searchers had left their car out on the dirt road and after viewing the bodies, Wiggins decided to stay by the car and wait for the authorities. He did not have long to wait.

Lt. Patrick Norris Duval (later Captain) was one of the first to arrive on the scene. Lt. Duval had already been with the St. Lucie County Sheriff's Department (SLCSD) for nineteen years. He is easily what may be termed a "seasoned veteran." Duval is tall and thin, and the weight of his job seems to have rounded his shoulders a bit, though he still holds them erect: an African-American man proud of his heritage and his position as a law enforcement officer. Duval's voice is deep and articulate, and his general demeanor commands quiet attention.

Gray is creeping into his dark hair now, but he still worked with the SLCSD in Ft. Pierce, when this author met him. Parking still cost a nickel on the meter and many people still remember when blacks were not allowed into established places of business. This being known, Duval's position alone was a statement of his determination. Duval liked to listen to classical music as he worked in his mahogany paneled office. It was a relaxing habit, for a job that on its slowest day would cause many to start gulping ulcer medicine. Duval was fifty-two in 1973, an age when many people begin to start planning their retirement. In a few months he would be promoted to Chief Deputy Sheriff and he wasn't even thinking about retiring. He was just trying to have a nice Sunday at home with his wife, when the case began for him.

"I was home, in fact, in the backyard. It was bright and sunny, and I was barbecuing with my wife, enjoying a Sunday off. Taking it easy. The kids were gone. I was just enjoying the day with my wife. Then one of the deputies came by and I had to go. It's part of the job. I left my wife and my barbecue and rode out to Hutchinson Island to begin a murder case. I didn't get home for almost four days."

Sgt. George Miller of the SLCSD was also dispatched to the scene. His job was to photograph and record any and all evidence as it turned up. The following report, written

by Miller describes the crime scene with
graphic clarity:

The undersigned officer was contacted at 2:00
p.m. April 1, 1973 by Dispatcher Reese Parrish
in reference to taking pictures of two bodies
in a wooded area located just north of Blind
Creek on South AlA.

Upon arrival at the scene, I was met by
Det. Sgt. Hinton of the Martin County Sheriff
Department, who proceeded to show me through
the crime scene. I started taking pictures of
an area located approximately 15 feet south
of the dirt road leading into the crime area.
These pictures show numerous articles of
women's clothing, partially covered by dead
leaves. From this area, we proceeded south
into a heavily wooded and undergrowth area.
Approximately 300 feet into the wooded area,
we came upon an open-type grave. Several
pictures were taken of this, showing the
length, width and depth being measured by
Lt. Duval (of the SLCSD) and Sgt. Bart Kanuff
of the Martin County Sheriff Department. Also
included in these pictures are two shots of
a white lace garment laying at the south
end of the open grave, partially covered by
dead leaves (one picture showed Sgt. Kanuff
measuring the distance from the south end of
the grave to the white garment).

The next area that photographs were taken
was located 39 feet 7 inches south of the
grave. These photographs show what was labeled
Body No. 1. Body No. 1 photographs show the
pelvic bone area, the left leg and foot bone,
thorax and a segment of a humerus bone. To
the southeast of Body No. 1 at approximately
30 degrees and the footage from Body No. 1
being 22 feet 4 inches. Pictures were taken
of the complete upper extremities of what
was labeled upper half of Body No. 2. These
photographs include the upper extremities
covered with dead palm fronds and also shows
upper extremities after being uncovered. In
these photographs can be seen both arms and
hands. One hand, assumed to be the left hand

and arm showing a piece of material, red-and-white in color, tied in a common knot around the wrist.

The next area photographed was to the southwest of Body No. 1 at approximately 55 degrees, footage being 25 feet 4 inches from Body No. 1, and this was labeled lower extremities of Body No. 2. These photographs show the lower extremities located next to a palm tree with the feet and legs to the south. Various photographs were taken showing the lower extremities of Body No. 2. One photograph shows Sgt. Kanuff holding up what appeared to be a belt found lying between the tree and lower extremities of Body No. 2. Also, a photograph of lower extremities of Body No. 2 shows two cloth patches found on the right front pant leg of lower extremities of Body No. 2. Patch No. 1 being a large cloth owl, red and black in color, and Patch No. 2 being a Roadrunner patch with the words "beep-beep" and emblem of Roadrunner, with the patch having a white background trimmed in yellow.

Next area photographed was 21 feet 10 inches south of lower extremities of Body No. 2. This photograph showing a complete right arm including finger and hand bone...this being labeled right arm for Body No. 1.

On April 2, 1973, this office again returned to the area to continue photographing any new evidence found.

At approximately 10:00 a.m. this same date, Det. Sgt. Richardson found a lower leg 10 feet to the east of Body No. 1. This was photographed showing how it was covered.

On April 3, 1973, this office again returned to the area to photograph any new evidence. This same date, officers searching started finding parts of a skull. Photographs taken include looking from the south end of the open grave to the area where parts of the skull were found. It also shows a view of looking directly down into several teeth and two vertebras located 24 feet 5 inches from

the north corner of the open grave. Also, a
photograph of a jawbone labeled Jawbone No. 1
with 3 teeth in place. This was found 28 feet
from the northwest corner of the grave.

A photograph was taken of what appeared to
be human hair, reddish-brown in color -- this
being 23 feet 9 inches from the northwest
corner of the open grave.

A photograph is also included of another
section of a jawbone assumed to be a front
section containing four teeth, labeled Jawbone
No. 2. This was located 33 feet 3 inches from
the northwest corner of the open grave.

More information will be added to this
report as new evidence is turned up and
photographed.

Signed: Sgt. George Miller

* * *

A good reporter establishes at least a daily routine check with local police and sheriff departments. This check informs reporters of the latest news on the "police blotter." A smart reporter tries to establish something more. A clerk in bookkeeping, a few friends in records, an officer willing to share some coffee and interesting conversation. Jayne Ellison maintained a professional, as well as friendly, relationship with most of the law enforcement agencies in Martin and St. Lucie Counties. She was more informed about what was going on in police circles than many of the people who worked within their policy-confining boundaries. Shortly after the bodies of two mutilated and, as yet, unidentified females were found on Hutchinson Island, Jayne Ellison knew about it.

Ellison called both St. Lucie and Martin Counties Sheriff's Departments to confirm the validity of the story and establish the identities of the dead girls. She found that indeed the story was true, but no one knew who the girls might be. A complete investigation into all missing persons throughout the last year or so would have to be executed. Then the narrowing down of possible victims would commence. It might take days, more probably weeks, to establish identification.

On a hunch, purely intuitive, Ellison suggested the authorities consider the Place/Jessup girls as possible victims. Their families could be reached in the Ft. Lauderdale area and were anxious to hear something. It was worth a try. She also mentioned that if foul play was involved, they had a possible suspect right there in the county jail. She referred to Gerard Schaefer. "After all, wasn't he currently serving time for abducting two girls last summer?" she asked.

Ellison then called the Places and asked if they'd heard from anyone yet. They told her they had not. She informed them that the bodies of two girls had been discovered on Hutchinson Island. They were not to be alarmed, but they should be prepared to answer any questions from police concerning their daughter. God willing, there would be no connection, the bodies could be anyone, but they should be prepared, perhaps for the worse.

At this time, the Places and the Jessups were notified by the authorities of the discovery. The families should stand by, but as of yet, there was no positive identification. Both families began to pray that the bodies were not their daughters.

As a matter of course, because the bodies were found in St. Lucie County, the case for the state came into the hands of Robert E. Stone, the State Attorney for the 19th Judicial Circuit which includes Martin, St. Lucie, Indian River and Okeechobee Counties.

Robert Stone was a heavy-set man in 1973.Thick shoulders and neck sat atop a barrel chest still, but he is thinner now. His hair is short-cropped, distinctively salt and peppered. He is tanner, more healthy-looking than he was in 1973. Upon first meeting, Stone appears to be a good ole boy Southern lawyer. It is a well-practiced facade. In truth, he is a skilled logician and his work in court confirmed this. An accomplished career filled with a history of accolades from his peers is a faithful reminder that success breeds success and its reward is a dynamic, juggernaut-like presence, unattainable by anything less. In Florida criminal history, Stone prosecuted some of the biggest cases to pass through the state's courts.

In 1973, however, Stone was new to the 19th Judicial Circuit, and enthusiastically eager to express his legal powers. He was about to get his chance.

Stone was born in West Virginia, the son of a mining engineer. His father worked in the tough steelyard business during World War II. At that time the Stones lived in Baltimore, Maryland, displaced country folk waxing out an existence in an industrial big city. At the end of the war, Stone moved his family to Virginia for two years, then to Kentucky, where he continued engineering work and supported his family in an environment more in tune with their simple, yet dignified heritage. Robert finished high school and attended a small college in eastern Kentucky. From there, he went to New Orleans, Louisiana, and studied law at Tulane University Law School.

Stone longed to return to Kentucky, with its rolling mountains and rich thoroughbred-bloodline horses prancing about in bluegrass fields. He intended to set up a small practice there and live the quiet, but good life. However, an uncle who already ran an established law firm in Ft. Pierce, Florida, offered the young Tulane graduate a place in his practice. Fresh out of school and eager to jump into the drama of courtroom battle, Stone accepted his uncle's offer and soon arrived in Ft. Pierce, briefcase in one hand, and a book of statutes in the other.

Florida was a fast-growing state, even then, with residential air conditioning becoming commonplace. It was fresh and clean, and families came down in droves, pushing their two-toned Fords along at seventy miles per hour, and marveling at the acres of sun-drenched orange groves and beaches thick with sea oats. It was a naive but wonderful and innocent time to be in the Sunshine State, and a young man with plenty of ambition could go far there. Stone worked with his uncle for over a year, but then his independent nature beckoned him to be out on his own, and so, he began his own practice. Soon, the young attorney began to get bored with private practice and longed to get his teeth into some criminal law. He was given his first bite as City Prosecutor for Ft. Pierce.

He held that position for two years and decided to take the challenge of defending some of the criminals he was helping to put in jail. He was appointed Assistant Public Defender in 1969 and maintained that job and his own private practice for three years. In l972, the State Attorney position for the l9th Judicial Circuit became open for anyone with enough experience, tenacity, and "killer instinct" necessary to do the job and do it right. Robert E. Stone was elected in November of '72.

By April of 1973, he began his first big murder case. It was to be an unforgettable experience, dealing with one of the most unusual and terrifying criminal cases in Florida history. By Tuesday, April 3, some notice of the story had been printed in the Palm Beach Post-Times newspaper, where Jayne Ellison was employed. The story, written by Dennis Lehner, the Times Bureau Chief, told of the discovery of the bodies on Hutchinson Island. It also mentioned there was a suspect but did not name him. The article quoted Lt. Patrick Duval with the following:

"An autopsy will be performed this week. The time period makes it a possibility that the bodies are those of the Place and Jessup girls. But, until we can get more positive identification of the bodies, all we can do is theorize."

Later, in the afternoon edition of the Post-Times, Chief Deputy Finis Parrish of the St. Lucie Sheriff's Department stated, "Without the skulls a positive identification will be almost impossible." And Lt. Duval added, "It was brutal, and it was weird. We believe they were cut up by a big strong man with a machete or axe. Several of the bones were cut clean through."

The article also stated that law department officers from Broward County had joined in the search, seeking a possible connection between the bodies found and the disappearance of Susan Place and Georgia Jessup.

State Attorney Robert Stone recalls the course of events as they fell into place.

"After the bodies were found, I followed the case closely, but did not want to interfere with the St. Lucie Sheriff's Department. I called the next day to volunteer my help. (Whereby, Stone observed the crime scene investigation). Wednesday of that week, it was April 4th, I was called by the sheriff's department about legality of obtaining search warrants. Thursday, we met with the St. Lucie County Sheriff (Lanie Norvell) and requested all authorities with interest in the case to attend. Friday, we met with Broward, St. Lucie and Martin Counties Sheriffs' investigators and my chief investigator, Mr. (Lem) Brumley. At that meeting we advised authorities of what we thought. Subsequently, search warrants were executed by the afore-mentioned sheriffs' departments.

"There was quite a bit of evidence gathered at the murder scene. We sent a bag of bones, that's what it amounted to, to Dr. Joseph Davis, the Dade County medical examiner. The bones had been scattered. We had some spent cartridges we wanted examined. We chopped down a tree at the murder site with knife marks on it."

Stone also told newspapers that, "Based on my knowledge and my intuition, I feel this may be the biggest crime in the history of the United States. I may be proven wrong later."

Dr. H.L. Schofield was the medical examiner for the 19th Judicial Circuit. Because the murdered girls were suspected of being Broward County residents, and because Dade County (which is just south of Broward) had better-equipped forensic laboratories, Dr. Schofield sent the remains to Dr. Joe Davis, in Miami. Dr. Davis studied the skeletal remains, and one of his advisors, Dr. Richard Souviron (who was the only forensic dentist appointed by the Justice Department of the United States at that time) studied the teeth and jawbones that had been discovered at the crime scene. Within a few days the medical examiners had concluded their examinations and called Stone to relay the results. Dr. Souviron's discoveries were most valuable in attaining the identification of the bodies, as dental records are as conclusive as fingerprints to the trained examiner. He positively identified the bodies of those of Susan Place and Georgia Jessup and sent his report to Stone. Dr. Davis also finalized his examination and sent the following letter to Stone:

Dear Mr. Stone:
    April 1973, I received, in two separate body pouches, the incomplete skeletonized remains of two females. On 15 May 1973 an additional vertebra was received.
    Enclosed are copies of my reports pertaining to these skeletonized bodies. In neither of these cases is it possible for me, at this time, to furnish a cause of death based upon examination of the skeletonized remains received on 7 April 1973.
    Identification of these remains is circumstantial by virtue of the fact that partial lower jaws were found in association with, but not attached directly to, these skeletal remains. The identification of these lower jaw fragments is the subject of a separate report by Dr. Richard Souviron, forensic dental consultant to this office.
    Georgia Jessup (73-962) sustained a fracture of her left forearm at eleven years of age, approximately five years ago. Preliminary X-rays of the forearms reveal such perfect healing that it is difficult to be certain that an injury had occurred at the site. However, I plan to seek additional roentgenological consultation in an effort to find evidence of previous injury which would coincide with the orthopedic records which I have received from Det. Sgt. Carruthers on 12 April 1973. The injuries to the bodies consist of cutting mutilations by a sharp instrument. No X-ray evidence of knife or bullet fragments were found within the skeletal remains.
    The dental identification by Dr. Souviron has also revealed metallic radiopaque

fragments corresponding to a defect in the
mandible identified as belonging to Susan
Place. The size of the defect is consistent
with a small caliber bullet such as a 0.22.

It cannot be determined whether the bullet
was fired into the jaw before or after death.
Although there is some black stain at the
dismemberment cut sites of the skeletonized
remains, there is no conclusive evidence
that these cuts in the bone were inflicted
prior to death.

Despite the inconclusive evidence of a
cause of death, I believe that there is ample
evidence to indicate a criminal agency.
However, the proof of a criminal agency is a
legal matter, not a medical responsibility.
It depends upon the sum of all the evidence
whether it be medical or not.

I enclose, for distribution by you to all
concerned parties, the reports upon the bodies
received by me on 7 April 1973 and copies of
the dental description by Dr. Souviron who
received his jaw fragment evidence from Lt.
Patrick Duval on 4 April 1973.

Signed: Sincerely yours,
JOSEPH H. DAVIS, M.D.
Dade County Medical Examiner

The following dissertation is a cooperative analysis of events as they most likely took place on the night of the murders. These conclusions are based on reports by investigators from all law enforcement agencies involved, and from the medical examiners, from comparative interviews with those people most closely connected with the case, and of course, speculative conclusions are drawn where no witnesses were available to either confirm or deny circumstances or evidence. In addition, Schaefer's own writings piece together what horrors probably occurred that fateful night.

On the night of September 27, 1972, after 8:00 p.m. and before 9:30 p.m., Susan Place and Georgia Jessup left the Place home with their male friend, who was introduced to Mrs. Place as "Jerry Shepherd."

(The state would later enter evidence, during the trial, that "Jerry Shepherd" and Gerard Schaefer were one in the same, and of course both

Mr. and Mrs. Place would identify Schaefer as being the man that left with Susan and Georgia.)

"Jerry," Susan, and Georgia would have headed east toward the beach to relax, play guitar, and perhaps drink a beer or smoke some marijuana. Susan would not have been overly upset, but she would have been at least agitated enough (from the brief conflict with her mother about "going away to Colorado") so that when an offer for a longer ride came up, she would not have turned it down.

Georgia, already "running away," having packed her clothes and always ready for some fun or "an adventure," would have been open to suggestions as well. A longer ride, perhaps to see "an old Spanish fort" on Hutchinson Island, would be fun and give Susan some time to think. She would not have been planning to leave home yet, as she had not packed any clothes, nor did she have any of her medication, Dilantin, with her to offset a grand mal seizure brought on by her epilepsy.

It was a pleasant evening, the weather fair, the cool night air blowing into the open windows of the blue-green Datsun as it headed north, probably along highway A1A, next to the beach. In less than two hours, providing they didn't stop too much for beer or bathroom visits, they would have been as far north as Martin County, or southern St. Lucie County. There, "Jerry" would have pulled the Datsun off A1A, onto the dirt road that led toward the beach. They would have been laughing, having a good time and drinking beer, because as Schaefer wrote, "Beer is useful to induce urination and make the victim groggy and more cooperative."

"Jerry" would have turned the car south going into the woods about three hundred feet, according to Sgt. Miller's report, to "an isolated area, assessable by car and a short hike away from police patrols" (which, as a deputy sheriff of Martin County, Schaefer would have been well aware of).

Susan and Georgia would have gotten out of the car with "Jerry," perhaps to follow him so he could show them the "Spanish fort" that Nancy Trotter and Paula Sue Wells had seen. They would not have known they were walking into "the execution site" that "must be carefully arranged for a speedy execution." There probably were "2 saw horses with a 2X4 between them", that "Jerry" would have offered for a bench seat. The girls would not have seen "the noose attached to the overhanging limb of a tree" or the other "rope to pull away the 2X4, preferably by car." Although the girls may have stumbled in it, they would not have suspected the large hole, already dug out as "a grave prepared in advance." At this point they still would not know that they were intended victims, though "the victims could be anyone of the women who flock to Miami & Ft. Lauderdale . . . even 2 victims would not be difficult to dispose of since women are less wary when travelling in pairs."

Now "Jerry" may have suggested a game to the girls, who were probably "groggy and cooperative," or he might have pulled the concealed .22 caliber out of his pants pocket and told them they would have to let him tie them up, or else he'd shoot them.

In either case, the girls would have found themselves tied, and probably gagged. Now, he may have separated the girls, but if he did, it is likely that he did not put too much space between them, because that plan had already proved itself to be totally inadequate, as with the Trotter/ Wells incident, it would give the captives too much time to think out their situation, and possibly escape. There is no way to be sure, and anyone with even a partially normal mind would not want to know exactly what "torture or defilement was planned for them," but Schaefer's his writings are descriptive enough to define the probable events of that terrible night.

One can only hope that Georgia lost consciousness, due to fear or intoxication, or whatever, and that Susan, perhaps, had an epileptic episode and that in either case they would not have known what atrocities would befall them. It is possible that Susan went into a grand mal seizure, and "Jerry" not realizing what was happening to her, might have become aggravated enough to aim his .22 pistol at her face, and fire. We know that at least one bullet struck her in the jaw, that may have rendered her unconscious, or he may have shot, possibly several times, into her skull and killed her then.

There is no way to be certain, as the upper portions of the skulls of both girls were never located. And, it is possible that he struck one or both girls a lethal blow to the head with either "a machete or an axe" as Lt. Duval would later point out.

By his own writings, "a white pillow case" (very much like the one found with "stains," at his Martin County home) "should be placed over her head." Once positioned, with pillowcases, gags, and wrists bound, and "subjected to further indecencies," one or both girls were probably hanged. We can be relatively sure that "Jerry" did not have sex with either of the girls, while they were alive. But they were probably "violated" after death, before they were "mutilated and carried to the grave and buried."

On April 5th, 1973, the Place and Jessup families were notified that their daughters had been murdered.

*   *   *

It was some twelve years later when this writer met the Places. Ironically, I found them living in Stuart, Florida. Stuart, the place where they found Schaefer's home on Martin Street. The home is also very close to where Susan was last known to be alive, and where she died. Perhaps that is the reason they chose to live there, so that in some way they'd still be close to her. I met them at their home there. Their house filled with beautiful and spotless antiques, and cherished family photos, and memories, both good and bad.

Lucille Place was small compared to Ira Place. Her reddish-blonde hair is fading to white. Her eyes, big, blue, and watery, reflect the sorrows she's had to bear. She was soft-spoken, but firmly decided with her opinions. Ira Place was a huge man. His hands were callus-thickened from years of carpenter work during his youth, and one could still feel the strength of those hands when I was greeted, pleasantly, into his home. They both are gentle, loving people, a fact made concrete when one learns that they'd been married over forty-five years.

There was an old piano in their home, given to them by an aunt, on which Susan performed. It was kept immaculate, and on the top was a framed photograph of Susan in a white graduation gown and cap. Next to the photograph, frozen still in a gaily choreographed dance, is a porcelain harlequin. A wonderful figure poised as if waiting for the girl of the piano to return and finish out her melody so that it can continue its dance.

It was near that figure, that photo, that piano, where we first talked; about Susan, her life and her death. And even with so many years passed, the emotions, the anger, the sorrow, the understandable want of vengeance were still very strong.

Mrs. Place sat in a chair, leaning forward, elbows on knees, hands clasped together as she spoke, her voice trailing off now and again as she'd stop to cry. Mr. Place sat, back erect, gray-black hair swept back from his forehead, a stoic rock of information, adding his thoughts only sporadically and briefly. Mrs. Place carried most of the conversation, as Mr. Place quietly stared forward into space, occasionally exhausting, audibly, a long breath of air.

"Well, you know when I reported this license plate, they put it in the computer wrong. They got that all screwed up. We were going to sue the city for that. But, I . . . we just . . . didn't.

"He (Schaefer) was a man that just gave me the creeps. He had a weird look in his eye, that said you just couldn't trust him. Something told me, you'd better just go and check this out (his license tag). He was sort of slovenly looking, but arrogant at the same time. He just looked as though he didn't care about himself much.

"What advice would I give to other parents? Well, if they don't have any forewarning like I did, in my own mind, I don't know what to tell them. But I knew something was wrong with this man and that's the only reason I took this (the tag number) down. But I still think you people just have to keep a better watch. You just can't let them . . . You must know who they're going out with and myself . . . (now) I'd go down and take everyone's tag down, and let them know you're doing it, and beware of the fact that they can be traced.

"Susan was fun-loving, outgoing. But she was somewhat introverted because of her epilepsy and because she was new to the area. She used to like to sing and play guitar. She composed some music. I don't know how good it is because I'm not a musician myself. And she wrote poetry . . .

"All the other children are married now. Susan was the baby. The youngest next to Susan, Kristen, is an attorney now, as well as a CPA and an interior decorator. She just finished all her schooling. She and Susan used to play and sing together. She (Kristen) mentions her (Susan) quite often. She asks, 'I wonder what she'd look like now?'

"She (Susan) was a real compassionate girl. I mean she cared about little things. I had some varicose veins in my legs, and she worried about them. She'd touch them and say, 'I just wish you didn't have them, Mom.'"

Mr. Place added, "She was a prankster, though. She loved to pull pranks on people." Then gesturing toward a picture of Susan, he said, "Just look at her, that face ... so full of life."

"Every once and awhile, I'll have some dreams again," said Mrs. Place. "But she (Susan) is whole again . . . and herself. But in my dreams, I know she's not real. I mean, it seems like it's real, but it, uh, still in my dreams, I know it's not. She's gone."

The Places recalled April 5th, 1973. Mr. Place was in the house when an officer, Sgt. Charles Hemp, from the Oakland Park Police Department, who "looked like the fellow that plays the judge, Hardcastle, Brian Keith," came to tell them the news. Mrs. Place was in the backyard, and Mr. Place called her in. Sgt. Hemp then told them the medical examiner's findings and said that Susan had been identified.

"I remember thinking," said Mrs. Place, "that I wasn't even there to hold her hand while she was dying."

Chapter 6

The Search

The guilt of my dark deed disturbed me but little. A search had even been instituted, but of course nothing was to be discovered, I looked upon my future felicity as finally secure.

From *The Black Cat*, by Edgar Allan Poe

A letter, sent to Shirley Jessup, Georgia's mother, from her sister-in-law. (The punctuation and spelling are as written in the original letter):

4-25-73
Dear Shirley, Ann & Kids,

I just received a letter from Ace telling me about Georgia.

I'm sick over this, I just don't know what to say to you, it's just a terrible thing to happen. Georgia was such a sweet girl & very pretty, I was very fond of her.

I wish I could come back there & be with you, but I don't have the money, or I would.

How is your Mom taking this? I sent our Mom a Christmas card & a letter & it came back to me. Where is she at?

How is George? Do you see him?

We are all fine.

Dan is almost 18 now, he is about 6ft 4 in. & skinney like Ace used to be, he is a good boy, but is a little on the lazy side, he quit school he only had 1 year to go but didn't want to finish, so he is looking for work.

Bob is 15 yrs. about 6 ft 2 in. & weighs 205 lbs he is really a big kid, he is doing better in school now. Cindy is 8 now she is real tall. She is real good in school.

Please write me when you feel better, I would love to hear from you if you can ever come to Calif. I would love for you to come visit us & spend some time here. We have a 10 acre farm & we love it here in the country, it's very peaceful & beautiful.

This letter is for your mother too. Please tell her to write us, we thought something had happened to her because the letter came back to me.

Shirley if I can do anything please let me know. Please write to me.

Ace's letter was quite brief about Georgia. So I don't know too much, did they find out who did this?

God Bless you.
Lots of Love
Donna & Family
Larry, Dan, Bob, Cindy

* * *

Although Gerard Schaefer had not yet been charged with the murders of Susan Place and Georgia Jessup, he was the most likely suspect.

Primarily of course, because the Places identified him as the man they'd last seen with their daughter. Additionally, he was, indeed, serving time for abducting two girls, and although this fact was circumstantial within legal rhetorical standards, it was nevertheless a strong suggestion that Schaefer was the type of man who was at least capable of committing a forcible crime.

Schaefer, already half-way through his six-month sentence, was informed that he was a suspect in a developing murder case. He declared himself indigent and requested legal aid in the form of a public defender. The man appointed to take his case was Elton H. Schwarz.

Elton H. Schwarz was born in Duluth, Minnesota in the late spring of 1928. Duluth is a harbor city that spreads out along the southwestern tip of Lake Superior. It lies at the end of Interstate 35 which races north, up out of the twin cities of St. Paul and Minneapolis. It is extremely cold there, and so, seeking warmer climes, the Schwarzes picked up young Elton only one and a half years old, and moved south, to Cleveland, Ohio, a city not so much warmer climatically, but certainly more temperate economically. Again, the Schwarzes chose to live in a harbor city, this chosen metropolis sprawled along the southern banks of another Great Lake, Erie. This was to be the home for Elton throughout his formative years and into his adolescence.

As soon as he was legally able, and perhaps because he'd lived in harbor cities his entire life and had become accustomed to living at least very close to large bodies of water, young Elton sauntered into the U.S. Naval Enlistment Office and joined up. He "did his time in the service," a stint lasting approximately two-and-one-half years. After the Navy, Elton attended college at Ohio State University where he graduated with a degree in business administration. His family moved to Florida, establishing residence in 1949, a move that delighted Elton as once again, he'd be near the water, and so, that is where he decided to attend law school. This he did at the Law School at the University of Florida, in Gainesville, where he graduated in January of '54.

Elton Schwarz, attorney, moved to Martin County in the mid-50s and helped organize a group that would start the successful banking group, First Federal Savings and Loan of Martin County (now the First Fidelity Association). Schwarz practiced law for the next eighteen years until he "tired of the rat race of general practice." He enjoyed trial work tremendously, so in May of 1972 he began work as Assistant Public Defender, taking Robert Stone's former job, under Public Defender Irvin

Frank, Jr. Frank decided not to run for the office again that same year, opting to retire to Georgia. Schwarz ran unopposed, as he did many times thereafter, and took over the office of Public Defender of the 19th Judicial Circuit, in November of '72.

Schwarz, for all the pressure his job must place on him, is a laid-back character, a transplanted northerner who adopted the South and its ways. He speaks with a deep, almost comforting voice, and if a cartoonist was to personify an animated creature with his character, it would probably be a sophisticated basset hound. Given some time, he'll tell you about his children, his grandchildren, and now and then, he likes to mention the fact that his oldest son and his current wife are the same age.

As Schwarz better acquainted himself with the Schaefer case, Stone, in collaboration with all involved law enforcement agencies, trudged forward to deal with the legalities involved in a murder case of this magnitude.

This was Stone's first substantial case as a state attorney, and he did not want to commit any errors that would later come back to haunt him in trial. He diligently researched issuing search warrants and instructed interested police agencies on how they should be executed. The effort was conscientiously undertaken. They "redid those search warrants four and five times, dotted every 'I' and crossed every 'T'. We didn't want to make any mistakes."

Even so, Stone felt they could not be too careful. A search warrant is a key element in a trial, if improperly issued, or executed, it could mean freeing the guilty party. As Stone would later say, "There are no loopholes in law. There are, however, many legal technicalities, with which an attorney can either make or break a case. I didn't want those search warrants to be rendered useless by such technicalities."

A warrant must first be properly petitioned, by an investigating officer, to a judge whose jurisdiction contains the property for which the search warrant is being sought. These petitions must list items of evidence that the officer believes he may find in or on that property, based on previously collected evidence or information. The search is performed, and all evidence gathered is listed on a "return," which is then filed with the county clerk, to be used in the trial.

The following petition and return were completed by Lt. David Yurchuk, under direction from Robert Stone and Phillip Shailer. Shailer was the State Attorney for Broward County, who would co-prosecute the case, as it developed, because of the fact that Susan Place and Georgia Jessup were Broward County residents. The information on these pages accurately displays the detail involved in such legal paperwork, and more importantly, pieces together the events as they had taken place up to that point. The search took place at Schaefer's mother's house, where Schaefer kept a locked, private room, even though he no longer resided there.

```
GENERAL AFFIDAVIT AND APPLICATION FOR
SEARCH WARRANT
STATE OF FLORIDA
COUNTY OF BROWARD as:


    BEFORE  THE  UNDERSIGNED John  G.  Ferris
Judge,  of  the  Circuit  Court  in  and  for
Broward County, State of Florida, personally
came  Lt.  David  Yurchuck  who  after  being
first duly sworn deposes and says:
    That he is a duly and legally appointed
Deputy Sheriff in and for said County and State;
    That  he  has  probable  cause  to  believe,
and  does  believe  that  certain  evidence,
instrumentalities,  and  fruits  of  a  crime,
consisting of:
    1. One girl's yellow gold birthstone ring
with a ruby centered between two pearls.
    2. One old blue suitcase.
    3. One red, white and blue knit purse.
    4. Certain photographs of mutilated women.
    5.  One  1969  blue-green  Datsun,  4
door,  bearing  1973  Florida  42D1728,  VIN  #
PC510067286.
    6. Any and all items and/or personal effects
relating  to  the  death  and  disappearance  of
Susan Place and Georgia Jessup.
    7. Firearms.
    Relating to the death of Susan Place and
Georgia Jessup,  such death being  homicide
and/or unattended deaths which are against
the laws of the State of Florida, and that
such evidence, instrumentalities, and fruits
of  the  crime  are  presently  located  within
```

or on the surrounding jurisdiction of said officer and is presently located within or on the surrounding grounds or area of the structure described and situated as follows and/or within the above described vehicle #5.

2716 S.W. 34th Ave., Fort Lauderdale, Florida (Unincorporated Broward County, Florida). The 4th house on the East side of S.W. 34th Ave. going South from the intersection of S.W. 34th Ave. and S.W. 26th Court, Fort Lauderdale, UNINCORPORATED BROWARD COUNTY, FLORIDA, further described as a one-story CBS dwelling house, light green in color with a white tile roof. The residence has a single column mailbox with the number 2716 on the column, said mailbox being located in the North West corner of the lot. The residence has a double front door, two tone green in color, facing West. A 1969, 4 door Datsun, blue-green in color bearing 1973 Florida 4D1728 in parked in the carport of the home located on the Northwest corner of the residence, in Broward County, Florida, and within the territorial jurisdiction of this affiant and the said Judge's Court of said County and State and,

That the facts upon which such belief of said affiant is based are as follows:

On April 1, 1973, the decomposed bodies of two white females were discovered in St. Lucie County, Florida.

This affiant was contacted by the St. Lucie County Sheriff's Department on 1 April 1973 in regard to the discovery of the bodies.

This affiant was conducting an investigation into the missing person reports of Georgia Marie Jessup, reference Broward County Sheriff's report number &2-9-3086. The affiant was working in conjunction with the Oakland Park Police Department in reference to the reported missing person of Susan Place.

Both Susan Place and Georgia Marie Jessup were last seen on 27 September 1972 at 9:00 P.M. by Lucille Place, mother of Susan Place, at the residence of 4451 Northeast 13th Terrace, Oakland Park, Florida.

Susan Place and Georgia Jessup left the residence with an unidentified white male who was introduced to Lucille by photo identification of one GERARD JOHN SCHAEFER as the person known to Lucille Place as JERRY SHEPARD the person with whom Susan Place and Georgia Jessup left the Place Residence on 27 September 1972.

Affiant learned from Lucille Place that the Martin County Sheriff's Department checked the 1973 Florida tag 42Dl728, which is the tag number obtained by Lucille Place on 27 September 1972.

The tag is registered to GERARD J. SCHAEFER, JR. of 2716 S.W. 34th Ave., Fort Lauderdale, Florida on a 1969 Datsun, 4 door.

On 4 April 1973, this affiant made record check of 1973 Florida tag number 42Dl728 and confirmed the registration of the tag to GERARD J. SCHAEFER, JR., of 2716 S.W. 34th Ave., Fort Lauderdale, Florida.

The affiant in conversation with the Martin County Sheriff's Department learned that Gerard J. Schaefer, Jr. is incarcerated in the Martin County jail as the result of an incident on 22 July 1972. Gerard J. Schaefer picked up two teen age girls, Nancy Trotter and Sue Wells, taking them to a remote area on Hutchinson Island in Martin County.

Gerard J. Schaefer is reported to have bound both girls with hand cuffs, cloth and gags. Gerard J. Schaefer threatened to kill the girls, one of them broke free of her binds and reported the incident to the Martin County Sheriff's Department who subsequently arrested Gerard J. Schaefer, Jr. He was later found guilty of the charges and sentenced to jail by the Martin County Court. The affiant in conversation with Lt. Pat Duval of the St. Lucie County Sheriff's Department revealed the two bodies identified as Susan Place and Georgia Jessup were located in a desolate part of Hutchinson Island, Martin County. The bodies were in advanced state of decomposition and tied binds were found on the deceased.

Lt. Pat Duval revealed that the two bodies of Susan Place and Georgia Jessup were located approximately six miles north of the location in Martin County where Gerard J. Schaefer, Jr. had tied Nancy Trotter and Sue Wells on 22 July 1972.

On April 1973 this affiant met with and had conversation with Theresa Schaefer, wife of Gerard Schaefer. She advised this affiant that her husband's blue Datsun is presently at the address of 2716 S.W. 34th Ave. Fort Lauderdale, certain information and physical evidence that may be associated with the deaths of Susan Place and Georgia Jessup, and that this physical evidence, instrumentalities, fruits of the crime may be vital to further the investigation into the deaths of Susan Place and Georgia Jessup.

WHEREFORE, affiant hereby makes application for a search warrant authorizing affiant Lt. David Yurchuck as such Deputy Sheriff of Broward County, Florida, to search the premises and search and seize the property herein described, and to search the surrounding areas and vehicle.

   Signed: David Yurchuck

   Sworn to and subscribed before me this 7th day of APRIL A.D. 1973.

   Signed: John G. Ferris Judge of said Court in and for

   Broward County, Florida

   RETURN ON SEARCH WARRANT

   RETURNED THIS 7 day of April A.D. 1973 SERVED by making search as within directed: upon which search I found (and seized) the following items:

   1) One white and red white owl cigar box containing various photographs of mutilated women and various letters and envelopes addressed to Gerard Schaefer

   2) Three spent bullets

   3) One hunting knife in case

   4) One 22 cal. Colt Magnum #G41951 and black holster and belt

   5) One 22 cal. Ruger #11-01193 and one black holster

   6) One bag containing miscellaneous paper, one red piece of rope, etc.

   7) One bag containing spent bullets

   8) One bag containing negatives

   9) Two hunting knives

   10) One newspaper, Fort Lauderdale News, Date: June 14, 1970, also Dec. 23, 1970, Dec. 26, 1970, Sept. 27, 1970, all Fort Lauderdale News.

   11) Seventeen magazines depicting nude women also pornographic pictures.

   12) One bag containing envelopes, handcuff case, empty, vial containing two teeth,

paper back history of torture, negatives, three small jack-knives, two envelopes, one containing photos of mutilated women.

13) One paper bag containing eleven 22 cal. bullets and five spent shells.

14) One knap-sack containing:

(1) One small light suede purse with identification and paper

(2) One stationary book

(3) Pens in case

(4) Letter opener

(5) One bracelet

(6) One paper back

15) Ten hunting knives

16) One machete

17) One Hippie belt

18) One Colt 38 Special #765 and holster

19) One Colt 45 #222016 and holster

20) One manila envelope containing various papers

21) One gold jewelry box containing various articles of jewelry

22) Two large boxes of pornographic books

23) One paper bag containing notes

24) One paper bag containing two bones and bracelet

25) Two sleeping bags

26) Seven Girl Magazines

27) Seven bank bags

28) Two cash drawers

29) One Remington 12 gauge automatic 2-3/4 chamber #1804079V

30) One single 16-gauge Eastern Arms Company 1929 Model 67A, no serial number

31) One 30.06 Remington Model 1903, #3099154

32) One single shot 22 cal. Winchester Model 67A No serial number

33) 410 shotgun Savage Model 311A Serial unknown

34) Nylon 66, 22 cal. long rifle only made by Remington Serial #412827

35) Large rifle foreign made, Serial 222811 MB 1

36) One paper bag containing wallet and papers—miscellaneous—belonging to Ted Greer

37) One jack-knife

38) One paper bag containing I.D. cards, drivers' licenses and evidence tags from Wilton Manors Police Department

39) One clear box containing spent casings

40) 1969 Datsun, four-door, blue-green in color bearing 73 Fla 42D1728

41) Four gun cases

42) Rope and duly inventoried the same according to law.

I further certify and swear that a copy of this warrant, together with a detailed receipt for the said property taken was given to Doris Schaefer the person from whom it was taken.

I David Yurchuck the officer by whom this warrant was executed, do swear that the inventory contains a true and detailed account of the property taken by me on the warrant.

Signed: David Yurchuck

Signature

Deputy Sheriff

Title

Previously, Lt. Pat Duval had petitioned for, and received, a search warrant for Schaefer's home in Stuart. Accompanied by Robert Stone and several officers from various police and sheriff departments, Duval searched the Martin County home of Gerard Schaefer. A few more interesting items were found.

```
INVENTORY AND RETURN
STATE OF FLORIDA
COUNTY OF MARTIN


Received this search warrant at Stuart,
Martin County, Florida, this 6th day of April.
Served the Same by reading and delivering
a copy to Teresa Schaefer (Gerard's wife),
and making search as within directed; upon
which search I found:
     #1l-White Pillowcase with stains
     #2l-RG - 23 22 cal. revolver serial No. 207063
     #3l-Large canvas bag containing assorted
ammunition, and cloths
     #4l-Pair blue men's tennis shoes
     #5l-Large man's belt-brown
     #62-Teeth (Human, as yet unidentified,)
     #73-Bullets
     #8l-Swedish fishing knife.
     #9l-Vehicle inspection certificate receipt
     #10l-Instacora-F2 camera with film exposed
     #11l-Pair man's boots
     #12l-White cloth bag
     #13l-Bag of rubber balloons
     #14l-Bag of misc. papers
     #15l-Styrofoam cooler-white with blue top
     #16l-Handy-wipe towel
     #17l-Hunting knife
     #18l-Note book
     #19l-Note book
```

The evidence gathered at both locations in Stuart and in Fort Lauderdale would be used by the prosecution for the trial. The items had to be labeled "Exhibits" and filed for reference during the trial. The following Exhibit list further details the investigators' findings, and we are also given the names of suspected victims of foul play, by which the so called "List of 28" possible victims was compiled. (This, along with missing persons reports from nearby police agencies, people thought to have "disappeared" while in the company of a man answering Schaefer's description, or known to have been in places he frequented, altogether combined to make up the list, that is explained further in this chapter.) Certain points of interest are underlined.

```
EXHIBITS LIST
EXHIBIT 1
    Item A - Paperback book, title "History
of  Torture".  Inside  cover  of  paperback,
Schaefer's  name.  Attached  to  paperback,
handwritten  pink  note  addressed  to  "John
from Cindy'' reference lending book to Cindy
    Item B - Paper folder containing 17 strips
of negatives depicting naked women
    Item  C  -  One  envelope  addressed  to
Schaefer  from  Candar  Pub.  Corporation,
Valleystream,  New  York,  postmarked  May
15,  1970  containing  two-page  letter-  FAU
letterhead with note attached, saying "can't
help  you  with  information  you  requested."
Letter  attached  from  Schaefer  requesting
information  on  women  being  executed  and
wearing of waterproof underwear
    Item  D  -  Airmail  envelope  with  return
address  FAU  containing  fourteen  black  and
white photographs of the buttocks and crotch
of a figure dressed in women's undergarments
    Item E - Small vial containing two teeth,
gold fillings

    EXHIBIT II
    Item A - Negative Kodak film, four pictures
in  strip,  bears  number  5584  of  what  appears
to be a female buttock and crotch area
    EXHIBIT III
    Item  A  -  Empty  handcuff  box  with  V
17093  stamped  on  bottom  of  box  and  #6.95
which  appears  to  be  price  of  box  -  brand
name Detective
```

Item B - One pen knife with simulated black tone handle

Item C - One pen knife, brown bone handle

Item D - One penknife name Ballow, brown handle

EXHIBIT IV

Item A – seven-page typed paper with handwriting on some pages stapled together. Paper appears to be about the hanging of a woman, in a swamp area, victim is stripped, pillowcase over her head, noose around neck, dresses her in rope shroud, terrorizes the woman description of her death is given. Descriptions of various incidents involving women. Tells about his life and sexual feelings and experiences

Item B – Five-page handwritten letter on lined stationary, last page written on page of Distribution Service Form. Details killing of unknown female dressed in a white waitress dress in area of Powerline date and time unknown

Item C - Four pages of handwritten material on yellow lined paper and two pages plain white stationary (No writing on white stationary) All this attached to *a manilla envelope with name Jerry Shepard 2716 S.W. 34th Avenue, Fort Lauderdale, Florida 33312.* Address on front of manila envelope. Letter tells of a story taking place in Hamburg Railroad Station, talking about executing women and women urinating. Vivid description of imaginary story of hanging women. Some names are mentioned

Item D – One-page handwritten letter on lined paper. Story taking place in London in June 1760, mentions name Eleanor Hussy, talks about hanging girl

Item E - Three pages yellow lined legal paper handwritten. Story of German woman being taken to gallows to be hanged. Mentions name of Michelle Dumont. Goes into detail about female defecating etc.

Item F - One handwritten page on white lined paper, both sides describing in detail the proper method for execution and for mutilating a female body

Item G – Three-page typed pages on back of mimeographed paper. Another story of woman *being hanged, mention female Carmen*, blond pubic hair, dressed in a pink nightgown. The maid, Margarita, also name Sonora Nia. Margarita is tall, mentions a triple hanging. Talks about execution in Latin American Countries. Mentions "I" as the hangman, burying the bodies mentioned.

Item H - Eight typed pages talks about a female being driven to deserted area and hanged-vivid description - female in black chiffon dress, hair done up, black pantyhose and high heels. Talks about what he saw after hanging her. Talks about molesting women after death. Woman wearing a slip, wants to find a pile of defecation, becomes very excited, talks about a Grove area - wrapped her body over an orange crate, dumped in canal, kept going back to body to skull, pulled out teeth, spread them around. She was scattered over thirty miles. Another story, Commandants Summer House - another story of killing etc.

Item I - Eleven page handwritten on back of long-distance toll call record from # 10 38 RVP. 668. Another story of Jimmie being executioner of young girl who is just a kid, mentions name Clyde, mentions age of victim, 18 or 20 mentions Harry & Bob. Says drug pushers, all ought to hang, worst type of criminals. Says hand cuffed behind her. Names Torn & Pete. Apparently, girl is being executed in prison. Names Barbie, a prostitute from Miami, 5'5" blond bleached, 38-22-37. *Says Sam works with pliers deftly and comes out with gold fillings. States we a ways salvage something from the bodies.* Talks again about gold fillings. Inmates taking down dead girl Linda, talks about Sam & Pete again, gold fillings out of Linda's mouth. Names Sam, a young black man. Keeps jumping from story to story throughout pages- Linda's blue pants pulled down to observe pubic hair. Official execution time 8 a.m. *Keeps talking about a white hood with blood spots.*

Item J – Three-page type paper, title Eleanor Hussy (The Irish Harlot Refused to Hang) *Historical account by Jerry Sheperd December 1970, attached to manila type folder* - this was also found handwritten among personal effects-story of girl about to be hung leaped off gallows trying to escape and broke her neck.

Item K – One-page typed story of woman being killed and dumped into grave, a girl in a white maid's dress. Executioner removed all I.D. She was a blond, had on rings, talks about orange crate assaulted her annaly. Says we picked her up, body covered up.

Item L - Three pages handwritten notes on white lined paper, mentions names Mrs. Oudry being hanged by Nazi's. Talking about white female shapely collaborator found hanging nude from back streetlamp post. Mention Schmidt in hanging girl by driving a truck to pull stand from under her causing her to hang

Item M - One handwritten page on yellow legal paper. Another story about young white girl

Item N - Three pages handwritten notes on white lined paper, another story of hanging-female had two chain bracelets, keeps talking about white things (Gallows, Gloves) Name Jack mentioned as Executioner. Mentions a blond girl again talks about using a truck in the hanging, talks about himself in school etc. Jumps around goes back to description of death and hanging.

Item O - Three pages white lined notebook paper, handwritten, another story mentions Roberto and a massacre-woman bound with wire or cord. Talks whipping-red light district by Revolutionaries. Mentions white slacks being bunched around ankles, and mentioned remains of ripped white shirt, mentions 30 Calle Roos in this letter. Mentions a garroting cord. Mentions Rigata Puta

EXHIBIT V
Item A - (1) One manila envelope

(2) Cover magazine with male and female, female has a noose around her neck Black and white photograph of white female having intercourse with two white males.

(3) Black and white photograph of white female having intercourse with two white males.

(4) Page from magazine (handwritten notes on page) page of a woman posing nude also depicts bullet hole and blood.

(5) Page from magazine of woman in black negligee

(6-7) Index cards with poems about hanging women

(8-12) Condemned woman's attire, dated 1955, Mrs. R. Ellis, also described death of woman. Talks about hot August sky on these cards-talks about Sheriff springing track. On back of card 11 is numbers HU 8694.

(13) One handwritten page, a story of another hanging woman in tight green skirt and waterproof underwear. 120 lbs of woman hanged, hosed down, rolled in plastic bag taken to her grave.

(14-34) Typed pages telling about hanging women. Page18 tells about coming face to face with or meeting a missing woman in a closet. States she was preparing for bed when the killer struck. Mentions Top-less Club 38-23-36 were her measurements. Page twenty talks about N.Y.P.D., imaginary stories, names mentioned in the above pages, Lola Ewing, Mary Hopkins. Describes one victim, heavy eye make-up, red dress no underwear. Another woman in late 20's dressed in white shirt and slacks which were too big for her. Page 28 speaks of lady paying the price because she is a tramp, makes pottery. Page 32 and 33, one girl that gave him a thrill.

Talks about being in apartment with girl-slipped nylons around throat and strangled her while having anal intercourse

(35-40) Handwritten pages on white lined paper, more about hanging women, mentions August afternoon, page 37 mentions hanging outside of London in summer of 1592 mentions body of Mary Former.

(41-45) Hand drawings of woman being hanged and other sketches. These drawings have writing on them. Hangmen are males, the writing is conversation by the Hangmen.

(46-74) Drawings of woman being hung, shot, etc. Pages 50-51 show blood etc. Page 55 has some interesting captioned writing. Page 57 has woman watching hangings, many comments. Page 73, woman on toilet

Item C - (1) Magazine Todays Nudist, various writings entered under pictures.

(2) Magazine "Wow Nude", check entries made nooses drawn around necks of models.

(3) Picture of male and female together

EXHIBIT VI

Item A - (1) Newspaper Fort Lauderdale News, Saturday December 26, 1970.

(2) Newspaper Fort Lauderdale News, Sports section dated Wednesday December 23, 1970, just one page

(3) Fort Lauderdale Newspaper, Sunday Sept 27, 1970 page 1 B "Mood of Campus at Kent State" Page 11B, Jury probes hanging death.

(4) Newspaper, Fort Lauderdale News, dated Sunday June 14, 1970, section C. Main story two women lost in mystery web, *Leigh Bonadies* maiden name Hainline disappeared from Davie Blvd, Sept. 8, 1969, 5'7" 130

lbs. brown hair, second girl was *Carmen Marie Hallock*

EXHIBIT VII
Item A - (1) Small gold jewelry box
(2) Bracelet gold in color, gold mesh braid with safety clasp and safety chain.
(3) Silver colored charm bracelet with safety chain with pad lock charm (flower design) Five heart shaped charms with names and initials.
(a) Initial D.R., flower design on back·
(b) Initial "B'' on back initial "E" scroll designs around edge.
(c Name "Ruth" on back name "Sterling"
(d) Initial "M.T.N." outer edges, a scroll design, on back work sterling with scroll work.
(e) Name "Papa" on back up in left corner of heart word sterling.
(4) Bracelet silver in color with eleven rose designed beads. At clasp end a religious cross and Madonna medal.
(5) Bracelet with a series of brown leather type links attached to a four-leaf clover design (color red leather)
(6) Gold chain (fine) 17 3/4" long
(7) Charm bracelet silver colored chain style with one charm in silver with outline of State of Louisiana, on one side a star appears with name "New Orleans" on medal. At top of charm sterling below that initial C.P.A.I. and date of 1960
(8) Pair of women's earrings, the screw on type clasp attached to each clasp with a pink circular design with cut out of the center.
(9) A woman pin in the shape of a man. The metal is silver in color surrounding a green glass color of a man.

10)   Medal gold colored with initials (CX) at top two swimmers on front of medal, the words Participant Exchange Meet at the bottom

(11) A Tri Hi Y Pin with a triangle sharp, a torch surrounding blue set in red. Pin attached to a small gold chain

(12) A pin green in color with red cross in upper left corner, words "Home Nursing" on pin

(13) A round pin with a silver clover leaf design on a blue background

(14) A round pin with a face designed on a blue colored background

(15) A pin in the design of a fish, colors blue, green and orange.

(16) A wooden cross, very small

(17) A tiny jack knife with imitation pearl grips approximately 1/4" long

(18) A tiny pair of gold scissors or cutters about 3/4"

(19)   A   tiny   reindeer   pin approximately 1/2" long

(20) Two small gold nut crackers approximately 1" long

(21) A small gold pin with word "pep" on it looks like a cheerleader's horn

(22) A   small   gold   jack   knife approximately 1/2" long

EXHIBIT VIII
Item A - One canvas knapsack
Item B - Two red pens
Item C - A paperback book titled "Scorpio"
Item D -Box of Firechief matches
Item E - One silver Indian bracelet with Indian designs
Item F - One letter opener, brass handle
Item G - One Curad bandaid

Item H - One suede tan woman's purse small

(1) Passport belonging to Colette Marie Goodenough

(2) Iowa driver's license #445-54-7538 issued May 17, 1972 with name Colette Marie Goodenough, W/F 4 November 53, 1312 Birch Avenue, N.W. Cedar Rapids Iowa

(3) Air dependents ID card #AF o, 356, 114 name Colette Goodenough, DOB 4 November 53 sponsored by T. Sgt. Harvey J. Goodenough, issued May 20, 1971

(4) I.D. card on Colette Goodenough (special problems Center)

(5) A paper in French name Colette Goodenough possibly French birth certificate

(6) Birth certificate on Barbara Ann Wilcox, white female DOB 8-17-53. Father Ray Alfred, Mother Loretta Jean, address: Ellis Terrace Trailer #63 Cedar Rapids, Iowa, St. Lukes Methodist Hospital, Cedar Rapids, Linn County, Iowa issued birth certificate.

(7) Miscellaneous coupons, etc.

(8) Stationary book containing various poems signed Collette, last entry December 7, 1972

(9) A paperback in leather folder entitled "Secret Path"

EXHIBIT IX

Item A - One White Owl Ranger cigar box

Item B - (1) One Airmail envelope addressed to G. Schaefer, postmarked 30 Mar 71, from Victoria, Australia. Return address John O'Riley, P.O. Box 38, East Brunswick Victoria, Australia, 3057

(2) A handwritten letter to Buddy describing the killing of women and mutilating of their bodies in the Sahara by the WOGS in Morocco.

(3) 37 black and white photos of women naked being hanged and mutilated. Some of pictures marked on back numbered as reflected with letter giving details on each photo.

(4) Four airmail envelopes, not addressed, cancel stamp 3825 MURREN. The stamp on envelope is green with Helvetia, possibly Switzerland. Envelopes contained five strips of negatives of woman being mutilated Note: Exhibit IX, Item B #4 appears to be the same as those negatives in Exhibit I, Item B

(5) A plain envelope addressed to Gerald J. Schaefer, Jr. 2716 S. W. 34th Avenue, Fort Lauderdale, postmarked with what appears to be an Australian stamp, containing 54 black and white photos of mutilated women and naked women. On back of six of photos there are notes written in pen describing things about the pictures. Eight photographs are numbered with 6, 6c, 1c, 9c, 4c, 3b, 3c, 3, appear to be numbered mentioned in letter.

(Note: Item B #2 picture #3 indicates in letter that it is getting rid of a girl who overdosed on heroine into a ravine.

(6) Envelope addressed to G. J. Schaefer, 2716 S. W. 34th Avenue, Fort Lauderdale. Cancellation stamp from Victoria Australia in 1971.Envelope contains 13 black and white photographs of nude women 11 appear to be of women being hanged, one woman is decapitated. Two pictures of a woman with white panties, one seated on a stool.

(7) One blue Florida Power & Light envelope, no addressee, return address of Holfelner Gonia Crouse PA, 2505 N. Andrews Avenue, Fort Lauderdale, Florida 33311 stamped on front. A phone #524-0926 or 525-0926 appears handwritten on front on envelope.

EXHIBIT X

Item A - (1) One black cash drawer

(2) One black cash drawer

Item B - (1) A canvas bag (bank bag) with Federal Reserve Branch, Jacksonville, Florida

(2) Canvas bag, Federal Reserve Bank, Jacksonville, Florida

(3) Blue zipper coin type bag with First National Bank of Fort Lauderdale on the front.

(4) A canvas bank bag First Security Corporation Banks Utah, Wyoming and Idaho

(5) Brown bank bag, zipper top Farmer's Bank & Savings Company, Pomeroy, Ohio

(6) Green colored zipper bank bag Peoples National Bank Myrtle Beach, S.C.

(7) A green bank bag, Albuquerque, National Bank, New Mexico

EXHIBIT XI

Item A - (1) Stapled sealed plastic bag containing a draft card, Civil Service belonging to Steven Douglas Kindig, DOB July 13, 1950 (appears to be changed) Selective Service #8 150 52 648, born Gettysburg, Pa.

(2) A Maryland driver's license belonging to Steven Douglas Kindig, 14309 Baver Drive, Rockville, Maryland. Appears with a crime evidence slip made out G. J. Schaefer Jr.

(3) Birth Certificate #154541, State of Penn. Name of child Steven Douglas Kindig, Borough Gettysburg address handwritten on back 14309 Baver Drive, Rockville, Md. 20853. Also two phone numbers 871-7598, 744-9584.

(4) Florida temporary operator permit for Michael Joseph Angeline 4-4-49 of 3001 N. Dixie Highway, Fort Lauderdale, Exam date 1-27-72, Examiner 329

(5) Wisconsin operator license for Kirk Phillip Duckwitz, 827 S. Park Avenue, Milwaukee, DOB 3-9-50 RK580320880

(6) 3 items stapled together, two courtesy cards for Cash-ones, checks belonging to Kenneth Canshaw and a certificate of good health for Ken Canshaw, 1329 S. W. 31st Street, Fort Lauderdale, Savrin Restaurant issued 8-25-71 #4288.

(7) A crime evidence slip given by G. J. Schaefer for a birth certificate.

(8) Another crime evidence slip, a note on Kenneth Canshaw appear on back apparently involves a police investigation.

EXHIBIT XII

Item A - Brown vinyl wallet containing miscellaneous papers and I.D. on Ted Greer, 1092 N. E. 38th Street, Fort Lauderdale. Full name Edward Mell Greer, DOB 4-15-46, also a vehicle registration belonging to a Dennis Caudill, 47 N. W. Commercial Blvd, Fort Lauderdale, on Chrysler, two door 72-Fla-10W151942.

EXHIBIT XIII

Item A - Five spent 38 cal. casings

Item B - Eleven 22 cal. live shells

Item C - Seven spent projectiles possibly four 38 cal wad cutters and three 45 cal. Projectiles

Item D - Three spent projectiles

Item E - One projectile unknown cal.

EXHIBIT XIV

Item A - A letter to John from his first wife Marti in which she tells him she can no longer live with him.

Item B - A mimeographed satire regarding a game about intercourse with wife

Item C - One piece of red rope (braid)

Item D -Small monthly calendars for years, part of 1972 and 1973

EXHIBIT XV

Item A - One silver bracelet with a heart shaped charm attached name "Leigh" on one side and Disneyland on the other side, has a small key attached to heart charm

Item B - (1) Pieces of bone four inches long (2) Piece of bone 3" long

EXHIBIT XVI

Item A - One handwritten letter describing the death of two girls, one blond and one brunette

EXHIBIT XVII

Item A - Fourteen assorted knives and cases

Item B - One large machete type knife with curved blade

EXHIBIT XVIII

Item A - Rope

EXHIBIT XIX

Item A - One hippie type belt

EXHIBIT XX

Item A - Three boxes of magazines depicting nudes, pornographic literature and sadistic art

EXHIBIT XXI

Item A - One 22 cal Colt Magnum #G41951 and black holster and belt

EXHIBIT XXII
Item A - One 22 cal Ruger #11-01193 and one black holster

EXHIBIT XXIII
Item A - One Colt 45 #222016 and holster

EXHIBIT XXIV
Item A - One Colt 38 Cal. revolver #765 and holster

EXHIBIT XXV
Item A - Remington 12 gauge automatic #184079 U

EXHIBIT XXVI
Item A - One 16-gauge Eastern Arms Company 1929 model no serial#

EXHIBIT XXVII
Item A - One 30.06 Remington Model 1903, #3099154, with case

EXHIBIT XXVIII
Item A - One single shot 22 cal, Winchester model 67A no serial #

EXHIBIT XXIX
Item A - One 410 Shotgun Savage Double-barrel Model 311A, no serial # and case

EXHIBIT XXX
Item A - One Nylon 66 22 cal, rifle Remington serial 412827 and case

EXHIBIT XXXI
Item A - One rifle serial # 222811 M 8 1

EXHIBIT XXXII

```
    Item  A  -  Cigar  box  containing  empty
cartridges various cal.
    Item B - One handwritten poem on white
lined paper

EXHIBIT XXXIII
Item A - Two sleeping bags
```

The significance of the underlined items in the Evidence List are as follows:

Exhibit I, Item D. These photographs were later shown to be that of a man dressed in female garments, and in several of these photos, the person appears to be hanging or suspending himself from a nearby tree. (This fact has greater significance when one looks over the psychological evaluations of Schaefer performed by psychiatrists and psychologists at the Florida State Mental Hospital, earlier in this book.)

Exhibit II, Item A. Again "what appears to be a female," is in truth a man dressed in female garments. It has been suggested by several authorities involved with this case, that the man dressed in female garments is indeed Gerard Schaefer.

Exhibit IV, Item A. Here is the mention of the use of a pillowcase in a murder. One of which was found "with stains", at Schaefer's Stuart home.

Item C. An envelope, with the name Jerry Shephard, which is how the Places were introduced to the man who left with their daughter. The address is that of Schaefer's mother's house.

Item G. The name Carmen, which would later be one of the names of the missing girls, Carmen Hallock, on the List of 28.

Item I (l.) The first sentence underlined describes pulling fillings with pliers. The Place/Jessup bodies and the Briscolina/Farmer bodies (two other murders being investigated) were found to have their teeth pulled. Also, the teeth found at Schaefer's Stuart home were identified as Carmen Hallock's. (2.) "We always salvage something", would indicate that the many items found in the Fort Lauderdale residence, particularly the jewelry, were taken from the victims, or suspected victims. (3.) The mention of "a white hood," again could refer to a pillowcase used in one of the murders.

Item J. Again, the name "Jerry Shepherd," ties Schaefer to the Places' testimony.

Exhibit VI, Item A - 4. A newspaper clipping telling of the missing girls, Leigh Hainline Bonadies, and Carmen Marie Hallock, both of whom knew Schaefer, and both would appear on the initial List of 28 missing persons.

Exhibit VII, Items A-4, A-6, and A-9. These pieces of jewelry would later be identified by the Briscolina family, as having been worn by Mary Alice Briscolina.

Exhibit VIII, Item C. The book "Scorpio" is a book about serial, or multiple killings in California.

Exhibit XVI, Item A. Susan Place was blonde-haired, and Georgia Jessup was brunette-haired, as were many of the missing female couples.

There are other items of great importance among the evidence collected, and they cannot be overlooked. However, the few items explained in the above are "hard evidence" that lend themselves to little or no ambiguity in their meaning to the case. Other items become more significant later in the case and will be discussed further in this chapter.

*   *   *

The search was a tedious and lengthy procedure, involving labeling, fingerprinting, photographing, evidence collecting, comparison tests, ballistic testing, and more. The actual search of the suspect's home, or homes in this case, is one of the most trying experiences for the investigator.

There is no subtle way to approach a family of a suspect and tell them you're there to find evidence that will help the state convict him of murder. Carl Ragucci, an investigator with the Plantation Police Department, was one of several investigators involved in the search of both of Schaefer's homes. Plantation Police, like so many other law enforcement agencies, had a special interest in this case. They were trying to find the killer of two more South Florida residents, Mary Alice Briscolina, age 14, and Elsie Lina Farmer, age 13. Again, the victims, two young girls known to hitchhike frequently, were found brutally murdered and mutilated. Additionally, as with the Place/Jessup murders, one girl was blonde-haired and the other brunette. Ragucci's deposition, given to both prosecution and defense attorneys, details the search of Schaefer's Stuart residence and his former residence in Fort Lauderdale. His involvement in the case along with, of course, the joint efforts of collaborating police departments, would be instrumental in helping piece together the List of 28.

The assistant public defender, Bruce Colton, a man with an uncanny resemblance to Chad Everett, the film actor, began the questioning. Also present were Elton Schwarz, State Attorney (of Broward County) Philip Shailer, and his assistant Richard Purdy.

"State your full name, please."

"Carl A. Ragucci."

"And your occupation?"

"Police Officer."

"With what department?"

"The City of Plantation."

"And are you a resident of Broward County?"

"Yes, I am."

"As you probably know, this deposition is for discovery purposes in the case of the State of Florida versus John Gerard Schaefer."

"Yes."

"Have you been involved in any aspects of the particular case pending against him right now? That is, for the murder of Georgia Jessup and Susan Place?"

"Yes, I have."

"Could you state what, in chronological order as best you can, what participation you have had in this case and what your activities were? Rather than me asking you specific questions, you just go through it."

"I was involved in both search warrants, the first being up in Stuart, Florida, at Schaefer's wife's apartment. The following day, I was involved in a search warrant at his mother's home here in Fort Lauderdale."

"Before we get too far into this, you are a detective with the Plantation Police Department?"

"Yes, I am."

"How long have you been employed there?"

"Three years at the Plantation Police Department."

"Where were you employed before that?"

"Everett, Massachusetts, and Tamarac Police Department here in Florida."

"So how long have you been in police work?"

"Close to fifteen years."

"Go ahead with what you were saying about the searches. How did you first become involved?"

"I was invited up to Stuart to attend a meeting up there with Attorney Bob Stone and police officers and investigators from Stuart and Martin County investigating the deaths of the Jessup and Place girls."

"Can you tell us why you were invited up? Had you been involved in the missing person's reports for these two girls prior to that?"

"No. The only reason I was called up was the similarities in the two cases, the Briscolina and Farmer girls and the similarity of the deaths of the two girls, the circumstances which they were found and where they were found and so forth."

"In regard to the Briscolina and Farmer girls, were you in charge of the investigations of those cases?"

"No. "

"Were you involved in the investigations of those cases?"

"Yes."

"Of both of them?"

"Yes, I was."

"Did this begin with a missing person's report or after they had been discovered?"

"It was after they had been discovered."

"Was it your department which had been involved in the missing person's reports regarding those two girls?"

"No, it was the Broward County Sheriff's Department."

"And you came into that case when the bodies were discovered?"

"Yes."

"Go on, you were involved with Martin County?"

"We attended the meeting. Well, I attended a meeting and a search warrant was drawn up and I was invited to go on the search warrant."

"And that was the search of where?"

"That was the apartment of Schaefer's wife, the apartment he had been living in before he was incarcerated up in Stuart."

"Prior to that time when you were invited up there to that meeting, had Gerard Schaefer been a suspect in any way in the murders of Miss Briscolina and Miss Farmer?"

"No. "

"So, the first that you knew of Schaefer was when you went to this meeting in Martin County or immediately preceding that?"

"Yes."

"Go ahead. You were invited to go on the search of his apartment in Stuart?"

"Right."

"And did you actively participate in that search?"

"Yes, I did."

"Can you tell me who was in charge of that search?"

"At the time, I believe it was State Attorney Robert Stone."

"Was he present when the premises were searched?"

"Yes, he was."

"Do you know who else was present when the premises were searched?"

"There was a Detective Lieutenant Duval. Offhand, I don't remember the other detectives that were there. I believe there was Sergeant Hemp from the Oakland Park Police Department."

"Were there any members of the Martin County Sheriff's Office there?"

"I believe there was."

"Do you know who they were?"

"No, I don't. Their names escape me right now."

"Were any of Mr. Stone's assistants or investigators there that you know of?"

"I believe there was one of them."

"Do you know who that was?"

"No, I don't know the name."

"Who actually executed the search warrant, do you know?"

"I don't recall who did read it at the time."

"Were you one of the first officers to enter the house? Did you all enter as one group?"

"We all entered as one group."

"And Mr. Stone entered at this time or did he arrive later?"

"No, he was there."

"Was there one officer, one person, who was making an inventory of the items which were found there?"

"Yes, there was. I do not know his name. He was a detective. He might have been an assistant of Stone's. I don't recall."

"But it wasn't Mr. Stone who was actually making the inventory?"

"No. He was with the officer or the investigator that was categorizing the evidence as it was brought into the middle of the room at that time."

"Why don't you go ahead and tell us exactly what you did in that search."

"I was with Lieutenant Duval in the master bedroom and I did search a closet along with Sergeant Hemp. I was present when Lieutenant Duval found two teeth in a plastic type capsule.

"Can you describe those teeth?"

"One appeared to be a molar and the other one appeared to be a front tooth."

"I know you are not a dentist, but could you tell whether these appeared to be human teeth or not?"

"To me, they appeared to be human teeth."

"And you say they were in some sort of a container?"

"I believe at the time they were in a plastic capsule."

"And where were those taken from?"

"I believe the top drawer of the dresser in the master bedroom."

"Was there just one dresser in there?"

"I believe there was only one dresser."

"Were there items of clothing in that dresser? When you were looking in that drawer, were you able to determine from looking at it whether it appeared to be Mr. Schaefer's belongings or Mrs. Schaefer's belongings?"

"I believe it was both of them. If I recall right, there were articles of clothing belonging to a man and a woman."

"In the particular drawer that the teeth were found?"

"Yes."

"You were present, but they were actually taken out by Lieutenant Duval; is that right?"

"That is right."

"Go ahead with what else you did."

"I also searched a closet in the hallway. There were numerous boxes on the top shelf containing miscellaneous household items such as pots and pans."

"Was any of that seized?"

"I don't believe so at this time, no."

"Anything else?"

"We went out into a utility shed to the rear of the apartment and we did search numerous tackle boxes and stuff like that; and at that time, I believe there was a couple of fishing knives or hunting knives that were confiscated at this time,"

"Did you yourself actually take any of these things?"

"No, nothing."

"You were just observing?"

"Observing."

"Was there a vehicle there belonging to either Mr. or Mrs. Schaefer?"

"There was a vehicle in the carport to the rear of the house or the utility shed and, at this time, I can't recall what it was, I believe it was a white Mustang."

"Was that identified as belonging to one of the Schaefers?"

"Yes. It was at that time."

"Was the car searched, do you know?"

"I do not recall. I do recall Mrs. Schaefer moving the vehicle at that time."

"Did she appear to be moving it to get it away from the police or was she..."

"No, just moving it so we could get into this door, the utility shed. It was blocking the door, I believe, at that time."

"Do you know what happened to the items which were seized at that house after they were taken from the house?"

"No, I don't."

"Did you then return to Plantation or did you have another meeting or any discussion?"

"No. I returned to Plantation that same night."

"That was on a Friday, wasn't it?"

"Friday, April 6, I believe it was."

"What was your next involvement in this case?"

"The following morning."

"Excuse, let me ask you was anything seized there that you felt might have some relation to the Briscolina and Farmer cases?"

"Yes."

"Can you tell us what those items were?"

"The teeth we found in the room because Mary Briscolina was not missing a front tooth." (Not missing a tooth while she was alive.)

"Do you know if any identification of those teeth has been made at this time?"

"No, they have not." (These teeth were later identified as Carmen Hallock's.)

"Were there dental charts supplied belonging to either of these two girls?"

"Yes."

"And these tests are still taking place, to your knowledge?"

"No. We did take these teeth from a doctor's office in Coral Gables, I believe it was, and took them up to our medical examiner here in Broward County and they were not, neither one of the teeth belonged to Mary Briscolina."

"And the Farmer girl either?"

"No. The Farmer girl had all her teeth present."

"Did you notice any other evidence seized there which you felt might have had a relation to these two cases you were working on?"

"No, not at this time."

"Why don't you go on then?"

"The following morning, it was me, Sergeant Hemp from Oakland Park, Lieutenant Yurchuck from the Sheriff's Department, Detective Renje, from Oakland Park, and Sergeant Carruthers from the Sheriff's Department, we did serve a search warrant at the mother's home of Gerard Schaefer."

"Would that be Doris Schaefer?"

"Right."

"Did you take an active part in this search?"

"Yes, I did."

"Did all of the police officers involved in that search go to the house together?"

"Yes, we did."

"Did you all enter his house at the same time?"

"Yes, we did."

"Can you tell me how you gained entry to that house?"

"We met the brother at the front door. He still had the chain in the door, I believe, and said his mom is getting dressed."

"Who was the officer that was in charge of that?"

"Lieutenant Dave Yurchuck."

"Did Mrs. Schaefer appear at the front door at all, to your knowledge?"

"I don't believe so, not at this time, no."

"Did you go in through that front door?"

"No."

"Do you know any particular reason why you didn't go in that front door?"

"He closed the door, I believe it was, and said wait a minute; and if my memory is right, he called from the utility room door, the carport door, and we entered that way and walked in through the kitchen into the living room and the mother was standing there and Lieutenant Yurchuck did read the search warrant to her at this time."

"Was it announced to the boy, Gary, I believe it was?"

"Right."

"Was it announced to him when he came to the front door that you were police officers and were there with the search warrant?"

"Yes."

"And that was done by Lieutenant Yurchuck?"

"Yes, it was."

"And you did take an active part in this search?"

"Yes, I did."

"Can you tell us what parts of the house you searched and what you found personally and what you did with what you found?"

"I searched a back bedroom first. It was me, Detective Renje, and Sergeant Hemp. We found numerous items such as guns, knives, a newspaper dated June 1970, and all these items that we found were laid on the bed and then were initialed by the officers finding each respective item."

"Do you know which bedroom this was?"

"It was the east bedroom; I believe it was."

"Do you know which member of the family occupied that bedroom?"

"It was Gary and a girlfriend, to our knowledge."

"Did the girlfriend appear to be living there?"

"I didn't see any other female's clothing there. It appeared that she stayed overnight."

"Was Gary present in the room when you were making the search?"

"Most of the time, he was."

"Did he identify any of the items that you found as being his?"

"Yes. There were two or three rifles and some handguns I believe that were his."

"Now, the items that you stated that were found in that room, were these items all found by you personally or were these just all of the items that were found in there?"

"Just all of the items found in there."

"Was there any found by you personally?"

"I think the only thing I did initial in that room was a cigar box with spent bullets, different caliber type bullets."

"You did initial that?"

"I believe I did, yes."

"What did you do with it?"

"It was brought out into the front room and we had all the evidence on the front room floor, and it was being itemized and numbered by Lieutenant Dave Yurchuck."

"And did you search any other parts of the house, you personally?"

"Yes. The second bedroom down the hall from there, just west from there. At that time, Detective Renje and Sergeant Carruthers from the Sheriff's Department were in the process of searching that room and I did assist.in the search of that room, also, by going through books on a bookshelf."

"Was this a bedroom, also?"

"It was a bedroom. It had a bed in it, but it had numerous boxes, and looked like it was being used more as a storage room for the family."

"When you went to that bedroom, had any other officers entered that bedroom before you?"

"Yes."

"Do you know if the door to that bedroom was locked?"

"I do not know."

"Do you remember anybody saying whether it had been locked or not?"

"No, sir."

"There weren't any signs that entrance had been forced?"

"No, sir, not at all."

"Did you notice any signs of any sort telling people to stay out of there?"

"No."

"We are referring now to the bedroom which appeared to be used as a storage room, is that right?"

"Right."

"You say you found some books on a bookshelf?"

"There were numerous books on the bookshelf of different titles. They were, I believe, Readers' Digest condensed books, hunting magazines."

"These books that were found on the bookshelf, do you feel that any of these could be referred to as being pornographic in nature?"

"Not on the bookshelf, no."

"Were these books confiscated?"

"No, not those books."

"Did any member of the family identify who those books belonged to?"

"No."

"Was any member of the family present in the room at this time?"

"No."

"Go on with what else you did in that room."

"I noticed a jewelry box on the top of a dresser in the room and it was unbeknownst to me at this time Sergeant Carruthers had found it in the drawer of the dresser. I still don't know which drawer. I took this jewelry box out after opening it up and noticed numerous pieces of women's jewelry in it and put my initials on it and the date and took it out into the living room; and at that time, I believe I asked the mother if the jewelry box was hers or any of the contents of the jewelry box was hers and she said no."

"Can you describe that jewelry box?"

"It was a box about six or seven inches long, a couple of inches high. It was cloth with some type of design on it."

Colton paused for a moment. He was contemplating before asking any more questions that might, when answered, injure his client. Schwarz waved him over and whispered some directions. Colton, hesitantly, regained the questioning.

"Go ahead with what you were saying."

"I opened the box and, like I say, there was numerous pieces of women's jewelry in there. There was a women's bracelet with the name Leigh on it, L-E-I-G-H. There was a Girl Scout pin in there and what appeared to be a nurse's pin, chains, women's chains, assorted bracelets, a pep rally pin. And I gave this to Lieutenant Yurchuck, and he listed it down as being confiscated."

"Is there anything else that you found in that room?"

"Not that I found personally, but I believe it was Renje and Hemp at this time in the closet of the room took out a couple, two boxes, I believe it was, of nudie magazines."

Again, Colton hesitated and turned to Schwarz. Would it be advisable, they wondered, to admit those magazines in Court? They decided to detail what was in the jewelry box first, in hopes that some of the jewelry would be revealed to be that of Teresa Schaefer's, or Doris Schaefer's. If so, it might be proven that the box was not Gerard's. Schwarz and Colton whispered excitedly at one another a full twenty minutes before Colton continued.

"I would like to go back for a few minutes to that jewelry box you said you found. Do you have a picture of that with you?"

"Yes, I do."

"Could we see that, please?"

"Where did you obtain these pictures you have here?"

"Lieutenant Neil Rasmussen, Broward Sheriff's Department."

"These were pictures taken by him?"

"Yes, they were."

"Do you know where these pictures were taken?"

"I don't know where they were taken, no."

"They were pictures of the evidence taken from the Schaefer residence in Fort Lauderdale?"

"Yes, they are."

"Why don't we mark this picture depicting the jewelry box as Defendant's Exhibit One for Identification for this deposition," Colton requested.

Mr. Purdy, the assistant prosecutor who, up until now had been quietly listening, interrupted, "For the record, also, that is Number Fifty-one in the deposition of Rasmussen or a copy of the same photograph or of the same item." Purdy, it would be noted, was very astute with observations.

"Okay, Detective Ragucci, this is Exhibit Number One. Would you identify that, please? It is a picture," Colton continued, wearily.

"It is a color photograph of a jewelry box. The color of the jewelry box is light blue with gold inlay flowers and stems on it. Up in the right-hand corner it is dated 7 April '73 and my initials CAR, and underneath that is 'north bedroom'."

"Do you have any other pictures of that jewelry box with it open or another view of it?"

"No. This is the only one that I do have."

"This is the jewelry box that you obtained?"

"Yes."

"Do you know if it was ever determined who the owner of that jewelry box was?"

"No. "

"You don't know, or it was not determined?"

"I do not know who the owner of this jewelry box is."

"Do you want to go on with what else you did at the house that day? You had gotten to the point where you had come across the boxes of, I believe, magazines."

"Right. There were numerous magazines, girlie type magazines, that were found in the closet by Sergeant Hemp and Detective Renje."

"Did you examine these magazines?"

"Yes, I did, in the bedroom and also at the Sheriff's Department after the search."

"Do you have any idea how many magazines there were?"

"Roughly, 1,000."

"Were all of the magazines which were found at the Schaefer residence taken to the Sheriff's Department?"

"Yes, they were."

"Did you find anything unusual about these magazines?"

"Yes, I did."

"Can you tell us what that was?"

"On many of the magazines, there were nooses drawn around female figures. There were bullet holes, drawn bullet holes, on female figures.

There were drawn feces and urine coming out of the vaginas of these photographs of females.

"I remember one specifically where, real painstakingly, the face was drawn a light blue as in death and a noose around her neck. Also, another magazine had a cartoon caption where supposedly the female was talking to somebody in the room and, if I recall right, it was please don't kill me and words to the effect where the female would have oral copulation with the man in the room and, at the end of a couple of pages, this supposedly man in the room does shoot her and it has got bullet holes all in the woman who was sitting on the couch at this time."

"Was it obvious to you in these various pictures that these bullet holes and these ropes and so forth had been drawn in and were not part of the picture?"

"Definitely. They were drawn in."

"Did you ever determine who owned these magazines?"

"No, not at this time, no."

"Did you ever determine who drew these things into these magazines?"

"No."

"Would you say that most of the magazines were marked in that manner?"

"Most of them were, yes."

"Do you want to go on with what else you did there?"

"That is about all I did on the search."

"Were there any vehicles made a part of this search?"

"Yes, there was. There was a blue Datsun, I believe it was, sitting in the carport. I do not know if this was searched at the time. I knew it was towed because I left the residence and went back to the Plantation Police Department to get a Xerox copy of the search warrant and, when I came back, the vehicle was on the hook of the tow truck. At that time, whether they searched it, the officer present at this time searched the vehicle there or searched it at the police garage, I don't know."

"Did you have any conversation with Gary Schaefer while you were there?"

"Yes, I did. I found a plastic bag of marijuana. I take that back. I don't know if I found it. Somebody else found it in a nightstand. I believe it was myself and I asked him if it was his and he said yes."

"You didn't make an arrest in regard to it?" Colton asked, keenly.

(If Ragucci had made an arrest at this time, it is possible that the whole search would be rendered useless, as "illegal search and seizure.")

"No, not at this time."

Colton pressed on, "You didn't go back and make an arrest, did you?"

"No, sir."

"Was that the extent of the conversation with Gary?"

"I believe it was."

"How about with Doris Schaefer, Mrs. Schaefer? Did you have any conversation with her?"

"I believe the only conversation I had with her, I asked her if the jewelry box was hers and she said no."

"Were you present when she made any statements to any of the other officers there?"

"No."

"How about Gary?"

"He might have been talking to the other officers present, but I can't recall really what the conversation was."

"How about this girlfriend of Gary's? Was she there then?"

"Yes, she was."

"Didn't she make any statements that you know of?"

"No."

"Were they the only three present who were not police officers?"

"Yes, they were."

"What did you do with all of these items after they were all marked and placed in the living room of the house?"

"They were transported, they were brought out to the vehicles, unmarked police units that were parked outside, and they were transported to the Broward County Sheriff's Department, Lieutenant Yurchuck's office."

"What did you do after that in regard to this case?"

"Nothing."

"That was the extent of your involvement in this case?"

"Right. Not actually. I did obtain a photo of Gerard Schaefer and did recontact all people I had contacted in the initial investigation of the homicide of Briscolina and Farmer and tried to find somebody that had seen Briscolina or the Farmer girl with Schaefer but was unsuccessful at the time. I am still in the process of doing it."

"You viewed all of the evidence after it was taken to the Sheriff's Office, didn't you?"

"Yes."

"From the evidence which was found at the Schaefer residence in Fort Lauderdale, were you able to determine that any of this had any relation to the deaths of Miss Farmer or Miss Briscolina?"

"Yes, I did."

"Would you tell me what that was?"

"Oh, I believe it was May 13, I had in my possession some color photos which I obtained from the Broward County Sheriff's Department and took these photos to the Briscolina family."

"Do you have those photos with you?"

"Yes, I do. I did show the family numerous photos of jewelry which was taken out of the room in the Schaefer residence and, at that time, they expressed concern over three photos. One was a metal female's chain with two miraculous medals on it."

"Is that the photo you have in your hand?"

"Right. And the family did tell me that Mary Briscolina had one like it and that she was also fond of miraculous medals, but they could not say if that was her chain."

"Why don't we have this marked for identification?" asked Colton.

Colton continued, "All right, now Exhibit Number Four is a...Well, what is that?"

"The family describes this as a poodle or a man, green glass on a silver background."

"Can I see that for a minute, please?" Colton asked before adding, "This is Exhibit Number Four and there is a tag attached to this piece of jewelry. It is marked 73-4-669 and then it says exhibit item number and the number is not shown in the picture. And at the bottom are the initials CWC and the date 4/9/73."

"Do you want the item number on that?" asked Ragucci. "Do you have it?"

"Yes. It is item seven. Then, I got parentheses, nine, described as a woman's pin in the shape of a man. The metal is silver in color surrounding a green glass."

"That is Exhibit Number Four you are referring to?"

"Deposition exhibit," Richard Purdy clarified.

"*Deposition Exhibit* Number Four," Colton stressed, as he turned and acknowledged Purdy. Purdy grinned briefly. Begrudgingly, Colton continued.

"Now, deposition Exhibit Number Three, would you describe what that is and also read into the record the identification number that you have on that."

"It is a fine gold chain seventeen and three quarters inches long, a type of which a female would wear around her neck," Ragucci answered.

"And your identification on it?"

"That is item number seven, parentheses six, described as a gold chain, parentheses, seventeen and three quarters inches long."

"And this other picture, which is *Deposition* Exhibit Number Two?" asked Colton.

"That is item seven, parentheses four, bracelet, silver in color with eleven rows designed beads at the clasp and a large cross and Madonna medal."

"Now, you say that you showed the Briscolina family several pictures and they expressed some concern about these three pictures we are referring to here, Exhibits Two, Three and Four?"

"Yes, they did at this time."

"Did they positively identify any of these as belonging to their daughter?"

"Not at this time, although they said that the pictures of the poodle, they would like to see the actual thing."

"Were they shown the actual item?"

"Yes, they were the following morning, which I believe was either the 16th or the 17th of May at the Broward County Sheriff's Department."

"Did they make any positive identification at that time?"

"Yes, they did, on the green glass poodle, or man. As soon as it was shown to Lisa Briscolina, the daughter, she became very upset and said that was 'my sister's.' And the father and the mother Mr. and Mrs. Briscolina positively identified this pin as belonging to their daughter."

"How about any of the other items you showed me?"

"They said that Mary Briscolina did have a chain and was fond of medals, but they couldn't be sure that this woman's chain was Mary's... excuse me, the bracelet. And Mr. Briscolina said that Mary did have a similar chain to this that he used to fix all the time."

"That is Exhibit Number Three?"

"Exhibit Number Three. But he couldn't positively say that it belonged to his daughter."

"And the only positive identification they made was of the..."

"The green glass poodle. And supposedly, it was given to Mary Briscolina by a girlfriend in New Jersey. And I did obtain the name of this girlfriend from Lisa Briscolina and I did telephone this young girl up there and she didn't remember giving it to her. She said she would have to see a picture of it."

"Was she sent a picture?"

"No, she wasn't."

"How old was Miss Briscolina?"

"The deceased?"

Colton nodded his head affirmatively.

"Fourteen years."

"And Miss Farmer?"

"Thirteen years old."

"In your investigation of this, of their deaths, and the information you received concerning the deaths of Miss Place and Miss Jessup, do you feel that the type of deaths which took place would indicate a link with John Schaefer other than this pin?"

"Yes, I do."

"Can you tell us what aspects would lead you to that conclusion?"

"Okay. Mary Briscolina and Elsie Farmer were known hitchhikers. The last we knew they were alive was about three or four days after they were seen in the motel. They spent a night in the motel in Lauderdale by the Sea and, the last they were seen, they were heading for the beach. And as I say, they were hitchhikers, known hitchhikers. Their bodies were found in the wooded area. Both girls were separated by approximately 200 yards. Their teeth were scattered about the body and our search for the teeth, which were out of the skulls, we found teeth up underneath the back and as far away as two and three feet from the body."

"In conversation with numerous dentists, they tell me that it is almost impossible for any type of an animal to pull their teeth out of their mouth, a rodent or a possum or something like this.

"The similarity between our case here and the cases up in Stuart sort of fell right into place on us. For instance, the two girls that got away from him, they were hitchhikers, they were out on the beach. All of the girls were known hitchhikers, the teeth being scattered around, the wooded area, the bodies being separated. As he did in the case of the two girls that got away from him, he separated those two girls. This was real puzzling to us when we found the two girls, why were they separated like this."

"Were you ever able to determine how long these girls had been dead when you found them or when they were found?"

"We have them up until, we think, the last Thursday in October." (Of 1972)

"And when were they found?"

"The first party, Mary Briscolina, was found January 17 and the second body, that being Elsie Farmer, was found February 15, almost a month apart."

Mr. Purdy interrupted: "Of what year?"

"1973," Ragucci answered.

Colton continued, "Was the cause of death ever determined for either of these girls?"

"No. No cause of death was ever determined by our medical examiner."

"Was there any indication that they had been tied in any way?"

"No."

"Was there any indication a hanging could have taken place?"

"No. The only visible injuries on the skeleton forms was that of Mary Briscolina. She had two severe fractures of the lower jaw, one on the front of the jaw and one on the right-hand side."

"Was there any indication of either of them being shot?"

"No."

"Cut with a knife?"

"None whatsoever."

"Did it appear, when these girls were found, did it appear as though they were killed there or that they had been taken there after they were killed?"

"It appeared that they were killed there, especially the first party, the Briscolina girl."

"What led you to that conclusion?"

"The position of the body lying on its back with the legs open. We found panties nine feet away from her left leg and the hip-huggers approximately twenty yards away from the body."

"I take it by the time they were discovered, it was just skeletons."

"All skeletal remains."

"And you say that you have been unable to link through witnesses these girls with Gerard Schaefer? In other words, you have not been able to find anybody that has seen them in his presence or is able to say that they have mentioned him as being a friend of theirs or an acquaintance?"

"No, not at this time."

Purdy, getting anxious, tried an offensive move, "Were the bones intact?"

"No, they were not. They were all broken up," Ragucci answered.

"Cut up?" asked Purdy.

"Scattered," said Ragucci.

Purdy pushed further, "Were their heads found?"

Ragucci swallowed before answering, "The heads were found, but their heads were detached from the bodies."

Colton jumped back into the questioning. "Did it appear as though either of them had been buried or an attempt had been made to bury either of them?"

"This was hard to tell because, during the course of the investigation, we believed that different type of animals out there in the area had gotten to the bodies and there was brush growing over the bodies although, in the Briscolina case, her right hand was approximately an inch underneath the ground where the right hand was mummified and there was still skin on the fingers of the right hand."

"Were there any holes or anything which would lead you to believe that someone had attempted to dig a grave?"

"Again, this was hard to tell although there was a small gully where the body was, and you couldn't tell if it was shoveled out or whether it was from the body fluids eroding the dirt away or from animals digging at the bodies."

"Were there any parts of the bodies that were missing that were not found?"

"On the Briscolina girl, there was a right front tooth. I believe the medical examiner classified it as a number nine tooth. We never did find this."

"How were their bodies discovered?"

"The first body was discovered by a surveyor surveying the land in the 7200 block of West Sunrise Boulevard. The second body was discovered by a bulldozer operator as he was clearing the land."

"And how far apart were the bodies?"

"About 200 yards."

"I am not sure if I have asked you this already, but were you able to determine whether it appeared as though both bodies had been there the same length of time?"

"In the opinion of the medical examiner, they were."

"And they were last seen together?"

"And they were last seen together."

"Did you take part in the investigations of any of the other girls who have been reported missing that have been possibly linked to Schaefer such as Leigh Hainline or Mona Dice or Carmen Hallock?"

"No."

"Belinda Hutchins?" asked Purdy, curiously.

"No," Ragucci answered, almost apologetic.

"Collette Goodenough?" Colton continued.

"No."

"These are the only two you have been involved in."

"Yes, sir."

"Is that right?"

"Yes, sir."

"I am not familiar with the Fort Lauderdale area, but is Plantation nearby Wilton Manor?"

"It is approximately seven, eight miles away."

"Had you ever had any contact with Gerard Schaefer when he was a police officer at Wilton Manor?"

"No, I did not."

"And you did not know anything about Mr. Schaefer until you were called to Stuart the day of the search of his apartment, is that correct?"

"That is correct."

"And he had not been even remotely considered as a suspect in the two cases that you were involved in up until that time, is that right?"

"That is right." Colton smiled.

"Other than the written...You have made written reports regarding this, haven't you?"

"Yes, I have."

"Other than these written reports which I imagine have been turned over to the State Attorney's Office..."

"Yes, they have."

"Other than those reports, have you been called upon to give any sworn testimony regarding either the Place or Jessup case or the Farmer and Briscolina case before either the State Attorney's Office of Broward County or of St. Lucie County prior to today?"

"No. "

"Have you submitted any sworn or notarized statements?"

 "Not sworn statements. I cannot be sure if I got any notarized statements in my reports. I might have one or two notarized statements in my reports, Xeroxed copies of notarized statements from other people in my reports."

"Other people?"

"Right."

"Have you ever given sworn testimony as far as information by yourself?"

"No."

"Is there anything that I have not asked you here today which you feel would be important that either the defense or the state should know, anything you would like to add?"

"I do have a statement from a police officer in our city, a working police officer in our city, Leon Webster. He did have conversation with Gerard Schaefer in the City of Plantation the last week in October and I believe that was either Tuesday, Wednesday, or Thursday, the 25th, the 26th, and the 27th of October of '72 when he had conversation with him. And it was a brief conversation and it took place in a parking lot at West Broward Boulevard and north State Road Seven."

"Can you tell me do you know what the essence of that conversation was?"

"I have a statement, I believe, by Leon Webster."

"Has that also been supplied to the State Attorney's Office?"

"No, it hasn't because I don't even have the statement with me. The statement is down at the State Attorney's Office along with the tapes. I haven't received a copy of it yet."

"When did you give that to the State Attorney's Office?"

"It must have been about two or three weeks ago. I didn't actually give it to the State Attorney's Office. I gave it to one of the girls in the office in the detective division. She was going to type it up for me."

"You did not give it to the State Attorney's Office?" asked Purdy.

"No."

"You gave it to whom?" Purdy continued, irritated.

"The girl in there in the detective division that does all the typing," Ragucci answered, sheepishly.

"In the Sheriff's Office?"

"Yes, up in Carruther's office."

"And what was she doing, typing it?"

"She was typing it."

"Now, do you have a copy of it?"

"I don't have a copy of it, no."

"I assume that will be turned over to the State Attorney's Office, "said Colton, with a notable impatience.

"Yes, it will. In essence, if I remember right, it was how you are doing and how do you like your job. And he told the officer at that time he was working in the Martin County Sheriff's Department."

"This was in October of '72?" Colton continued.

"Yes, the last week in October."

"This Leon Webster, is he still employed by the Plantation Police Department?"

"Yes, he is."

"And he can be reached through the police department, is that correct?"

"Yes, he can."

"Did Mr. Webster indicate to you that he had known Schaefer before?"

"Yes, he did. He once went to the Broward County Police Academy with him."

"Did he say whether they had been friends?"

"No, he didn't say that he was friends. In fact, I believe he said that he was not friends with him, just an acquaintance attending class."

"Did he indicate whether it was the only contact he had had with Schaefer since leaving the police academy?"

"I believe he did."

"He didn't state that he had seen him on any other occasions in the area, did he?"

"No."

"Do you have anything else that you would like to add?"

"No, not at this time."

"Anything you would like to add that you feel should be added?"

"Just that his family, his in-laws, don't live too far from where the crime scene was, approximately two miles."

"You say his in-laws. You are referring to Schaefer?"

"Right."

"And who are his in-laws?"

"I can't think of their last name now."

"Would it be Dean?"

"Dean, right. The Dean family lives on Holly Lane, I believe it is, and it is only a couple of miles from where the crime scene was."

"Do you know his brother-in-law Henry Dean?"

"I met him once."

"What were the circumstances of that meeting?"

"He had a conversation with Lieutenant Yurchuck when we were en route up to Stuart for that first meeting in April."

"You were with Lieutenant Yurchuck?"

"Right."

"Did you meet with Mr. Dean at that time?"

"Yes, I did."

"Where did you meet?"

"He met us at the toll gate at Tamarac in the City of Tamarac, Commercial Boulevard and the Florida Turnpike."

"Did you receive anything or did Lieutenant Yurchuck receive anything from him at that time?"

"I believe, at that time, I don't know if he received a pocketbook at that time or not. It seemed to me he did or there was conversation about Mr. Dean turning over a pocketbook to Lieutenant Yurchuck and supposedly this pocketbook was given to Gerald Schaefer's wife."

"The gist of the conversation was that Schaefer told his wife to get rid of it and I guess she turned it over to her, brother, Mr. Dean."

"Have you had any other occasion to speak with her or meet with Mr. Dean since then?

"No. That is the first and the only time I ever seen the man."

"How about Mr. Schaefer's in-laws, his wife's mother and father? Have you ever met or spoken with them?"

"No, I don't know the people. Never met them."

"You have never contacted any members of Mrs. Schaefer's, John's wife's family?"

"No."

"Is there anything else?"

"No."

"I have nothing further."

* * *

The List of 28 possible victims is, at its best, an educated guess. It was first canonized on the front page of the Palm Beach Post-Times, Sunday morning, May 13, 1973 edition. There, in one-inch bold letters, was the title: "6 Dead; 28 May Be: A Trail of Butchered Girls." The article, written by Jayne Ellison, states:

"A total of 28 girls and young women in South Florida, four others in West Virginia and Iowa and possible other victims in Europe and North Africa may be involved in the case . . .

"Sheriff's investigators in St. Lucie, Martin, Broward and Palm Beach counties believe the final death toll of hacked and butchered girls may reach or surpass 28 in Florida.

"No one has been charged in any of the murders, but a former policeman in Broward County and later a Martin County sheriff's deputy is a suspect."

The article does not mention how the number "28" was arrived at, nor the "6 Dead, "and even Robert Stone was "not exactly sure" how they came up with twenty-eight possible victims. However, the following explanation is probably accurate as to where the numbers came from.

If we take the list of persons known dead and/or missing, based on information collated by all the police and sheriff departments involved, we can arrive at a figure of nineteen, and maybe twenty possible victims. They are:

1.)Susan Place, known dead.

2.)Georgia Jessup, known dead.

3.)Mary Briscolina, known dead.

4.)Elsie Farmer, known dead.

Two young women the Palm Beach Post Times listed as "evidence of death, no body found":

5.)Carmen Hallock, missing.

6.)Leigh Bonadies (Hainline, maiden name.), missing.

Two young women from Cedar Rapids, Iowa, whose personal effects were found in the Schaefer's home:

7.)Collette Goodenough, missing.

 8.)Barbara Wilcox, missing.

Two co-eds from Morgantown, West Virginia.

9.)Karen Ferrell, missing.

10.)   Mared Malarik, missing.

One young woman from Fayetteville, Arkansas, last known to be in South Florida:

11.) Elizabeth Wilt, missing.

The remainder of the list includes names of girls missing from all over South Florida and/or girls known to have come into contact with Schaefer, now missing:

12.) Katrina Bivens, missing.

 13.) Sandra Bivens, missing.

14.) Bonnie Taylor, missing.

15.) Belinda Hutchins, missing.

16.) Deborah Lowe, missing.

17.) Peggy Rahn, missing.

18.) Wendy Brown Stephenson, missing.

19.) Patricia Wilson, missing.

These were the names of missing or known dead that Robert Stone had compiled on his list of possible victims. One more girl was added, whom Ragucci had mentioned in his deposition, and who was missing from the Fort Lauderdale area.

20.) Mona Dice, missing.

The other names, to come up with a List of 28, probably came from the Exhibits List, Exhibits XI and XII, which we will call the "Men's List," as all the names are those of young men. Identification for most of these men were found among Schaefer's possessions. How thoroughly their status of missing was investigated is uncertain, but their names do help to make up the List of 28.

21.) Michael Angeline, listed as missing.

22.) Kenneth Canshaw, listed as missing.

23.) Dennis Caudill, listed as missing.

24.) Kirk Duckwitz, listed as missing.

25.) Edward Greer, listed as missing.

26.) Steven Kindig, listed as missing.

27.) Leonard Masar, known dead.

Masar, whose body was found on Hutchinson Island with both hands cut off, is attributed to Schaefer, though none of his personal belongings were found among Schaefer's.

And finally, there is number:

28.) Kay Price, missing, a girl whom Schaefer was known to have dated for some time shortly after his divorce from his first wife.

We do not know exactly how the number 28 was arrived at. Probably, the number developed when Robert Stone spoke to the press and told them, "there were at least twenty-eight possible victims, and maybe many more," and this gave the press free rein to print any number, but particularly twenty-eight.

At any rate, there were at least twenty-eight that could be named. This does not, however, mean that even that number was accurate. As it would later turn out, a few of the names would be dropped from that list. Conversely, there were the many pieces of jewelry found at Schaefer's former home, which may have come from just a few people, or from many. Many, who may have been victims of foul play, and again the jewelry may have been gifts of friends, though that is unlikely. Whatever the case, there were more missing persons reports coming in from all over the state, and the nation. Many, like Elizabeth Wilt, had taken trips to South Florida and never returned.

Furthermore, Schaefer had purportedly traveled extensively throughout Europe and Morocco, and in a letter to Jayne Ellison, wrote that, while he was not involved in white slavery in the United States, he was at least indirectly involved with some aspects of it overseas, and that he did some things that he was "not proud of."

Additionally, there were the photographs, confiscated from Schaefer's mother's house, that showed dozens of women shot, stabbed, hung, or tortured to death. To be sure, many of these were "faked." That is, they are pictures with stab, or bullet holes drawn onto the photos. However, many are authentic pictures of women, either dead or dying. Where did the photos come from? Did Schaefer take them? If there were more victims, where were the bodies? This last question was on the minds of every police officer involved with the case. With so many possible victims, there had to be more bodies, though according to Schaefer's own writings, they could have been "scattered over thirty square miles. "And if the bodies were deposited out in the Everglades' wilderness, where Schaefer used to work as a "guide," they would certainly never be found.

Authorities mobilized a massive investigation, and began to search in remote, desolate areas where it was suspected Schaefer may have visited. An article from the Fort Lauderdale News describes one of the many searches that was conducted at that time:

"GRAVE" SITE PROBED FOR MORE VICTIMS

DAVIE - Three years ago it was a brief sensation, quickly written off as a college kid prank: a burial mound beneath a hangman's noose sequestered by a melaleuca thicket in an undergrowth area of Davie not far from Broward Community College.

But macabre scribblings and grisly finds that resulted from a search of the Fort Lauderdale home of Gerard Schaefer's mother resurrected the memories of the mound and noose.

Yesterday, detectives from the Broward County Sheriff's department probed the area for clues which could shed some light on the strange case of accused murderer Schaefer.

Schaefer, in a state hospital at Chattahoochee for 30 days of court-ordered psychiatric testing, is charged with murder in slayings of two Broward County teen-age girls, Susan Place, 17, and Georgia Jessup, 16, whose bodies were found in a remote lover's lane section near Fort Pierce two months ago.

Schaefer also is suspect in several other cases of missing young women.

Among the findings in Schaefer's locked room at his mother's home were bits of human bones, gold tooth fillings, feminine attire and trinkets, and five or six photos of melaleuca thickets.

These photographs, according to Lt. David Yurchuck of the sheriff's juvenile department, are blurred but show vaguely discernible female figures, one of which appears to be hanging.

Because of these photos, officers of the Florida Game and Fresh Water Commission (GFWC) have been on the lookout for similar stands of melaleuca.

Their pinpointing of the Davie site, plus recall of the old "prank" burial ground mystery of three years ago, and reports about two years ago of other strange happenings led yesterday to a search of the area here. Three years ago, a butchered pig had been found buried in the mound, along with blood-stained female undergarments. It was written off as a college prank.

Recently a nearby resident who hunted in the sector, recalled seeing a motorcyclist leave girlie magazines and female underwear in a tin coffee can at the mound.

The hunter said that, over a period of several months, he checked the coffee can several times and there were different magazines nearby.

Yesterday's search and investigation of the site, with the aid of metal detectors, recovered the coffee can containing five or six pairs of women's panties and a pantyhose, according to Yurchuck.

The garments were not bloodstained, he said, but had been there, he estimated, about two years. He said the can had been covered with a piece of Styrofoam, protecting its contents from the weather. What was possibly a girlie magazine, but now too rotted to process, was nearby.

"We didn't find what we were looking for," said Yurchuck. But, he said, the area will be searched further. Yurchuck did not say exactly what investigators were looking for.

He said the area is "similar" to that shown in the photographs, but identification is difficult, "because we may be dealing with a three-year lapse of time."

Three years ago, the site was practically inaccessible. Now people have moved nearby, and it is used frequently as a dumping ground.

A number of .38 caliber cartridges, some bullets and spent shotgun shells were also uncovered in yesterday's search. These will be checked against weapons which belonged to Schaefer.

Perhaps a more significant clue found yesterday was a board that might have held the hangman's noose.

The timing of two old mysteries may be even more provocative. The noose and buried pig were found in the fall or winter of 1969, sometime after Schaefer left BCC, where he was a student.

Around that time two pretty, young Fort Lauderdale women, Leigh Hainline Bonadies, 25, and Carmen Marie Hallock, 22, disappeared.

A gold-filled tooth, identified as Carmen's, was found in Schaefer's locked roan.

This article brings up several significant facts about the case. First, it mentions that Schaefer had been placed in a state hospital, a mental institution in fact, for "30 days of court-ordered psychiatric testing." This testing, a result of both Stone and Schwarz agreeing to determine if Schaefer was mentally competent (though Stone opposed transferring Schaefer to a state hospital) to stand trial, was the recommendation of Dr. R. C. Eaton. Eaton (whose evaluation is covered more thoroughly in a subsequent chapter) found that not only was Schaefer mentally disturbed at the time of his evaluation, but that he was expressing suicidal tendencies. Eaton felt that it would be beneficial for Schaefer to be "tested" for two reasons: It would be determined if he was competent to stand trial, and they could keep him from killing himself if the attempt was made.

Secondly, there is the mention of a "butchered pig . . . along with blood-stained female undergarments." Throughout Schaefer's 30-day testing at Chattahoochee, in several interviews with various psychiatrists, he admits to several sexual perversions. One of which was having sex with dead animals, and often these animals met their death by his hands.

Thirdly, the hangman's noose that was found is interesting to note. Schaefer did use a rope knotted into a hangman's noose to incapacitate Nancy Trotter on Hutchinson Island. It goes without saying most people never have the occasion to form a hangman's noose, and most do not know the technique to form the knot.

Fourthly, the article mentions that "a number of .38 caliber cartridges... and spent shotgun shells were also uncovered..." A .38 pistol and a shotgun were only two of many firearms found at Schaefer's Fort Lauderdale home. It is interesting to note also, that almost all of the weapons seized in this case were found at the Fort Lauderdale home, and not at his home in Stuart. One would believe that such an avid gun collector would keep his cherished possessions close at hand, rather than locked up many miles away.

It seemed the more investigators investigated this case; the more questions arose. Questions like: If there were twenty-seven or twenty-eight victims, where were all the bodies? Was there really that many people killed, or was the media and an over-zealous state attorney blowing the case out of proportion? Conversely, were there many more bodies, perhaps transient travelers carrying no identification, or children who would not have any, who were picked up by a benevolent policeman only to be murdered and mutilated, their bodies scattered across the South Florida wilderness? If this were true, the number of dead could far exceed twenty-eight.

Many more questions arose: If there were dozens dead, what was the motivation? How could these murders go so long undetected? What was the common denominator with all of these people? The answer to this last question was becoming more and more obvious to the authorities. Because these people were so varying in physical types, especially so in age, but also in sex, financial background, location of residence, and more, it was extremely difficult to tie them together, to find a common denominator.

However, they all seemed to have one thing in common: Gerard Schaefer (or in some cases, a man at least resembling Schaefer) had touched their lives. The most baffling question in the case began to present itself, and oddly, no one seemed to be able to clearly answer it. The question was: Exactly who was Gerard John Schaefer? Or, more importantly: What was he?

Chapter 7

The Suspect

The fury of a demon instantly possessed me. I knew myself
no longer. My original soul seemed at once to take flight
from my body, and a more than fiendish malevolence . . .
thrilled every fiber of my frame.

From *The Black Cat,* by Edgar Allan Poe

On May 18th, 1973, Gerard J. Schaefer, Jr., was charged with two counts of murder in the cases of Susan K. Place and Georgia M. Jessup. The day came almost seven weeks after the grisly discovery of the two Fort Lauderdale youths decomposing bodies on remote Hutchinson Island. In less than one month, Schaefer would have been freed from the Martin County Jail, where he was incarcerated in January, 1973, for abducting Nancy Trotter and Paula Sue Wells.

Just three days prior to the official charges being filed, an agitated State Attorney called a press conference. Robert Stone, accompanied by Lt. Patrick Duval, and an oddly quiet Chief Investigator, Lem Brumley, waited for the din of the crowding reporters to hush before carrying on with the conference.

Brumley, who would remain silent throughout this conference, had spoken with a reporter from the Palm Beach Post-Times, just the day before. The chief investigator was a tall man, six feet, two inches. He was lean, but not thin, and broad shouldered. He was a typical native of the area, speaking with a deep southern drawl, and entertaining pastimes such as hunting and fishing "every chance I get." He was a twenty-year veteran, a good investigator, who held a teaching certificate that enabled him to teach upper-level law enforcement classes, and who, at one time, was named southern region supervisor for the Florida Department of Law Enforcement. He was forty-one when the case began for him; married and father to four children. The former tractor- trailer driver wore the typical "Florida Cowboy" look, his leathery, sun-darkened face framed with long pork-chop sideburns, hair parted on the left side and immobilized with thick applications of tubed hair cream. His attire was polyester-western.

Perhaps he stood quietly because the weight of the investigation was beginning to take its toll on him. The day before, he'd told the Post-Times reporter that, "I would say in scope and bizarreness, this is the biggest case I've ever worked on." He added, "I've been involved in some big cases on dope and loan sharking, but nothing like this." Later, Brumley's name would be scandalized, and throw suspicion upon the State Attorney's office, when he would be connected with one of the biggest drug smugglers in South Florida. A personal, and career, casualty that would not go unnoticed by Gerard Schaefer. But for now, Lem Brumley was, for all appearances, a diligent, hard-working investigator who stuck to his job and got results.

"I called this press conference for several reasons," Stone began. The Sun-Sentinel, a local newspaper, had apparently leaked information about the case and, Stone felt, had misquoted him. "I haven't talked to anyone at the paper," he said. He then went on to attack the paper that printed ". . . Schaefer would make Jack the Ripper, and the Boston Strangler, Boy Scouts by comparison, and the Manson Family murders small potatoes."

Stone told the press conference that Schaefer was the only suspect, but he also let them know that he was worried about the media's coverage of the case. He was concerned that the defense would apply for, and receive a change of venue, which would mean the case would have to be tried in another part of Florida, presumably where it had not received so much adverse publicity. In truth though, the story had already "gone nationwide," indeed it had gone international. Besides being run in almost every big city newspaper, in North America and Canada, the German magazine Bunte, had run a lengthy story about "the killer cop," giving the story European appeal. Despite all the coverage, however, the story was secondary to either headlines of the Watergate conspiracy, or the Skylab with its many problems. For all its notoriety, the story was, somehow, slowly but surely, being overlooked. Later, cynics would go as far as saying, it was "covered up."

During this conference, Stone told the press that if Schaefer did go to trial, and was found guilty, he probably would not receive the death penalty. This caused more than a little murmur amongst the newsmen who were packed into the small press room. Stone went on to explain that there was no death penalty at the time the murders were believed to have been committed. It was assumed, though impossible for medical examiners to say, exactly when the girls were murdered on the night they left home. That night, of course, was the night of September 27, 1972, and Florida did not have a capital punishment sentence for murder, until October 1, 1972, just four days after the proposed murder. This technically, while a godsend for murderers up until that time, was an unfortunate and inadequate retribution for the surviving families of victims, and also for the State Attorneys who would be put into a frustrating position of following the letter of the law, while holding against the wishes of most of the victims' families, who were also usually a part of the populace that voted him into the office.

Stone, for the first time since he took office, was beginning to feel that he was in the position of "being between a rock and a hard place," with no place left to turn. This entire issue would go on to haunt Stone for years to come, because his critics would state that it is "easier" for the prosecuting attorney to try to get a life sentence rather than the death penalty for a convicted murderer, and that by relinquishing the chance for a death sentence the prosecution does not have to use a grand jury. And, by not using a grand jury (which is a jury of at least twelve members) the State Attorney's case is "easier" to try. Because of the smaller number of people who are selected for jury duty: a selection process which is arduously long and tedious, avoiding a grand jury typically makes for a more expedient trial.

Stone would soon find out there would be nothing "easy" about this case.

Continuing with the press conference, Stone told reporters that "investigators from at least fifteen other states" had called his office seeking information on missing persons, and unsolved murders, that may have been related to Schaefer. He confirmed that the Place and Jessup murders, for which Schaefer was the only suspect, could possibly relate to "the dozen or more" other cases being investigated. He quickly added those suspicions still came "under the category of speculation," and that "you don't rule out any person missing under similar circumstances and that's why some of these cases are being considered."

When asked if he could give an exact number of cases that he was investigating, he replied, "about 20 or more," and ". . . we have linked some of these murders, but not to one individual."

Once again, the number of dead, or presumed dead, could not be agreed upon, nor would it be throughout this entire case. At one conference the number had gone from a "dozen or more" to "about twenty or more," leaving many families of missing persons to wonder in anguish over what happened to their children, sisters, or wives. They would still be wondering years after this case came to a standstill.

*   *   *

While the investigation, or investigations, as it were, continued, Schaefer remained in Martin County Jail. Both the defense and the prosecution wanted Schaefer to be examined by psychiatrists to determine if he was competent to stand trial. Stone desired only a declaration of competence.

Elton Schwarz, on the other hand, requested that Schaefer be sent to the State Mental Hospital to determine if he was sane enough to stand trial. Because of the bizarre nature of the crimes, and the subsequent findings at Schaefer's mother's Fort Lauderdale home, Judge C. Pfeiffer Trowbridge, the justice who would rule the case, declared that Schaefer would undergo psychiatric examination, at the state's facility. He added, however, that it would have to be deemed necessary by at least three psychiatrists. In the end, two letters from psychiatrists, Dr. Mordecai Haber and Dr. R.C. Eaton, along with requests for voluntary admission from Schaefer himself, and affidavits signed by both Teresa and Doris Schaefer stating that Gerard "is going through a mental breakdown and has definite suicidal tendencies," together would be deemed sufficient by Trowbridge. Schaefer would be given a 30-day evaluation at the Florida State Mental Hospital, in Chattahoochee. As evidence mounted against Schaefer, it became clear to him, and his family, that if he should stand trial, his best defense would be a plea of insanity.

It is these psychiatric evaluations that are such important elements in the bewildering case of Gerard Schaefer. Though many of them are quite similar, it is interesting to note how each psychiatrist diagnosed Schaefer, and how he presented himself to each doctor. Each evaluation is only slightly different from another. But these differences, usually found in the patient's "history" section, are significant in helping to decipher the mystery of Gerard Schaefer.

This first evaluation was performed by Dr. R.C. Eaton. He was the first psychiatrist to examine Schaefer, for the purpose of concluding whether Schaefer should undergo the 30-day evaluation at the State Mental Hospital in Chattahoochee, to determine if he was sane enough to stand trial. Particularly, whether sane or not, the court must know if the defendant knows the difference between right and wrong.

PSYCHIATRIC EVALUATION

This 28-year-old, married, white male was examined on the order of Circuit Judge C. Pfeiffer Trowbridge dated April 9, 1973. The purpose of the examination was to determine his present mental condition.

The patient was brought from the Martin County Jail and was examined in my office alone. The purpose of the examination was explained to him, and that a written report would be sent to the court. He was cooperative and answered questions clearly and relevantly. He stated he presently is serving time in jail for an incident which occurred in July 1972. He was charged with False Imprisonment and then Aggravated Assault. He said he got six months and then two years' probation. He has approximately two to three months to serve. He went into considerable detail explaining why he had picked these girls up, and said that he had felt that they were run-aways. He had picked them up twice, and the second time had bluffed them into admitting that they were run-aways. He was going to take them back to the police station and was lecturing them, and then he said they laughed at him, and this apparently is when he tied them up.

PAST HISTORY:

He stated he had lived in various states until the age of thirteen, when they moved to Fort Lauderdale. Family: His father, he thinks, is about age sixty. His parents were divorced in 1967, and he said his father was a severe alcoholic and a salesman. He stated his father was always running him down and expecting him to do better than other people. He said his mother works as an executive secretary, and is about age fifty-two, and said that he both loves and hates his mother. He added that his father tried to kill himself when the prisoner was about twenty years of age by shooting himself. He stated that he feels they were forced into marriage, because his mother was pregnant with him at the time. He was born approximately six months after the marriage. His sister, age twenty-four, is married and has two children. He stated he used to be close to her, but one time lost his temper with her, and since then has stayed away from her. He has a brother 19, who is single.

School: He finished high school in 1964, and then went to Broward Junior College. He received a BA degree also from Florida Atlantic in 1971 in Social Science and Geography, and also got a teacher's license. Then, in 1972, got an Associate Degree at the Broward Junior College in Criminal Justice. He said he was an honor student and on the dean's list. During high school, he said he had thought of going into the priesthood. He stated he put himself through school and worked off and on at various jobs. He worked some time as a guide and ran a guide service in the Everglades. He also was with a musical group for a while. He worked as a salesman for a magazine company.

Marital: He stated he was married for the first time in 1969. His wife was about two years younger than he. He said this lasted only about one year, as they did not get along sexually, explaining that his wife was frigid, so he gave her an ultimatum to either produce or get out. Apparently, their divorce was arranged by mail. He married for the second time in September,

1971.His wife was about 19 at the time. He said they got along well and have normal sexual relations and are perfectly compatible sexually. He said they came to Martin County in about June 1972, stating this was to get a better job and a career. He had worked as a policeman in Wilton Manor in Broward County before that. He said he tried to get on the Broward County Police Force but had been turned down.

From an early age, he has had numerous sexual hang-ups. He stated that when he was in Atlanta at the age of twelve or thirteen, he would tie himself up, and fantasize that people were torturing him. He said he would get satisfaction from this, especially the struggle of getting out. This gradually progressed, until after he finished high school and the girl he had been going with during high school had dropped him, his sexually deviant behavior continued, and he would go out in the woods and tie himself up, and sometimes even suspend himself from a tree. He said at times he had to fight to get out of the rope, and once almost didn't. He said this would excite him, and at times these urges would become quite uncontrollable. He also had a considerable preoccupation with death and would get excited when he would dream about killing people. Sometimes he did not know what fact was and what fantasy was. He also became interested in pornographic literature and would draw gory pictures, which would excite him.

MENTAL STATUS:
He was well oriented for time, place, and person. His memory for both recent and past events was good. He seemed to be of above average intelligence. Rather interestingly, he did poorly in serial sevens. He had difficulty concentrating. Mood: During the interview, he cried considerably, stating he felt there was no use in going on. He did admit that the present newspaper publicity had upset him. He had definitely been thinking about suicide, and talking about this in a very matter-of-fact tone, without any great show of emotion. For the last seven days, he has not been eating and definitely plans to go ahead with killing himself. He said he had written letters to his mother and wife. He admitted that in 1968, he had previously threatened suicide, and was seen by a psychiatrist at that time. Also, back in 1966, he went to a psychiatrist, because of his sexually deviant behavior and also because he was getting thoughts that he wanted to kill someone. There were no definite delusions or hallucinations noted. He admits that he has never trusted anyone in his life, has never had a close male friend, and admits that any hostile feelings have been primarily directed toward females.

```
SUMMARY:
```

```
    This 28-year-old white male was seen for
evaluation for 2&1/2 hours. It is my opinion
that this man is definitely depressed, partly
as a reaction to the present situation. He
definitely has been ruminating about suicide
and is making definite plans about suicide.
It is my opinion that he is definitely
depressed and potentially suicidal. It is
recommended that he be sent to a state mental
institution for treatment and observation
and further evaluation.
```

```
R.C. Eaton, M.D.,
Psychiatrist
```

The significant points of Dr. Eaton's evaluation, which was completed while Schaefer was still in the Martin County Jail, are that: One: It reveals the fact that Schaefer had been fasting. Later, it would be suggested that Schaefer lost weight in a conscious effort to disguise his appearance. Indeed, this may have been the case. For by the time Schaefer went to trial, less than six months after he was charged with two counts of murder, in addition to wearing a newly grown moustache and longer, darker hair, he'd lost over sixty pounds. The reason for this chameleon-like metamorphosis is obvious. If the Places (who were the only eyewitnesses who could place Schaefer with the victims on the last night they were known to be alive) could not identify the suspect as being the same man at their house on the evening of September 27, 1972, then by and large, the state would not have a case.

Two: Schaefer admits for the first time since his incarceration, that he was getting thoughts that he "wanted to kill someone," and that "he would dream about killing people," but that there were no "delusions or hallucinations noted." At this point his "preoccupation with death" is described by him as merely an "urge," and that in no way had it physically manifested itself, at least not beyond himself and his self-administered sadomasochism.

One of the first psychiatrists to see Schaefer after his transfer to the state mental hospital in Chattahoochee, was Dr. Hector Gianni. Dr. Gianni's observations correlate similarly with Dr. Eaton's, with a few new variations and details of events. One variation is that now Schaefer expresses he has an "ability" to judge women "that should be eliminated for the welfare of society," similar to the objective of Jack the Ripper, the 19th century, wherein the Ripper felt compelled to rid society of what he considered immoral women. Additionally, Dr. Gianni suspected that Schaefer may have been beginning to enjoy the status of having "committed one of the largest crimes in the criminal history of the United States," though Schaefer had still not confessed to the murder charges.

Later Stone would remark that Schaefer was most likely trying to fool the doctors into thinking he was "sicker than he really was." When asked to elaborate on that statement, Stone said he felt Schaefer wanted to be diagnosed as a paranoid schizophrenic, or "split personality." The reason would be obvious: if he was a true multi-personality, then it would be difficult for a conscientious jury to declare him guilty for crimes committed while his mind was under the direction of an "alter ego," or some other equally obsessive "psychological master."

DR. GIANNI'S EVALUATION:

Dear Judge Trowbridge:

The following is a report on Gerard John Schaefer, Jr, a 28-year-old, married male, who has an education which includes a Bachelor's Degree in Social Science from Florida Atlantic University in 1971 and a Bachelor's Degree in Geography and a degree as an Associate of Science in Criminology at Broward Junior College. He obtained a teacher's license to teach Social Studies at a grammar school level. In August 1971, he held a job as police officer in Wilton Manor for eight months but was fired for Civil Service violation. In May 1972, he obtained work as a Deputy Sheriff in Martin County, a job he liked "because everybody was honest." He lost this job when he was charged, convicted and sentenced to six months for Aggravated Assault for tying two girls (hitchhikers) to a tree. He handcuffed both of them and later on tied them to different trees with a rope. The explanation of the patient about these facts is that he was trying to teach them the risks involved in hitchhiking on the road. He was trying to put fear in them in such a way that they will not repeat it. Meantime, he was in jail, and the police found a diary in which the patient wrote about different crimes, always related to sexual aberration, a lot of pornographic material and drawings by the patient of women hanging from a rope, dead. There were drawings and other material that indirectly linked the patient to two different women which disappeared and later their bodies found. Consequently, the patient was charged with First Degree Murder, 2 Counts.

Family History: His father was a salesman, who usually made sales trips every month, being far from home for a whole week. They moved to another house and at that time his work caused him to be out on sales trips three out of four weeks a month. He did start drinking a lot and at that time patient was 5&1/2 years old. The father was too strict, asking for perfection all the time (mother says) but he was proud of John, telling other people about it, but never to John. The mother tried to fill in for John's father, "she feels sorry for him because he did not have a father." She behaved possibly in an overprotective way toward him. This conflictual relationship between the parents aggravated by the father's alcoholic problem found the family morals going down to the point the father brought his girlfriend home to introduce her to his wife, pretending they could become good friends. In that shocking appearance, John, age 22, was present, and mother says, "he took it all right because he knew what he could expect from his father." Consequently, they divorced in 1968. "The marriage was a forced marriage because my mother was pregnant with me," patient said. The patient felt upset talking about his parent's relationship. His siblings are his sister, Sara, who is younger than he. She is married and has two children and is a nurse. The patient said she was the father's favorite. He said, "my father always favored her, so I wanted to be a girl." He was pretty close to her. He has a brother, age 19, to whom the patient said he had always tried to be an example.

Psychosexual development began with masturbation at adolescence. Since the 6th grade, at the age 12, "I'd tie myself up to a tree, struggle to get free, and I'd get excited sexually and do something to hurt myself." When he was asked how he could hurt himself he replied that he would masturbate and fantasize hurting other people, women in particular." At that age, "I discovered women's underwear, sometimes I wore them. I'd want to hurt myself." From age 14-17 he had regular sexual intercourse with a steady girl, but she went off to college and left him. That day he went into the woods and tied himself with a rope in the trees and hurt himself in the masochistic way he used to do when he was younger. This was the first time in more than two years. When he was 24, he married Marion

Fogg, who patient's mother says was quite an intelligent girl, but childish and this marriage ended in about one year. Later, he married Theresa Dean in September 1971, to whom he was actually married. Patient said that in the first marriage he did not have any kind of sexual satisfaction. She did not understand him, but in the second marriage he is very successful from a sexual point of view.Mental Examination: The patient showed himself with short hair, and a tidy appearance. He was cooperative, coherent and relevant and showed an intelligence of above average. He was alert, responsive and oriented in time, place and person. His recent memory was good, his remote memory was poor about many different things. Immediate retention and recall were intact. In general his affect appears appropriate, but sometimes he has an inappropriate smile in describing criminal fantasies that he wrote about or when he was referring to killing those people. Mood seems slightly depressed. He will talk mostly about and shows a lot of preoccupation with his sexual experiences and fantasies. Patient did not show any hallucinations, auditory or visual, and it is possible that he is deluded about the purpose of his actions in his criminal fantasies. He is able to do abstractions. Insight about his problem is partial.

In summary, I disregard physical etiology of his disease based on the negative results of the electroencephalogram, skull x-rays and neurological examinations instead of based on the long and gradual development of an intricate conflict, an elaborate paranoid system based on often preceding logically

from misinterpretation of a natural event.
The patient states the wrongfulness of
prostitution in indecent women in society
(again, replicating the Ripper murders.)
Patient indulged himself with a unique and
superior ability to decide which are the
women that should be eliminated for the
welfare of society. Despite a long chronic
curse possibly since patient was a child
this condition did not seem to interfere too
much with the rest of the patient's thinking
and personality. As shown by the statement
of his mother, wife and friends, they said,
also neighbors did not see anything unusual
in the patient's behavior.

During my interviews with the patient,
I never saw any thought disorder or
inappropriate affect. He would not touch
the subject of sexual morals of society.
In such discussion the patient would show
himself deluded and sincerely convinced
that indecent women and prostitutes should
be destroyed for the welfare of society.
Patient would also show inappropriate affect,
smiling or laughing inappropriately when he
will recall his sadomasochistic thoughts
and ideas about the subject.

(This author observed similar reactions when I interviewed him,
years later.)

In his paranoid line of thought the
patient will show obsessive compulsive
tendencies for example, patient relates to
me that when he see a prostitute on the
street he feels the urge to destroy her and
usually will convert this feeling with the
practice of a whole sadomasochistic ritual

to the point that he will dress himself as
a woman, will tie himself to a tree and
punish himself this way most of the time
reaching the orgasm. Afterward the patient
began to relax and was free to behave in
a normal way. Instead if he is prevented
by the circumstances from completing his
compulsive ritual or if he is concerned
about being unable to control himself, he
will feel great anxiety and distress. That
is why usually the patient will carry in
his car, all the time, rope and all the
necessary materials for his sadomasochistic
ritual to be used at any time he feels the
urge to do it. The patient never denied
or confirmed the charges against him. I
think the patient is in the dilemma to
admit or deny the charges because in his
paranoid line of thought it is hard for the
patient to face the charges and lose the
opportunity to be suspected of committing
one of the largest crimes in the criminal
history of the United States, which brought
him the attraction of newspapermen and the
consequent fame, that in his paranoid mind
he enjoys so much. Of course, this tendency
is not to the point as usual to overpower
his self-preservation drive. The patient
also expressed to me several times that he
is more worried about finding out whether
or not he killed these girls than if he
is found guilty or not of the crime. He
claimed to me several times that it is hard
for him to recall past events; whether he
actually did it, or fantasized he had, or
wrote about it. This claim of confusing
fantasy with reality evidently at this point
could be seen as convenient for the patient
to pretend. I found that the patient is

consistent with this assertion because on the psychological evaluation done at Florida Atlantic University on May 17, 1968, by Mr. McConnick, psychometrist. In one part of his report he informs "Bender-Gestalt Tests reveals preservation of the fundamental outstanding Gestalt principles by the use of a primitive loop as a unit symbol. This is indicative of decreased ego control and of impairment in reality which is often found among psychotics or individuals with intracranial pathology." In the post-testing interview the patient was asked how he felt, and he indicated he felt fine now but that he would have times when everything feels unreal. "I feel fine, but at times I feel different like it isn't real, not like I black out, but things just go." John motioned with his hands downward toward his head with fingers extended. This confusion between fact and fantasy create doubts in my opinion if he will be able to aid his lawyer in his own defense.

Yours very truly,
Hector D. Gianni, M.D.
Staff Psychiatrist

The next person to see Schaefer was Dr. Benjamin Ogburn, acting superintendent for the state hospital. By the time Dr. Ogburn came to observe Schaefer, the evaluations were becoming almost identical. Indeed, there seemed to be a set formula: the description of the abduction of the Trotter and Wells girls and subsequent incarceration; the family history as illegitimate child with alcoholic father, and so on; the patient's sexual development, including the perverse hanging ritual (which at that time had no reference name, but is now known as "autoerotic asphyxiation"); and his college and marital histories. Dr. Ogburn's evaluation would achieve some notable originalities. These would include the following: 1.

Schaefer's relationship with his mother, now being described as one of "love-hate." 2. In addition to his obsession with autoerotic asphyxiation, Schaefer describes killing animals and having sex with their corpses. 3. He describes hearing "voices" telling him to kill people, while still denying that he ever did so. 4. Dr. Ogburn, in opposition with a few of his colleagues, diagnoses Schaefer as Paranoid Schizophrenic, a diagnosis that would be agreed upon by other psychiatrists who would also evaluate Schaefer. 5.Dr. Ogburn talked to Teresa Schaefer, one of the few psychiatrists to do so, and obtains a brief profile of the woman married to the man accused of such unspeakable atrocities. 6. Schaefer is now to be considered "a very dangerous person . . ."

DR. OGBURN'S EVALUATION:

CONSULTATION

Re: Gerard John Schaefer, Jr. A 69 653
June 20, 1973

This patient was seen by me for evaluation for primarily two reasons, (1) At the suggestion of the Superintendent of Florida State Hospital, Doctor Milton J. Hirshberg and (2) Because of my interest as Chief of the Forensic Unit at Florida State Hospital and the widespread interest concerning the patient. The patient was seen on several occasions on the ward, but only for a few minutes, but was seen in a psychiatric interview situation for approximately one hour and fifteen minutes on June 9, 1973. In addition, the patient's wife was interviewed for approximately forty-five minutes on June 10, 1973. It had been my original intention to see the patient for an additional interview, however, my combined duties as Acting Superintendent and Chief of the Forensic Unit prevented the time necessary. At the time the patient was interviewed, he was advised as to his rights and the issues of confidentiality. I advised the patient that he should discuss any issues which he felt might be incriminating with his attorney, prior to revealing anything of this nature to me. The patient was well aware of his present situation and his reasons for admission to the hospital. He denied any knowledge of the charges for which he is being held, although he did talk about the previous convictions for assault and related that this time, he did feel his behavior had been inappropriate, however, he was quite angry at the girls who he eventually tied up and felt that he was teaching them a lesson. He was particularly angered when they laughed at him and he felt that triggered his reaction and he was intending to show them the dangers of the two of them wandering around the countryside hitchhiking. The patient had some concerns about the period of time which had elapsed between the time that he had left the girls and they escaped. He stated it seemed more like five minutes to him, whereas they had indicated to him it was an hour. The patient describes his time in jail since his sentence as being uneventful, however, he has been more depressed in the past few months, since being charged with murder, and has had some suicidal ruminations, particularly when he thinks that there might not be any way out, or any hope for him. Pertinent past history on the patient reveals that he was an illegitimate child and always felt that he was rejected by his father. He remembers the father as being a harsh, cruel man, who drank extensively and was often away from home. The patient remembers sleeping

```
with his mother on many occasions, until
he was approximately eight years of age. He
describes his relationship with his mother
as being a love-hate relationship and that
he has been unable to reconcile the many
feelings he has about his mother.
```

(Authors' note: Indeed, in an interview with an investigator with the Broward County Sheriff Department, who chose to remain nameless, it was revealed that Doris Schaefer "used to find notes, on her bed or in her bedroom." These "notes" would tell her that "she would be killed" and, were usually found when Mr. Schaefer, the father, was away. No one signed the notes, but she felt in her mind, that her son was the anonymous author. She became concerned enough, so that at one point, she went to the sheriff's office to make a complaint. The investigator added though, that all of the notes had been lost since that time, as was the original complaint form. One can only speculate and wonder if these papers were truly "lost" or perhaps stolen, or "misplaced" by say a patrolman—Schaefer—from a nearby police station requesting an unauthorized file search. It is conceivable and quite possible.)

```
    He always described himself as a loner
and stated that he had few friends as a
child. He has always tended to distrust
other people. He first became involved with
sexual activity about the age of puberty,
twelve or thirteen. He often masturbated,
using women's clothing, dressing in them.
In addition, he often tied himself to a
tree, or would allow himself to be suspended
from a tree by a rope, either around his
neck, or sometimes around his waist and
would get sexual gratification from this.
During this time, he would have fantasies
of killing himself, and at times he would
almost lose consciousness. He felt that he
almost killed himself once by this means. He
became interested in the Catholic religion
more intensively during his teenage years
```

and eventually applied for the Priesthood at age seventeen but was rejected and has turned from the church since that time. The patient describes some normal heterosexual sexual activity during his teenage years however, in the past four to five years his sexual behavior has become more of a concern to him. He describes killing horses and cows with a machete and then having sex with them later, sometimes after cutting off their heads. He remembers feeling invincible when he attacks the animals and has the feeling that he is a third person and he is looking at himself. Mr. Schaefer attended college and has received a Degree (B.A.) in social science. He also has an associate degree in criminology. While he was attending college, he became increasingly concerned about himself and his impulses and eventually sought psychiatric help and saw a psychiatrist on several occasions. He was particularly concerned about his hostile feelings and he recalls vague voices telling him to kill people, however, he was able to not respond. He stated that at the suggestion of the psychiatrist, he began writing and drawing some of his fantasies. He also began shooting and killing inanimate objects, feeling that these activities would help relieve some of his feelings. He also describes having some blackouts and feeling disoriented and not knowing how he got to a particular place after he found himself there.

Mr. Schaefer has had a poor work history. He has worked some as a Guide in the Everglades. He has also attempted to teach school, however, this lasted only a very short period of time. In addition, he has worked in law enforcement jobs, however, none of these lasted very long; he would eventually be involved in some conflict and he usually felt he was unfairly treated. He has been married on two occasions. His first marriage only lasted about one year. He states that there was much incompatibility, primarily in the sexual area. He and his present wife were married in September 1971 and he states has been a good marriage. States he and his present wife have many activities which they share, that there have been no significant problems with the marriage and describes a compatible sexual relationship.

As noted earlier, the patient's wife was also seen to evaluate the entire situation. She impressed me as being a somewhat naive twenty-one-year-old white female, who seemed to have a genuine positive interest in her husband and has been shocked and quite dismayed and upset over the charges. She had considered a divorce, however, at this time she feels that she will stand by her husband. She tends to deny any particular problems with their relationship or marriage and the only concern she had was at his inability to hold a job. However, she has seen this as "he has been unable to find himself." She denies any indication of psychiatric illness in her husband and has many doubts about the charges. However, she felt quite concerned about the material which he had written.

The patient presented as an alert, cooperative white male, who initially showed some reluctance to talk, had many concerns about the reasons for the interview. However, as the situation was clarified, he became more open and talked quite freely. He tended to ramble at times, and it was difficult for him to always deal with the particular issue, however, there was no gross disorganization of thought. There was no evidence of delusions or hallucinations, although he did describe some voices in the past telling him to kill people. There tended to be a paranoid trend to his thinking and a tendency to mistrust and to withdraw from people. His affect was usually appropriate and animated, however, on occasion there was noted some inappropriate responses, particularly when he was talking about some of his sexual acting out and sadistic behavior he would seem to smile inappropriately. He seemed to have some difficulty in always distinguishing between the reality of the situation and some of the active fantasy life he has participated in. He was felt to be intelligent, with reasonable judgement. He certainly had insight into his need for treatment and to the bizarreness of some of his behavior. There was considerable ambivalence noted, particularly in his relationship with women, more specifically with his mother. The ambivalence seemed to be more than would normally be seen in an individual.

In summary, Mr. Schaefer gives a background of a very traumatic childhood with a punitive father and a very difficult relationship with his mother. There was early evidence of bizarre sexual acting out, together with poor identity as a man.

There is noted a schizoid type of character with a paranoid element. For the past few years, the patient seems to have become more disorganized with periods of active fantasy life, in which some of his behavior was very bizarre. There has been evidence of considerable paranoid feelings, hostility, and anger, which erupts and explodes with little stress. The patient's behavior at this time and during the interview with a consideration of his history appears to be indicative of a psychotic illness, mainly paranoid schizophrenia. He appears to have a very marginal ability of tolerating normal stresses and becomes very disturbed with little stimulation. In addition, there seems to be a very active fantasy life which is just beneath the surface and also is immobilized with little stimulation. It is noted that past examiners have seen this patient as representing a character disorder and itis my feeling, in consideration of his background, the mental status of the patient, and a review of the psychological evaluation done at this hospital, that a more appropriate diagnosis would be Paranoid Schizophrenia.

Recommendation: It is my impression that this patient will require long-term in-patient psychiatric treatment. He is considered to be a very dangerous person, both to himself and to others.

Benjamin R. Ogburn, M.D.
Acting Superintendent

One of Dr. Ogburn's colleagues, Dr. Patrick E. Cook, a psychologist, also observed Schaefer. His evaluation was brief, perhaps more concise, but correlates closely with Dr. Ogburn's conclusions. He too was given certain original insights that had not been revealed to some of the other examiners.

Among his observations he wrote of Schaefer:

"From once fantasizing mass-murder he now believes he is the 'eliminator' of wicked people = immoral women = all women . . ."

"He claims to hear voices and these 'advisors' give him instructions which he must follow. He sees himself as the helpless agent of the directions of his advisors (which he named) Matthew and Jack. (Speculation: Jack the Ripper?)

"Mr. Schaefer was reasonably cooperative on the testing, although he did not take much time to work on items he considered to be beneath his dignity. He has delusions of persecution, grandiosity and external control of his actions."

And, in correlating with State Attorney Stone's assumption at that time, Dr. Cook added:

"On the basis of his interview behavior and test results, it is also felt that Mr. Schaefer may be exaggerating some of his symptoms. He is bright enough to do so effectively. It is my impression, however, that the underlying personality disorder is so serious as to render any malingering relatively meaningless.

"Because Mr. Schaefer is clearly psychotic, and due to his sadomasochistic sexual perversion, he must be considered to be extremely dangerous. He is suffering from a paranoid psychosis and sexual deviation.

"Mr. Schaefer understands the nature of the charges against him and can assist counsel in his defense. Consequently, I feel he is competent to stand trial."

So, while the psychiatrists differed somewhat in opinion as to Schaefer's credibility, all more or less, agreed that he was suffering from some form of mental illness, that most likely being severe enough to be considered serious, possibly psychotic, and definitely warranting his segregation from society. They all agreed, too, that for a complete diagnosis, all elements should be considered, including, of course, a complete physiological and neurological examination. They concurred that if these examinations proved to be within "normal" standards, that regardless of whatever mental illness Schaefer was suffering from, he did know the difference between right and wrong, and according to Florida law, would be eligible to stand trial.

Dr. Merton L. Ekwall, M.D., performed the neurological history and examination on Schaefer and put together the following report:

The patient is considered to be a fairly reliable historian but much of his history is guarded and early life illnesses and diseases and family history may need to be checked with the mother.

Family history indicates the father has been alcoholic but is probably recovered. The mother has no known neurological illness. The family history is negative for migraine or epilepsy or other neurologic disease. Diabetes is present in the father, paternal grandfather, and paternal aunts and uncles.

Past personal history indicates that he was born in Wisconsin, raised in New York to the age of 6. Oldest of three siblings. The patient does not know his birth weight, history of gestation or any unusual childhood diseases. He feels he had the usual childhood diseases without residual. At age 8 or 9 he was "going deaf" in school and grades were suffering. On physical examination he was found to have enlarged adenoids and had a T&A (tonsil and adenoid removal) age 8 or 9. At the same time he also had scarlet fever with an unknown amount of delirium or encephalitic reaction. At about age 10 he dove into the shallow end of a swimming pool and sprained his neck without unconsciousness. Age 14, fractured left great toe in football practice requiring surgical reduction. At about the same age he was a passenger in an auto accident with no fractures and no known unconsciousness. Age 18, auto accident with the car rolling over but patient sustaining only sprains and bruises, no unconsciousness. Age 16, was struck on the head near the eye with a sandstone rock with pieces of sand embedded in the left eye requiring surgical removal. Age 20, was struck over the posterior occiput (rear lower portion of skull) with a 2 by 4. No unconsciousness but was dazed for several minutes. Age 27, intermittent high fever over 4-5 months, not responding to Tetracycline but eventually responding to Terramycin. (odd as they are the same drug)

According to the subject he has no major neurological complaints. He has had a mild ringing or buzzing in both ears over a long period of time which is exacerbated by fatigue, headache, etc.

In addition, the history indicates episodes of amnesia over periods of time varying from a few seconds to as high as one day at intervals since age 16.

General status: Patient is a well-developed, well-nourished white male six feet one inch tall, weighing 190 pounds. Body type is athletic, and he seems well coordinated. The only visible scars are residuals of an old abrasion of the left lateral lower leg and a 4 mm. old burn scar over the right lateral biceps area. The patient states that within the past year he weighed up to

240 pounds and has had more than 50-pound weight loss which he associates with the chronic fever of undetermined origin. He denies the use of excessive amounts of nicotine, alcohol, Coca-Cola, coffee, or drugs.

The cranial nerves were examined serially and found to be intact. There is no alteration of smell. Visual acuity is good. Pupils are round, regular, and equal and react to light in a combination directly and consensually. Fundoscopic examination shows no myopia or hypermetropia and visual fields are adequate to direct confrontation. Extraocular movements are normal. The fifth and seventh cranial nerves are intact with no alteration of sensation or muscle movement. Auditory acuity is good and testing with a tuning fork shows Rinne and Weber tests are negative. The ninth, tenth, and eleventh and twelfth cranial nerves are intact.

Deep tendon reflexes are generally hypoactive but equal bilaterally. Superficial reflexes are hypoactive but equal bilaterally. No pathological reflexes are elicited. All coordination tests and sensory modalities are intact.

No evidence of focal or disseminated neurological disease on the neurological examination.

By history, there is a suggestion of emotional storms in early childhood with temper flare-ups and loss of temper with "red-outs" together with a history of periods of amnesia in the mid-teens and throughout the twenties. These seen to be more psychologically connected but the possibility of a neurological etiology should be kept in mind. Electroencephalographic tracing is recommended for any possible cerebral dysrhythmia.

And so, in his thoroughness, Dr. Ekwall scheduled an electroencephalogram, a diagnostic device which records "brain-wave activity." One important element should be noted in Dr.

Ekwall's report thus far. That being Schaefer's severe weight loss of "more than 50 pounds." Again, it would later be suggested that Schaefer consciously underwent this drastic physical change in order to become unrecognizable to the Places and the Jessups, if they were to testify against him in court. The Places and the Jessups being the only living witnesses that could place him with the victims the last night they were known to be alive. If this were true, it would account for his having grown a mustache, and allowing his hair to grow as well. And, if this were true, then this "human chameleon" would further add to his "disguise" when he would lose an additional nine pounds by the time of his electroencephalogram (EEG) recording.

Dr. Ekwall's delineation of Schaefer's "EEG," is most likely too scientific for the average laymen's understanding, but of significant interest to the case in at least two sections of the report. The first section, describing the patient, and the last "Impression" section, that concludes that Schaefer was "normal'' at least inasmuch as his neurological health was concerned.

Description of EEG:
EEG is requested for routine evaluation for possibility of cerebral abnormality. The patient is 6'1" in height, weighs 181 pounds, and blood pressure is 130/80. He

is quite suspicious of the examination but cooperates fairly well. He is reported to be taking Valium 10 mg. and Noctec 500 mg. prn.

The EEG shows a basic pattern of moderate voltage fairly well regulated and modulated 10 COP fundamental Alpha with normal distribution over the hemispheres. The fundamental frequency is almost constantly modified by underlying mixed 20 and 50 CPS semi rhythmical Beta which is attributed to medication effect and muscle tension artefact. The hemispheres are essentially synchronous and symmetrical and no true focal, unilateral, or paroxysmal abnormalities are noted. Hyperventilation stimulation is fairly well performed and does not significantly alter the stable background pattern. Photic stimulation shows normal Alpha blocking and no paroxysmal discharges are evoked.

Impression:

Well within limits of normal variations for this age group except for medication and muscle tension artefact. There is no electrical evidence of an expanding lesion, focal cortical abnormality, or epileptiform activity at this time.

* * *

Throughout Schaefer's recorded psychological history, he'd undergone a battery of tests to better evaluate his mental health. During his years in college when he first sought psychiatric help, beginning in 1968, through his 30-day confinement at Florida State Mental Hospital in June of 1973; hundreds of tests had been administered by dozens of psychiatrists and psychologists. A survey of these tests is in order, if only a brief look, to better understand the nature of psychological testing and thusly, peer a little further into the mind of Gerard Schaefer. The following is an abbreviated list of some of the key tests that Schaefer was given and that, along with many hours of doctor-patient discussions, enabled the evaluators to better diagnose their bewildering, and now infamous patient.

Rorschach test
Minnesota Multiphasic Personality Test (MMPI)
Bender Gestalt Test
Wechsler Adult Intelligence Test
Figure Drawing Test
Thematic Apperception Test (TAT)
Word Association Test (Shipley)
Serial Sevens Test

Miss Debra Patterson, a practicing clinical psychologist agreed to help us to define these tests in laymen terms.

"The Rorschach, TAT, MMPI, Bender, and figure drawing tests are part of a battery of tests given to evaluate some specific question asked by a referral source, (In this case, the court who was trying to determine Schaefer's sanity level.) For example, someone like a psychiatrist might be working with a client whose symptoms are somewhat psychotic and also neurotic. The psychiatrist needs to come up with a diagnosis and asks the psychologist to evaluate to determine at what level of intellectual functioning the client is performing and what is revealed about the client's personality.

"Usually the referral question calls for an IQ score. This is the most routine kind of testing done at a mental center. The Wechsler and Bender are usually enough to suffice (for intelligence testing).

"Some people give all these tests in a battery. I, myself, and most of my colleagues will give only a few of these tests as a battery, depending, again, on the referral question.

"The projective (Rorschach, TAT, sometimes the Bender, and the figure drawing tests) are usually used when there is a diagnostic question and the therapist can't get a handle on the person just from the clinical interview."

Patterson wrote that the Shipley Test and the Serial Sevens Test were tests used to determine if there might be neurological damage" in a patient. Further, she went on to quote several reference sources that correlated with the information she gave us, information which in some instances can be considered subjective in nature, depending on the examiner.

Perhaps the most useful test in Schaefer's diagnosis was the TAT, or Thematic Apperception Test. This is a test whereby the patient reveals to "the trained interpreter some of the dominant drives, emotions, sentiments, complexes, and conflicts of his personality." The test is able to "expose the underlying inhibited tendencies which the patient is not willing to admit or cannot admit because he is unconscious of them." The test is usually administered before a series of psychotherapeutic interviews or psychoanalysis begins. It is used, often, with the Rorschach Test (commonly known as the Inkblot Test) as they yield a combination of information that is peculiarly effective in helping arrive at a diagnosis.

As with the Rorschach Test, the TAT procedure consists of presenting "a series of pictures to a subject and encouraging him to tell stories about them, invented on the spur of the moment." Particularly interesting in relation to the Schaefer case is that these "stories" reveal two psychological tendencies: "the tendency of people to interpret an ambiguous human situation in conformity with their past experiences and present wants, and the tendency of those who write stories to do likewise: draw on the fund of their experiences and express their sentiments, and needs, whether conscious or unconscious."

"If the pictures are presented as a test of the imagination, the subject's interest, together with his need for approval, can be so involved in the task that he forgets his sensitive self and the necessity of defending it against the probing of the examiner, and before he knows it, he has said things about an invented character that apply to himself, things which he would have been reluctant to confess in response to a direct question. As a rule, the subject leaves the test happily unaware that he has presented the psychologist with what amounts to an X-ray picture of his inner self."

The TAT reflects ten areas of evaluation, among them are: "significant conflicts, nature of anxieties," and most interesting, "adequacy of superego as manifested by punishment for crime."

Also, interesting to note is the MMPI (Minnesota Multiphasic Personality) Test, which Schaefer also took, and which is "designed to provide an objective assessment of some of the major personality characteristics that affect personal and social adjustment." In other words, they help to determine a "category" under which the patient may be listed. Among the nine possible categories are: Paranoia, Psychopathic deviate, and Schizophrenia. Schaefer scored high in all three of these categories.

Undoubtedly, the combination of the Thematic Apperception Test and the Minnesota Multiphasic Personality Test, along with the clinical interviews (psychotherapy-type discussion), and in light of the fact that Schaefer displayed no neurological, or otherwise physiological, maladies, altogether helped the staff doctors to conclude that Schaefer was indeed a paranoid schizophrenic, with psychopathic sexual deviations. However pathetic his "overall personality crisis" might have been, he was deemed "normal," in that he could distinguish right from wrong, and thus stand trial for two counts of murder.

* * *

While the doctors busied themselves with their final deliberations over the anomaly known as Gerard Schaefer, they also began to prepare to release him to authorities who would transport him to his new residence, the St. Lucie County Jail, where he would wait until his court date was set.

Robert Stone, too, had been busy. During the time Schaefer was being studied at the Florida State Mental Hospital, in fact shortly after he'd been taken from the Martin County Jail for his 30-day evaluation, Stone paid a visit to the jail. He wanted to talk to a man, a former cellmate of Schaefer's, named Spencer Buckelew, Stone was beginning to form a picture of the type of man he believed Schaefer to be. He felt that if Schaefer shared a cell with a person he thought he might be able to impress, and particularly someone who did not seem to come close to grasping a low rung on the social ladder—a fellow criminal as it were—then Schaefer would be enough of a psychotic egotist to share his tales.

Bragging about criminal deeds, however heinous, is not uncommon in prisons, and if Stone was right, he'd be able to form a clearer picture of the type of man Schaefer was. Stone, up until this meeting with Buckelew, had not been sleeping well. Although he'd collected enormous amounts of evidence against Schaefer, and the Places said he was the right man, and Stone had told the newspapers Schaefer was the only suspect, he still found it hard to believe that a former policeman and deputy sheriff could perform the terrible crimes he was accused of committing. After all, Schaefer's wife, mother, family, and friends were all standing by him, and swearing stern-faced that he was the friendliest, loving, all-American boy that they'd ever known.

There was reason for doubt, but it would soon be eliminated at least in Stone's mind, after his discussion with Spencer Buckelew. The following is an excerpt from that discussion, recorded on June 4th, 1973. (NOTE: All questions and comments by Robert Stone are prefaced with an abbreviation, S. All answers and comments from Spencer Buckelew are prefaced with B.)

S: Like I said this has nothing to do with you, you were in the cell with Schaefer, and I would like to know what he talked about?

B: I was in the cell with him about a month, I think.

S: What did he talk about, what did he say to you?

B: He used to be real skittish, used to rapping about little shit, just start rapping about something, like I was talking about this dude I know that passes a lot of dope and he said that he could knock him off easy you know. Anyway, he says, he start talking about, like you know mister he just got into shit, when he talked about it, like he talked about knocking off people and shit like this.

S: How do you mean knocking off people?

B: You know like knock them off, get their money, fuck it and never know about nothing, you know? He says if you ever want some quick money, let me know, I says what do you mean? He says these frigs you know you can knock them off and keep all the dope and shit for yourself. He was talking about over in Viet Nam and you could kill people, like he would get a real expression in his face about it, like he really digs on it.

S: Like he really digs on killing people?

B: Yea. Like he was talking about this woman he killed you know over in Vietnam, in the shit house, he killed her and fucked her and knocked her down.

S: He killed her and then he screwed her?

B: Right, he pushed her back down in the shit thing and put the lid down, he was a creep.

S: When did he talk about this?

B: When I was in the cell with him, we used to stay up all night.

S: Was he bullshitting you?

B: No, he was dead serious, he says like he had a lot of financial problems on the outside and he needed some money when he gets out, at first I thought he was talking about dope, different people we know and things we did, and he says maybe we could get something going, like these people that goes and picks up dope and stuff, always has money on them, knock them off and keep it for yourself or something.

S: When was he in Nam?

B: I don't know, he told me all about these foreign countries he used to go to before he was married, he used to work for a man in Africa, Spain or something, some knock off man, told me he used to be a knock off man over here, used to knock off whores, told me about this one whore he knocked off in Fort Lauderdale.

S: Did he ever mention her name?

B: Yea, Annette or some shit like that.

S: Jeanette, in Fort Lauderdale?

B: I don't know, something like that, I can't remember shit like that.

S: Come on now, it's important.

B: It's not important to me!

S: It's important to me, I'm just asking you to help me out.

B: Okay.

S: When was this supposed to have happened, this killing in Fort Lauderdale?

B: Let's see, he said he was a policeman, some kind of cop over there, says she was a prostitute and she was holding out on the man and he kinda took her out for a date, and they said they was going to this café, and she said hey, this ain't the way to the café and he said, I know it baby, you just shut up, and they went down to the swamp, some swamp there was there, down by a boat ramp where you put a boat in the water an airboat or something and he got behind there and he says I'm going to kill you, do you want it fast or slow or what, now he had a gun and this wire thing with two fingers in it, two little circles in it, and he got behind her, put it around her neck and choked her to death, she started shitting all over and she died and he said he was drunk, he took her out and put her in the trunk and he woke up and he fucked her and he cut her head off and said how do you get rid of the bodies so no one ever finds them, he said the swamp does miracles, does funny things.

S: In other words, first of all he talked about the woman he killed in Nam, then the woman he killed in Fort Lauderdale, possibly named Jeanette, something like that, was supposed to be a whore there, right? He was supposed to be talking to her? He was supposed to have killed her?

B: Yea.

S: Was this when he was working as a policeman?

B: This dude got him to do it for him.

S: This dude got him to do it for him?

B: Yea.

S: You mean Schaefer killed this whore for somebody else?

B: This guy got him to do it, got him to do a lot of shit like that, he said that's how he got all this money and bought this car.

S: What car?

B: He said he had a, some other car some little foreign car, Datsun, I don't know, some foreign car, he said that guy helped him get that car and make a lot of debts, the dude paid him good. See the M.F. and me was going to get together when we got out, we was going to bust out the same day and a this ain't going to put in a bad word for me? Alright, we was talking about different people I know, they carry a lot of money on them, like I know truck brokers, and that's how we started talking and when he told me he was capable of doing this kind of thing.

S: Do you believe what he was telling you?

B: Have you ever sit down and talked to somebody about fucking a broad, and the expression on their face, you know, they're digging them, you know what I mean, they like that kind of thing.

S: You said he killed this whore down there in Fort Lauderdale, we'll call her Jeanette, you said he killed her for the man she was pimping for?

B: Right.

B: Dave Martin can tell you the same thing, me and Dave Martin all three of us were talking together.

S: Then after that, he was supposed to have screwed her then.

B: Yea, screwed her and . . .

S: She was dead?

B: Yea.

S: Cut her head off?

B: He said he put her in the trunk, the band thing did that (cut their heads off), after he did that he threw her in the water and he put his foot on her, she wouldn't go down, so then he picked her up and put her in the trunk and he got in his car and went to sleep, he was drinking he said, then he got back up, got out and before he got rid of her, he fucked her and then he said and I said how did you get rid of her so people don't find her? And he said the swamp does funny things or something like that.

S: Who was the man he was supposed to be doing this for?

B: I don't know.

S: Did he ever mention any names?

B: He mentioned lots of them.

S: Give me some of them?

B: I don't know none.

S: Come on now, after all of this stuff?

B: I forgot, I forgot.

S: Are you feeding me a line, is this a bunch of bull?

B: This is true, I forgot, I don't pay no attention to shit like that you know.

S: Well, you said you thought he was telling the truth?

B: I'm talking about names.

S: Alright, what else did he talk about?

B: Just strange things, people he did for and all this shit like that when he was in Spain, I think it was Spain, some faraway place like that, he worked for this dope man, like going to Africa and getting black dope, black market dope and bringing it back into Algeria, some place similar like that. When they find out what they wanted they would just knock them off, fuck it and take their money and go.

S: About here in the U.S., did he talk about killing any other ones?

B: He just said he made a lot of money doing this kind of shit, knocking off these prostitutes, queers, homos and different things like that.

S: Queers? Did he ever talk about killing any men? Or is it all women?

B: That includes women I guess, whores, prostitutes and queers.

S: Some men are queer too?

B: That's all he ever talked about is shit like that, you know gory, messy jobs.

S: Messy, like screwing them after they were dead?

B: Yes, let them shit in their britches and all and fucking them in the ass and all kinds of shit like this, he just liked to get down to the nitty gritty.

S: Did he ever talk about any other times he did it, any other women he killed?

B: There was this one he used to tell me over and over would really give pussy.

S: What was that one about?

B: It was a spade chick, he knocked off.

S: A black girl and a white girl?

B: It was a spade and a white girl he knocked off, he really dug on them, he always said that pussy was really good. He killed two of them, I suppose he did, he told me this. Dade County is Miami ain't it, well he said these two broads was doing their man wrong and he knew the girls and found out where they lived and he went there one night with his little gun and told them to come on, got them out in the car and took them for a long, long drive.

S: This black and white, were they supposed to be prostitutes too?

B: I don't know, he said they was doing the man wrong, the man wanted to do away with them.

S: Who is this man you keep talking about, did he ever mention his name?

B: Yea, I don't remember, I'm serious, I can't remember names, places, addresses, now if I go there, I can remember.

S: But you don't remember who this man was?

B: He said it a lot of times, but I don't remember no damn names.

S: What about this white girl and black girl.

B: What is was, he killed them.

S: How did he kill them?

B: He just knocked them off and fucked them?

S: How?

B: He cut them all to hell and back, that's what he told me.

S: How? Did he use a hatchet or knife?

B: What do you call them things, goes on the end of a gun? One of them kind of knives.

S: Like a bayonet?

B: Bayonet, that's it. He says one of them tried to get away and he had to run her down.

S: When was he supposed to have done this? In other words what I'm trying to say did he ever associate times with these, did he ever tell you when he did this?

B: Two or three times he said I did this job a couple of months ago. I did this job for this man maybe that was about the closest he ever come to saying time.

S: Anything more about this black and white in Dade County? Does he say where he took them, what their names were?

B: I don't know, I forget.

S: Did he talk about this to everybody in the cell?

B: No, always nighttime when everybody was sleeping, he started talking, well David Martin, two or three times, David woke up and come over and listened in on it.

S: Where is Dave now?

B: I don't know, he's out, free.

S: What else did Schaefer talk about?

B: Just gory shit like that.

S: Give me any example you can think of? You say he enjoyed talking about this?

B: Oh, shit yea, the expressions on his face, you know.

S: Any other girls, women, incidents?

B: He'd date the bitches and take them out to the beach and rip them off, just do away with them.

S: Who were these women? Where did he get them?

B: Sometimes it would take a week, two weeks to get a date with her you know, he would get a date with her, take her out and he would talk to her, tell her what he was going to do and do it. Like he would say, now baby you know it's time for me to do this to you, you have been doing the man wrong you know, made them suck his dick and all this before he, you know. Give me a minute to think back to when we was talking, I'm trying to remember that name, Bah haj or something I keep getting it mixed up with the one he was talking about over in Africa.

S: What did he talk about in Africa?

B: He was just over there having a nice time, knocking off, fucked a lot of prostitutes over there and wouldn't pay them, things like that, he knocked off a lot of dope men they'd go to buy big quantities of hashish and then when they would find out where it was at and all.

S: What about these two girls that he is charged with?

B: Yes, I asked him about that, he said he wasn't going to do nothing to them. I said why did you have them all hogged tied? He said he was trying to scare them, and I said I know better than that and he said well you know, I said, I guess there was more to it and he wouldn't tell me.

S: What about the two girls' bodies they found in St. Lucie County?

B: I never did talk to him about that, I was down, I was down from there then.

S: Do you remember when to when you were in the cell with him?

B: I've been downstairs with Sam about two months. It was February I was up there; it was either March or February. Take your pick, which one do you want.

S: You think about it, I'll talk to you tomorrow.

B: I'll try to remember it.

S: Don't give me a run around now, don't play games.

B: I ain't giving you a run around, I'm pissed off, if I can't remember it, I can't remember!

* * *

Shortly after Schaefer's release from the Florida State Mental Hospital, and his subsequent incarceration at the St. Lucie County Jail, Elton Schwarz began an aggressive defense plan. Having heard of Spencer Buckelew's accusations, and considering the results of the 30-day evaluation, Schwarz knew he would have to reformulate his plan of action. He still believed the best defense would be one of insanity, though Schaefer resisted this idea wholeheartedly. He still maintained he was innocent, and now the doctors at Chattahoochee had declared him "eligible to stand trial," despite his obviously worsening mental condition. No, he told Schwarz, he could not see using a plea of insanity, at least not this early in the game. But Schwarz needed time. He did some digging and came up with Dr. C. W. Long.

Dr. Long was now the Chief of Psychiatry at Polk (County) General Hospital in Bartow, Florida, near the west coast. However, throughout the late sixties, in fact up until June of 1971, Dr. Long had worked at the Henderson Clinic in Broward County, as well as maintaining a position at Florida Atlantic University. He'd known Schaefer during his student years at the school, knew of his previous mental problems, and along with doctors Killinger and McCormick, had seen Schaefer as an outpatient. Why Dr. Killinger and Dr. McCormick did not now get involved in Schaefer's case is unknown. But, Dr. Long, after listening to Schwarz's desperate plea or his client, agreed to see him, and if, in his opinion Schaefer was "sick" enough, he would write a letter to Judge C. Pfeiffer Trowbridge, asking that Schaefer be hospitalized.

The following is the letter that Dr. Long penned after seeing Schaefer.

Re: Mr. Gerard John Schaefer, Jr.

Dear Judge Trowbridge:

I interviewed the above named for approximately 2&1/2 hours yesterday, July 6, 1973, at the St. Lucie County Jail in Fort Pierce, Florida. In my opinion, Mr. Schaefer is a definite danger to himself. He is suicidal and has the motivation and ability to kill himself. In my opinion he is in urgent need of hospitalization.

Mr. Schaefer is well known to me. I had seen him regularly from 1968 to May 1971, as a private psychiatrist, as a psychiatrist working for Henderson Clinic Broward County Inc., and as a psychiatrist employed by Florida Atlantic University, Boca Raton, 1969 to 1970. I first saw him in 1968 following the

discovery of his suicide note written while
he was attending Florida Atlantic University.
I understand that Mr. Schaefer has received
a great deal of notoriety in newspapers,
magazines, etc., but I was unaware of any of
the recent events until I was informed by
Mr. Schwarz . . .

    Again, I would like to repeat that in
my opinion Mr. Schaefer is in urgent need
of immediate hospitalization in a State
Hospital such as the one in Chattahoochee
or any other psychiatric unit equipped to
give adequate supervision, observation,
and treatment of mentally ill patients with
a court hold.

Respectfully Submitted,
C. W. Long, M. D., Chief of Psychiatry

Judge Trowbridge, having just heard from a staff of doctors at the Florida State Mental Hospital, disregarded the letter.

Desperately, Schwarz began to question Schaefer's friends and family, anyone who might be able to shine a more favorable light on his hapless client. He was also looking for someone who might know something about some of the missing persons thought to be Schaefer's victims. One person who, like Schaefer, knew several of the missing girls, presumed dead, was John Dolan, Schaefer's former roommate. Schwarz talked with Dolan in July of 1973, at Florida Atlantic University in Boca Raton, where Dolan was a student. There, on a typically sweltering summer day, in an air-conditioned secluded study room, the two men talked at great length.

Schwarz displayed his traditional laid-back style of interrogation, but Dolan was quite the opposite. Throughout the questioning, he was defensive, and though the tape-recorded session is often inaudible and indistinguishable, it is clear enough, at least to this listener, to say Dolan's answers were, at times, evasive. Though that may be a subjective interpretation, it is a fact that Schwarz would, in the end, choose not to use Dolan in the trial. The reasons? The following excerpt from that deposition speaks for itself. (NOTE: All questions and comments from Elton Schwarz are prefaced with an abbreviation, Q. All answers and comments from Dolan are prefaced with an A.)

Q: Did he (Schaefer) ever...

A: He showed me that article in the paper about Carmen Hallock disappearing, you know, and the other girl. I knew Carmen Hallock.

Q: You did know her?

A: Yes.

Q: How well did you know Carmen?

A: Pretty well.

Q: How did you happen to meet her?

A: Through school.

Q: She was going to school with you?

A: Yeah.

Q: Where was this? Broward Community?

A: Yes.

Q: Do you know where she lived at that time?

A: Yea, she lived over on...somewhere off of Commercial, you know, Eighteenth Avenue or fifteenth or something off of Commercial. (In Fort Lauderdale.)

Q: Did you ever date Carmen at all?

A: Yeah.

Q: For how long a period of time?

A: About...brief time, not too long.

Q: Do you recall about when that was?

A: It was when I was going to Broward.

Q: That was before or after you went in the service?

A: After.

Q: After you got out of the service. Was it a short time before she disappeared?

A: I really couldn't say as far as, you know, in relation to when she disappeared, you know.

Q: Were you dating her while you and John were living in the apartment?

A: No, no, no.

Q: It was before you lived in the apartment or after?

A: It was a long time before.

Q: Did you ever know Leigh Hainline or Leigh Bonadies (married name)?

A: That blond girl. He showed her to me, you know, and said he really liked her a lot, you know, but kind of held her off, you know. Like he would never go up and ask her for a date or anything. He was like, you know, kind of restraining from doing it, but he really wanted to go over, you know, and –

Q: Had he ever dated her at all?

A: I have no idea. No, no, it was just something that he would be sitting around his house at night, I guess. This is the impression I got. He would be sitting in his house at night with nothing else to think about, and he would think about her.

Q: It has been at least probably a couple of years since you have seen John?

A: Yes, yes.

Q: Did he ever talk to you about going to law enforcement work at all?

A: Oh, the last time I talked to him about that was when he was working for Wackenhut, (a security guard employment agency) you know. He said he was going into law enforcement from Wackenhut because he submitted this report, and everybody thought it great. I thought he was kind of nuts.

Q: Did he ever...about how many times would you say you visited John in his home where his mother lives?

A: Oh, quite a few times. I am familiar with the home.

Q: Would you generally spend the time back in his bedroom or out in the front room, living room or what?

A: Between the kitchen and, not too often in the bedroom, occasionally, but not too often, you know.

Q: Did you ever happen to see, or did he ever show you any of these...I guess you would have to call them for lack of anything else pornographic magazines, nudist magazines of one type or another.

A: Nudist magazines?

Q: Yes. They are not actually pornographic magazines; they are just nudist magazines.

A: I don't recall.

Q: Do you recall if he ever showed you any of them where he had mutilated the pictures as they existed by drawing a noose around the necks of women or by drawing bullet holes or blood?

A: Not that I recall.

Q: You didn't see anything like that? If you had seen a magazine of his with these drawings in it, you would have...?

A: Right I probably would have. Yes.

Q: He never showed you any photographs of mutilated women or anything?

A: Photographs of mutilated women? No, no.

Q: Actually, mutilated women or where he had mutilated pictures of women and photographs'?

A: Mutilated pictures of women and photographs? No. No.

Q: How about stories that he had written involving killing of women or persons being attacked. Did he ever show you any of those stories?

A: No, he just said he was a creative writer. I never read any of his junk.

Q: You never read any of his writings?

A: No.

Q: About how long a period of time would you say it was that you were dating or acquainted with Carmen Hallock?

A: Two or three weeks. That's about all. It was just a two, or three, week period there.

Q: You say John showed you or he saw the newspaper when she disappeared?

A: John showed it to me, and I said, "Boy that's weird," you know. So, what I did was I called the restaurant, you know. I said I was some credit agency to find out if they knew where she was, you know. They said, no, she just took off, you know. So, I didn't know anything more about that. This was right. There was another article in the paper. Maybe it was the same. I don't know. Anyways, when I was going up to school my mother had shown me this article about these...it must have been the second article in the paper about these two girls that were missing and everything like that.

Q: Did you ever meet personally Lee Hainline?

A: Lee Hainline, is this...

Q: The girl that lived a couple of doors from John, from his mother's house.

A: Maybe just to say hi, that's all, you know.

Q: Did you ever hear of a girl by the name of Kate Price or something like that?

A: Kay Price. I don't know. He introduced me to one other girl whose father was a piano player. OH, wait a minute, Kay Price. He was going with a girl when we were rooming, you know. Yeah to think about that too, he said that he didn't want me around that night, you know. So, I said I could dig it, you know. I left, you know. I came back, and she wasn't there. John made this big thing about telling me that they had had intercourse, but she had been menstruating, you know, so there was blood all over the place. I didn't ever see any blood because he had cleaned it all up. Is that supposed to be one of the girls that he murdered?

Q: We don't know as yet. She is not one of the ones that is listed as being attributed to him.

A: Is it a girl that is missing?

Q: We haven't been able to locate her. Let's put it that way. We have got very little identification.

A: After that I asked him where is that girl that you used to see? Oh, I just go over to her house now he used to say, but I never saw her after that.

Q: Have you seen her at all?

 A: Well no. The only reason I knew her was through Gerard.

Q: You had only talked to her. You hadn't seen the two of them together?

A: What do you mean together?

Q: Have you ever seen her?

A: Oh yeah, I've seen her, right.

Q: How would you describe her?

A: Red hair.

Q: Redhead?

A: Yeah.

Q: About how tall.

A: She was kind of a small girl. Maybe about 5'5" or something like that.

Q: Was she fairly slender build?

A: Yes, slender build. Not real good looking.

Q: Did you ever know John when he was friendly with or going with a crippled girl?

A: Right, right. I knew that girl. I can't think of her name.

Q: How long did John go with her?

A: I have no idea. That was one of the reasons why I left. She left, and then I left, you know. That was one of the most disgusting parts, you know, the whole thing was...

Q: Why? Why do you say that?

A: First of all, I couldn't figure out what the hell this girl, who could not take care of herself at all, was doing living here, you know.

Q: Where was she living?

A: Huh?

Q: Where was she living?

A: With us.

Q: She was living in the apartment?

A: Yeah. In this house. It was no apartment. It was a house.

Q: Where was this located? This is the place you were telling me about when you and John were staying together?

A: Right. There was only one place. It was that house over there.

Q: How long did she live there?

A: Quite a while. Almost as long as I was living there. She had a friend that was...it was real bad, you know, because she couldn't do anything for herself.

Q: Who would take care of her?

A: I would ordinarily, you know.

Q: Did John help take care of her at all?

A: John was usually at work or hunting or something. I don't know where he was, you know, but he was never around in the daytime. Man, that was a real...I didn't want any part of that, you know.

Q: Where did she sleep?

A: She slept with John.

Q: Did John ever discuss the nature of their sexual relations?

A: How should I know? I have no idea.

Q: He never mentioned it to you?

A: What? What they did?

Q: Yeah.

A: No, not that I can recall.

Q: Did John ever mention anything to you about any unusual sexual acts? Anal intercourse or anything of that type?

A: Unusual sexual activity? No, No.

Q: How about sodomy with animals? Did he ever mention anything about that to you? Killing any horses or cows?

A: Killing horses and cows?

Q: Cutting their heads off and having intercourse with them?

A: No, no. That would have blown my mind. I would have remembered that.

Q: I am sure you would have. How about some of these other girls that have been missing?

A: No, nothing.

Q: Did he ever mention Belinda Hutchins to you?

A: Belinda Hutchins. I don't know these names.

Q: Alleged prostitute.

A: Alleged prostitute. I don't know about alleged prostitutes or anything. There was a girl that he said he met in the library in...Mike has met her too. Her father was a musician and John was dating her. Then this other Kay Price, I believe it was, that girl that John was going with the red hair, kind of slight girl, right? That was another one that he was going with.

Q: Do you know where this Kay Price lived?

A: I have no idea. I never knew a thing about her except that she was going with John, you know.

Q: And he asked you to leave the apartment one night?

A: Yes.

Q: Did...were you dating any specific girls at that time?

A: No.

Q: Do you recall any occasion at all when you and John had had a disagreement because there was some question as to who some girl up there wanted to be with, whether it was with you or John?

A: A disagreement as to who...

Q: And John left, left you with the girl.

A: A disagreement as to who...

Q: Who the girl had to stay there with. She was hot for somebody, and John wasn't too interested in her, and he figured she was interested in you, so he left.

A: Who? Who was that?

Q: I don't know her name.

A: I think you are probably talking about this...the crippled girl whatever her name was. If you got that story from John, it must have been from her because there was no other girl living there, but okay. As far as that crippled girl goes, right, I was taking care of her. I didn't want to take care of her, but I was taking care of her, you know. As far as I could see, the best thing for her to do was to move out. She had no business living on her own, right.

Q: Did she have a family that you know of?

A: I had to drive her down to her family. I walked into this thing, you know. All of a sudden, I was nursemaid and chauffeur and everything else, you know. It was a real...I wasn't ready for any of this stuff. When I moved in with John, he had pills, man, and everything. There was people he knew doing marijuana. I didn't know about any of this stuff, you know. When I walked into this– as a matter of fact I had never lived, you know, had a roommate, you know, and that type of situation. I had been in the Navy, you know, but never, you know, just had a roommate and that type of deal. This whole thing was kind of like new to me, you know. I was trying to learn it, and it turned out to be a real . . .

Q: Real bummer?

A: A big bummer, right.

Q: Had you ever had sexual relations with this crippled girl while she was staying in the house?

A: Yes, yes. I'll tell you how it came about too. You know, like we were sitting in the kitchen, you know. All of a sudden, she said, do you want some or something like that? We were talking. She like...I figured she had a dress on, you know, but I didn't know whether to say yes or no, you know. I figured well, might as well say yes, you know. That is the way it came about.

Q: How old a girl was this?

A: I don't know. She was in her twenties.

Q: She may have been crippled, but she still knew what she liked?

A: I would guess so, yes. She was pretty intelligent. They said in the paper that he had some poetry, and she wrote a lot of poetry.

Q: She did?

A: Yeah. John had some. She wrote some pretty good poetry. I'll tell you what, personally I thought she was pretty decent, you know, for what she had to put up with.

Q: How was she actually crippled? I mean to what extent?

A: She didn't have voluntary control over her limbs.

Q: Both her arms and legs?

A: Yeah, right.

Q: Do you know what ever happened to her?

A: I have no idea. She wanted off at this woman that she knew, you know, but I thought it was a better place for her. At least this woman could take care of her properly.

Q: Did she have any means of support that you know of?

A: No. It was the damndest thing I ever saw. It was ridiculous. I really thought that when John brought this girl in that he really got himself into something, you know. He's really, you know... (It is interesting to note here, that if the accusations against Schaefer were true, particularly those derived from his own writings about sex with the dead, then the crippled girl may have been his own way of dealing with his bizarre urges. Perhaps to him, having sex with a girl who was virtually paralyzed from the neck down was as close to having sex with a corpse as he would come, at least at that point. And if this were true, after the girl's departure he would have had to resort to other ways of dealing with his psychopathic sexual urges. Author's notes.)

Q: Do you know where he ever met her?

A: At Henderson Clinic I think he said.

Q: Are you familiar with John's attendance at the Henderson Clinic?

A: I knew he attended.

Q: Did he ever discuss why he was attending?

A: No, that was one of the things I could never figure out about John. You know, he seemed all right to me, you know. I used to always tell him he was all right and everything like that, you know. But then he came up with this stuff, you know.

Q: Did he ever tell you that he heard voices at all?

A: No, no, nothing like that.

Q: Had you ever had sexual relations with this Carmen Hallock?

A: Yes.

Q: Frequently?

A: When I was dating her, yes.

Q: Did you ever have occasion to...this may sound stupid but...to observe her teeth?

A: No.

Q: Did you ever notice whether, or not she had any gold inlay work done at that time?

A: I don't even know what inlay is.

Q: Gold fillings, caps on her teeth.

A: She might have. I don't know.

Q: Do you recall ever having a conversation with John after Carmen disappeared concerning what happened to her as to her having been killed or killed and mutilated and her remains destroyed in any way?

A: No.

Q: Did you ever see any teeth in John's possession at all?

A: He had some stuff that he said he had collected, you know.

Q: Did you ever see any that had gold caps on them?

A: No, I never saw nothing like that, no. As a matter of fact, it was before I went in the service that he had shown me these little bones and everything. It was a long time ago.

Q: Did he tell you those were the Indian bones that he had brought back from Tennessee?

A: Yeah, yeah, something like that.

Q: Did you ever recall him making any mention at all of having... Carmen Hallock having been chopped up and disposed of at the city dump down there?

A: Jesus, no.

Q: You never made any such statement to John?

A: What? What was my statement supposed to be?

Q: That she had been chopped up and disposed of at the city dump?

A: That I said that to John? No, no. Wow. This is turning into kind of a bummer, man. I mean I am sitting here telling you my God damn life story, and I don't know you from Adam; right?

Q: Right.

A: Jesus.

Q: I got the job of trying to defend John and trying to do what is right for him. All I can do is try and find out everything that I possibly can. I am not trying to implicate anybody. I didn't even have to tell you that, but it is not an easy job. I sure don't enjoy working on the fourth of July. As a matter of fact, I have been working eighteen, twenty hours a day solid for three weeks just trying to find out all I can about what may have happened. How about, well you haven't known John in the last two years roughly?

A: No.

Q: Did you know his first wife, Marti, at all?

A: I met her a couple of times.

Q: What kind of girl did she seem to be?

A: Well I think she would have turned out to be a pretty good wife if John didn't, you know, move into that slum he moved into, and had treated her half way decent and didn't go hunting all the time and everything, she might have turned out to be a decent wife. She was not ready-made, you know...

Q: Did she appear to be a highly intellectual type?

A: Oh, yeah.

Q: Were they living in the same house that you subsequently stayed in there for about three or four weeks?

A: They had lived in that house. That's why he got the house originally. He was still living there after Marti moved out.

Q: You never heard of any girls by the name of Briscolina, Farmer, or Wilcox, Goodenough or Hutchins?

A: I don't recall any of those names.

Q: How about Susan Place and Georgia Jessup? Did you ever know them?

A: Susan Place and Georgia Jessup. No.

Q: Those are the two girls that he is charged with killing now. Is there anything else unusual that you ever noticed about John?

A: No. I—including my family, right—we all thought John was a little bit different, you know. We didn't know why, you know, but we figured that this is the way I thought, you know, that if he was a little bit different, you know, that he had been doing a lot of things. I can't help but thinking that there wouldn't have even been a golf team at Aquinas if he didn't want to play golf, you know. That kind of deal, you know.

Q: Pretty good athlete?

A: He wasn't in anything except golf, you know. And anything that he wanted to do, he could do. But it was always, you know, not something that was already doing. It was a new thing that just started. John was right there, you know.

Q: Did he appear to socialize readily with other people and in groups or did he prefer to be a loner?

A: I didn't know who his friends were. I assume that his friends were high school people in his neighborhood, you know, and not necessarily from school.

Q: How about afterwards when he was in junior college?

A: I didn't know who he knew in junior college or anything like that. Aside from the one date that we doubled on in high school and the fact that I had moved in, you know, with him for three weeks or so, right? This was the—the only real close contact like—I wasn't like his confidant. I know he had...he had this guy, yeah. What was his name? Webster. He was good friends with this guy, Webster, Jerry Webster.

Q: Is he the one that is up in Carolina some place?

A: Is Jerry Webster in Carolina?

Q: Have you seen him lately at all?

A: No. I haven t even seen any...I'm just up here, you know.

Q: Did John ever meet Carmen Hallock do you know?

A: Meet her?

Q: Yeah, know her?

A: No, I had no idea that John knew Carmen Hallock. There is no way that...if he knew her, he knew from sources outside of the place that I knew her. She used to hang around at the Veteran's Club Table. That's where l met her. John was nowhere near this Veteran's Club Table because he was up at FAU, so if he had met Carmen Hallock, you know, it was through ways and different set of circumstances from the way I met her.

Q: Do you know where she worked while you knew her or while you were dating her?

A: Yeah. That was the place I called. It was the Round Table.

Q: Was she a waitress there?

A: Yeah, I guess so.

Q: And the first time that you knew that John even knew Carmen Hallock was he showed you the newspaper clipping of the article on her disappearance along with Lee Hainline?

A: The first time that I knew...I had always been saying, "You know I ought to go back and see Candy Carmen), you know." But I never did it, you know. Then I found out she was gone, you know. But I always had in the back of my mind that I would go back and see her again some time. I didn't know, you know...John shows me this article and said she is gone.

Q: How did you and she happen to break up?

A: It was more having to do with...she told me that she had met this guy, you know. She said that this guy had...she really dug this dude, you know.

Q: Did she ever mention his name?

A: No, no. She said he was a sailor or some shit. I, you know, couldn't find out if she was really into it, you know.

Q: Did she mess around with drugs at all do you know?

A: Not that I know of. We never did.

Q: You ever smoked pot together?

A: No, no.

Q: After she told you about meeting this sailor or whatever he was, that was pretty much the last time you saw her?

A: Right, right. We never had an argument, though, but you know, it was just kind of like, you know...

Q: She went her way and you went yours?

A: Yeah. Like your time is up, you know.

Q: You say John never knew her at the time you were going with her to your knowledge?

A: No, no.

Q: He never expressed an interest in going out with her himself? He might have been jealous of you or something?

A: No, I didn't even know John at the time. I was living at home. I had not seen John for quite a while, you know, when I was dating this Hallock girl.

Q: You had known John prior to that time?

A: Oh yes. He would have no way of knowing that I was going with her at the time I was going with her.

Q: Had you ever talked to John at all about her after you had stopped going with her?

A: Yeah, I might have one or two times. But, you know, it was just passing conversation.

Q: So, John did know that you had been going with her?

A: Right, right.

Q: What I am trying to get at, Jack, is trying to figure out why John would have been considering making these statements that he made concerning her and you.

A: What statements?

Q: The fact that you may know something about her disappearance.

A: John says that about...well I'll tell you. I don't...I am not into, you know, I haven't talked to John, right, or anything like that.

Q: In the past two years?

A: Right. I am not killing anybody, right?

Q: No one other than John has made any...tying it in with anybody. I am not trying to at this time, but I am trying to figure out why John would have made this statement. What he knew about you and Carmen's relationship that would cause him to even...

A: The only thing that I could think of is his maybe kind of guilt transfer, you know, that type of thing, you know. That is the only thing that I can think of, you know.

Q: Had he ever given any indication of this regarding anybody else in the past while you knew him? Something that you may know that he had done, and that he tried to pass the buck on to somebody else?

A: Pass the buck on to somebody else? See I didn't know him that well. I'm sure he was capable of doing that though. Oh yeah, there might have been some things with this fraternity we were in, you know, that... somebody said he stole a gun or something like that, you know. He was pretty...if you asked him about it, you know, he had something set up, you know, where somebody else did it or something like that. He was pretty good at that, I would say.

Q: You don't recall any specific instances though, other than possibly a gun situation?

A: Yeah, we had a little gun in this house we had, and it was gone, you know, stolen.

Q: Do you recall what kind of gun it was?

A: No, I never saw it except it was in this box.

Q: During the time that you knew John, did you ever suspect that he may have had any homosexual tendencies of any type?

A: Homosexual? No, no, I never thought of John as a homosexual. I just thought of him as kind of messed up. I mean he got married, you know, right? He tried to do the best he could, you know, he was just messed up. As far as I could see, you know, he was just messed up. I don't put that blame any more than fifty per cent on anyone else. It was at least half John's fault.

Q: Let's see, you knew his sister, Sadie, I think also, didn't you?

A: Yeah, I dated her a couple of times or once or twice. I don't know.

Q: Did she ever mention anything unusual about John?

A: No, no. See Sadie, you know, if it could be avoided, wouldn't want to talk…Sadie, the only thing that Sadie would ever say to me about John, you know, was some nice thing, you know.

Q: There appeared to be a fairly good brother and sister relationship between them?

A: No, no, it didn't appear that way. But I mean, you know, they weren't about to let me know about it.

Q: Do you have any idea what the problem was between the two of them?

A: I had no idea that there was a problem. They just seemed to me, you know, just knowing like with my own sister and me, you know, that's it both about the same, you know, or something like that, you know.

Q: Did you ever see John collect articles of women's clothing at all or have any unusual amount of women's clothing in his possession?

A: Unusual amount of women's clothing, no.

Q: For a single man, I assume any amount of women's clothing would be somewhat unusual.

A: No, no, I don't recall anything like that.

Q: From all appearances, John was completely heterosexual. He was normally interested in girls?

A: As far as I could tell, yeah.

Q: Was there anything else about John that you could think of that might be of value in trying to recreate his life history or try to figure out what kind of problem he might have had?

A: Just that I would be reluctant to testify in his behalf.

Q: For what reason?

A: I think, you know, I think that there is twenty some odd dead people who were in separate little files, you know. Then they ran through his movements and put them all together. There wouldn't be these twenty some odd murders if there wasn't a John Schaefer. So, in—just from the things that he had said to me and everything like that, and his attitude towards me, right, I feel in some ways, you know, that I have been the brunt of a pretty bad joke in some cases.

Q: Has anybody ever mentioned before I had now about John making any statements concerning you at all?

A: No, but I would assume...I would have guessed in fact that he would.

Q: Why do you say that? You as opposed to any other friends that he might have. Were there any ill feelings between the two of you that you can remember?

A: Right, right. If somebody asked me about John Schaefer, would have to say he's...I get that feeling of animosity, you know, after...I really did not have anything to do with him, you know. After I moved out, I had gone to see him a couple of more times. Then I said, this is, you know...

Q: But you never recall any specific arguments or disagreements that you had other than the one argument that you don't remember what you were arguing about? You had just taken opposite views?

A: Right. That's about it you know. I didn't take an opposite view. He assumed that I had though. I really don't know what he was arguing about. There was things like that—when I moved out of there, I had said to myself, you know, when I move out of there, I can't tell him like I am going to move tomorrow, you know. I have just got to get my stuff and move out right like that, get out, you know.

Q: Why?

A: I was afraid of him. I don't know, I really don't know why I was so afraid of him, you know, but I was afraid of him.

Q: I am sure you read in the newspapers and that the manner in which these two girls, Susan Place and Georgia Jessup, were mutilated. They were decapitated, various limbs removed, the torso of the body was cut in half. From your relationship with John, would you consider him the type of an individual that would do such a thing to an attractive young woman?

A: Well who would, right?

Q: That is what I am getting at.

A: Well, who would? So, you can't say that John is as good as anybody, you know. I mean just to look at a person and say, this guy does that, you know, or this guy does that, you know.

Q: Did he ever talk to you at all about how wrong it was to allow loose women to be walking around the street—girls hitchhiking and prostitutes, picking up guys and rolling them?

A: No, no.

Q: Did you ever see John really lose his temper at all?

A: Just one time that I really felt, you know, I never expected John to really swing on anybody. This is one thing about John, you know. When I was in the service, you know, you kind of learn to size up a person, you know, by should you get into a fight with him, you know. Would that person, you know, like if you were losing, would that person just keep on you? Would that person fight you and wait and hit you in the back of the head with a pipe or something like that, you know, that kind of a person, you know. Just exactly what type. It always appeared to me that John was the type of person that wouldn't fight no matter what you did to him, you know. He would wait and get you some other time.

Q: Did he ever tell you about an instance where a woman ran him off the road, and he later went back and slashed her tires up?

A: He told me one time that he blew up a car, but I don't know about any tire slashing.

Q: Do you recall when it was, he told you about blowing up a car?

A: This is when I was living with him. All of this stuff is going in my mind, and then got to get out of there, you know.

Q: Have you talked to any law enforcement officers or representatives of the State Attorney's Office at all either concerning John, or Carmen Hallock?

A: No, no, no.

Q: Nobody has ever contacted you concerning your relationship with John or any of these other people?

A: No. You are the first person who has contacted me, and I would be reluctant to get involved at all, but I would...

Q: Any particular reason why you would be reluctant to get involved in it?

A: To get involved in this thing?

Q: Other than the fact that it is time consuming to have to go sit around and wait.

A: Right. That one and...I don't think that there is much point to it. I think that I probably could get myself into trouble doing it.

Q: Why?

A: Because I see myself as that dude, you know, that John is trying to slip it to.

Q: I don't know why he would select you over any other friends.

A: Okay, has he selected me over any other?

Q: You are the only one that he has mentioned.

A: There.

Q: Of course, from what I know you are the only friend of his that knew Carmen Hallock. He has never referred to Mike or Webster.

A: I knew Carmen Hallock, but I didn't know her at the time—no, no, I only knew her for a short period of time, a couple of weeks, right? How did John say that he knew that I was going with Carmen Hallock at the time that I was going with her? That would be an interesting question.

Q: I haven't gotten into the point with him yet as how he knew it.

A: That would be something I would like to know myself.

Q: John never mentioned anything at all about killing anyone?

A: No, no.

Q: Or a desire to kill women?

A: The only killing that you can relate to him is by virtue of his going out and hunting animals?

A: Uh-huh.

Q: Did John carry a gun at all that you know of?

A: Oh, he always had guns, knives, axes, and machetes, and everything in the back of his Volkswagen, you know. That is another reason why I left. He had that dog—I had a convertible you know, with the bucket seats like this. He put his dog in the back seat, and the dog would just drool all over everything you know, puke in the back seat, you know, and everything. He was so disgusting, you know. He was just unbelievable.

Q: Do you recall the dog's name off hand?

A: Spot or something. I don't know.

Q: Did you know John when the dog died? John put it out of . . .

A: No. I didn't know that the dog had died.

Q: You say you knew that John was undergoing psychiatric treatment at Henderson Clinic?

A: He had told me that, right.

Q: Did he tell you that his wife, Marti, was also receiving consultation with the psychiatrist?

A: No.

Q: Did you ever know John's father?

A: No, never met him.

Q: How about his brother, Gary?

A: Yeah, I knew him.

Q: Did you ever notice anything unusual about Gary?

A: He seemed to me to be a little bit kind of weird when he was younger, you know, but he seemed to get kind of squared away when he got older.

Q: You never noticed him talking about anything strange?

A: No, no.

Q: Would you say that John was basically a lazy type individual?

A: He was slow moving, yeah.

Q: The type of individual that would go out and dig a hole 3x 5 foot and four feet deep without using it?

A: You couldn't tell about John. John would do what he wanted to do, you know. Like I say man, the dude would get up at 3:30, you know, and load all that stuff into his car and head out into the Everglades. You know, that is some effort, you know, to be doing that stuff.

Q: Hunting trips?

A: Yeah. If he wanted...there was nothing, you know, that I would...if he wanted to dig a big hole, he sure wasn't you know...

Q: Did you ever notice him carry his shovel around with him at all?

A: A shovel. He might have had one in the junk in his car.

Q: You don't recall ever specifically seeing one?

A: No.

Q: I'll tell you there are a lot of weird things about this case. Nothing fits into place, especially how these things could have possibly gone on over such a period of time without somebody suspecting something.

A: I don't think that the girl that lived two-doors...

Q: Lee Hainline?

A: Right. Didn't her father or anybody ever—I would think that that would be the first clue, you know. Her father would have suspected something, you know, with John.

Q: Was there anything unusual about their relationship? She did live a couple of doors from him, and she was about the same age as John.

A: He didn't think of her as the same age. He thought of her as older, I think. I think that was the deal.

Q: What do you recall him ever telling you about Lee?

A: That she was really sharp, you know. He said he can stand up and watch her change her clothes sometimes from the window, you know.

Q: Did he invite you over to watch?

A: I was never over there at the right time,

Q: To your knowledge, you never saw Lee at all?

A: Oh, I met her, you know, she was working at the (indistinguishable), you know. I saw her every once in a while, you know. I didn't even know her well enough to say hi if I saw her, you know. She...

Q: You never dated her or anything?

A: No. If she came up and took my order, I would just give her my order and, you know, that would be it.

Q: I know once I leave, I will think of a million questions to ask you. I don't want to inconvenience you having to come back later on. Is there anything else that you can think of that might be of any assistance or value at all to try and make heads or tails out of the situation? Did you ever see anybody ridicule John or laugh at him? Make a joke out of something he was trying to be serious about?

A: Something he was trying to be serious about. I don't know when John—I might have done that myself, but I really don't know, you know, if there was something funny that John said, you know, something that John would start to talk about or anybody. If they start talking, they start getting weird, you know, you laugh and you say, you know, get out of here, and all this stuff, you know.

Q: Did any girls do that to him while he was trying to carry on a serious conversation with them about something and they tried to make a joke out of it or tell John he doesn't know what he is talking about or laugh at him?

A: No, no.

Q: There is nothing else you can think of about John?

A: No, I can't think of ...

Q: Well I sure appreciate your taking the time to talk to me about it, Jack...

A: I wish you luck, you know, but not too much, you know.

Q: John, the doctors that have been examining him the last several years, actually pretty well agree, that John is sick. Obviously if he did these things, he is very sick. If he did them, I think he belongs in a mental hospital rather than in jail. It would take a pretty sick person to do these things.

A: If he did them, the way I look at it, I don't see any way how they could ever, you know, rehabilitate him good enough to let him out, you know.

Q: He is still sick. Some of the things we have found in his possession. Do you think of there being any possible way with the time that you spent over at his house and that he could have had anywhere from 175 to 200 of these nudist magazines that obviously he spent years or many months at least drawing pictures in.

A: I never saw, you know, any nudist magazines over there, but that is not to say that I saw everything that John had, you know. He had boxes all over the place. He had this big desk that he brought over from his house real thick, strong, not too well painted desk. He had all his shotgun shells and knives all over the place. There was a lot of junk, you know, kind of like he moved his whole side of his bedroom, you know, right into there. It looked exactly the same, you know, the same junk all over the place and everything.

Q: He never actually discussed having intercourse with dead bodies.

A: No, the only thing that he said to me that one time was that he drank blood. I was trying to think of it in relation, you know, something that—I don't know—hunting, you know, they take the blood and put it on their forehead or some shit like this, you know, and kind of got carried away or something. I don't know, you know.

Q: A little bit far out?

A: Yeah.

Q: Okay, well I have got to get back up to Stuart this afternoon to get ready to take more depositions tomorrow.

A: Yeah.

Q: So, I do appreciate talking with you, and I've got your phone number if I do have to get a hold of you some time. I'll give you a call. You will be here at least until December, I assume.

A: EHow long is this thing going to go on for John here?

Q: We have no idea at this point.

A: Are you a regular criminal attorney?

Q: I am a Public Defender up there for the 19th Circuit.

A: Oh.

Q: I have taken over this case myself mainly. I've got a couple of my assistants working with me, but most of the stuff I am doing personally. So, I will be following it through until it is over with, I imagine.

A: Man, this is a real bad thing, you know. There is not too much I can say about it. I can see how it is going to get drawn out and everything. I don't see that there is anything really material that I could add, you know, to any part of the, you know.

Q: The only thing that I might mention is that I would probably have to list you as being one person who may have known John during a relevant period of time involved here, in which case the State Attorney may want to talk to you.

A: I'll be glad to talk to him.

Q: You don't think that if he talks to you that there is anything that you could possibly tell him that you can think of now that you haven't mentioned to us?

A: No, as a matter of fact, I've said about more than I think I should say, you know. I could have probably held a couple of things back, but this is about the whole story that I know.

Q: All I care about is that everybody tells it the way it is.

Here we must make some observations. One: It is interesting to note that Schwarz asked Dolan if he knew K-a-t-e- Price. Dolan, after stammering around a bit, says, "K-a-y" Price, before a sudden recall of his memory. Two: The story about the ". . . blood all over the place" Could it have been that the girl was murdered that night and Dolan stumbled innocently onto the scene only to be misdirected by Schaefer? Or, did Dolan know more? Had he really just turned and left the scene, no questions asked? Was Dolan one of the other persons Stone was investigating? After all, Stone had said they had "linked some of the murders, but not to one individual," Who were the other suspects?

For now, Dolan was ruled out as a suspect. But Stone wondered who was "John-O," real name John O'Riley, who scribed the following letter to Schaefer from East Brunswich, Victoria, Australia. Local authorities and Interpol agents could not answer that question, and Schaefer was quite vague as to the identity of his Aussie friend. He mentioned only that he was a friend he had met in his overseas travels, a mercenary soldier and guide whom he befriended. But we can clearly see at least three points of interest in the following letter.

One: that Schaefer used drugs (hash) or that he at least associated with people who did. (A fact of his character that he would consistently deny). Two: that Schaefer was indeed in Morocco. Though his actions there are still unknown, the letter would suggest that he, and his friend "John-O" had witnessed and photographed some type of massacre. The psychological effects of such a sighting can only be the subject of speculation. Three: that Schaefer had, and possibly shared with others, a perverse interest in death. The pictures sent with this letter were terrifying photographs of grotesquely mutilated women. Some of them hacked apart vertically, from crotch to cranium, almost in half.

```
July 20, 1971

Hey Buddy!
    How's the action in the USA these days?
Bloody quiet here in Victoria. What ya say
we head out to the Sudan you and me and
check out the coup there. We can drift on
South into Kenya and see the animals and
maybe get a boy to guide us up Kilimanjaro.
    I'm sending another bunch of pictures.
Most are from that village in the Sahara
the wogs massacred while we were in Morocco
last summer. Lots of nice European stuff died
```

there. You ever send your pics to the U.N.? I don't think they could do much anyway.

I numbered the ones you didn't see. The others are mostly just shots of those murdered Europeans. Some Arabs too. Pics 10-86 you probably remember yourself. I'm sending these in case some of yours didn't come out. You know these are probably the only pics around of that massacre. Lot of European stuff on film as well as some of the Arab talent too. Hope I don't get in trouble for sending this stuff through the mail. I hear your gov't is tough on the nude women scene. I've got a lot of other pics. Some you missed out on, so I'll have to mail you copies if these get through OK.

How was the hash in the last envelope? Good Stuff that Lisbon Red. Keep the faith brother.

John O'

P.S. You know any blokes who want to go into the bush in Sept.-Oct. Let me know I'll be in touch. They've gotta be tough and wonna make (indistinguishable) you know the type.

Chapter 8

The Victims

It was this unfathomable longing of the soul to vex itself
. . . to offer violence to its own nature, to do wrong for
wrong's sake only . . . that urged me to continue . . .

From *The Black Cat* by Edgar Allan Poe

The fate of Georgia Jessup and Susan Place was known. But what of the remaining "List of 28" possible victims? How accurate was the list? Was the list a compilation of unconnected missing persons, and unsolved murders, a desperate "grabbing at straws" attempt, as Schaefer's defenders would say, to discredit the defendant and make up for an inadequate, circumstantial, and insecure prosecution case by a state attorney who'd been in office only a few months? Or was the list completely inaccurate, not only in "selected victims" but in sheer number; was it, in truth, only the tip of the iceberg?

The whole truth will forever be subjective theorizing at best. Whenever there are multiple versions of any one story, the real story becomes more and more elusive as the multiplicity expands. For each person there is a different story, a different truth. With almost one hundred people subpoenaed by the prosecution alone, it goes without saying there would be many "truths" told in this case.

However, a basis of *a* truth, of what had to have happened does exist. A logic based "common sensing" if you will. Hundreds of people are listed as missing in South Florida every year. Many are found dead, their killers found only some of the time, and successfully prosecuted even less than that. The basis of truth that we can reasonably believe, in Gerard Schaefer's case, must be assembled from several sources, and it must be kept in mind that we initially worked only with the State Attorney's "List of 28" as our guide. Those sources were the facts as presented to this reporter, as found in police and forensic reports, personal interviews with as many people connected with this case as possible, and of some speculation to be completely honest, based on knowledge of the case and the killer that I came to know. Schaefer's version of "facts" became more unreliable as his story changed to manipulate the truth. This then, is the basis of the facts as we came to know them.

The following dissertation of who the victims were and what happened to them, or was believed to have happened to them, is not conclusive. It is simply our best effort to present as accurate a picture to the observer as is humanly possible, of events that most probably happened in some cases, and absolutely did happen in others. We did investigate some additional cases and possible victims that Schaefer, himself, provided to us. Such evidence is presented to the readers to allow them to form their own opinions and make up their own minds about the strange case of Gerard Schaefer, and the fate of these twenty-eight people.

In presenting this information, we listed the names in the same order as they have been previously listed, earlier in this book. This is for reasons of clarity only, to present information in a logical order and is not, chronologically, the order in which the information was obtained, nor is it arranged in terms of priority.

Though some of these cases yielded little or no information, all were equally important as the next. Some cases are clearly more detailed, simply because more information was existent, and available for those cases, while others were inconclusive, or led to dead ends. All the persons named on the List of 28, as we came to know it, were investigated. The following is a register, if you will, of those people and what happened to them, as best as we could uncover, given the length of time elapsed since the Schaefer case began, and consequently the information that time (and other factors) invariably obscured or erased up. I write this to caution those who still seek an answer that cannot be finalized due to lack of records, and/or little to no investigations into those individual cases.

In fact, when Schaefer finally looked at this list and commented on it, he wrote, "Turning to your list, the correct number is 34, not 28. '6 DEAD, 28 MAYBE' that equals 34. Let us not be selling the numbers short after all these years." Schaefer was referring to the headlines of the May 13, 1973 Palm Beach Post-Times' article, though in truth, he misunderstood the content of that article. But, upon quoting the 34 number, Schaefer went as far as issuing a few more names, to be "put on the list," that I had not seen before. These names he said, he drew from letters, sent to him by investigators, from agencies interested in his possible involvement with these girls' disappearances and/or homicides.

The additional names he gave this writer were: Nancy Leichner and Pamela Nater, who disappeared in Ocala National Forest on October 2, 1966. While it is commonly believed they drowned while swimming, their bodies were never found and for reasons, upon which we can only speculate, Schaefer decided to add them to own his list of suspected kills (while also proclaiming his innocence). Could he have wandered up to the central Florida forest and murdered them? It's a possibility, but there is no hard evidence to come to that conclusion other than some similarities to his usual method of operations: two young women gone missing at the same time and his penchant for abducting two girls at once.

Leichner and Nater, were on a diving trip in Ocala National Forest. The water was too cold for them, but their boyfriends dove in, then took a canoe ride. When they returned, all they found were some personal items of the girls who seem to have vanished. Nancy was seen by other hikers on a trail about 12:30pm and Pamela about an hour later by another hiker. The Lake County Sheriff's office does believe they were abducted and killed but there were no bodies found nor any physical evidence to tie them to Schaefer.

Two others were sisters, Maggie and Mary Jenkins, whose remains were found in a wooded area in Key Largo, Florida on May 3, 1973. They were last seen near Stock Island, just north of Key West the night before, hitchhiking. While their profile fits that of Schaefer's victims, he was already incarcerated in the Spring of 1973. I talked to Lt. James Newton of the Monroe County Sheriff's office as recent as July, 2019 and he followed up with the DNA database from the Florida Department of Law Enforcement and confirmed that they did compare Schaefer's DNA to that which was found at the Jenkin's crime scene but it did not match and there was a new investigation into another serial killer that might shed light on the girl's fate.

So, that is a total of four which, if we included them in the list we already had, would give us a total of 32, not 34. In truth, at that time, we could find no police agency that had any information that would connect Schaefer to those four cases, any more than any unsolved disappearance or murder in Florida, pre-1973.

Now, it is possible that some of the persons named, on the list of 28, are alive. If that is the case, and we were able to find them, then it is noted. However, there were inevitably, a few missing who remained elusive to our investigations, and it is quite possible that following the publication of this story, these people may surface. Here then, is what we know of the "list of 28," in numerical order.

* * *

The destinies of both (Victim 1) Susan Place, and (Victim 2) Georgia Jessup have been dealt with previously in this book. This is not an attempt to belittle their cases, nor their short and tragic lives. Rather, for the sake of brevity, we will not again go over their cases here, and in keeping with the theme of registration for this list, we will say at this point that both girls were known to be dead, victims of foul play. Their accused killer, Gerard Schaefer, incarcerated and awaiting trial for two counts of murder in the first degree.

* * *

The city of Plantation is a nice community. A suburb of Fort Lauderdale that is spruced up and washed behind the ears. Here, the powers that be don't mind paying the extra dollars it takes to maintain good, smooth roads and manicured landscaping. The police department is an elegant building and, of course, very clean. People like to live here and vacation with friends who reside here. Like so much of Fort Lauderdale and its surrounding suburbs, it has had its problems. The transients. The drugs, and, a few murders. Victims number three and four, Mary Briscolina and Elsie Farmer, schoolgirls, aged 14, were killed here.

At approximately 4:00 p.m., on Wednesday, January 17, 1973, James Christian and Dominic Bengivengo were surveying an empty lot in preparation for the future construction of Apple Creek Condominiums. At a site, approximately forty yards north of the main road, Sunrise Blvd., Christian spread open the legs of a transit, a surveying tool that resembles a three-legged spider on stilts and planted its pointed feet into the sandy soil. Bengivengo went ahead with the survey stick that measures the relative elevation of the land. He chose a random spot, to get a quick elevation check and as he turned, he noticed Christian cautiously probing into some bushes near the transit. As Christian was setting up, a flash of burgundy appeared out of the corner of his eye. It was a pair of hip hugger slacks. They belonged to the corpse that lay approximately twelve feet to the west.

The corpse still wore a shirt, red, white and blue, the buttons still neatly closed. The body lay with its legs spread wide apart, badly decomposed, except for the hands which were partially covered by the soil, and so, miraculously well-preserved. Those hands would tell the story that this body had not gone down without a fight, the fingernails were broken off and several of them were found nearby, rain-beaten beneath the soil. The corpse's head had been battered; the lower jaw broken into numerous pieces. It would later be theorized that the head blow was indeed the death blow, and its extremely violent nature was because of the victim's struggling. She had not wanted to be sexually assaulted while alive and was not. However, due to the placement of the limbs of the body, it is almost definite that she was assaulted after death, while her head lay in a puddle of blood and splintered bone fragments, having been severed from the body. It would take a particularly demented killer to perform such an atrocity, one that was not only a necrophiliac, but one who would deliberately kill the victim in order to have sex with the dead bodies.

This corpse, who met such a tragic and violent end, was Mary Alice Briscolina (Victim 3). She was fourteen.

Detectives Ben Butler (now Capt. Butler) and Carl Ragucci were dispatched to the scene to begin the investigation. Later, Detectives Tom Edwards and Carl Carruthers would also join in. The investigation began and went smoothly enough, the detectives combed the area for clues until dark, posted guards to secure the area, and went home for a good night's rest. The following day they returned, accompanied by two city employees for help with labor, and several excavation tools, including "rakes, shovels, and large and small screen wire." The detectives found a small pair of ladies' pink stretch panties, nine feet-two inches from the body, under some bushes. They dug an area around the body in a square, approximately 6 feet by 6 feet, and 8 inches deep, and began screening dirt, first with the large screen, then with the small. During this process they found three fingernails, one tooth (the only one missing from the victim's battered skull) and several small bones.

All evidence was turned over to the medical examiner, Dr. G. Mann. Dr. Mann quickly deduced that the body was that of a white female, approximately 16 to 22 years old, 5' 5" to 5'7" in height, weighing about 120 to 135 pounds, with medium to dark brown hair. Estimated time of death was between 1 and 6 months, but probably closer to 2 or 3 months. The identity was unknown. And so, it would go. No one would find the identity of this female corpse for some time. Not until after they found the second corpse, about one month later.

On February 15th, as plans got under way for the construction of Apple Creek Condominiums, the land clearing process began. A bulldozer operator spied another body, just before plowing under it with his "bucket." This body was almost identical in its placement, state of decomposition, and the method used for its untimely demise. This body was Elsie Lina Farmer (Victim 4), though again it was impossible to identify yet.

When the first body was found, it received some attention in the local newspapers, but when the second was found only 200 yards away from the first, all of the news media began to develop an interest. Who were these young girls who were mysteriously whisked away, brought to a vacant lot off a heavily traveled boulevard, bludgeoned to death and sexually assaulted? Were they murdered at the same time, or was one forced to endure the painful wails of the other as she was systematically raped and beaten to death? The news coverage was, at first, relentless, but just as suddenly—without any suspects in custody, and the identities of the murdered girls still unrevealed—the news media lost interest.

One man had not lost interest, however; Mary Alice Briscolina's father. Anthony Briscolina had been watching the news, carefully, since hearing of the discovery of the first body. His daughter had left home in October of '72 and neither he nor Mrs. Briscolina had heard from her.

Mr. Briscolina went to his daughter's dentist and requested a copy of her records, to be furnished to the Plantation Police Department. Dr. Paul Talchik complied and sent a copy of Mary's records to the medical examiner's office. They were immediately compared to the teeth of the girls who'd been found in the empty lot, and a positive match was made, identifying the first body as that of Mary Briscolina. Then, things began to come together.

Mary Briscolina and Elsie Farmer were not angels. The weeks prior to their murders were spent in the company of several older boys and men, some well into their twenties, many with records of prior drug arrests. Gerard Schaefer is quick to point this out, and add that it is possible, that these two girls were murdered in connection with a drug deal gone awry, or for being "narcs" working with local authorities. But it should be noted that he levels the same accusations at Susan Place and Georgia Jessup, and investigations have shown no concrete evidence that would support those accusations. It should also be noted that it is not the moral judgments of Mary Briscolina and Elsie Farmer that is under investigation here. It is the question of who murdered these girls. Once again, Schaefer is the prime suspect.

These are the facts as we came to know them:

According to Mary's younger sister, Alicia, Mary was "running away." She'd come in late, "stoned...both from drugs and alcohol," and she'd argued with her mother. Elsie was with her, and two boys, Bob Wyatt, and John Higgins, waited outside, in a car. Mary and Elsie both took showers, and Mary had already packed some clothes which she took with her when she left. The following day, October 22, 1972, Mary returned home; her parents were not there. Mary told Alicia she wanted her to help her run away, and picked and picked out some additional clothes, including some "maroon hip-hugger pants." The same pants that would be found nearby her body a few months later.

Alicia saw her sister again, for the last time, at John Higgins' house in the company of several older boys, who would later be found to have had drug arrest records. Both Mary and Elsie were "stoned," and Mary was argumentative with Alicia who pleaded with her to return home. Mary said she would return home the next day. That was on Wednesday, and when Mary failed to return home, Alicia asked around, and friends said they'd seen her on Thursday night. Then she vanished, as did Elsie Farmer. Elsie lived with her half-sister, Linda Walker, 22, and her husband, Robert Walker, 29, in a mobile home just north of Commercial Boulevard, in Fort Lauderdale. Mrs. Walker recalled the last day she'd seen Elsie was at their trailer, the morning of October 24, 1972. She was with Mary, John Higgins, another boy, Russ Coleman, and they had Bob Wyatt's car, a white Buick. Mrs. Walker had a doctor's appointment and she left. Upon returning, Elsie and her friends were gone, but she'd left a note on the refrigerator that said she'd be back shortly. She never returned. By that evening, when Elsie had not returned home, Linda and Robert Walker got in their car and began searching for her, investigating all her hangouts, with no luck. They filed a missing person's report the next day.

It has been established that the girls and their male friends, Higgins, Wyatt, Coleman and several other young men went to an apartment at Lauderdale by the Sea, where they all "hung-out." This was a popular place for this group, and they would sit around and play music, get stoned, and meet there when they wanted to get away from their homes and authority. This is also the place both Mary and Elsie were last seen. Several people stayed there, transiently, and the apartment and its occupants had a record of complaints filed with the local police. When Mary and Elsie went missing, the police interrogated everyone they could find who had any connection with the "party apartment."

At first, the investigation went nowhere, and eventually came to a dead end. Then, several months later, investigators Carl Carruthers and Carl Ragucci were given the name of Raymond Cummings. Cummings was a friend of John Higgins, and when the Place/Jessup murder trial began to seize media attention, Cummings recognized a picture of Schaefer in one of the local newspapers. Cummings showed the picture to Higgins, who also recognized the face, but both Higgins and Cummings had known the man in the picture as Gary Sheppard, not Gerard Schaefer. Furthermore, Cummings recalled that "Gary Sheppard" worked at the Becker Window Company in Oakland Park, and that on two separate occasions he did see "Sheppard" with Mary Briscolina. At those times, "Sheppard" was driving a '68 or '69 blue Lincoln convertible. Cummings also stated that "Sheppard" had told him that he was an ex-Wilton Manors police officer. Additionally, Higgins stated that he'd seen "Sheppard" with Mary Briscolina and that he'd been driving a blue Lincoln. He added that Mary was dating Robert (Bob) Wyatt at that time and that Wyatt had split up with Mary, because he thought she was "seeing this guy Gary. "Higgins and Cummings agreed that as far as they knew, the driver of the blue Lincoln had an apartment over the Becker Windows Company, where he lived for a brief time. Higgins went on to add that it was his sister Sharon who lived in the apartment at Lauderdale by the Sea, the "party apartment" and that Mary and Elsie had asked her if they could stay there since they had run away. Their request was denied, and Sharon Higgins told her brother that the last time she'd seen the two girls, they were getting into a blue Lincoln convertible with a man known as "Gary."

Ragucci then went to see Bob Wyatt. Wyatt stated that he did see a Becker Window Company truck, not a blue Lincoln, pick up Mary at her residence and he did break up with her because of this. Though he had not seen the driver, he assumed it was William Becker, the son of the owner of the company. He also said he'd seen the blue Lincoln at the Becker Window Company but did not know who owned it.

The next person questioned was Alvaney Munroe, then an employee of the Becker Window Company. Munroe told Inspector Ragucci that he did know a Gary that worked at Becker, "about a year ago"(which would have been in the fall of '72). When shown a picture of Gerard Schaefer, Munroe immediately identified him as the man he knew as "Gary." Munroe added that "Gary" had stayed in a room over the company building, which was also shared by Bond Electric Service.

Edmund Casoria, the owner of Bond Electric, was contacted next. Casoria told Ragucci that he had not rented the room in question to anyone, but he did remember on one occasion he'd let a man use it for three days "about a year ago." He did not remember the man's name, but when shown a photograph of Gerard Schaefer he positively identified Schaefer as the same man.

Next, Ragucci questioned William Louis Becker, Sr., the owner of the window company. Becker said that he did have an employee at one time, who drove a blue Lincoln, whose name was not Gary, but Ronnie Ray Minton. Minton had worked for Becker "approximately 12-13 months ago," (again, the fall of '72) but was terminated after only about a week because of a "disagreement." Minton had also told Becker that he'd been a police officer before but did not say where. When shown a picture of Gerard Schaefer, Becker told Ragucci that that was the man he'd known as Ronnie Ray Minton. Becker added that Minton, or Schaefer as the case may be, never drove a Becker truck, but that he, himself, had drove Mary Briscolina home in a company truck. Becker also stated that the only thing he ever saw "Minton" drive was a blue Lincoln convertible.

Later, two cashed payroll checks were found, payable to Ronnie Minton. The checks were dated March 31, 1972 and April 6, 1972. A notation was made, by Ragucci, to compare the signature of Minton on the back of the checks to that of Gerard Schaefer, but apparently this was never done. Nor is there any record of an attempt to compare the Social Security numbers of Schaefer and Minton. For that matter it is not documented how extensively Minton or Gary Sheppard were sought. But the following facts stand out:

1.) Within the evidence seized in the Schaefers' home, no title or registration were found linking Schaefer with a Lincoln convertible, which some investigators suggest may have been stolen or borrowed. Additionally, no identification was found with the name Ronnie Ray Minton, nor Gary Sheppard. However, there was the one letter from Georgia Jessup to "Jerry *Shepard*," and this is also the name with which Schaefer was introduced to Lucille and Susan Place.

2.) At least four separate people identified Schaefer as being "Gary Sheppard" (similar enough to "Jerry Shepard) and Shepard knew Mary Briscolina. Also, of note is that even though Becker identified Schaefer as Minton, not Shepard, the fact remains that it is very possible, based on photo identification that Schaefer worked at Becker Window Company. That connection being made, it is also easy to reasonably assume that Schaefer could have known Mary Briscolina.

3.) The most damning evidence against Schaefer came later when the Briscolinas positively identified some of the jewelry found within Schaefer's belongings, and this was pointed out in a deposition taken from Carl Ragucci (earlier in this book), who assisted in the search of Schaefer's mother's house. These three pieces of jewelry: the silver bracelet with eleven rose-shaped beads and the cross and Madonna metal; the 17 ¾" long, fine gold chain, and the very distinctive silver pin, in the shape of a man (or poodle) made of green glass, all belonged to Mary Briscolina.

With these facts one can only wonder why Schaefer was never brought to trial for the murders of Mary Briscolina and Elsie Farmer. When asked this question, Capt. Ben Butler said, "I couldn't say for sure." Was it a lack of evidence? "No, I wouldn't say that," Butler told me.

Any speculations? "Seems to me, it would be a waste of taxpayers' money to try a guy for homicide who's already in a state prison now . . ."But do you (Butler) still consider him a suspect? "Absolutely," said Butler,

Later, in March of 1983, Butler, along with detectives Brian Flynn (Plantation PD) and Frank Carbone (of Pompano PD) put Schaefer through a polygraph test concerning the murders of Briscolina and Farmer. Schaefer would say that the polygraph "cleared his name" in connection with that case. Butler would say, "Not in my opinion."

So, who killed these two young girls, and why was the killer never brought to justice? We may never have an answer, but Gerard Schaefer is still, in the eyes of many investigators, the most likely candidate. One investigator suggests that Mary and Elsie were his "typical victims." With this in mind, a closer look at the girls and their short lives is in order.

Mary was the daughter of much older parents, her father was forty-seven when she was born, her mother, forty-two. Their relationship to Mary was described as "living in the same house but being in two different worlds," Mary liked fast or expensive cars, and it would seem looking at a list of her friends, older males. Young men who Mr. Briscolina described as "sniffers"(of transmission 'Go'). But both parents insisted Mary did not use drugs, though evidence would show she at least used marijuana, so there is a basis to assume that she may have been emotionally vulnerable, that being a correlation with many of Schaefer's proposed victims. Physically, Mary was "making the transition from adolescence to womanhood . . . just starting to develop... with a firm bust. She had the body of an 18-year-old..." Her relatives said that she "probably would have become a model." She weighed just over 100 pounds and stood five feet, two inches tall, a bit short for a model, and liked to exercise. She had "olive skin," and long black hair. Elsie also had dark hair, and so this makes this pair different from the usual blonde/brunette victims ordinarily associated with Schaefer.

Emotionally, however, Elsie could be said to have been a very likely candidate for Schaefer's craving. She was described as "a child no one ever wanted." At ten years old, she came home from school one day to find her belongings outside her home, from which she'd been thrown out. She became a ward of the state, but eventually settled in with her half-sister, Linda Walker. Elsie became quite heavy, 160 pounds at age thirteen. This was probably a result of her emotional crisis that began with her "getting bounced around from one place to another." At any rate, she and Mary became inseparable, relying on each other for friendship and emotional stability as they grew into young women.

The two of them hitchhiked together, dated boys together, and "hung-out" on the infamous "Lauderdale Strip" together. And, in living together, they died together.

According to authorities, their case is "not closed, yet."

* * *

The cases of Carmen (Candy) Hallock (Victim 5) and Leigh Hainline Bonadies (Victim 6), are perhaps two of the strangest, and most mysterious, of all the "possible victims'" cases.

Mysterious, because of the nature of their disappearances, and because even though these girls were not supposed to have known each other, there has been some evidence which may link the two young women. Additionally, in both cases, and among other correlations, there has been alleged FBI and/or CIA involvement. At any rate, both girls became missing persons in late 1969, the year many experts believe Schaefer began killing, and both disappeared under unusual, but somewhat similar circumstances. Hallock vanished leaving a bathtub full of water, and a puppy uncared for. Hainline similarly vanished, leaving a husband of two weeks and a note on the refrigerator that said she was going to Miami but would return shortly. Both women were Fort Lauderdale residents, and both, according to friends and relatives, were offered high paying government jobs involving narcotics undercover work.

Carmen Hallock was a twenty-two-year-old, extremely attractive cocktail waitress. She had auburn hair, penetrating dark eyes and weighed a trim 120 pounds. She was single, living only with her new puppy, and when last seen was described as "happy" by one report and "depressed" by another.

Nancy Bauer, Carmen's ex-sister-in-law, felt that Carmen was depressed having recently broke up with her boyfriend. But Irene Johnson, with whom Carmen (also known as "Candy") worked at the China Doll restaurant, said that Carmen was happy when she last saw her, having dinner at the Brave Bull with a male companion. No one seemed to know for sure whom the male companion was. One friend thought it must have been Dick Meier, a merchant seaman, whom Carmen dated a few times. But ships' records show that Meier was in Louisiana, on board his ship at that time. Another friend thought Candy may have been out with Dan Mayer, an Air Force officer whom she'd been out with before, but he too had an alibi.

Regardless of whomever she was with, Carmen was seen again on December 18, 1969, by Nancy Bauer, who would later report her missing, and was the last to see Carmen alive. That day, Nancy and Carmen had lunch together at which time Nancy invited Carmen to her house for Christmas festivities. Bauer ·reported Carmen missing on Christmas Day, 1969, when Carmen failed to show up. When Nancy, concerned over her friend's absence, went to her apartment, she found the door open, Carmen gone, but all her clothes were still there, and the tub was filled as if in anticipation of a bath. The puppy, ecstatic to see another living being, jumped and yipped and Nancy took it home to feed it and clean it, because it appeared to have been uncared for, "for about a week." It was as if Carmen Hallock had stepped out for a moment, having forgotten to buy some soap, or shampoo, and simply vanished. Her beige-and-white Ford Fairlane was found parked on the south side of George English Park parking lot. No one in the vicinity of the park could shed any light on how the car got there, or where its driver had gone.

Throughout the missing person's report, filed on Carmen "Candy" Hallock, there is not a single reference to Gerard Schaefer. However, there are several items of interest concerning Hallock and Schaefer.

1.) Though no one seems capable of remembering with whom Carmen had a date the night before the last day she was seen, a friend and fellow worker remembers Carmen wearing "a black dress and black shoes." Items of clothing that would not be recovered in searching Carmen's apartment. Earlier in this book in one of Schaefer's "stories," he described one of his "fictional" victims as "wearing a black chiffon dress, with her hair done up and black pantyhose and high heels. She was wearing perfume and was very sexy." Then, after a brutal description of hanging the girl, and sodomizing her after death, he wrote ". . . for the first time (I) really noticed her auburn V covering her cunt." Carmen's hair color was auburn, though of course, that cannot conclude what her genital hair was. Still later, in this morbid tale, he wrote, "The lower jaw I buried and the rest of her skull with the face smashed in and the teeth out, I put in another canal some ten miles (from) the rest of her body." And, "there is no possible connection between us." But within the evidence seized at Schaefer's homes, there were two teeth belonging to Carmen Hallock. Teeth that would later be described by forensic dental specialist Dr. Richard Souviron, as having been healthy teeth with no reason whatsoever for their extrication.

Additionally, the name Carmen appeared in at least one of Schaefer's "stories."

2.) Schaefer, according to his ex-roommate, John Dolan, knew Carmen Hallock, because Dolan used to go out with her. (Later, Schaefer would tell me that Dolan had killed Hallock and had told him so, but that he was afraid to tell anyone.)

3.) Carmen attended Broward Junior College at the same time Schaefer did. Additionally, Nancy Bauer remembered in her last conversation with Carmen that she "had been offered a government job by one of the teachers at BJC." Schaefer was, for what it was worth, a student teacher at that time. Also, Carmen listed Professor Neil S. Crispo of BJC, as a reference on a job application. Crispo was also one of Schaefer's professors.

4.) Lucille Carbone, another friend of Carmen's, came forward with some interesting, if not baffling information, six months after Carmen disappeared. She stated that just before Christmas (which is the approximate time that Carmen vanished) she'd seen Carmen at a House of Pancakes restaurant, and that "Candy"(her name for Carmen) had been in the company of Leigh Hainline, another missing person. Carbone had seen articles in the newspapers chronicling the two girls' disappearances. The stories said that the cases were unrelated and that there was no connection between Hainline and Hallock. Up until Carbone presented her information there was no link between the two women. However, Carbone stated that she not only recognized the picture of Hainline in the paper, but "Candy" had introduced her friend as "Leigh Bonadies," Hainline's married name.

Carmen had one sister as family, Martha Borman, who lived in Hinsdale, Illinois. Their mother had died shortly before Carmen disappeared. In one of their last phone conversations, Carmen had told Martha that she had been offered a "high paying government job." A job that would earn her $5,000 a month. She was to be an undercover narcotics agent and was to travel out of the country frequently, and particularly to the islands (Bahamas) and to South America. Furthermore, in Carmen's last known conversation, with Nancy Bauer during lunch at Britt's department store in Coral Ridge (near Miami), Carmen had mentioned she had an appointment at 5 p.m., about a "new job." She left Nancy at 2:30 p.m. and was never seen again.

Martha Borman, would frantically search the Ft. Lauderdale area in January of 1970, looking for her sister with no leads whatsoever. The last time they talked she warned Carmen of her "new job," telling her it sounded "shaky." Carmen replied, "What have I got to lose?"

Leigh Hainline, victim numbered "six" on our list, may very well have been victim "number one" in reality. Chronologically, she is the first person reported missing, having disappeared on September 8, 1969; her disappearance attributed to Schaefer. She was twenty- five, an attractive blonde, who had been married to Charles Bonadies, about one month when she disappeared. It was Leigh's second marriage. The young couple had lived together for a few months before marrying, along with two other female roommates, who eventually moved out prior to the marriage. The newlyweds lived off of Davie Boulevard in Ft. Lauderdale. Leigh, like Carmen, was a waitress. Charles was a former schoolteacher who had entered "private enterprise" and was working with Linton Industries, a company that dealt in typewriters.

Leigh was reported to have been unhappy at the time of her disappearance. It is easy to imagine she would've been. Both her female roommates had been described as "unstable." Both used drugs regularly, and either one, or both, had attempted suicide at least on one occasion before moving out. And the newlyweds began to use marijuana frequently, and Leigh used barbiturates for a "weight problem" that began to develop, rapidly, around the time of her marriage.

Of the fact that Leigh knew Gerard Schaefer, there is no doubt. The two grew up together as neighbors just a few houses apart. They met in their early teens and often played tennis and went swimming together. Although Schaefer's name appears only once in Leigh's missing person's report, a private investigator, William Marshall, found evidence that linked the two just prior to her disappearance. Marshall was hired by Paul Forward, Leigh's brother-in-law, who took a keen interest in her case. Marshall reported that Schaefer said that Leigh had called him (the day she vanished) and had asked for a ride to the airport, but she never called back. One week prior to that, she'd sent Schaefer a telegram, but its content is unknown.

The Hainlines remembered Schaefer well. Mrs. Hainline recalled, "I never cared for the boy. He did foolish things. One time he and Gary (Leigh's brother) went fishing out on the ocean, and he (Schaefer) threw away the oars. The boys finally drifted in with the tide." She added, "you never knew where he was. He was sneaky. He sort of dropped by all the time." She remembered Schaefer as being "excessively" polite. "He was kind of a pest. I found him in the bedroom all the time. He was coming in and running up the stairs, into Gary's room, and Leigh's room . . . He was kind of a high-tempered fellow. He wasn't a quiet boy . . ."

But Mr. Hainline liked Schaefer, and Gary, Leigh's brother, used to hunt and fish with him. They were all close friends. Later, the Hainlines would identify jewelry found in Schaefer's possessions; a gold locket with the name LEIGH on it, and a swimming club pin and a Disneyland pin, all having belonged to Leigh Hainline. Her yellow Mustang was found in a city parking lot near the S.E. 7th Avenue boat ramp. Perhaps not coincidentally, Leigh's car and Carmen Hallock's were within a stone's throw of the Intracoastal Waterway where a view would be blocked by the waterway itself, unless a passing boater happened to look inland. And both the S.E. 7th Avenue boat ramp, and the George English Park parking lot are remote and, for the most part, uninhabited after dark.

Leigh was different things to different people. To her parents she was "a good girl who was brought up religious, but could be led the wrong way . . ." To her employer, she was "strange and goofy, but happy." To a fellow worker she was, "on drugs . . . speed, pot, and acid . . . " To her brother, to whom she was probably closest, she was "mixed-up and unhappy." Leigh had told Gary that she was not happy with her marriage. She also said that she had the opportunity to make a lot of money working for the CIA . . . as an undercover agent. "She seemed serious," he said.

Charles Bonadies was not happy with the news of his new bride's undercover job. He told her flatly to forget it. But this is where this story becomes increasingly baffling.

On the day Leigh disappeared, she left a note, according to Charles Bonadies, that said she would be back in time to play tennis and go to their planned dinner date at Paul Forward's home. She said she was going to Miami. Later, Charles is reported to have called Paul Forward to say that Leigh was ill, and they could not make the dinner date. Even more baffling is that Charles did not report Leigh missing until 9/23/69, about two weeks after her disappearance. By March of 1970, Charles had divorced Leigh.

Then in June of 1970, Barbara Blaikie, Charles Bonadies' new girlfriend, made out a complaint with the Ft. Lauderdale Police Department. She stated that at approximately 3:00 p.m. on 6/20/70, two white men, dressed in conservative business suits, knocked on her door and asked to see her. The men both showed her badges and identification that read: Federal Bureau of Investigation. One man was 6'2", over 200 pounds, about 35 years old and had black hair.

Once inside the house the tall man began to ask about Charles. Where was he? When would he show up? Then the men pushed her into the living room. They asked if they could search the house. Barbara said yes, but she did not like how they were questioning her. Then they began to ask about Leigh Bonadies, whom Barbara had never met. They questioned her extensively, and finally, apparently satisfied, they left. Or so Barbara thought. She began calling around looking for Charles but could not find him. As she turned to hang up the phone, she found the two men had re-entered her house, and had been listening to her.

At this point the men, who had identified themselves as FBI agents began to slap her. They continued even after she fell across a table in the living room, knocking glasses and ashtrays to the floor. Then they started kicking her. After a while, the two men left again. When she was able to collect herself, Barbara located Charles, then called the police.

Barbara told the police of the incident and told them that over the past few months, she had received mysterious phone calls from someone she believed to be Leigh Bonadies. The caller had called long distance from somewhere in Miami. Barbara heard the operator's request for 40 cents, then the caller asked her if she was the girl dating Charles Bonadies. Barbara said yes. Then the caller said she would give her advice, "Did she know what it was like to be in love with Charles and to follow Charles all around." She added, among other things, that Charles would "make her suffer."

The police were ready to pass the whole incident off as a lover's triangle gone awry. But another friend of Charles', Vinny Bonvino, told police that two FBI agents had come to his house as well. He had been gone at the time, but his mother was there. Mrs. Bonvino verified the story and added that the two men "upset" her, and they matched the description that Barbara Blaikie had given.

The FBI became interested in this, and the Carmen Hallock case, but their extent in the investigation has not been made available. The Ft. Lauderdale Police Department took fingerprints and investigated further, but the results of their findings, if any, was not made available to this reporter. The FBI did say that the two men were not theirs, and added that the F.B.I. does not carry badges, but special ID cards.

Barbara Blaikie awoke a few days after the first assault, to find two men whom she could not identify standing over her bed and pummeling her head with their fists. After her second beating, she told police, she had her two children to worry about, not to mention herself, and that she was breaking off all engagements with Charles Bonadies.

When asked what he thought happened to his wife in 1970, Charles Bonadies stated he thought she'd "been rubbed out," being somehow involved with narcotics. Because of the conflicting testimonies in this case, Charles Bonadies was, at least at one point, and possibly without his knowledge, a suspect in the disappearance of his wife, However, his status in the case changed, in light of the fact that Schaefer, a suspect in so many other cases, was found to have several pieces of Leigh's personal jewelry, and was known to have talked to her, at least by phone, on the day of her disappearance.

By and large, Schaefer became a logical suspect in this case, a viewpoint that is strengthened by yet another of his fictional stories. The story describes the torture and subsequent death of a female dressed in a white waitress dress, killed in the area near Powerline Road. Leigh was expected at work the day she vanished and may have been wearing her work clothes which would have been a white waitress dress. That "story" was part of the evidence list, Exhibit IV, Item B, found at Schaefer's mother's home in his old bedroom. Furthermore, in 1978, nine years after Leigh's disappearance, a group of men hunting off Powerline Road, in Palm Beach County, came across a macabre discovery. They found the upper half of a human skull, riddled with at least three large bore bullet holes. The skull remained unidentified for some time, but eventually made its way into the able hands of Chief Medical Examiner, Dr. Joseph Davis and his equally adept collaborator, forensic dental specialist Dr. Richard Souviron. The doctors concurred, positively, that the skull was indeed that of Leigh Hainline Bonadies.

* * *

Collette Marie Goodenough became medical examiner's case number 77-2978, Barbara Ann Wilcox, is 77-2979. They are proposed victims, 7 and 8, respectively, on our list. However, if they are, in fact, victims of Schaefer, they would have been, in all probability, his last. They were last known to be alive between January 8th and 11th, 1973, just a few days before

Schaefer began his jail sentence (January 15th, 1973) for the abduction of Nancy Trotter and Paula Sue Wells.

Collette and Barbara were both nineteen and attractive, one blonde, one brunette, both looking for a change in their lives. The two decided to hitchhike mid-western homes to Florida in January of 1973. It has been suggested they met a young man from Florida, a college student, who invited them down with a promise of a place to stay. They could stop and rest a few days in Biloxi, Mississippi, where relatives lived, then continue on. An aunt of one of the girls reported they had been at her home sometime between the 8th and 11th of January 1973, in Biloxi. After that, they left, hitchhiking, and were never seen alive again.

Schaefer, while out on bond, awaiting his trial for the Trotter/Wells incident says he left the state, (another violation of the law) to go on a hunting trip. Destination? His first story said he went to Iowa. Later, he began saying he went to "South Dakota, or somewhere up there." State Attorney Robert Stone has stated that he has seen a long- distance phone bill listing a call made from Cedar Rapids, Iowa, to Schaefer's home in Stuart, supposedly made while he was on that hunting trip. But what was he hunting?

Both Collette and Barbara lived in Cedar Rapids, Iowa.

Schaefer said that the time he was out-of-state was the "actual, real time that the Place and Jessup girls were reported missing . . . somewhere near the end of October. (The first missing person report on Susan Place, that this reporter has seen, is dated October 1st, 1972. A very revealing report that will be looked at later in this book. Schaefer said this report has been "falsely written.") At any rate, Schaefer was definitely out-of-state sometime in the fall of '72 and it is possible that he could have met the two Cedar Rapids girls, on this "hunting trip," in the

North.

Collette Goodenough was an "Army brat." The daughter of an Air Force sergeant, she was accustomed to replanting her roots time and again. She was a coupon saver and a lover of literature, who also took the time to try her own hand at writing poetry. She liked to travel. Unfortunately, she also possessed several characteristics that correlated with Schaefer's proposed victims. In addition to the fondness for poetry, she may have also experienced some emotional problems. A common denominator that many of the persons, throughout the List of 28, shared. Among Collette's possessions, which would be found in the April 6th, 1973 search of Schaefer's Ft. Lauderdale home, was an identification card in the name of

Collette Goodenough, to attend a "special problems center." An outpatient center that, among other things, dealt with problems of an emotional or psychological nature. Her other possessions, found in that same search, were her birth certificate, passport, several identification cards, and some of her poems signed, "Collette."

Not much information was available on Barbara Ann Wilcox, other than she was a friend of Collette's, and they were traveling together. They were both last seen leaving Biloxi, Mississippi on January 11th, 1973, headed south, for Florida.

In January of 1977, a truck driver strolling along a canal bank in St. Lucie County, Florida, spied what appeared to be the skeleton of some sort of animal. Upon closer observation, he noted that there were actually two skeletons, commingled, and they were human bones. The upper skulls were both missing, however, and the skeletal arms appeared to have been bound together with baling wire. The truck driver called the sheriff's office.

The St. Lucie County Sheriff's Department called in a group of anthropologists from Florida State University, an archaeologist from the Florida Park Service, and several investigators from the Florida Department of Law Enforcement (FDLE).The FDLE investigators took possession of the skeletons, assigning them case #770-110-115, and labeling them A and B,A local dentist, working with medical examiner Dr. Schofield, kept the mandibles (the lower jaw) of the skeletons for identification purposes. One of the mandibles was tentatively identified as Barbara Wilcox.

Nearly one year later, Dr. Dan Morse, one of the anthropologists from FSU who had originally observed the bones, was in Miami for a conference. While in Miami, Dr. Morse met with Dr. Joseph Davis, and subsequently Dr. Richard Souviron. Dr. Souviron is a renowned forensic dentist, an expert witness who has testified in dozens of criminal cases, including serial murderer Ted Bundy and, Gerard Schaefer. Dr. Davis, an internationally respected leader in the field of pathology and forensic science, also worked on the Schaefer case in 1973.Dr. Morse had again obtained the mandibles from the St. Lucie County medical examiner, Dr. Schofield, and along with doctors Souviron and Davis, began to look at the skeleton again.

On January 8, 1978, after carefully charting the teeth on both mandibles, Dr. Souviron positively identified the remains as Collette Goodenough and Barbara Wilcox.

In June of 1981, a particularly hot summer produced a dried-up canal, the same one along whose banks a truck driver had strolled some four years earlier. Another discovery had been made: the upper skull of a human body. The St. Lucie County Medical Examiner's Office, now headed by a Dr. Walker, contacted doctors Souviron and Davis, and after a few days of comparing mandibles and records, positively identified the newly found skull section as that of Barbara Wilcox. The upper skull, from the maxilla (upper teeth) up to the top of the head of Collette Goodenough has never been found.

St. Lucie County is located just north of Martin County, where Schaefer used to live and work as a deputy sheriff. It is also the county where the remains of Susan Place and Georgia Jessup were found. Although Schaefer went to jail on January 15, 1973, just four days after Collette and Barbara were last seen, their possessions were found among the evidence gathered at Schaefer' mother's home in Ft. Lauderdale, on April 6, 1973.

* * *

Victims number 9 and 10, Karen Ferrell and Mared Malarik, were two college students from Morgantown, West Virginia. The two young women were missing, and police authorities in Monongalia County heard of the Schaefer case and took an interest in it. Because the authorities had contacted Robert Stone's office inquiring about Schaefer, the two girls were added to the list of proposed victims. Later, when their bodies were found, it was quickly determined they were indeed murdered. Schaefer again became prime suspect. However, authorities could not place Schaefer in or around Morgantown at the time of the girl's disappearance.

In October of 1981, Eugene Paul Clawson confessed and was convicted of the murders of both Malarik and Ferrell. In December of 1982, prosecuting attorney Thomas H. Newbraugh wrote to Schaefer and told him the outcome of that case, and in so doing, cleared Schaefer of any suspected connection with that case.

* * *

The case of Elizabeth Wilt, proposed victim number 11, is certainly one of the most baffling.

The Arkansas School for the Blind, in Little Rock, Arkansas, was established in 1859.It closed for a short while during the Civil War. Other than that brief hiatus, the school has been teaching visually handicapped youth, from ages five to twenty-one. Many of the children there are above average intelligence; they don't have the distraction of video games or TV. Their red-tipped canes tap, amazingly proficient, about this magnificent campus; a group of redbrick buildings whose prominence is embellished by their placement on top of the hill, the apex of the sprawling 40.4 acres which belongs to the school. The grounds are rolling hills, softly covered with long, but manicured, grass and speckled with millions of dainty yellow field flowers.

I met with Mrs. Rosetta Sykes at the school. She is a petite woman, silver-haired, with sky-blue eyes that are enlarged by her horn-rimmed glasses. She is a schoolteacher, and possesses that unique, undying energy that many of the very best of teachers retain all their lives. It is an energy that is fed by helping others and she had done that, for over thirty years when we met. Mrs. Sykes was the adoptive mother of Elizabeth Wilt. She agreed to talk to me because "even if it couldn't help Elizabeth, it might help other people in the same situation."

The day we met, she was wearing a pale-colored dress, with a pattern of dainty yellow flowers that matched perfectly with those on the campus grounds. She spoke with that wonderful Arkansas, southern dialect that captures the listener with its warm throatiness and told me the plight of her missing daughter.

Mrs. Sykes was teaching a first-grade class at the Arkansas School for the Blind, when she first met Elizabeth. She was brought to Mrs. Sykes as a student, though she could see "lights and shadows and some colors," she was legally blind and could not attend regular public schools. Elizabeth's real name was Caroline Anne Marrs, though no one knew that at the time. Elizabeth was born by a midwife in the home of sharecroppers. Her mother was very ill during the pregnancy and it was believed she would die. Her the father could not feed another hungry child, so Caroline Anne was given up for adoption and her name changed. It is unclear where "Elizabeth" came from, but it is assumed the state gave her that name. Orphanages often name their children to keep them from finding out who their biological parents are. Elizabeth was staying with a foster family, the Levys, when she came to the school for the blind.

Rosetta Sykes recalls Elizabeth as being "quiet and withdrawn, and not intermingling with the other kids." At the end of a particularly difficult day for Elizabeth, Mrs. Sykes held her after school and tried to encourage the child to explain what it was that troubled her so. Elizabeth stared at the floor, with her unfocused eyes for many long moments, scuffling her feet and biting her lip. Finally, she blurted out, "Well, I'm a welfare child, you know." At that moment, she stole Mrs. Sykes' heart.

The kindly schoolteacher began to look into Elizabeth's case, and found that her foster family was not going to keep her. When they finally gave the child back to the state, Mrs. Sykes simply "just took her home one day, and kept her ever since." It was not quite that simple, however. Legal adoption took over three years simply because "the authorities refused to believe anyone would want to adopt a child with bad vision."

Elizabeth grew up in Little Rock, and eventually graduated from the Arkansas School for the Blind, which teaches grades 1-12. She enrolled at the University of Arkansas in nearby Fayetteville as a music major. She soon met Richard Wilt, and after two months of dating, and against the wishes of Mr. and Mrs. Sykes, she married him. She was eighteen. Richard was also a student at the university, though several years older than Elizabeth. He often made fun of Elizabeth's singing voice, so she dropped music, and took up English as a major.

They were married just over a year when Elizabeth became pregnant. She was elated. Mrs. Sykes visited her often during the pregnancy and recalls Elizabeth constantly wanting to be photographed, showing her pregnancy. She wanted to show her child that she was indeed its mother, to prove it wasn't adopted, as she was. It was important to her,

The marriage lasted about three years before ending in divorce. Elizabeth continued to attend the university, Richard did not, and their child, Christian, went to live with Mrs. Sykes at fourteen months old. Elizabeth visited her mother and child often. It was during these visits, that Mrs. Sykes began to notice her daughter's growing depression. She was not taking the divorce well. Once an "A" student, her grades began to fall, and when she visited, she often sat in a room by herself, not talking to anyone, and staring into space. Mrs. Sykes was worried, but felt Elizabeth found strength from her child, and was relieved when Elizabeth began to express an interest in politics.

Elizabeth told her adoptive mother she wanted to go to Miami as a delegate for the Republican Convention in August of 1972. As it turned out, she missed being elected as a delegate by a few votes, but decided to go anyway, for a vacation and to see what a big political convention was like. Classes were out for the summer, so she wouldn't miss school and the breakaway might do her some good, so she left for Miami and its big city life.

On August 24, 1972, Elizabeth called Mrs. Sykes and told her she would be staying a few extra days. Classes were to begin again on September 5, 1972, her rent was due the same day, so she would have to be back at least by then, and she hoped to be back for Labor Day weekend with the family. That was the last time Mrs. Sykes would ever talk to her daughter.

On August 29, Elizabeth sent a letter to her "landlady" at the rooming house where she lived with some other girls who also attended the university. She said she would be back in time to pay her rent and begin classes. On the same day, August 29, she penned the following note, and sent it to the Sykes in Little Rock, Arkansas.

August 29, 1972

Dearest Parents:

Forgive the nature of the stationery (or -ary?) I ran out of note cards. Everything here is fine. Did you get my post card?

I still hope to see you Sunday, or Monday, partly about Christian & to see how you are.

I long to see & hope to see Christian. I hope he is not giving too much trouble to you,

Say hello to Aunt Reba for me.

Love always, will see you soon. Take Care,

Libby

"Libby" or "Liz" was a nickname that Elizabeth was fond of and asked that friends and family refer to her as such. "Libby" never returned home.

When Mrs. Sykes did not hear from Elizabeth, she assumed she'd changed their Labor Day plans, and went on back to school and home in Fayetteville. Still, after a few days, she was getting worried, and began calling around to find her. Elizabeth's friends at the rooming house said "she wasn't in right now," though none of them said she had not come home. Finally, after several calls over several days, Mrs. Sykes told one of the girls that she was "Libby's" mother and she was worried and wanted to talk to her. The girl told Mrs. Sykes that Elizabeth had never returned from Florida, that they had just assumed she had gone to Little Rock to visit her child and mother, and that put Mrs. Sykes in "a real tizzy." But when Rosetta Sykes called the local police, they just "fluffed it off." They told her they would notify the Miami PD, but Miami would later say they never received any notice from Little Rock P.D. Whether they did, or did not, is not the point, what is important is that if any police department was looking for her, they were not finding her.

The Sykes hired private investigators, but to no avail. One investigator told them that a girl, probably Elizabeth, had been "hit in the head with a bottle at the Republican convention." This prompted Mrs. Sykes to begin believing that perhaps her adopted daughter was suffering from amnesia, as they so often do in the movies, and that Elizabeth was wandering about South Florida not knowing who she was. Then, late in October of 1972, the Sykes received a shipment notice from the bus depot in Fayetteville. The notice told them that some baggage was being stored at the depot, sent ahead prepaid by "Liz" Wilt, and to come pick it up, or notify her to do so, to avoid further storage fees. Mrs. Sykes had the bus depot ship the baggage to Little Rock. She would pick it up at the depot there. Mrs. Sykes brought Christian, Elizabeth's son, with her to the depot to pick up the baggage. The man at the depot showed Mrs. Sykes the original prepaid receipt. It was in her daughter's handwriting, shipped by "Liz" Wilt, from Miami Beach, Florida on 8-30-72, several days after the convention. Elizabeth would have had to have had the presence of mind to send the bag; she was not suffering from amnesia. When Christian saw his mother's distinctive red suitcase, he became very excited, jumping up and down exclaiming, "Mommy's coming. Mommy's coming." But she never did.

Soon, the Sykes received another surprise in the mail. This time it was a bill from Jackson Memorial Hospital for services rendered on August 29, 1972 for Elizabeth Wilt. The balance due was for twelve dollars. But, try as she might, Rosetta Sykes could not get any information from Jackson Memorial as to the nature of Elizabeth's emergency treatment, only that it wasn't "serious." Once again, Mrs. Sykes began to panic, believing the "bottle-to the-head-amnesia theory." Despite private investigators and police departments who were supposed to be looking into this case, it would be thirteen years later, when this investigator presented legal authorization to the hospital for observation of records, before we could determine what had happened to Elizabeth, at least at this hospital. She was treated for pain to her "upper and lower right jaws." Elizabeth had told them she thought her gums were infected from recent wisdom teeth extraction. She was given Darvon and told to see her dentist upon returning home. This removed any doubt that the amnesia theory was not true.

What is true is this: 1) Elizabeth sent her suitcase home, but not her overnight bag. Presumably she did this because she had a ride arranged with what would have been a newly found friend. Her suitcase contained her evening clothes and dress wear, along with tourist knickknacks from Miami. Mrs. Sykes stated that she knew Elizabeth packed her bathing suit, and other "light" apparel, and her toiletries in her overnight bag. Things that would be adequate for a two-day car trip to Arkansas. 2) Elizabeth was slight in stature, five feet, two inches, 110 pounds, and she was somewhat handicapped both physically and emotionally, with her blindness, and more recently, her rather difficult divorce. These facts and her open and friendly attitude would have made her an easy target for a killer who chose his victims with these same characteristics. A killer, many investigators would point out, much like Schaefer. Susan Place could be compared to Elizabeth, both in size and because they both shared a handicap, Susan being slightly paralyzed on one side and emotionally stunted from her epilepsy. In fact, almost all of the proposed Schaefer victims could be termed emotionally handicapped. All would have been easy prey for a killer whose warm, heartfelt charm would take keen advantage of these people, so many of whom seemed only to be seeking some friendship and understanding.

There is no physical evidence linking Schaefer to Elizabeth Wilt, however one may consider the following. Elizabeth became missing about one month after the discovery of Schaefer's abduction and the subsequent escape of Nancy Trotter and Paula Sue Wells. A time when he would have been, according to investigators and psychologists viewing the case, particularly aggravated and "active." Additionally, we can look again to Schaefer's perverse "stories" that state: "The victims could be any one of the many women who flock to the Miami and Fort Lauderdale area." It can be pointed out, too, that Elizabeth's disappearance came just over a month prior to the murders of Susan Place and Georgia Jessup, and about two months prior to the murders of Elsie Farmer and Mary Briscolina.

It is believed that the summer and fall of 1972 was Schaefer's most active periods. That like most serial killers he was executing a "sweep," piling up victims and adding to his list in an almost uncontrollable rage. A rage that would become a flame fanned to intensity by Schaefer losing his deputy sheriff's position in Martin County.

* * *

The headlines read "2 Vanished Sisters May Be Alive." Along with the headlines were two black- and-white photographs of the Bivens sisters, Katrina Marie, 14, and her younger sister Sandra Elaine. The story ran on May 14, 1973, a Monday following a Sunday newspaper's heavy coverage of Gerard Schaefer's case and his many "possible victims." The story, though not actually accusing Schaefer of being their abductor, suggested the girls were a "possible link to a series of brutal crimes in the area." The suggestion was enough to put the girls' names on the infamous List of 28.

The truth is, however, that Sandra and Katrina Bivens, victims thirteen and fourteen on our list, should never have been on the list in the first place. Exactly how their story came to the paper is unknown, but it can be theorized that the reporter (who will remain anonymous) tried to tie as many missing people to Schaefer as was possible, for publicity reasons. Consider this: The girls were listed as missing in January of 1970, but they were known to be returned home in June of 1970. It was common knowledge at the Palm Beach County Sheriff's office that the girls were repeat runaways, and they were often reported as "missing." In all likelihood, the reporter looked at the missing person's blotter at the sheriff's office but failed to research any further into the case. At any rate, the girls were not murdered and should not have been on the List of 28.

Sgt. Steve Newell of the Palm Beach County Sheriff's Office had this to say:

"We had a single missing person's report for both of these girls, from January of 1970, and both girls were recovered on June 16th, 1970. If there were any reports after that, we (Palm Beach County Sheriff's Office) don't have them. But I do know that one of the girls, Katrina, was alive by December of 1982, she filed a complaint of a larceny."

So, we know that at least one of them, and probably both, were alive as of 1982. One officer thought he remembered one of the girls being killed in an automobile accident, but we could find no reports to substantiate that claim. The point to be made here, is that the Bivens sisters were alive years after Gerard Schaefer's incarceration, and the names of victims 12 and 13 can be omitted from the list.

* * *

Several other names of "possible victims" should be dealt with here for purposes of simplification and clarity. This group has been taken out of context from the List of 28 and lumped together, if you will, for several reasons. They all are females and were at one time listed as missing, but unlike others on the list, there is little to no hard evidence to nonexistent. That said, in some cases, we did find some information that may tie them to Schaefer and the logical conclusion is that if a person knew Schaefer and went missing, he became a suspect in their vanishing.

Again, this is in no way an attempt to belittle the significance of these people in relationship to Gerard Schaefer's case. It is simply an attempt to bring to light that these people, too, were suspected of being possible victims of Schaefer, but little to no information was obtained to clarify their status and so, at this point we can only still consider them "missing." That said, in the opinion of this porter, anyone who had contact with Schaefer, then went missing, should be considered another victim of his. Coincidence with serial killers, is not an acceptable conclusion.

Bonnie Taylor (number 14), a woman listed as missing as of March 19, 1972. She was a Wilton Manor resident. Schaefer was reported to have stopped this woman for speeding. No other information was available.

Deborah Lowe (number 16) listed as missing February 29, 1972 from Pompano, near Fort Lauderdale, Florida. She was last seen walking to school between 7:30 and 8:00AM, on February 29, 1972. Deborah was 13 years old. She never arrived at school and was never seen again. Her schoolbooks were found in a trash bin one block from her home. She was last seen wearing a tan poncho, a yellow blouse, black slacks with vertical rose-colored stripes, and a ring with an aquamarine stone. The ring was shaped like a flower with eight, off-white petals and gold wire around them, a blue dot in the center, and a gold band. Schaefer had worked with Deborah's father at one time and had visited their home and 1972 was one of Schaefer's most active abduction years. No other information available and this remains a cold case with Broward County Sheriff's Office and the Pompano Police Department.

Patricia Wilson (number 19) listed as missing from Cocoa Beach, Florida, specific date unknown. This woman is reported to have had an automobile accident in Wilton Manors. Schaefer may have been the attending patrolman. No other information is available.

Mona Dice (number 20) was a name pulled from a deposition given by Carl Ragucci. She was, at least at one time, listed as missing and was a resident of the Fort Lauderdale area. No other information available.

Kay Price (number 28) listed as missing. The only information obtainable on this woman was that she was reported to have dated Schaefer, after his divorce from his first wife. No additional information has been filed in relation to these five girls, inasmuch as this reporter was able to find. But again, her connection to Schaefer then her to going missing, can hardly be considered coincidence.

* * *

Belinda Hutchins, possible victim number 15 on our list, was last seen on January 4, 1973.She was twenty-two, a wife and mother to a ten-month-old daughter, and a prostitute. Her husband, a dark-haired short man, who made a living as a mechanic and liked to wear "flashy clothes," was the last to see her as she stepped out of their Fort Lauderdale home into the night, and a waiting car. The car was a "light-blue or white Toyota or Datsun." Gerard Schaefer drove a light-blue Datsun.

Belinda was gorgeous. The night she disappeared, she was wearing a pink dress, white high-heeled shoes and a small clutch purse, containing only her cigarettes. She wore no make-up and according to Bill Hutchins, her husband, "she didn't need any." She was not a streetwalker, but a high-priced call girl who was making between $40,000 and $60,000 a year. She left expensive clothing in her closet at home, and a Corvette and Cadillac parked in the driveway, fully paid for. The couple and their baby lived in a nice apartment and according to friends and family Belinda was happy, despite what one might obviously conclude from her chosen profession. "She was proud of her profession," her husband said. "It was a job."

Belinda was the daughter of an Italian mother and Spanish father. She was one of eleven children. She drew her olive-skinned beauty from her Latin-combination heritage, though her hair grew blonde as she got older. She was not tall, but developed into womanhood early and by the age of 14, she worked as a go-go girl in Baltimore. She lied about her age and "learned the ways of the world fast." She learned that if she wanted to keep her job, she would have to follow instructions." That is also when she learned that the prostitution "business" was profitable. Belinda and Bill met when she was 18. She lived nearby a gas station where he was employed as a mechanic. He knew she was a "working girl," and accepted that fact. She quit the "business" for a while after they were married but went back to it when the young couple found themselves financially strapped. She did not, and would not, use a pimp, and Bill was to know as little as possible about her work. With the money she earned, she helped her small family get the things they wanted and needed, and usually had enough left over to help her parents and brothers, too.

Her family did not look down on her, and upon her disappearance, they made a concerted effort to find any information leading to her whereabouts. A private investigator was hired but found no leads. But other leads did develop. A girlfriend said that Belinda had once told her of a policeman, named Schaefer that she "dated." A sister-in-law identified a picture of Schaefer as the same policeman that Belinda occasionally brought to her friends' homes. When Bill heard Belinda was "dating" a policeman, he asked her about it, fearing she was being set up for a vice squad arrest. She said she was going to see the policeman that night and not to worry. His name was Schaefer, and "he was okay." That was the night she disappeared.

Besides the car Belinda was last seen getting into, which resembles Schaefer's in description, and the accusations of family and friends, there are some other interesting correlations to Schaefer in this case. In several of Schaefer's macabre and bizarre writings, the name Belinda appears as one of the helpless victims who is tormented, killed and violated, and finally, mutilated. Furthermore, there are many numerous references to killing women who are prostitutes in these same "stories." Indeed, while being psychologically evaluated by Dr. Patrick Cook.

Schaefer revealed that he believed he was the "eliminator of wicked people, immoral women," and that he was the helpless agent of his advisors "Matthew and Jack." In other words, an exterminator of prostitutes or, if you will, a modern-day Jack the Ripper. With this in mind, one can only wonder how many prostitutes, or for that matter homeless girls, might have fallen prey. With no families, or with families that did not care, or did not know where their daughters were, who would have reported them missing?

Despite any information that might have linked Schaefer to the disappearance of Belinda Hutchins (and it must be pointed out that none of it is "physical" evidence) she has never been found. Her case, according to authorities is still "open."

* * *

Peggy Rahn and Wendy Stephenson (numbers 17 and 18 on the list) were the youngest of all the "possible victims." Peggy was nine years old. Wendy was eight. It should be pointed out right away, though, that there have been so many stories (most of them misleading and false) about these two girls that is not fair to say Gerard Schaefer is the only suspect in their disappearance. Nevertheless, because these girls vanished from Pompano Beach (as did Deborah Lowe, number 16 on the list) near Fort Lauderdale, and because they were a young female couple, one blonde, one brunette, Schaefer did become a suspect in their case. Consequently, when the numbers were tallying up against Schaefer, by the media and the state attorney's office, these two girls, having been missing since December 29, 1969, were put on the list.

A few days after Christmas, in 1969, Peggy Rahn and Wendy Brown Stephenson went to the beach, along with several friends and relatives. The weather was good, clear and sunny, and the ocean looked more like a lake than the turbulent Atlantic. It was warm enough in fact for some ice cream. The girls pleaded with their guardians for some change, and upon obtaining a few quarters, ran off for treats. They never returned.

The story that was finally handed to the families of the girls, and was begrudgingly accepted after years of hopeless wondering, was that the girls must have drowned. However, the bodies were never found, leaving room for not just a little speculation. Speculation that bears some looking into in because more than one person has sworn, under lie detector tests, to have seen the girls. Then too, one must realize the unlikelihood of two girls, who were accustomed to swimming, to drown at the same time on a crowded beach, with the ocean as still as glass. Of course, there is always the possibility of an undertow beneath the calm surface of the ocean, and there were signs posted warning of heavy jellyfish infestation in the area, but we must consider this an unlikely disaster befalling both children.

The stories as to what did happen to these girls were numerous. The girls received much media attention, due in part to the initial massive search, and subsequent manhunt that followed their disappearance.

A cashier at a Seven-11 store swore that the girls had come into her store, still in their bathing suits, in the company of a man. The man was described as 6'2", 190-200 pounds, gray-blue eyes, sand-colored hair, with a "scar on the back of his right hand." (Schaefer did not have a scar on either hand, and the rest of the description, including "a bump on his nose," does not fit Schaefer, either.)

A few days later a camera shop owner reported the girls were in his shop. Still later, a man in north Georgia, a police chief, reported that he'd seen the girls, again accompanied by a man who talked on a pay phone as the girls quietly waited in the car. These stories may have been true, and if so, it would appear that the two girls were kidnapped and taken out of state. It has been suggested that Wendy's true father (hence the name "Brown") took the girls because he was denied custody of Wendy. However, evidence that he was in a military stockade that day in December 1969 does not support that theory.

Other stories had the girls kidnapped, murdered, locked in car trunks, buried in the woods, and so on, by every criminal with a child molestation record, or every confessed killer who was captured by authorities for the next several years. Once again, Schaefer's adamantly denied and spurns any wrongdoing where young children are involved. (In a subsequent chapter of this book, evidence is revealed that shows Schaefer as a state's witness in conjunction with Senator Paula Hawkins' department against child abuse. Their collaborations helped in the arrest and conviction of a major child pornography ring being operated out of Avon Park Correctional Institution in Florida.)

But, in 1989, Schaefer once again, playing his media game of Jekyll and Hyde, wrote that he was curious about the cannibal killer, Albert Fish, so he hinted he "ate the girls with sautéed onions and peppers," but never sexually molested them.

Once again, the case of these two girls is still "open," and any information that might help to clarify this case is welcome. As of this writing, these girls are still listed as "missing."

* * *

Finally, there is the "Men's List," within the List of 28. This list, except for Leonard Masar, should not have been used to make up the number of possible victims attributed to Schaefer. However, it was utilized by because some personal items, i.e.; drivers' licenses, etc., were found in Schaefer's possessions. But, in truth, there were no missing persons reports filed on any of these people and again, with the exception of Masar, many have documentation attesting to their being alive, after Schaefer's incarceration. Of course, this does not explain why, or how, Schaefer obtained their personal belongings, or in what way they might have been linked to his case. It has been suggested by a few investigators that worked on this case, that Schaefer may have stolen these identification papers and used them to misrepresent himself. At any rate, this is what I have found:

Michael Angeline was killed in a plane crash in 1981.

Kenneth Canshaw and Dennis Caudill were still in Fort Lauderdale, at least until after Schaefer was incarcerated.

Kirk Duckwitz may have returned to Milwaukee, though there is no current listing for him. While his exact whereabouts are unknown, no one has filed a missing person's report on him, and it is likely according to some investigators, that he is still alive somewhere.

Edward Greer is still living in Fort Lauderdale.

Steven Kindig was presumed to have returned to Pennsylvania.

These six names should be omitted from a list of possible Schaefer victims, and once again should never have been placed on it to start with. However, there is the case of Leonard Masar . . .

On January 3, 1973, a Martin County road worker, diligently worked his shovel and rake; an effort to maintain the dirt road that ran off highway A1A, toward the beach. The "road," hardly wide enough for a car to travel, was a lover's lane that ran in a snakelike line to a beach, not usually frequented by the general public. The area was a part of Hutchinson Island, the long, narrow jut of land that ran along the east coast of Southern Florida. The island lay partially in Martin County, but extended well into St. Lucie County to the north where in April of the same year, the bodies of Susan Place and Georgia Jessup would be discovered. But for now, the road worker had no knowledge of the grisly secrets this remote, seemingly peaceful, island beheld,

As the worker labored slowly toward the beach, having just returned to work from the New Year's holidays, he spied what he thought was a turtle shell barely protruding out of the soil. He kicked it and in doing so, uncovered it from its sandy bed, a skull that turned out to be what remained of Leonard Masar. The worker uncovered the rest of the body and found it to be lying in a shallow grave, wrapped in plastic. Only the upper part of the head had been exposed to time and the elements, the remainder was remarkably well preserved, but for one significant deletion; the hands had been removed. He was completely naked except for shoes and socks.

Masar had been missing since the night of August 11, 1972, about five months before the discovery of his body. He was last seen by an acquaintance named James Walker. Walker, a garage owner, saw Masar leave the Dutchman's Lounge in Riviera Beach at about 9:30 p.m. Other reports placed him at Carlson's Bar, also in Riviera Beach, later that night. He was also reportedly seen entering a Yellow Cab taxi, in which he frequently traveled. However, Yellow Cab had no record on their trip sheets that would substantiate that story.

Masar ran a small coffee shop in Riviera Beach, which is located just north of West Palm Beach. An average breakfast of two eggs, toast, and potatoes or grits, ran about fifty-two cents at that time. Masar made only about a hundred dollars a week at the shop, which his mother owned. However, he was known to carry a "roll of bills," usually about five to six hundred dollars, with which he would cash checks for a fee. He was a man who could make ends meet.

Masar was 5 feet, 5 inches and weighed about 140 pounds. He was not a large man, and his childhood polio had left him with one leg shorter than the other. That, and a metal plate in his shoulder from a previous surgery and his dental plates, helped to identify the corpse left in the shallow grave. Masar was 45 years old when he was murdered. Speculative theories were plentiful.

James Walker told police that Masar had said he was going to "meet a broad in the parking lot," when he left the Dutchman's Lounge. Therefore, police were inclined to look for a female killer. Then, too, many people felt that one of his "check-cashing clients" might have murdered him for his roll of bills. A killer was never found, nor any leads, and reporters covering the case, including Jayne Ellison, felt compelled to ask the opinions of several experts in the field of forensic science. Two psychiatrists, (among the specialists) both members of the American Academy of Forensic Sciences, were asked, "What kind of man killed Masar?" The following are excerpts from their answers.

"Very amateurish . . . between 25-38 years of age . . . probably a fairly muscular laborer."

"The hands make you think of a paranoid schizophrenic. Cut off the hands to get rid of evil things. Like in Macbeth. I would think we are looking for one man, a white man."

"He would not stand out in a crowd. He is not unusual. Not fat. Not lean. Relatively nondescript."

"A smart, itinerant boy isn't going to take a chance on such a crime . . . a smart crook wouldn't pick on such a little fellow (Masar). The killer is a young man, about 25 years of age. He hasn't learned how to do a thing in the field of crime. He is a loner. You can't imagine that he would have friends who would participate in such a crude act."

"There is always the possibility that the dead man's short leg made him despicable or a deformed character, therefore, a threat to the killer."

Speculation, for what it's worth, is still speculation. It would be several months later when the bodies of the Place and Jessup girls would be found, and because of their proximity of the location with that of Masar's grave, Schaefer became a suspect in Masar's death. Some psychiatrists who examined Schaefer have suggested that one of the reasons for his compulsion to murder girls, was because of an underlying hate for women, borne out of a latent homosexual drive that he would have been constantly battling, mentally. This being the case, it has been further suggested that Schaefer may have met with Masar and tried to engage in a homosexual tryst. A fling, if you will, that may have resulted in sexual failure for Schaefer, or is more commonly believed, rejected by Masar, whose sexual preferences were not known.

If this were true, then why cut off hands? Most investigators say it was an attempt to keep the body from being identified. But if this were true and Schaefer was the killer, why didn't he remove the teeth, which he certainly knew were as definite a means of identification as were fingerprints? At any rate, there is another theory, that investigators failed to see at that time.

In an earlier chapter of this book, we have part of a deposition taken of Thomas Stempkowski, a patrolman who attended the police academy with Schaefer. In that deposition, Stempkowski reveals that Schaefer owned an unusual set of handcuffs, which Schaefer repeatedly offered to place on one of the other academy students. None of the other students complied, because Schaefer never seemed to have a key to release the cuffs. Now, it is possible that Schaefer applied these cuffs to Masar, for whatever reason, to hold him captive, or perhaps for a sexual diversion. For whatever reason, once applied, it is likely that they could not be removed because there was no key. This would explain why Masar's hands were cut off, the handcuffs could possibly have been identified by policemen who knew, or had heard, that Schaefer owned such an unusual item. One must realize, too, that Schaefer himself told Stempkowski that he had obtained the handcuffs by cutting them "off the body of a dead person."

While this is only a theory, it should also be noted that to date no one has been arrested or convicted of Leonard Masar's murder. Later it would be suggested that perhaps Masar was connected with drug smuggling. Schaefer was quick to go along with this theory, adding that the deaths of Susan Place and Georgia Jessup were also the result of a drug deal gone awry. But there is no physical evidence, i.e., luxury cars, fancy clothes, swank apartment, that would support any allegations of drug smuggling with Masar, nor with Place or Jessup. These people lived meagerly, not extravagantly, and were for the most part simple people; a coffee shop owner, and two high school students. It is unlikely that any of them would be involved in drugs to the extent of getting themselves killed.

Jayne Ellison supported the theory that Schaefer killed Masar. She did so for three reasons: 1) The "handcuff theory; 2) The close proximity of the Masar grave to that of Susan and Georgia, and 3) The following letter, which was written by Gerard Schaefer while he was being psychologically evaluated at Florida State (Mental) Hospital in Chattahoochee. Schaefer wrote the letter in answer to a letter from Jayne Ellison, in which she requested Schaefer's opinion as to what happened to Masar. Grammatical errors are from Schaefer's original letter.

"Since you mentioned that this reply is confidential, I can give you theory about Masar. As you undoubtedly know, young girls are still being turned up missing and murdered since I have been incarcerated. The circumstances of my case, I mean everything falling into place so neatly. Casts a reasonable doubt on things if you care to look below the surface. I may be mentally ill, I may even be insane, only the doctors can know this; for sure. Remember, the beginning of my case on 7 22 72 with Wells-Trotter. I mentioned selling them into white slavery. I said I knew a man who would buy them. This is all in their statement to the police. I was arrested and he was murdered sometime between Aug 11- Jan. When his body turned up. The police don't talk much about the Masar murder, do they? But they do talk a lot about the Place-Jessup murders – Both on Hutchinson Island, near the beach. All kinds of information is being "leaked" out about my connections with missing women. A little evidence here, a little evidence there, all circumstantial of course. I understand that the state has very little of a case other than circumstantial but according to my lawyer, all the "lab" evidence is not in. Why rush on the part of the state if all the evidence is not in?

"Let me tell you a little story. The story should more than interest you but keep it confidential just in case something should happen to me. You have a daughter and should be at least be able to be trusted for her sake. I just hope all this business about the press keeping their sources confidential is true." (Ellison, at that time, believed that this reference to her daughter may have been Schaefer's way of threatening her. The wording could easily allow that assumption, but what is most interesting is that she had never told Schaefer about her daughter. Having been in jail for 3 months already - how did he find out she did have a daughter? He did the same thing with this reporter some years later.)

"Mrs. Ellison, reporter, all this began some time ago, centuries to be sure. But I will not speak in riddles. In 1969 two Broward Co. women disappeared under mysteriously similar circumstances. One of them, Lee Hainline was a good friend of mine. Older, more experienced and into drugs. She even attempted suicide at least once by an overdose. Life became too much to bear or was it guilty conscience? Late in Aug. or early Sept. 1969, she told me she was in fear of her life from someone who she did not mention because she was trying to "get away" and marry a guy by the name of Bonadies. She asked me to drive her to Miami airport so she could go to Kentucky and hide with relatives or her mother. Later she sent me a telegram that she had decided not to go and that was the last communication I had with her." (This telegram was never located.)

"We were confidants and lovers to a certain extent. I did have some of her jewelry in my possession but nothing valuable to be sure.

"Shortly after that the Hallock woman disappeared under mysterious circumstances dealing allegedly with drugs. I did not know her but according to the newspaper account in June of 1970 they visited a lot of the same places. Also in June of 1970 I flew to Luxemborg and was met at the airport by a Swede identifying himself as Costa Malm. Mr. Malm as it turned out dealt in international drug trafficking. I was out for adventure and ended up getting into more than I bargained   am an expert with a pistol and he needed protection so you might describe my job as one of "body guard" since it was necessary for him to carry extreme sums of money on his person.

"We made drug connections in Rheims, Paris, Avinignon, Aix en Provence, Arles, Barcelona, Malaga/and Torremolinos. The job paid me all my expenses and had an intrigue which appealed to me. Along the way we would pick up attractive young women hitchhikers and Malm would always phone ahead to get us a suitable place to stay. The women would always be left behind, with "friends" as we moved down through France & Spain toward Morrocco.

"Once into Morrocco we went to Tangiers where we went to a place in the Casbah right out of the Arabian Nights. I saw the transfer of 10s of thousands of dollars worth of Kilo Bricks of Hashish take place. The language was all in French so I could only get the drift of the conversation. I was also in Rabat, Casablanca, and Marrakech. If you do not believe in white slavery let me assure you that it does exist and large sums of money are involved. The main source is freewheeling teenage girls, here or in Europe. They end up in an Arabian Shiekdom somewhere on the African Continent. I am not an authority and don't wish to be. It is a nasty business.

"After I left Europe and returned here. Malm told me that I may be useful over here. I said "no". He said, "Think about it and I'd be contacted." I said, "Ok, but no deals." I came home, married my wife Teresa and got a job on a police dept. to further my ambitions in law, in short. (It's a long story) I got in trouble by sticking my nose into municipal police corruption in Broward Co. (Wilton Manors) and was blackballed into moving to Stuart.

"I know that the disappearances of Hitch Hiking females are not always rape & murder deals. White slavery runs out of this country too, but I have never been involved here. However, on 7 22 72 when I was trying to impress on Trotter & Wells the dangers of Hitching and told them they could be sold into white slavery. They laughed. I, knowing they could well be, decided to teach them a lesson and bound them and told them I knew someone who would buy them. I really didn't, but when the story got out someone figured that Masar was a fink to me, a Dep. Sheriff and he were hit (killed) unjustly. The business about him going out to "meet a broad" seems to fit. Check and see who is missing from where (female) around Aug. 11. It could be that he "delivered" someone to the beach to be boated away and then killed because he was suspected of having a contact with the police (double agent) His unexplained resources (the $500.00 roll of cash Masar was known to carry) seem to explain his job as delivery man, since all deals are cash on the line . . . "

The letter, what one can believe of it, is most interesting. But, if anything, it shows Schaefer more rather than less guilty, of at least complicity, rather than clearing him of suspicions. Once again no one has been charged for Masar's murder, and the case, according to police, is still open.

* * *

So, that is the List of 28, such as it is. Several of the names were omitted, while others led to dead ends, and still others remain surrounded by a veil of mystery. However, this is what we end up with, out of the given twenty-eight names that must have made up the original list, for which the media and the state attorney's office drew their body count number;

Susan Place and Georgia Jessup dead; Schaefer tried for their murders.

Mary Briscolina and Elsie Farmer, Leigh Hainline Bonadies, Collette Goodenough and Barbara Wilcox, Leonard Masar all dead; Schaefer a likely candidate for their killer.

Carmen Hallock, Elizabeth Wilt, Belinda Hutchins, Deborah Lowe, Kay Price, all still missing, but more likely than not, dead; Schaefer, again, a very likely suspect in their murders.

The rest of the list is compiled of people found, some never missing, some dead from various causes (including another killer who confessed to the murder of Malarik and Ferrel) and some who eventually returned home.

There are those, like little Wendy Stevenson, Peggy Rahn, and Deborah Lowe, as well as Kay Price, whose disappearances will always confound those of us who have looked for them. But after all the rhetorical smoke has cleared, the number that comes closest to being accurate that can be attributed to Gerard Schaefer with all existing evidence considered, is eleven. Again, this is not to say that Schaefer was definitely guilty of eleven murders; that was for a court of law to decide. This just concludes, for the sake of argument, that he was a very strong suspect in those eleven cases.

Once again, it should be mentioned that this list is not necessarily conclusive. There could be, possibly other victims that no one knew, or those that did, did not come forward with information to open a case on them. In the words of Dr. Joseph H. Davis, Miami's chief medical examiner, "There's always that possibility, that subsequent skeletal remains have been found . . . and have been by passed by other examiners." And so, their identity would forever be unknown. Be that as it may, we still have the existing eleven cases, for which Schaefer was tried for only two (Susan Place and Georgia Jessup) leaving the families of the other nine to wonder, "Who will pay for the death of my child?"

Chapter 9

The Trial

I saw the lips of the black-robed judges. I saw the decrees,
of what to me was fate, were still issuing from those
lips. I saw them fashion the syllables of my name, and I
shuddered because no sound succeeded.

From *The Pit and the Pendulum*, by Edgar Allan Poe

The teams assembled. Strategies were formed. Charges were filed. In May of 1973, Gerard John Schaefer was charged with two counts of first-degree murder. Even before that, since the discovery of the Place and Jessup bodies on April 1st, the legal machine's gears began to turn, and now were spinning, well-oiled, on both sides of the judicial automaton. The legal machine is, briefly, both amazing and tedious. It is in truth an intricate game, not unlike chess, whereas the defendant's innocence or guilt in the eyes of God and humanity are no longer the real issue; it is how well the game is played. Like the game of chess, one move in one direction sets off a whole chain of moves in opposing directions, each in turn effecting the other, and establishing new moves, new directions. In the end, one must wonder: yes, there was a "fair trial," as guaranteed by the Constitution of the United States, but did we really get to the truth of the matter? Ultimately, for the sake of sanity alone, one must accept the results of this system, or constantly doubt its authority and authenticity.

Before the trial can begin, there are many complicated procedures to perform, by both the prosecution and the defense. Every person who might (or might not) be called to the stand, must be on a list, which is presented to the court. Additionally, any evidence that might or might not be used (relating to the case, of course) or shown, or presented in court, must be labeled and listed and given to the court prior to the trial. There is little margin for error. There are few surprises. If anywhere down the line, the prosecution fails to have followed the designated procedure, one careless omission is committed, then the whole case can be dismissed, and the defendant, guilty or not, can take a walk. Likewise, if the defense is not watching the procedures very carefully, if he allows the prosecution to make an unfounded accusation without voicing his objections, then the defendant, guilty or not, may go to jail or die by the hands of the system that has promised him "due process of the law.".

It is not the intention of this author to omit the legal details of this trial, however, for the sake of brevity, a substantial amount of that information must be deleted. We will look at the key characters involved, the key witnesses called, briefly, the pre-trial hearing and jury selection, and of course, the outcome of the trial. Once again, this is to abbreviate the court's connection to this case, and thus outline, if you will, thousands of pages of court transcript, into a briefer, hopefully more readable chapter in the unusual case of Gerard Schaefer.

* * *

The team assembled to prosecute the case of Gerard Schaefer consisted of Robert Stone and Phillip Shailer. Stone had several years of experience within the criminal court system, but this would be his first murder case as the State Attorney for the 19th Judicial Circuit. To say he was concerned about the outcome would be an understatement. His humorous, Southern laid-back attitude belied his true feelings. From the time his office began investigating the case until the trial began, Stone lost over sixty pounds, from the stress of it. However, he felt he had prepared well, and he had confidence in his assistant, Phil Shailer.

Shailer was appointed by then Florida Governor Reuben Askew. The feeling was that a man was needed from the Broward County Stated Attorney's office, because much of the case involved either victims living in Broward or evidence seized from Schaefer's mother's house, also in Broward County. Phil Shailer was that man. Younger, perhaps not as experienced as Stone, and certainly less dramatic, with little to none of the Southern gentility that Stone had adopted and used to warm up the court and jurors; Shailer was more intense, and just as thorough. In opposition to Stone's style of "I'll get to it . . . in a minute, then I'll nail you;" Shailer often paced, tall and lean, hands in pocket, biting his lower lip as he stared at the floor, concentrating with his brow furrowed, selecting the most appropriate, and logical questions to pose to the witness. Years later, Stone would tell me, "off the record", that Schaefer knew Shailer from Schaefer's time as a patrolman down in Broward County. At one point during the trial, Schaefer leaned over to Shailer and said, "I had lunch with your wife at Lum's."

They felt, at that time, that Schaefer was trying to intimidate Shailer by indicating he knew what Shailer's wife looked like and where she dined frequently. However, there is no official record of this whispered conversation, and if it was a threat, it was worded carefully enough so as not to incriminate Schaefer any more than he already was.

For the defense, there was Elton Schwarz, appointed public defender. He would be assisted by Bruce Colton.

Schwarz was quiet, almost somber, but not at all a sheepish character. Indeed, though he often "operated on an even keel," his deep, gravelly voice was often heard, especially so in making persistent, sometimes annoying objections. Schwarz was a contradiction in appearance; wearing moderate to bold suits, with loud ties and white leather belt and shoes, and black-framed glasses. His outfits did not fit his rather sullen face, a look that may have been the result of a thankless, underpaid job, or perhaps because of his personal life where his marriage was now ending in divorce. He was a marked contrast to Robert Stone, with his stark, solid- colored blazers and rather aggressive personality.

Bruce Colton, Schwarz's assistant public defender, could have doubled for the actor Chad Everett. He would handle his end of the case smoothly, efficiently; perhaps a quieter, less conspicuous character in the legal drama's unfolding. He seemed to be absorbing, even learning as the case wore on.

Several other attorneys would assist in this case, intermittently. Richard Purdy and Anthony Young for the state, and James Brecker for the defense. However, though their assistance may have been invaluable in helping to form the case, track down more leads, or research law texts, these attorneys worked more in the background, and were not always present during the trial. Therefore, we will follow the legal maneuverings of the primary attorneys, Stone and Schwarz; while keeping in mind that there were many important players on both teams.

The overseer of these very different attorneys and their legal maneuvers was perhaps the most flamboyant character of them all. He was C. (Cyrus) Pfeiffer Trowbridge and he was the judge. Trowbridge was a true individualist. He had graduated head of his class in law school and at age 32, became the youngest barrister at that time to be named to a Florida Circuit Court judgeship. He was the son of a businessman, and the name Trowbridge is often connected with money in Martin County, Florida. He was the first to obtain a decision that a judge could carry a gun without a permit, and often did so underneath the folds of his judge's robe. A: robe that had gone from black to a faded purple hue over the many years that he wore it on the bench.

He was described thusly:

"He is quick and decisive . . . there are no dilemmas with Trowbridge."

"Always a jump ahead of the lawyers and their problems . . . he interprets the law as though he wrote it."

"Explanations are at his fingertips. Nothing is complicated. His logic seems faultless, like his speech: clear, easy, measured, with a surprising economy of words."

". . . a sense of adventure in his wit and firmness in his manner. He is a man born to be first."

But for all his wisdom and wealth, you'd never know it to look at the man. Besides the faded robe, he wore Chukka boots, and an ill-fitted toupee that often came back rearranged after chamber breaks or recesses for lunch. It seemed to be aligned more by the wind than by its wearer. He was likened to the television character Columbo; a disheveled, eccentric appearance disguising the intellect and wit of the underlying man.

Sitting at the center of these judicial tacticians, smiling benignly, some would say stupidly, ostentatious by his presence alone, was Gerard Schaefer. A: presence that grew considerably more and odder, compounded by his aloofness, and throughout the trial, his frequent haranguing of Robert Stone, and his persistent unblinking stare, which was usually directed at the state attorney, or whomever took the witness stand. The only time he would avert his gaze would be when a favorable point was made for him, either by a defense witness, or the legal semantics of Elton Schwarz; then he would turn to the present members of the media, grin widely and bounce his eyebrows up and down, Groucho Marx-style. Ira and Lucille Place would become so infuriated by Schaefer's boyish antics, it would be all they could do to restrain themselves from charging across the courtroom and strangling him.

His supporters were usually two: his mother, Doris, and his wife, Teresa. The two of them often exchanged hugged, with each other and the defendant, and whispered amongst themselves. On more than one occasion they were seen laughing and smiling outside the courtroom. Inside the courtroom they were stoic, sometimes tearful, always supportive of Schaefer, though Teresa showed signs of beginning to doubt her husband's credibility.

Jayne Ellison, who covered the case daily for the Palm Beach Post-Times, recalls Doris and Teresa as being so very different. Teresa was somber, insecure, doubtful and vulnerable, dressed conservatively as if she was going to church, sitting primly, at times crying softly, at times showing a quiet courage, and always displaying an air of properness. Doris changed her appearance, probably at the suggestion of her son's defense attorney. At the beginning of the trial, she appeared dressed in a purple miniskirt and white go-go boots, with a bouffant hairdo and flashing jewelry; the press was aghast. After her initial, shocking appearance, she returned the following days of the trial, dressed down, with a conservative hairstyle, no heavy make-up, plain shift dresses; the concerned mother of a young man wrongly being tried, she believed, for two murders. Thirteen years later, when we talked, she would still believe it was all some big mistake, or an even bigger conspiracy.

* * *

Before the trial could begin to start, the "pre-trial hearings" would have to take place. This is where time is voraciously consumed. During this phase, the evidence is listed, and the witness lists for both defense and prosecution, and the motions are filed, and this case had many. In fact, the motions, and their denials or acceptances, would take up nearly half of the court transcripts. Additionally, during this time, both the prosecution and the defense were feverishly looking for new evidence to either help the defendant, or condemn him,

Oddly, one of the most damning depositions at this time was taken from Henry (Hank) Lee Dean, Schaefer's brother-in-law, Teresa's brother. It would be used to link Schaefer with the "little brown purse" evidence that would figure heavily in connecting him to Georgia Jessup. Lem Brumley, Stone's chief investigator, conducted the deposition;

Q: I want to direct these questions, Hank, regarding Gerard John Schaefer. We will start off by asking do you know him, and how do you know him?

A: I know John through my sister. He is my brother-in-law. He married my sister.

Q: When was this?

A: This was what—in September? I don't remember when they got married. About a year and a half ago, approximately a year and a half ago from now.

Q: Okay, so you have been appraised of the present situation as far as John Schaefer is concerned, with him being arrested and suspected and charged with two murder charges. The following question is going to be directed to certain things that the statements that he has made to you and things that you are aware of:

On the day that John was charged, approximately two weeks ago last Friday, you were at the Martin County Jail with your sister, Teresa?

A: I was.

Q: Were you there for the purpose of seeing John, with your sister? If you will elaborate on that, and precisely why were you there?

A: My main concern at the time was the welfare of my sister in relationship to being divorced until this whole situation was cleared, or until John was convicted, one or the other. I talked to John, with my sister, and elaborated on the evidence which I had known to have been found, and I discussed this with John. Most of the things he did not know about. First of all, I had heard and read and been informed of some teeth that had been found belonging to one of the dead victims. And he asked me if this was out of the skulls of the girl's found in Martin County. I said I thought they were. And he advised me that they had not found the skulls of the girls up there and appeared to be very surprised that they might have come from those heads.

Q: Based on his actions and statements that he made to you that day, did you draw a conclusion as to the meaning that he put in behind the fact that he said that they could not or did not find those skulls, or it was impossible that the skulls were found of the two girls?

A: Yes. I got the impression that he felt that the skulls would not be found, for some reason or another.

Q: About the time that this conversation was being held did a deputy come in and serve him with a warrant charging him with the two present charges?

A: The deputies came in with the warrant, asking me to step out and Theresa to step out, and we did; at which time he was served with the warrant, fingerprinted, and booked on the charges, and then we resumed talking with John.

Q: What was the conversation about then?

A: Well, John appeared to be surprised that he was charged. (Schaefer was officially charged with two counts of murder on May 15, 1973.) He then asked Teresa if she wanted some money, which had been offered to him if he would give his story to Time magazine. He asked her if he should give them his story, and she said she didn't want any money.

Q: Did he make a statement to you to the effect that, or asking you, rather, should he confess to you?

A: He asked me if I wanted him to confess to me, and he said he could always just kill himself.

Q: Well, did he, in fact, confess?

A: No, he did not.

Q: Well, did you tell him that you did not want him to confess, or why didn't he go ahead? Or do you know why?

A: No. He turned to Teresa and told her that he was sure that I believed he did commit the crimes, and he asked her what she thought. And that was the end of that bit of conversation.

Q: Okay. Now I direct your attention to a period of time shortly after the two bodies were discovered in Martin County. I don't recall the exact date, and you may not either. If you do, please say so, but it was on or about April the 3rd. Can you tell us about your knowledge of a small suede leather clutch type purse?

A: I was talking with Teresa one day and asked—and told her that if John was innocent, we wanted to know, but if he was guilty we also had to know. Therefore, was there anything that she could think of that John gave her which might have belonged to one of the victims? She said that John had asked her to take some items out of the apartment, which at the time, he explained might be used just to make up some kind of evidence in that realm of thing. He specifically—well, she told me he specifically asked her to take some shells and a purse out of the apartment. Shortly after that I was in Teresa's apartment and observed a purse laying on the bed. I asked her if this purse was the one that John had referred to. She said yes. I asked her if she wanted it taken to mother's, or one way or the other, and I said that I would take it to mothers for her. And I took the purse. You want to know the disposition of the purse then?

Q: Yes. There was I understand that you have been a past deputy sheriff in Broward County and that you have friends or acquaintances there, and, to be more specific, Lieutenant Dave Yurchuck?

A: Right.

Q: And I understand that you called him one day to get briefed and get appraised of the present situation as to the investigation against John Schaefer there, and during this conversation the purse, or the fact that Teresa Schaefer had this purse, was brought out. Could you elaborate on that?

A: Yes. I advised Dave that I thought there was one or two items which may be linking factors in the case which he was working on. Therefore, I called Dave when I had possession of this purse. This was done on my own accord. And I turned this over to Dave for further investigation.

Q: When you turned the purse over to him did you make some type of mark on it so that you would know it in the future?

A: I did. I marked the purse, I believe, with my initials inside.

Q: One further thing, Hank, during the course of your conversation on the day that he was charged, was there conversation other than what you have already told us about that would lead you to believe, or did he, in fact, say that he was going to write a story, or collaborate with someone to write a story about his charges?

A: The only indication of giving a story was to the Time magazine. Which he appeared to feel confident that he did have a story to give, and would in turn receive money for, which he had offered Teresa. I asked him about—knowing that he was a religious person, I asked him what about his soul and what about God, and he said, "I just don't think of that at the times," or "I don't want to say that at the time." I tried to just ask him about what he thought about his soul, and he says he don't think about this.

Q: Hank, since you have known John Schaefer, I assume that you have on several occasions talked to him. This was prior to his arrest in Martin County on the Wells and Trotter cases there. Have you ever had a conversation with him concerning criminal acts, or crimes being committed?

A: Yes. I was talking to John late one evening and he asked me if I ever thought there could be a perfect crime where in fact all evidence was gone, and someone just disappeared. Did I think that there would be any chance of ever being caught? My reply was if someone committed a crime and they even left breath, someday something would come up and connect them to the crime. This conversation was over the course of, I guess, at least an hour, and probably more of questions, as far as evidence and things of this nature came about, and then that was the end of the conversation.

Q: How long ago?

A: This was right before John's involvement with the two girls up here that he is serving time for currently.

Q: And that was July of 1972?

A: Okay.

Q: So it would have been about May or June?

A: Right. Just maybe a month or two months before he was involved with these girls up here.

Q: Just in general terms, Hank, has he ever, in your presence, told you or anyone else, or discussed or explained the killing of human beings, either by persons or animals, or...

A: I have heard him tell stories of where bears had destroyed two teenagers in a mountain camp somewhere out west, and he went into detail as to how they had ripped the bodies apart. Now, if this was fantasy at the time, I don't recall, you know.

Q: Well, do you associate that in any way with a trip that he and Teresa took out to Yellowstone?

A: No. At this time, I believe that he was referring to times when he was out to Yellowstone before he ever met Teresa, and this was a story being related to smaller children.

Q: Was it a single story, or were there other similar stories?

A: There were other stories, but this one just stuck in my mind because it made an impression on me.

Q: By that, you mean it was a very gruesome type story?

A: It was an unusual story to be telling children.

MR. BRUMLEY: I have nothing further.

This testimony, which would be repeated during the trial, (with more than a few objections from Mr. Schwarz) would be one of the most damaging to Schaefer's case. Likewise, the testimony of Teresa Schaefer, which correlated with her brother's, was equally injurious. These two people were two of Schaefer's closest relatives, and their testimonies were some of the strongest reasons why Stone was convinced that he was prosecuting the right man.

Teresa Schaefer's deposition, also taken at this time, is rather lengthy, but is significant in that it gives us further insight into Gerard's history (much of which would not be allowed in court, because it did not pertain directly to either of the murdered girls he was being tried for). More importantly though, is the insight into the character of Gerard's young, naive wife. One can only wonder what feelings she must have experienced when faced with the growing realization that her husband was perhaps one of the most heinous serial killers in history. Daily, the news media began to label Gerard: "The Butcher of Blind Creek," the "Bluebeard of the Beach," the "Killer Cop," and so on. This, the man Teresa promised to love, honor, and obey, til-death-do-you-part. (All questions prefaced with a Q: are asked by either Robert Stone or Lem Brumley. All answers from Teresa are prefaced with an A.)

Q: Would you state your full name, please?
A: Teresa Dolly Schaefer.
Q: Teresa, you are married to Gerard J. Schaefer?
A: Yes.
Q: Known as John Schaefer?
A: Yes.
Q: When were you married to him?
A: September 11, 1971.
Q: Where were you married?
A: Should remember the name of the church—I think it's St. John's.
Q: What town?
A: It's in Fort Lauderdale.
Q: He's Catholic?
A: Yes.
Q: Are you Catholic?
A: No.
Q: What religion are you?
A: Methodist.
Q: After you were married, where did you live?
A: The address?
Q: Yes.
A: It's on Southeast 21st Street. I think it's 490 or something like that.
Q: And that's in Fort Lauderdale?
A: Yes.
Q: How long did you live there?
A: About six months, I think, something like that.
Q: Where did you live after that?
A: I think we moved up here after that.
Q: To Stuart.

A: Yes.

Q: When did you move to Stuart?

A: It would have been about July, '72.

Q: When did you say you were married, again?

A: September.

Q: Of '71?

A: Uh-huh.

Q: When did you first meet John?

A: January, '71.

Q: Where did you meet him?

A: Where I work.

Q: Where was that?

A: Econo-Way.

Q: You dated him from January until you were married in September? Did you ever leave the State of Florida with him?

A: Between January and September? No.

Q: Did he ever leave the State of Florida during that time, that you know of?

A: Not that I know of. Not that I recall.

Q: Then you say you moved to Stuart July of '72.

A: Approximately, yes.

Q: That's when he became—where was he employed when you first met him?

A: When I first met him? Wackenhut Corporation.

Q: And then how long did he stay with that job?

A: I don't know how long he'd been with it before he met me. I guess right up until we were married. He was going to school at the time, too.

Q: He stayed with them up until the time you were married?

A: As far as I can recall, yes.

Q: Where did he work after he worked at Wackenhut?

A: With Wilton Manors. (Police Department)

Q: And then how long did he work there?

A: I don't know how long.

Q: He was fired from there, isn't that correct?

A: Right.

Q: Where did he work after Wilton Manors?

A: I'm not sure. I think the other job would have been here. I don't think he worked anywhere else.

Q: What brought you to Stuart?

A: His job up here.

Q: He got a job?

A: With the Sheriff's Department.

Q: Did you know him when he applied for a job with the Broward Sheriff's office?

A: No. I was thinking he was working with some kind of grocery, but that was Wilton Manor.

Q: Have you ever been to West Virginia with him?

A: With John? No.

Q: Do you know whether or not he has ever been to West Virginia?

A: He's never said he's been there hunting or anything like that. Usually goes to South Dakota or somewhere.

Q: Do you know whether he's ever been to West Virginia? (These questions were in reference to the Malarik/ Ferrell murders.)

A: Through the State? I think he said he had driven on the Turnpike up there. I don't know where he was going.

Q: Did he say where?

A: No.

Q: Are you from West Virginia?

A: Yes.

Q: Where?

A: Bluefield.

Q: Have you been back to Bluefield since you have been married to John?

A: No,

Q: When you were in Stuart, did you ever go on any hunting trips with John or fishing trips?

A: We have been down to the Keys fishing. But I'm not sure whether we were here or still in Lauderdale at the time.

Q: You remember the camera, that man that came into your house and executed the search warrant, there was some film on there? Where was that fishing?

A: That would have been the other side of the State, but I don't think we were married yet. They have been in there for several months.

Q: Do you know where that was?

A: Around Fort Myers.

Q: Around Fort Myers?

A: I have got to get that film back. I keep asking.

Q: We'll give it back to you. Do you remember when John was arrested for the charge that he is now in jail for?

A: Yes.

Q: What did he tell you happened?

A: He really didn't come right out and tell it.

Q: Weren't you concerned about it?

A: He told me the same thing that was in the papers, basically. He said that—he said that he picked them up, and the same thing he had did the first—you know, he picked them up and called it in, you know, and I don't know what he did with the girls. But he said that he did not handcuff them or anything, you know. He was very upset at the time, so he really didn't say too much. I was more concerned about him.

Q: He didn't tell you he handcuffed them?

A: I think he said he didn't like tie them up with ropes and all that. But I'm not real sure about that.

Q: Those were his words, he didn't tie them up with ropes?

A: I don't know.

Q: Why would he say "ropes"?

A: Well, whatever he said. You know, I don't know really—I'm not the type of person that...Q: Weren't you a little bit curious why he would take two girls off in the woods and tie them up?

A: He said he was trying to teach them a lesson, and I took it for that.

Q: Did you really believe that's what he was trying to do?

A: Yes.

Q: Do you still believe that's what he was trying to do?

A: I don't know.

Q: That was in July. After he got out of jail on that charge, did you notice any change in him?

A: No.

Q: Did he ever discuss with you any of his relationships with other girls?

A: No, not really,

Q: After he got out in July, did you make trips with him to Fort Lauderdale?

A: We go down there, my family lives down there.

Q: Did he ever go down there without you?

A: He's gone down there to get stamps and things like that, the same day.

Q: He had a stamp collection?

A: (Nodding head affirmatively. No collection was ever found in his possessions.)

Q: You were working at Florida Power and Light at this time?

A: Uh-huh.

Q: He was dismissed from the Sheriff's Department after this incident he's in jail for?

A: Uh-huh.

Q: Where did he go to work after that?

A: He started work with a plumbing place for just...it only lasted for one day, and he got sick and he went to the doctor and was sick for a long time.

Q: What was he sick about?

A: I don't think the doctor really knew. Some kind of virus.

Q: Who was his doctor?

A: Dr. Davey.

Q: Then did he work any place else after that?

A: He worked with Kwik-Chek.

Q: When did he ever work there?

A: I think it was in November.

Q: In November? How long did he work for Kwik-Chek?

A: I imagine a couple months. I don't know

Q: He was sentenced in December. Do you know the date that he was sentenced?

A: It was before Christmas. I think it was around the 20th or something.

Q: Do you know why he did not start serving his time until January 15th?

A: No, I just thought they were going to wait until after the holidays and maybe he would start it. (In truth, the court did postpone Schaefer's servitude until after the holidays. In that time, it is likely that he murdered at least two more persons; Colette Goodenough and Barbara Wilcox.)

Q: Did he work any place else after the plumbing place, before he went to work for Kwik-Chek?

A: I don't remember if he did. I don't think so.

Q: What did he do for an income? Did you support the family during this time?

A: I worked steadily, yes.

Q: What did he do during the day?

A: He fished a lot, went looking for jobs, about all, I think.

Q: Did he ever make any trips to Fort Lauderdale?

A: Yeah, I guess that he has gone down.

Q: September 27th, do you know recall whether or not he was in Fort Lauderdale?

A: I don't remember whether he went, was going down or not that day.

Q: Didn't he take a hunting trip to South Dakota?

A: Yes.

Q: When was that?

A: It was in October – sometime in October.

Q: Do you know the date he left?

A: I think it was around the 13th or something like that.

Q: Do you know when he returned?

A: Around the 29th, I believe, I'm not sure.

Q: Did you go with him?

A: No, I didn't.

Q: Who went with him?

A: There were five or six in the car.

Q: Do you know their names?

A: Three of them.

Q: What were the names of the three you know?

A: His brother Gary, Ed and Jean Ferris.

Q: Ferris? How do you spell that name, F-e-r-r-i-s?

A: I believe.

Q: Who else?

A: There was another couple, but I don't know their names. They were friends of Mr. and Mrs. Ferris.

Q: Did he say anything when he went to South Dakota about going through Iowa or coming back through Iowa?

A: I received a phone call from him from Iowa.

Q: You received a phone call from Iowa? Do you know where it was?

A: No. I have it on my phone thing, slip I got from the phone company.

Q: Could it have been Cedar Rapids? (It was confirmed that it was from Cedar Rapids, and so it is possible that he met Goodenough and Wilcox there.)

A: I don't remember where it was,

Q: Do you know of anybody else that he knows outside the State of Florida, any names of friends or people that he knows?

A: Only his ex-wife. He hasn't been in contact with her for a long time.

Q: Did he use to travel with a singing group?

A: Yes.

Q: What was the name of that singing group?

A: I believe it was called Sing-out, I believe.

Q: Did they have a van...did they travel in a van?

A: I don't know.

Q: Was this before you met him?

A: Right.

Q: Has he ever been with these people since you met him?

A: Not that I know of.

Q: What bank have you banked with since you have known him, Teresa?

A: Plantation First Nations, I believe is one, Bank of Stuart.

Q: What other banks?

A: I believe those are the only two accounts we have both our names on.

Q: Do you know any accounts he has by himself? (Stone was inquiring about banks because of the number of bank bags that were found among Schaefer's belongings, coming from banks throughout the US)

A: I think he has one—oh, we had a saving account down there in another bank, First Federal Savings or somewhere,

Q: Do you have those savings books?

A: Do I have them? I closed our account in Lauderdale that I had, that we had.

Q: Do you have the cancelled checks from these accounts? Have you kept the cancelled checks?

A: Yes.

Q: He gave you a gold watch or a watch and a gold necklace, didn't he?

A: Yes,

Q: Do you have that with you?

A: (Nodding affirmatively)

Q: Is that the gold watch?

A: Uh-huh.

Q: Do you know where he bought that?

A: I believe he gave—bought most of the things from Leeds or Arden's down there – that wholesale place down there.

Q: Fort Lauderdale? How did he pay for them?

A: I believe he wrote checks for them.

Q: Do you have cancelled checks for them?

A: I believe I do.

Q: And you say "believe"? Are you pretty sure he bought them at Leeds or Arden's?

A: Yes.

Q: And are you sure you have cancelled checks for them?

A: I guess I do. I never really went and looked for them, but I remember him writing checks, because he had to use my checkbook and write down.

Q: When did he give you the watch?

A: In '71.

Q: Do you know what time in '71?

A: After we were married.

Q: Which would have been September? You know what month?

A: No.

Q: When is your birthday?

A: November.

Q: What day?

A: 17th.

Q: Would he have given it to you on the 17th of November?

A: No. I don't think it was given to me as a gift like that.

Q: What about the necklace, was it given to you the same time the watch was given to you?

(Stone pursued these jewelry questions so intensely because it was believed that the jewelry was that of one of Schaefer's victims.)

A: No, it was given to me at a different time.

Q: Do you know what month?

A: That might have been a birthday gift in '72, I'm not sure.

Q: Was he, between July and the time he went to jail, was he ever away from you overnight?

A: Not that I can remember. He always...never went anywhere, he would always be home at night.

Q: Think really hard on that, it's important.

A: I don't recall him being away overnight. Whenever he went anywhere, it would be both of us together most of the time.

Q: When he came back from South Dakota he had a .38 caliber pistol. Did he tell you where he got that?

A: You mean that he had gotten from there?

Q: Yes.

A: I really don't.

Q: Didn't you know something about a gun that was stolen? Did he ever...

A: It was stolen, it was stolen? I don't believe he ever stole anything, any gun or anything.

Q: Were you told it was stolen?

A: I had heard that there was a gun in his possession that was stolen. But I don't believe he stole it.

Q: Do you know where he was a week just before he went into jail?

A: Not exactly the week before.

Q: Would have been the week between January 8th and January 15th.

A: He might have gone somewhere or something, I don't know.

Q: Did he leave overnight?

A: I don't recall him leaving where he would stay overnight.

Q: Can you think of him being gone, knowing he was going into jail January 15th?

A: Not that I remember.

Q: Did he bring you any jewelry or gifts home just before he went into jail on January 15th, or any of those scarves you talked about?

A: He did give me a couple scarves, but those weren't like right before he went in or anything.

Q: How long before?

A: Just in the course of the time we were married.

Q: Do you know where he was between January 8th and January 15th? (Again, Stone was trying to determine if Schaefer had gone to meet Goodenough and Wilcox.)

A: I can't say specifically.

Q: He wasn't working then, was he?

A: He was working for Pantry Pride for around that time until in January some time before he went in.

Q: Were you working then?

A: (Nodding affirmatively)

Q: Right after they found the bodies of two girls over on the beach, he told you to get rid of some things. What did he tell you to get rid of—didn't he tell you to get rid of some things?

A: He told me that he did not do these things, which I believed him.

Q: You still believe him?

A: That, I don't know. He said that he just asked me to get—to bring some things down to Lauderdale, that they might—it might cause him to get into trouble like if they were trying to accuse him of something.

Q: What things did he tell you to take to Lauderdale?

A: Some bullets and things like that.

Q: And what else?

A: He said there was a purse with bullets, to take that down.

Q: It was a suede purse?

A: Yeah.

Q: Little hand suede purse?

A: Yes.

Q: What did you do with that suede purse?

A: My brother found it and took it down.

Q: And you told your brother what he had told you to do?

A: I just said I was—I was going to take it down to Lauderdale with some things.

Q: Didn't you think it rather strange he wanted you to get rid of something right after they found two bodies over on the beach?

A: No. Well, I mean, like a lot of time people are accused of things and they find things that might . . . and they try to put it together to make a case out of it.

Q: Where did he get that purse?

A: I don't know. He said he had found it somewhere.

Q: Did he say where he had found it?

A: No.

Q: When did he give it to you?

A: I believe it was some time in the latter part of '72.

Q: Once before when you told it to me, didn't you say you believed he brought it home for around your birthday?

A: It might have been. I don't remember.

Q: What else did he tell you to get rid of?

A: Said to take his guns and things down to Lauderdale.

Q: What about a trunk? Was that already down there?

A: There was no trunk up here.

Q: Your read some of the writings attributed to him, is that correct?

A: Yes.

Q: Did you recognize his handwriting on some of them?

A: They might have been written by him, I'm not sure.

Q: You recognized his handwriting? You'd recognize it if you saw it?

A: I imagine.

Q: You get letters from him almost daily, don't you?

A: Uh-huh.

Q: You got one just recently from him?

A: Yes.

Q: What else did he tell you to get rid of? Tell you to get rid of some scarves?

A: No.

Q: Did you get rid of any scarves?

A: Yes.

Q: Why?

A: I just wanted...I don't know where the other one...

Q: Why did you get rid of it?

A: Because I did not feel it had anything to do with the case at all.

Q: Why would you get rid of it?

A: I don't know.

Q: Did you keep one?

A: No, I don't know where the other one is.

Q: Do you know why he would have possession of another girl's passport and driver's license (Goodenough and Wilcox)

A: No, I don't.

Q: – who was last seen alive in Biloxi, Mississippi, on January 8th? Why would he have...

A: January, '73?

Q: January 8th of '73.

A: He couldn't have been up there at that time.

Q: But she was on her way to Florida January 8th of '73? Do you know why he would have something like that?

A: No, I don't. I have never gone into his belongings or anything.

Q: He ever give you any jewelry?

A: None other than my watch.

Q: You have been shown these photographs before. Don't you believe that photograph to be the photograph of your husband?

A: It could be. (These were the photographs of a man, dressed in women's clothing in some, partially naked in others, taken by the person in the pictures. The face cannot be seen, but the rest of the body is quite visible. In some of the pictures the man is hanging himself, in others he appears to have smeared feces across his buttocks.)

Q: Does he have a scar on his buttocks, his rump?

A: He has one, but I'm not sure exactly where it's at.

Q: What does it look like?

A: I don't know, just a scar.

Q: Is it Y-shaped, or fork-shaped?

A: I don't know.

Q: I'll give this back to you. Did your husband ever say anything to you about, talk to you about the fact that he liked to collect pins or things that belonged to women?

A: No.

Q: Did you ever see any teeth in his possession?

A: Only the ones that he pulled out of his mouth.

Q: You have never seen anybody else's teeth?

A: No.

Q: You wouldn't know the reason why he would have the teeth that belonged to some girl that had been missing for several years? (Carmen Hallock)

A: I don't know.

Q: Did you know a Bonadies girl when you lived in Fort Lauderdale?

A: No.

Q: A: girl named Hallock or Hutchins?

A: No.

Q: A: girl named Briscolina?

A: No.

Q: Farmer?

A: No.

Q: Did you ever know Susan Place or Georgia Jessup?

A: No.

Q: Did your husband ever discuss with you that he had a prior mental condition?

A: He just told me that he had seen someone out at a clinic, because of family problems.

Q: Do you think he's mentally ill now?

A: I believe he has a problem.

Q: What is his problem?

A: Well...

Q: What do you think it is?

A: I don't know for sure what type of problem he has.

Q: His letters seem to you to make you think that he doesn't know what he's doing?

A: He seems okay.

Q: In fact, didn't you just get a letter where he made the comment that he—there is no death penalty in this case, it makes him happy?

A: Yes.

Q: Do you also know that he wrote a letter saying that if we really got close, he'd have to get F. Lee Bailey or somebody else? Did you know that?

A: No.

Q: Has he ever discussed with you that he might hire another lawyer?

A: No.

Q: Did he ever tell you that he confessed to all these crimes to his priest?

A: No.

Q: Do you know who Collette is?

A: No.

Q: Have you ever seen this book of history of torture?
A: No,
Q: Do you know why he would collect money bags from all over the United States?
A: He has gotten coins from other countries and things like that, and it might have been included in them.
Q: Has he ever discussed pornography with you?
A: No.
Q: Has he ever asked you to look at pornography with him?
A: No.
Q: Have you ever seen those teeth before?
A: Just the picture.
Q: Did you ever see these newspaper articles that he kept?
A: No.
(The following questions were asked in reference to photographs of evidence taken at Schaefer's mother's house in Fort Lauderdale.)
Q: Are those your earrings?
A: No.
Q: Are those?
A: No,
Q: Is that your pin? (Shows her several various pins.)
Q: Those are the guns, aren't they, or appear to be?
A: Yes, appear to be.
Q: I don't want to show you these nasty pictures--is this your pin?
A: No.
Q: Do you know why he would have this passport of this girl?
A: No, I don't.
Q: I'm just going to go through them. If any of them are yours, say so... (exhibiting photographs). (Stone showed Teresa dozens of photos of jewelry, none of which was hers.)
A: No.
Q: Those are his sleeping bags, aren't they?
A: I have seen some similar to that at his home.
Q: But these aren't the ones he kept at the house where you lived? (In fact, the sleeping bag is believed to have belonged to Collette Goodenough.)
A: We had a double sleeping bag.
Q: Is that your gold jewelry case?
A: No.
Q: Is that pin of Louisiana yours?

A: No.

Q: Is that your bracelet?

A: No.

Q: That's not?

A: No.

Q: That's not yours?

A: No.

Q: Okay. You can sit back down. Have you ever seen any of those items before you saw these pictures?

A: No.

Q: Do you know that those items belonged to girls that are missing and some of them belonged to girls that have been found, same as these two girls were found?

A: I know that some of those people (family members) said they belonged to some of the girls.

Q: You know of any reason why he would have the pins that belonged to two girls that were found dead in Fort Lauderdale, and have items that belonged to girls that were found dead in Fort Pierce?

A: No.

Q: You just think there is nothing wrong with that?

A: I just don't know what to think.

Q: It's not what you would consider to be usual, is it?

A: No, I guess not.

Q: This is a question that I'm not sure even you can answer it correctly, to know what you mean. Was your sex life normal? What you consider "normal"?

A: Depends on what you'd call normal.

Q: Well, I mean did he ever ask you to do any real weird things?

A: No.

Q: We are all adults up here. And I understand he never wanted to beat you or hit you in any way.

A: No.

Q: He never wanted you to mistreat him?

A: No.

Q: You know what a masochist is, don't you?

A: Yeah.

Q: Was there ever any indication of that?

A: No.

Q: Didn't he tell you one time, and you didn't think much about it, that there was some day he wanted to sit down and tell you something? I think he told me that once before.

A: He said—it was about his problem, he wanted to tell me about it. He never said anything before.

Q: Could it be he also wanted to tell you he had a hang-up on death, too?

A: I don't know.

Q: Do you know what he told the psychiatrist?

A: A: few things, I didn't read the report or anything.

Q: Did you know that he liked to hang himself from trees, that he had sexual excitement like that?

A: Someone had told me something like that, yes.

Q: But he never told you that?

A: No.

Q: Did he ever discusses with you that he liked—did he ever kid around the house by putting on your clothes?

A: No.

Q: Did he ever tells you that a doctor ordered him to write down his thoughts and feelings?

A: Yes.

Q: In manuscript form? Did he tell you that he did that?

A: He told me that his writings were from other doctors that had told him to write about it.

Q: When did he tell you this, before or after the bodies were found?

A: I guess it was after they searched and everything, because he never said anything before.

Q: You didn't know anything about those before, did you?

A: No.

Q: It was after the search that he revealed that to you?

A: Yes.

Q: Did you know that he told those two girls, that got away, that he was going to bury them?

A: No, that's—no.

Q: You haven't been reading the papers, have you?

A: Just once recently.

Q: Did you know that he, in his writings, described, detailed, the exact situation that was found with the two girls over here on this beach?

A: In this particular situation?

Q: Yes.

A: No.

Q: You say, "this particular situation"? You know of some other situation?

A: No, I don't,

Q: Teresa, this record, I know when I talked to you before, that you had a good life with him. And I know you have some good feelings for him. Are you in a position now that you feel like that you want to do anything you can to help him?

A: I muchly want to help him, yes. But I don't know what you mean...

Q: Would you cover up anything to help him?

A: No.

Q: Would you hide anything or keep anything from us, because you think it might be damaging to him in any way?

A: No.

Q: If he were guilty of these things that he's accused of, you wouldn't want him back out on the street, would you?

A: That's not really for me to say.

Q: Lem (Brumley), do you have any questions you want to ask?

Q: Just a couple here, Teresa. On your watch, I understand there was a gold cross he had given you, or a gold filigree cross or necklace.

A: Gave me a necklace.

Q: Necklace?

A: Just a rose with a chip of a diamond in it.

Q: The one that you are wearing now? Is that the watch that you are wearing now?

A: Yes.

Q: Did he give both of them to you at the same time, or separate?

A: No.

Q: Separate times? Do you recall when he gave them to you?

A: One was in '71 and the other one was...

Q: Do you have the checks?

A: I imagine I do. I haven't thrown anything away.

Q: Did you see the checks, or do you recall distinctly any...

A: Well, I have gone through all my checks at the time I get them back from the bank, and none have been missing or anything like that. He had to write them down in my checkbook where they were from,

Q: My question is: Do you distinctly recall seeing the checks for the two items?

A: Not distinctly, no.

BY MR. STONE:

Q: Where is the gold necklace now?

A: (Teresa Exhibiting necklace around neck)

BY MR. BRUMLEY:

Q: I hate to keep on the same subject of the watch and the necklace there, but all the other things being considered, he had several items of jewelry that you are aware of. You just got through looking at photographs of them there. He gave you the pocketbook, which since has been identified as belonging to one of the girls over here. And we are interested in the watch and the necklace. Either to eliminate it, you know, if you did buy those, I certainly want to find that out.

A: These things were in new cases and everything when I got them.

Q: They were?

A: They were just handed to me.

Q: Was it an occasion in particular, birthday?

A: I think the necklace was for my birthday. The watch was not.

Q: There is no occasion for the watch?

A: Fight or something, I'm not sure.

Q: Just a make-up present?

A: Sure.

BY MR. STONE:

Q: Did you-all have fights very often?

A: No.

Q: What would you have had a fight over?

A: Maybe him having to sleep when he was working on duty, you know, coming in and sleeping—you know, different hours. Maybe once or something, but it was never anything...

Q: Is that the purse he gave you (exhibiting purse)?

A: I believe it is. Looks like the purse that John gave me.

BY MR. BRUMLEY:

Q: Did he mention to you about a singing group that he was with at one time? Was he a musician or a singer in the...?

A: He was a singer. It was either—I said Sing-out—it was Up with People Sing-out, one of them, I'm not sure. He had booklets in his room. I don't remember the name of it.

Q: Do you know when this was?

A: No, I don't know what year or anything. It was before I met him.

Q: Do you know what area of the country that he was singing in?

A: No.

Q: Have you ever been out of the State anywhere with him, any other State?

A: We went to Wyoming one time.

Q: Do you recall when that was?

A: The end of May it would be, '72.

Q: What town were you in?

A: We went to Yellowstone and back in one week.

Q: So you were only in Yellowstone what, couple days?

A: Right. Straight drive up and back.

Q: Did anything unusual happen while you were at Yellowstone?

A: No.

Q: Any of the people there, did you hear about anything?

A: No. We were together at all times.

BY MR. STONE:

Q: Does that appear to be his handwriting?

A: It looks like it might be.

Q: Does that appear to be his handwriting?

A: Yes.

Q: Does that appear to be his handwriting?

A: It could be, yes.

Q: You said "yes" on this and "could be" on this.

A: Because I know the letter.

Q: You know you got that, right?

A: Right, I know the letter.

BY MR. BRUMLEY:

Q: Teresa, are you familiar with the areas that he hunted in when he went hunting? Ever go with him?

A: I never went hunting with him.

Q: Did he ever tell you...

A: We went fishing together all the time, we didn't go hunting.

Q: What areas did you fish in?

A: Went to the Keys, sometimes, sometimes over across the State.

BY MR. STONE:

Q: When were you in the Keys?

A: Sometime...it was out of season on a couple of times. It wasn't in season.

Q: Did he own a big machete?

A: I've never seen one. I don't know whether he did or not.

Q: You saw a picture of the one we found?

A: No.

Q: Have you ever been married before?

A: No.

Q: How old are you?

A: 21.

Q: And your birthday is when?

A: November 17th.

Q: November 17th, right. Let me ask you this. This is a personal question; did he have any difficulty making love from what most people consider the normal way?

A: No.

Q: Did you have intercourse that way most frequently—more frequently than you did any other way?

A: I'm not sure what you mean, but there was never anything abnormal in our sex relationship.

Q: You know why he broke up with his first wife?

A: Basically.

Q: Because of sex?

A: Uh-huh. From what I understand, she was a Mormon or something.

BY MR. BRUMLEY:

Q: Teresa, do you recall the boots and the orange looking like hunting boots?

A: Yes.

Q: Do you know where he got those boots?

A: What store, you mean?

Q: Yes.

A: I believe it was K-Mart or Woolco, or something like that.

Q: Teresa, did you ever find or see any women's clothing of any kind in his car, in his possession?

A: There was never anything to indicate, you know, what they found, you know.

Q: Aside from what you have read in the papers, were there any clothing at all?

A: That were found like in the car or something like that, you mean?

Q: Yes.

A: No, there were nothing like that.

Q: Other than the purse in the way of wearing apparel and the two pieces of jewelry, the watch and the necklace, did he ever give you any other clothing?

A: No...now that I recall, there was some kind of a...there were a couple pair of underwear he gave me once a long time ago.

Q: Nothing that you could think of...

A: I think he said he had found them. I think they were in my car or something. He never used my car. They could have been like my sister-in-law's or something. He'd never drive my car. Put that cleaning in the back seat, or something, and fell out, that I ended up with them.

Q: Did they (sister in law) drive your car from time to time?

A: They had their clothing in my car before, I believe, to the laundry and things like that.

Q: Did he (Schaefer) ever drive your car at any time?

A: He always used his. If we drove, we might have driven my car out to dinner or something, but I was always with him when he took it.

Q: You never traded cars, like...

A: I don't know now to drive his car.

Q: The only way you are talking about, he told you that he had found them?

A: No, he didn't say...he didn't know where they'd come from.

Q: In other words, they appeared in your car and you asked him if he knew anything about them.

A: I asked him if he knew where they came from, he said "No."

Q: Are you afraid of him now?

A: John? No, I know he would never hurt me.

Q: Have you formed any opinion one way or the other about what you have been reading and what he said?

A: I don't know who to believe.

Q: That's understandable. Other than the camera we got those photographs, I might add there are a couple of them there as a matter of fact, there are three or four of them, one or two of you that are pretty good photographs, very clear. They are beautiful pictures. Other than that camera that they took from your apartment there in Stuart, did you own another camera?

A: I have a camera, yes.

Q: Is it the same type?

A: No, it's an Instamatic.

Q: I believe the one we got was a little Instamatic.

A: I believe it's another brand or something, this is a Kodak.

Q: This is the type of Polaroid shots you mean, or regular film?

A: Takes regular film.

Q: I understand your parents are in the glass and mirror business, or were at one time?

A: My father is dead. My mother's in it; the family, my brothers.

Q: It is your brothers' business?

A: Uh-huh.

Q: How long has he been in that business?

A: My father started it up north. We have been down here for twenty years at least, so it must be several...I don't know how many years, maybe thirty years or something like that.

Q: They are still in the business now?

A: Uh-huh.

Q: Did you know if John ever got any mirrors from them?

A: Not that I know of.

Q: Particularly large mirrors. (This refers to mirrors used in photos of a man hanging in the woods, in women's clothing. These photos were seized in the search of Doris Schaefer's home.)

A: No.

BY MR. STONE:

Q: You still have that one little elusive scarf we were talking about?

A: I don't know where it is.

Q: Are you sure you don't know where it is, or did you get rid of it?

A: I did not personally get rid of it.

Q: Who did?

A: I gave it to I someone. I don't know what they did with it.

Q: Who did you give it to?

A: You are not very nice . . . I believe I gave it to his family.

Q: Which member of his family?

A: His brother. He was up here, and I said it was something Gerard was questioning, and I gave it to him.

Q: That was Gary?

A: Or his sister or something. I don't know who.

Q: You said that was something there was a question about, so you gave it to him?

A: Yes. Somebody had said something about, you know...you want it, right? I don't even know. I can check and see. I don't care.

One of the most incredible aspects of this case is that Gerard Schaefer would never take the stand during his trial. Neither the state nor the defense called upon him to testify. This is particularly surprising when one discovers how extremely verbal Schaefer is. He did take the stand during the pre-trial hearings and though his testimony is brief, it clearly shows the animosity between himself and Stone, and Schwarz and Stone, that persisted throughout the hearings, and the trial.

DIRECT EXAMINATION BY MR. SCHWARZ:

Q: Please state your name.
A: Gerard John Schaefer, Jr.
Q: You are the defendant in this case, is that correct?
A: Yes, sir.
Q: Did you at any time kill Georgia Jessup or Susan Place?
A: No, sir.
Q: Have you ever seen either of these two girls in your life?
A: No, sir.

CROSS EXAMINATION BY MR. STONE:

Q: Were you in Fort Lauderdale on September 27, 1972?
A: I don't remember being in Fort Lauderdale on that date.
Q: You don't remember at all?
A: No, sir, I do not.
Q: Could you have been in Fort Lauderdale on September 27, 1972?
A: It is a possibility that I could have been. I don't recall being there.
Q: What kind of car do you own?
A: Pardon me?
Q: What kind of car do you own?
A: A: Datsun.
Q: What year is it?
A: 1969
Q: And do you know what the license tag number of that car is?

A: No, sir. I do not.

Q: All right, do you know whether you killed Georgia or Susan Place? Do you know whether you did or not?

A: Do what?

Q: Do you know for sure that you didn't kill those two girls?

A: I killed no one.

Q: You killed no one?

A: No, I didn't kill anyone.

Q: All right, do you know, did you authorize your attorney to file this notice of statement of particulars on your behalf today? Have you seen this before? Read it over closely.

A: (Witness reading document silently.) I don't understand some of the wording of this. I just—whatever my attorney advises me to sign, I sign.

Q: You didn't sign it. He signed it. Did you authorize him to do that?

A: He is my attorney and whatever he does he has my authorization to do it. I don't understand some of the words there in that, or anything.

MR. STONE: I would like to have that marked, even though it is filed, for identification.

Q: Do you know this says you are suffering from paranoid schizophrenia and you might have killed them and not even known it?

MR. SCHWARZ: I object to that unless he reads it verbatim. Your Honor, it is not evidence. The document is the best evidence of what it says.

MR. STONE; I will offer it into evidence.

MR. SCHWARZ: I object to it, your Honor, it doesn't bear his signature at all.

MR. STONE:

Q: Did you authorize your attorney –?

MR. SCHWARZ: It was filed by me as attorney for the defendant,

Q: Did you discuss it with your attorney and authorize him to file on your behalf a statement that you might have committed this act and not have known it?

MR. SCHWARZ: That isn't what the statement says.

MR. STONE: I think that is a fair question.

MR. SCHWARZ: I object to him inferring what it is. If he wants to show it to him and say, "Did you authorize the signing of this or the filing of it by you attorney," fine, but I don't like him putting words into the pleading that may or may not be there.

MR. STONE: He puts the man on the witness stand and denies he did something, then files a pleading and says if he did do it he doesn't know what he was doing, so if he didn't know what he was doing when he filed this pleading, he doesn't know what he is saying now, he doesn't know whether he didn't or not, now.

MR. SCHWARZ: It specifically states, "Without admission of committing any acts set forth in the Amended Information."

MR. STONE: That is correct, but the point is he is raising a defense that the man might have done it but didn't know whether he did or didn't, and then he puts him on the stand and is going to use him to say he didn't do it.

THE COURT: That is argument and not a question. You can make that argument at the conclusion. I will sustain the objection.

BY MR. STONE:

Q: Let me ask you. Did you authorize this being filed?

A: As I said, Mr. Schwarz is my attorney and he has the power to do whatever he feels necessary.

Q: Do you know what that is saying, what that suggestion is?

A: Like I said, I don't understand ...you asked me to read it and I read it and I don't understand the words.

Q: You don't understand it?

A: I am not a lawyer. I don't understand the legal terms.

Q: You don't understand the medical terms?

A: No, sir. I am not a doctor.

MR. STONE: We would like to offer this evidence, may it please the Court, just for this hearing, admit that into evidence specifically.

MR. SCHWARZ: I object to it, Your Honor. It is not signed by him.

THE COURT: All right, I will sustain the objection.

BY MR. STONE:

Q: Okay. In November of last year did you give your wife a brown hippie purse?

MR. SCHWARZ: I object to that. If we are going to start going into a full trial on this now, fine, but...

MR. STONE: He denies he ever knew these girls, and he said he never has seen them, and I am going to have evidence to show that he had in his possession belongings that belonged to those girls. He specifically asked him if he had ever seen these girls and he denied it.

THE COURT: Mr. Schwarz, I don't see how I can sustain that objection. You asked him did he kill these girls, and Mr. Stone has a right to cross examine him on that subject.

MR. SCHWARZ: He is asking him to identify something by a vague and indefinite term of a "hippie purse." If he has something to show him and ask if he gave this to his wife, fine, but I object to the form of that question.

BY MR. STONE:

Q: Did you give your wife a brown suede purse last year?

A: I would like to see it.

Q: Well, do you recall giving her a purse?

A: I have given her many gifts during our marriage. If you have something you would like me to identify...

MR. STONE: Will the Court give me about two minutes? I can get something.

THE COURT: Send Mr. Young out, or one of our assistants out. Can we go ahead with anything else while we are waiting?

MR. STONE: Yes, sir. I am just checking here on something.

Q: Did you make the statement to Hank Dean in the St. Lucie, or the Martin County, Jail, did you say to him, "You want me to go ahead and confess to these crimes?" Now, do you recall making that statement in the presence of your wife?

A: In the presence of my wife?

Q: Yes, do you recall making that?

A: No, I don't recall making that.

Q: Do you recall making that statement to Hank Dean that, "You want me to go ahead and make you a lot of money telling the whole story?" Now, do you remember making that statement?

A: No, I don't remember making that statement.

Q: Do you feel you are suffering from some type of mental disorder?

A: Yes, I do.

Q: And do you feel that mental disorder might be such that you might not know what you do at times?

A: Yes. Sometimes I am very confused about what I do.

Q: And do you feel that that mental disorder might be such that sometimes you can't separate fact from fantasy?

A: Yes, I will have to say that.

MR. STONE: Judge, I want to wait, if you don't mind, until I get that (purse) if we can wait just a second.

Then continuing:

Q: Do you recall asking your wife right after these two bodies, making the statement right after these two bodies were found, that, "They are probably going to pin these two on me, also"?

A: Making the statement to her?

MR. SCHWARZ: I object to that, Your Honor, as privileged communication.

MR. STONE: He is on the witness stand and he denied his guilt.

MR. SCHWARZ: That doesn't make any difference as to whether he denies his guilt. He still can't be required to disclose confidential communications.

MR. STONE: I think he waives it once he takes that witness stand.

THE COURT: I will sustain the objection.

BY MR. STONE:

Q: You don't recall right after April 1 telling her to get rid of that purse when the bodies were found?

MR. SCHWARZ: Object, Your Honor, confidential communication between husband and wife.

THE COURT: Sustain the objection. (Author's note: This should not have been sustained – because Schwarz waived confidential communications between wife and husband at the beginning of the hearing.)

BY MR. STONE:

Q: Where were you on September 27, between September 21 and 28 that week; where did you go?

A: Between September...?

Q: 21st to 28th, that week. Do you know where you were?

A: I would have to have a calendar in front of me and then perhaps I could recall. Do you have a calendar?

Q: Didn't you go to Fort Lauderdale quite often?

A: Quite often, no, very rarely.

Q: And your wife was working at that time, wasn't she?

A: Yes, she was.

Q: And you had just been charged with a crime in Martin County, isn't that correct?

A: Yes.

MR. SCHWARZ: Object, Your Honor. I don't see any relevancy or materiality as to any other...

Q: Were you working?

THE COURT: I will sustain the objection.

BY MR. STONE:

Q: Were you working at that time?

A: At which time, sir?

Q: Around September 27?

A: I believe I was employed around that time. I do work on and off doing things.

Q: And it is your testimony here today you have never seen Susan Place or Georgia Jessup in your life?

A: Yes, sir, that is my testimony.

Q: You have never seen them?

A: I have never seen them. Mr. Stone, I have seen a photograph that was allegedly said to be Susan Place, was shown to me by a detective.

Q: That was how you were in the Martin County Jail, correct?

A: Yes. That is just to get it straight. He was considering where I was on October 27. (Schaefer, once again tries to imply that the photograph of Susan Place he was shown while in jail, was originally marked "missing - October 27, 1972," then changed to September 27, 1972. This is a position he would forever maintain. It is pointless, however, as there are missing person's reports filed on Susan Place before October 27, 1972.)

Q: Do you recall ever making the statement to any individual that you had never been in Fort Lauderdale around that period of time at all, to any newspaper reporters?

MR. SCHWARZ: Around what time? He testified...

MR. STONE: September 27. September 27.

MR. SCHWARZ: Your Honor, I object to that unless he specifies the individuals, Your Honor. It is involving confidential communication.

THE COURT: I will sustain the objection.

MR. STONE: Judge, I have no further questions until we can get that... Judge, if we can wait it will just take one second.

BY MR. STONE:

Q: Didn't you used to visit with your wife with a friend in Oakland Park, Florida, to a friend's house in Oakland Park, didn't you and your wife visit them?

A: Who?

Q: You and your wife visit a friend in Oakland Park?

A: What friends?

MR. SCHWARZ: I object to the vagueness on that, Your Honor. The man lived in Fort Lauderdale for years, as the State Attorney knows.

MR. STONE: I just want to ask him if he had a friend in Oakland Park, Florida.

A: If you can state to me a name, I could probably tell you whether they lived in Oakland Park, but the Fort Lauderdale metropolitan area encompasses so many different municipalities, it is kind of hard to say when...

Q: You know where Oakland Park is, Mr. Schaefer. Weren't you a police officer in Wilton Manor?

A: Yes. It is adjoining Wilton Manor, yes.

Q: Didn't you have a friend who lived in Oakland Park around September 27?

MR. SCHWARZ: I object.

Q: Around September 27, around that time, didn't you have a friend who lived in that area of Oakland Park?

A: I have very few friends. If you could tell me who the person was, I could probably tell you where they lived, but...

Q: If you have a few, you ought to be able to remember the one you had in Oakland Park.

THE COURT: That is argumentative,

A: No, I don't remember having visited anyone in Oakland Park.

MR. STONE: Judge, may I be excused? Maybe I can speed it up a little bit.

THE COURT: If it is going to take any length of time let me know so we don't have to sit here.

MR. STONE: Mr. Schwarz, may we approach the Bench? (Whispered conference at Bench, inaudible, off the record.)

THE COURT: Why don't we call another witness?

MR. STONE: I can recall him?

MR. SCHWARZ: Yes.

THE COURT: Yes. Do you have any further cross examination?

MR. STONE: All right, that is all.

Later, when the brown purse had been brought from Stone's office, Teresa Schaefer was called, and recanted much of her original deposition. Finally, Gerard Schaefer was recalled.

BY MR. STONE:

Q: Mr. Schaefer, I show you what is marked State Exhibit B for identification, July 31, this hearing, and ask you if you have ever seen that purse before?

MR. SCHWARZ: May I examine it, please?

MR. STONE: For the record, we would show the purse is marked as 73-4-669, purse, Jessup's hair analysis, on the card, and initialed inside by Lieutenant Dave Yurchuck, Hank Dean, and Lieutenant Duval, among other initials.

MR. SCHWARZ: May I have just a moment, Your Honor? I merely wish to ascertain this is the same purse that was exhibited to me at noon yesterday by a State witness. Okay.

BY MR. STONE:

Q: Have you seen this purse before?

A: It appears to be mine.

Q: Where did you get it?

A: In the Country of Morocco, in North Africa.

Q: You got this in the Country of Morocco, North Africa, when?

A: 1970, I would believe is.

Q: What month of 1970?

A: Probably July, or it was June or July. In 1970, what city in Morocco?

A: In what city?

Q: Is Morocco a city?

A: Morocco is a country.

Q: Is there a city there? What city did you buy it in?

A: I bought quite a few things in different cities. Now, I can't think of what city it was. I believe it was in Marrakesh.

Q: Marrakesh?

A: Yes, I believe that was the city.

Q: Who were you with when you bought it?

A: Who was I with?

Q: Yes.

A: Well, I was with several other people that I was traveling with.

Q: Who were they?

A: One of them, his name was Yosta.

Q: Do you know any other name?

A: A: Canadian guy by the name of Steve.

Q: Do you have any other name other that Steve?

A: None, none that I can recall. It might have been McKenzie, I think.

Q: Do you know where he is now?

A: No, it is...I met him at the hotel, and we had gone to buy souvenirs at the Casbah, and I bought a number of things there.

Q: What did you do with this purse after you brought it back to the United States?

A: I used it to carry change in for quite a while, then I put it away.

Q: Did you ever give it to your wife?

MR. SCHWARZ: Your Honor, this is all very interesting, but I object to the relevancy of this until there is some relevancy shown with this purse.

MR. STONE: His wife said he gave it to her as a gift, and he found it in the woods.

MR. SCHWARZ: She never said that. I object and move that be stricken.

MR. STONE: We have got depositions to show that.

MR. SCHWARZ: We are not on deposition, Mr. Stone,

THE COURT: Okay, let's back up here. The question that was asked, I will sustain the objection too. Now, wait a minute. Now I am getting confused. What is the question?

MR. STONE: I will withdraw it.

THE COURT: All right, that simplifies it.

BY MR. STONE:

Q: Okay. Did you ever give it to your wife?

A: I was in Fort Lauderdale preparing to go to South Dakota on my trip. I came across my different souvenirs from North Africa, and I thought perhaps she would like to have it.

Q: So you gave it to her?

A: I brought it home and I...

MR. SCHWARZ: At this time, Your Honor, I want to caution him not to make any disclosure of any statements that were made between the two of them unless it was in the presence of someone else and that person can testify to it. I haven't had a chance to explain that particular to him regarding his testimony this morning. Make sure before you make any statements as to what you said to Teresa or her to you. Give me a chance to object to it.

BY MR. STONE:

Q: Mr. Schaefer, you were a deputy sheriff of Martin County, is that correct?

A: Yes, sir, that is correct.

Q: And you are familiar with the Hutchinson Island area?

A: Yes, sir, I am, in Martin County.

Q: Right. And have you done any hunting or fishing over there?

MR. SCHWARZ: Object to it, being irrelevant and immaterial, Your Honor, unless there is some relevancy as to point of time or location, something. Hutchinson Island is a big area.

Q: Did you ever do any fishing over there around the month of September of '72?

MR. SCHWARZ: Where?

Q: Hutchinson Island, St. Lucie County?

A: In St. Lucie County?

Q: Yes.

A: I rarely –

Q: North of the power plant.

A: I very rarely ever got up that far fishing, because the fishing is much better down in Martin County.

Q: But you said rarely. You did get up that far on occasion?

A: I don't know whether I have been north of the power plant or not, fishing or hunting. I think there was a road that goes in south of the power plant that I used to go in on.

Q: The beach or river side?

A: On the beach side. I am a surf fisherman,

Q: When you went to Morocco you had to use your passport, didn't you?

A: Yes, sir, I did.

Q: Do you have your passport?

A: Do I have it with me? No, I don't even know where it is.

Q: Now, in your mother's house they found a little gold jewelry box. Where did you get that?

MR. SCHWARZ: I object, Your Honor. It has not been established that it was his. It is totally irrelevant and immaterial, and if he is going to start going through some 3,000 exhibits, they have got sent down to the Broward County Sheriff's Office, we will be here until next January, because I am going to insist they be identified and made some way relevant. He hadn't been in that house for over ten weeks at the time they went in and seized those, and there are many objections to all those things that I don't think are pertinent at this point.

BY MR. STONE: I will withdraw that.

Q: There was a trunk of belongings in your mother's house. Was that in your mother's house in September, on September 27, 1972?

MR. SCHWARZ: I object unless it is exhibited to him, and unless it is established where it was and that he would have knowledge of it, whose it was, and there is some relevancy shown to it in this case, that it contained anything that would in any way relate to this case. It is totally irrelevant and immaterial.

THE COURT: Well, without describing it better or presenting it for his view, I will sustain the objection.

BY MR. STONE:

Q: All right, were any of your personal belongings whatsoever in your mother's house on September 27, 1972?

A: Yes.

Q: Were any of them in your home in Stuart?

A: Of course.

Q: Were they moved to your mother's house after April 1, 1973?

MR. SCHWARZ: Object. He would have no way of knowing, Your Honor. Mr. Stone knows the man was in jail at that time. He would have no way of knowing what anybody had done with this stuff.

MR. STONE: If he told them to move it...

MR. SCHWARZ: If he told them to move it, it would be privileged communication, too. You are not going to get around it like that, Bob.

BY MR. STONE:

Q: Do you have personal knowledge about whether any of your personal belongings were in your mother's house after April 1, 1973?

MR. SCHWARZ: Personal knowledge?

MR. STONE: That is right. I am asking him.

A: Do I have personal knowledge that any of my belongings were at my mother's house?

Q: Were moved to your mother's house from your house, after April 1, 1973?

A: No, I have no way of knowing that.

MR. SCHWARZ: Your Honor, I object to the State Attorney thumbing through all these photographs with the press sitting right behind looking over his shoulder, until they are either offered in evidence or their relevancy is some way established in this case.

MR. STONE: You can object all you want to. If you want to move the press out of the jury box you can ask the Court, but you don't object to me looking through anything at my desk.

THE COURT: Well, the press is sitting in the jury box, but they are not the jury for this hearing today, so I will overrule that objection.

BY MR. STONE:

Q: Have you ever seen any of these before, Mr. Schaefer? (Indicating a group of photographs.)

MR. SCHWARZ: I object unless he has them marked for identification, Your Honor, so they can be properly referred to. It is a group of photographs there.

MR. STONE: Okay, we will mark all of them.

(Whereupon, said group of photographs were marked State Exhibits C, D, E, F, G, and H for identification on motion hearing.)

MR. SCHWARZ: Your Honor, unless Mr. Stone tells me to the contrary, it is my understanding these are photographs that have been paid for by the, or charged to, the Public Defender's account and delivered to us. I am going to object to him using my photographs in his case.

MR. STONE: These are mine. I have got yours in here. You give me $85.00 and you can have them.

THE COURT: All right, gentlemen.

MR. SCHWARZ: It so happens they are charged to my account at the photographer's, Mr. Stone. As a matter of fact, the officer who charged them is in the courtroom. (Whereupon, Mr. Stone handed Mr. Schwarz a package of photographs.)

BY MR. STONE:

Q: Mr. Schaefer, I show you what has been marked as State Exhibit C for identification and ask you if you have ever seen any of these items?

A: No...well, no, no, no; I have never seen any...anything like that.

Q: State Exhibit E, have you ever seen that?

A: Absolutely not. What is it?

Q: Well, State Exhibit D, have you ever seen that?

A: No, I haven't.

Q: State Exhibit F, have you ever seen those shoes?

A: No, I haven't seen them. They are certainly not mine.

Q: State Exhibit H, have you seen them?

A: No, I haven't, and I don't even know what that is, either.

Q: Have you ever seen State Exhibit G? Have you ever seen those jeans on that body? (This was a photograph of Georgia Jessup's remains.)

A: Which way does it work? Is this...have I ever seen the jeans? No, I have never seen the jeans. There is not much to the jeans. Is this supposed to be a leg, or what?

MR. STONE: That is all the questions I have.

MR. SCHWARZ: Are you through?

MR. STONE: Yes.

MR. SCHWARZ: I have no further questions. You can step down,

Again, up until now, all testimony had been in depositions or pre-trial hearings, though in truth some of the arguments and objections drifted into the realm of actual trial work. Still, before the trial began, to be heard and decided upon by a jury, motions had to be filed and a jury selected. In order to get a better grasp of the complexity of this case, we must afford at least a brief look at some of the motions filed, and finally the jurors selected.

The motions were numerous, voluminous, but a significant part of this trial. However, they can, and should be, abbreviated in order to consolidate this information. Largely, the motions were introduced by the defense, as is customary as an effort to provide the best possible case for their client. The state, too, files motions, as is needed in the legal process, and also in rebuttal of motions filed by the defense. There are motions filed throughout the trial, but the following were presented in the pre-trial hearings, and are the bulk of them.

There will not be a lengthy explanation of each motion. To do so would make this book too voluminous to print and turn it into a transcript of trial procedure. That is not my desire, nor intent, and so, the motions are simply listed and some of them are explained for clarification.

Motion to Dismiss: Schwarz introduced this motion right away (as would any good attorney) stating that the state had improperly charged the defendant. Firstly, by an improper "joinder" of two separate and unrelated offenses. One, the case of Susan Place, and two, the case of Georgia Jessup. The court ruled against this, saying that the two counts (of murder) grew from the same act, or transaction.

Within the same motion, the state should have been prosecuting by "Indictment" (charges filed by a grand jury) rather than by "Information" (the state attorney filing charges). This point had some merit, and in truth this case should have been tried with the use of a grand jury, because it was a capital crime. As such, the sentence of capital punishment could be sought (which the state did not seek). This is a significant ruling, as it is controversial.

Eventually this motion caused the state to amend their Information. The state filed, finally, saying that there was not a death penalty in Florida until December 8, 1972, (according to the U.S. Supreme Court) and that the girls were killed on September 27, 1972, therefore, they did not have to use a grand jury, because Schaefer had committed the capital crime before capital punishment was instated in Florida. However, the Florida State Supreme Court had ruled that October 1, 1972 was the date when any capital crime would be tried by Indictment (with a grand jury). So one could argue that Schaefer could be tried by Indictment because he was tried after October 1, 1972 (and after December 8, 1972 for that matter) or one could argue he could be tried by Information, because the actual crime was committed before October 1, 1972. If this were the case, (and this is

306 - American Ripper

how the case was tried) then we are talking about a difference of three days. Three days, that would determine whether Schaefer would get life imprisonment or the death penalty, if he were found guilty.

Law is a nebulous thing. One could argue the state should have pushed for the death penalty. Almost every serial killer convicted in Florida has received the death penalty, including Ted Bundy, Aileen Wuornos, Danny Rollins, Otis Toole, and more. Grand juries, because of the number of jurors, mathematically make it more difficult to convict and sentence a killer to death. Yet, with overwhelming evidence, it has become the norm for a state where serial killers seem to be a more common phenomenon. But, because of the aforementioned motion, the death penalty was not sought.

Motion for statement of particulars: Basically, Schwarz asked that the state give a more definite date as to when the crime was committed. The state held with September 27, 1972.

Motion for suggesting insanity at time of trial: Three psychiatrists were called and testified that it might be possible that Gerard Schaefer was insane and might be at time of trial. (They were not allowed by the court to say that he "definitely" was insane.) In rebuttal, the state called one psychiatrist who testified that Schaefer could possibly be faking his insanity. The court ruled to set a time for a hearing on the question of sanity to stand trial, later.

Motion to strike defendant's disclosure to prosecution: This was filed by Robert Stone, in an effort to strike the defense's witness list. He contended that the list was a direct Xerox copy of his list, and as such he could not subpoena people on his list without having the defendant present. This was simply a semantics game between Stone and Schwarz. The court ruled that the defense could call the same witnesses, but they had to notify the state of any new witnesses, or evidence that might benefit the defense. During this time, it is interesting to note that documentation shows that Schaefer had begun to yell names at Stone, their exact nature is not in the court transcripts, but the animosity between these two men had begun and it was growing.

Motion for protective order: This was simply Schwarz asking for all original depositions to be sealed, until ordered open by the court. The state agreed and the court accepted the motion.

Motion to restrict: This was basically a reinforcing of the motion for statement of particulars. The state had to hold with the time span of September 27, 1972, until December 7, 1972, that the crime would have been committed.

Motion to permit free access: Schwarz asked that anyone on his witness list have access to visiting Schaefer in jail. The court left the decision as to who could, or could not, to be determined by the Sheriff in charge of the jail.

Other motions filed are relatively self-explanatory: Motion to dismiss (again by Schwarz – more legal rhetoric), motion to prohibit censoring of mail (to and from Schaefer), both motions denied by the court. Request for transcripts was okayed. A: motion by Schwarz to strike the state's psychiatrist (who testified Schaefer may be faking insanity) was denied.

The defense filed a motion to "compel disclosure," which asks that all lab tests and state's evidence be available for the defense to look at before the trial. The court approved.

The state filed a motion to strike demand of a speedy trial, holding with the fact that it would take more time for both the state and the defense to establish their cases. The rules of the Criminal Procedure state a "speedy trial" is executed within sixty days, which would have been impossible in this case. The court went with the state's motion.

The defense filed numerous motions to suppress evidence which they contended were illegally obtained. They included: the deposition of Teresa Schaefer (the court denied the motion); the evidence seized at Doris Schaefer's home in Fort Lauderdale, which after capacious citing of legal text by the defense, the court denied the motion. Likewise, evidence seized at Schaefer's home in Stuart was rendered admissible, though once again, Schwarz did try to suppress the evidence with a motion of unlawful seizure.

Schwarz then filed a statement of particulars, relating to defense of insanity at the time of offense, but without admitting his client had committed an offense. The court recognized it but did not rule on it.

Motion to set bail or release defendant on his own recognizance: The defense filed this motion, of course, and in so doing had to call several witnesses to testify on behalf of Gerard Schaefer, including Schaefer himself. The court ruled that it would set bond at $100,000.00 on each count.

Motion resolving costs: the court ruled county taxes would pick up part of the tab (a large part) of Schaefer's defense. The state's cost of prosecuting Schaefer was also taken into account. Basically, the court ruled depositions, and certain professional witnesses, and court transcribers would be paid, as well as some miscellaneous items.

The state filed a motion to resolve Schaefer's bond, and witnesses had to be called for that. Additionally, evidence was looked at, including the elusive "little brown-hippie-purse," and some photographs, including those of the remains of Susan Place and Georgia Jessup. The court granted the motion and vacated the bond motion previously heard.

Finally, two of the most significant motions were filed. One, the change of venue and two, the mental status of Gerard Schaefer, which was filed more as an "application" than a motion; both filed by the defense, but argued, extensively with Stone.

A: change of venue simply allows that the defendant would receive the benefit of an impartial jury, jurors who are not prejudiced or opinionated about the man on trial. It was believed that anywhere Schaefer went in Florida, the people probably would have heard of his case, and so, the likelihood of finding an impartial jury would be just as good in the 19th Judicial Circuit as anywhere else in Florida.

As for Schaefer's mental status; after listening to the testimony of several psychiatrists and psychologists, (all of whom agreed that Schaefer was a "mentally disoriented sex offender") the court ruled that Schaefer was competent enough to stand trial.

Other motions were filed, to be sure, but the last before the trial began was a motion to sequester the jury (which means to seclude them from outside sources and media attention which may sway their decisions). This was denied by the court.

* * *

On September 19, 1973, the double murder trial of Gerard John Schaefer began.

The jury had been selected quickly, in just two days, which greatly pleased Judge C. Pfeiffer Trowbridge. He had expected the voir dire (jury selection) examination to go on for some time. There were six jurors selected (and alternates in case of something happening to one of the original jurors causing him or her to be replaced) and they were:

Julian R. Arkin: a real estate salesman, 74 years old. His face as wrinkled as a raisin, and almost as dark, baked by the Florida sun. He was intense and logical, often leaning forward in his seat to hear every word spoken.

Betty P. Haugh: she too was in real estate. But at 44, she'd also been a nurse for many years. Her face still reflected the caring yet solemn expression of the world-weary medical professional. She was awed by her selection, but confident, even appearing relaxed in the jury box. She was selected as superintendent of the jury.

Kathy Wockley: 42, intelligent, soft-spoken woman. She worked at Indian River Community College. At times, as she listened to testimony (particularly that of the medical examiners) her face drew tight to her skull, her color paled.

Paulette Tompkins: a 19-year-old newlywed. At her young age she'd never been called for jury duty, and didn't particularly want the position, yet she'd answered the questions put forth by the attorneys. Now, though she was obligated to sit through this trial, she'd rather have been back at the soft-drink plant where she worked or, better still, with her new husband at home.

Warren Wrobleski: a 40-year-old businessman who managed an electric parts business. He showed no emotions throughout the trial except, perhaps, for some agitation for having to sit for so many hours on hardwood seats. He would rather have been conducting business than sitting in a stuffy, crammed courtroom.

William J. Forbes: 30, a former construction worker who had suffered a back injury, and thus, was forced into a new field, that of a trainee at a savings and loan association. Though he was worried about losing his new position at the bank, and his injured back began to ache after hours of sitting, he did not mind being a juror. In fact, he had already formed opinions of the man on trial, a cardinal sin for a juror, and he felt it was his duty to justice to stay on as a juror. Later, he would become a critical element in this case.

Of these six jurors, Forbes, Tyson, and Wockley had no children. Arkin had a middle-aged son, Wrobleski had two boys, 13 and 14, and Haugh was the mother of two girls, 16 and 17, and one boy, 13. They were selected from thirty-five candidates that had been questioned, from a list of 102 names drawn. There were also two alternate jurors; Joanne E. Harten, 21, a nurse's aide, and Mildred M. Loveglio, a mother of five children ranging in age from 18 to 26. The group represented a random sampling of people from various walks of life; Gerard Schaefer's peers.

The trial had officially begun the afternoon of September 18, 1973, immediately after the jury selection. Judge Trowbridge had given the instructions to the jurors, but by the time he'd finished, it was already 5:14p.m. and time to adjourn for the day. The wily judge kept a strict schedule in his court; court convening at 9:30a.m. promptly, and just as promptly adjourning for the day at 5:00p.m., with a lunch break from noon until 1:30p.m. But that first day of instruction to the jury was most important, and if it took his honor an extra fourteen minutes to adequately explain court procedure, then by God, he would take it. He made it very clear from the beginning, that he was the kingpin of this judicial operation, and with selected logic and eccentric manners, no one would dare second-guess him.

The actual trial, that being where witnesses are called and the jury listens to their testimony, began at 9:30 sharp, on a bright, hot Wednesday morning. Stone started things off with his opening statement:

MR. STONE: May it please the Court, ladies and gentlemen of the jury: This is the time during the procedure of the trial where the attorneys have an opportunity to make an opening statement and the Court, I think, outlined to you yesterday what you are going to do here procedurally during the course of this trial. This is the time when we have a chance to tell you what we expect to prove, because this is what you were selected for as jurors, to hear the evidence and to decide on that evidence what your verdict will be.

There are several reasons for an opening statement. One is to give you some idea as to what you can expect during the course of the trial, and the other is to outline what we want to prove, because during the course of the trial sometimes we may have to call a witness out of sequence, so that unless you have some perspective of the over-all view when you hear that particular witness's testimony you might not know where it fits in.

It is especially true when you have expert witnesses who have schedules and who have subpoenas to go other places, and they may have to come in out of schedule to testify and then you are going to have to put it in proper sequence at the close of this trial. Simply, it is sort of like an index to a book that you look at and see where you want to go in the particular part of that book to get to this particular phase of the trial, and I want to caution you, as the Court has cautioned you, what I say and what Mr. Schwarz may say in these opening statements is not evidence. You are not to consider that in your deliberation of your verdict whatsoever.

The only evidence you are to consider is what comes from the witness stand and whatever documentary evidence might be, and I think what the evidence is going to show you, and briefly I will outline to you right now, what you are going to hear as far as the State is concerned.

We are going to present to you evidence that shows on April 1 of this year, in this county, that there were a couple men out looking for beer cans and bottles and just tramping through heavy underbrush over on Hutchinson Island, which is off AIA, just north of the power plant, that while these men were doing this, they stumbled on and they found part of the remains of a human body, and that they say the remains of, several remains of a human body which were bones, is what they saw, parts of a body. They saw them scattered around.

That one of the men called a friend of his or called somebody he knew who came to the scene and viewed what he saw, and before he came he called the Sheriff's Department, and this is the first person we will put on the stand, Mr. Holley, and the second person he called was a Mr. Wiggins. That the Sheriff's Department came there, and they found scattered the remains of two human bodies. They found a grave. They found a tree near the grave, and then for the next three or four days through an intense search of that area, maybe two or three days later, they were able to find scattered parts of jawbones and teeth and these were later identified, and I think it has already been stipulated by the defendant's attorney that these belonged to Susan Place and Georgia Jessup, two sixteen and seventeen year old girls that had been missing from Fort Lauderdale since September 27, and had never been seen by the parents since that night.

The evidence is going to show that on September 27, the last day that they were seen by their parents, that the defendant, Gerard John Schaefer, Jr, using the alias of Jerry Shepard, went to the home of Susan Place. That he met Mrs. Place. That he had a conversation with Mrs. Place. That he talked to her. That she talked to him. That they talked about her daughter leaving and she was afraid that her daughter was going to leave. Her daughter had left before, and she was afraid her daughter was going to leave. She became concerned about it.

During the conversation it appeared maybe they were only going over to the beach to play the guitar for a while, but she didn't want her daughter to leave the house. The mother became so concerned about it that she was afraid she might never see her daughter again, that she went outside and looked at the car, and she will be able to identify for you the car itself, and she even went so far, because she was so concerned, to write down the tag number on the car. She wrote it down on a piece of paper on that particular day, on that particular evening, she wrote it down so she would remember it. The evidence and the testimony will show you that that tag number and that car belonged to the defendant, Gerard John Schaefer, but even more so, she will be able to identify him for you personally.

I think the evidence will also show that Dr. Davis, who is a forensic pathologist, who has had extensive training, he works for the crime lab, the Dade County Crime Lab, was sent the remains and asked to examine them, and asked for him to give us a report on what he discovered and what he determined from his examination.

His testimony will be that because of the long period of time since the death, that he is not going to be able to give you an exact cause of death, but he is going to be able to tell you that the condition they were in was inconsistent with death by self-infliction or natural causes, although he can't give you the exact cause of death, was caused by the violent act of another, and we are going to show you that this violent act was caused by Gerard John Schaefer.

We are going to show you also, the evidence to show that there was a purse, a little, small hippie purse that belonged to Georgia Jessup, and there will be three people that can positively identify that purse as belonging to Georgia Jessup. The testimony will show you that that purse was taken by Hank Dean, the wife's brother, the brother-in-law of the defendant, Gerard John Schaefer, it was given to him by the defendant's wife, and that the wife got that purse from her husband, and that that person, Hank Dean, took that purse then to a friend of his who was a lieutenant, Dave Yurchuck, with the Broward Sheriff's Department, and we are going to show you that other evidence that this man had a scheme, a mode of operation, a plan of murder and a plan of premeditation and that through his plan, through this scheme and this design, he put it into effect and into operation, and that sometime after September 27 and before December 7, and probably more likely closer to the September 27th date, but between those dates, that he murdered these two girls on Hutchinson Island in St. Lucie County, and we are going to ask that you keep your mind open, you listen to the evidence, because when it is over, as I said yesterday, I am going to stand up here before you and I am going to ask you to return a verdict of guilty of murder in the first degree as to both counts. Thank you.

Stone had been talking directly to the jury. Not in a lecturing fashion; he was more relaxed, confident, and as he spoke, he managed to look into the faces of each of the jurors, He wanted them to feel as though they could trust him, his instincts, his authority. He did not want to seem cold and domineering, but neither weak nor unsure. He kept one hand in his pocket, the other rested on the rail that separated the jury from the rest of the courtroom, as if leaning against the mantle of a fireplace. When he mentioned the Places or the Jessups, he would glance back at the families, and his face would echo the sorrow of their loss. Just as effortlessly, he could grasp the jurors' focus with his eyes, and upon mentioning Schaefer's name, glance fortuitously but contemptuously at the defendant.

Schaefer would usually smile back at the open faces of the jurors, who would then, quickly, avert their eyes to a more comfortable berth, usually the face of the protective prosecutor. When Stone finished his opening statement, he walked briskly back to his seat at the state's table and began going through his papers. The jurors looked to Schwarz, who was conferring with Schaefer at the defense table, expecting and anticipating his opening statement. To everyone's surprise, it did not come.

Schwarz stood up and confidently asked the permission of the court to reserve his opening statement until the close of the plaintiff's (the state's) case. The court gave approval and Stone had no objections.

The state immediately called the first witness: Jesse Holley. Holley described what he and his father had found on April Fool's Day, 1973. Holley explained how he and his father had been searching for beer cans, and whatnot, when his father had found the remains of Susan and Georgia. He explained with a southern drawl, how after the discovery they'd gone to Calvin Wiggins' house, called the sheriff's office (both Martin and St. Lucie Counties) and along with Wiggins, returned to the scene. On cross-examining Holley, Schwarz was able to ascertain that the Holleys visited that area on Hutchinson Island quite often, in fact sometimes a half dozen times a week. He also established that Jesse had been born in Fort Lauderdale. People in the court began to wonder what Schwarz was getting at. Events became more curious after Stone released Holley. Schwarz asked the court to keep Holley on subpoena because he might want to recall him. The court okayed Schwarz's request, but it was anybody's guess what he was up to.

Calvin Wiggins was called next:

DIRECT EXAMINATION BY MR. STONE:

Q: Would you state your full name, please?
A: Calvin H. Wiggins.
Q: What is your address?
A: 1600 East 9th Street, Stuart, Florida.
Q: And your: occupation?
A: Chief Ambulance Attendant, Stuart Ambulance,
Q: Did you know Jesse Joe Holley?
A: Yes.
Q: How long have you known him?
A: Eight or nine years.
Q: Did you have an occasion to see him on April 1 of this year?
A: Yes, I did.

Q: Can you tell this jury what the occasion was that you saw him and what transpired and limit it to what you can testify you saw or did, not what someone told you?

A: May I ask you a question to that?

Q: Yes.

A: Do you want the time he did come to the house and what he told me then?

Q: You can tell us he came to your house and what you did. Don't tell us what he told you.

A: He come to my house on that date. After he had come to the house, I did call the St. Lucie Sheriff's Department.

Q: Then what did you do?

A: After the St, Lucie Sheriff's Department, I called the Martin County Sheriff's Department and I had them meet us up on Hutchinson Island by Blind Creek.

Q: Did you go up there?

A: Yes, I did.

Q: What did you observe when you got there?

A: When we got there, I observed a shallow grave.

Q: I am going to show you what has been previously marked as State Exhibit No. E, (The photograph of the grave on Hutchinson Island.)

MR. SCHWARZ: I object to the use of the word "grave," Your Honor. He is not an expert on things such as that, and I think it is an opinion and conclusion on the part of the witness not supported by the evidence. A: hole in the ground.

MR. STONE: That is what it was.

THE COURT: I will overrule the objection.

Q: Go ahead. Tell us if you can identify that picture.

A: Yes, I can.

Q: Is that the shallow grave you saw?

A: Yes, it is.

Q: All right. What else did you see?

A: There was a portion of a body, the torso part, the lower section of the body.

Q: Did you see any other portions of a body?

A: Yes, there was one section appeared to be part of a leg we seen, also.

Q: And in what proximity were these to the grave? How close?

A: I would say approximately fifteen to twenty feet away,

Q: How many parts of a body did you actually see?

A: Three.

Q: Three. All right, did you stay there then until the Sheriff's deputies got there?

A: I did go back out to the road then where the car was parked and stayed there.

Q: All right, were you there when Lieutenant Duval or Sergeant George Miller of the St. Lucie County Sheriff's Department got there?

A: Yes, I was.

MR. STONE: That is all the questions I have.

CROSS EXAMINATION BY MR. SCHWARZ:

Q: Mr. Wiggins, this photograph, Exhibit E (the photo of the gravel road for identification) were any portions of the body found or seen in there?

A: No, sir.

Q: So when you say it is a grave that is an assumption on your part, right?

A: Yes, sir.

Q: It is a hole in the ground, right?

A: Yes, sir.

Q: It could have been used for burying trash, right?

A: It could have, yes, sir.

Q: It could have been used for any purpose?

A: Yes, sir.

Q: Does this generally depict the way that hole looked at the time you first saw it?

A: It appears to be, yes, sir.

Q: Was there any indication that the sides had washed down or collapsed from rain or anything of that type?

A: Some. Not too much.

Q: Not very much?

A: Not too much, no.

Q: Did it appear to you that hole had been there very long?

A: I couldn't actually say just how long it had been there,

Q: Months or weeks?

A: I couldn't say. I am not an expert in that field.

Q: Are you related to Jesse Joe Holley?

A: Yes, sir, I am.

Q: What is that relationship?

A: Brother-in-law.

Q: And you are married to his sister, I believe, right?

A: Yes, sir.

Q: How long have you been married to his sister?

A: Seven years.

Q: And you have known Jesse pretty well through that time?

A: Yes, sir.

Q: About how tall do you think Jesse is?

A: About six-one.

Q: About how much does he weigh?

A: About 215 or 220 pounds.

MR. SCHWARZ: No further questions.

REDIRECT EXAMINATION BY MR. STONE:

Q: Could you tell us, in relation to this grave you have described how far away those bodies were, parts of bodies, and in what direction they were away from it. You say you found three pieces. Tell me where you found each piece and describe it for us.

A: The lower section of the body was approximately, I would say about twenty feet south. It was more or less to the right side facing south. The upper portion of the body approximately, I would say, about twenty feet south. It was more or less to the right side facing south. The upper portion of the body was approximately the same distance away. It was to the left side facing south. The portion of the leg that appeared to be part of a leg portion was between the other two sections in this section here.

MR. STONE: All right, fine. Thank you.

RECROSS EXAMINATION BY MR. SCHWARZ:

Q: Do you know the defendant, Gerard John Schaefer, Jr.?

A: No, sir. I have never seen the man up until this time.

Q: This is him sitting here.

A: Yes, sir.

Q: He looks a lot like Jesse, doesn't he?

A: Wiggins looked perplexed. He looked at Schaefer and then at Schwarz, then back to Schaefer, and finally at Jesse Holley. He raised his eyebrows but said nothing.

Schwarz smiled and said, No further questions.

Stone, smiling back said, "Good try, Elton. That is all."

It had become obvious what Schwarz was trying to do. If he could show that Schaefer looked like any number of young men, even one of the witnesses called, he could put some doubt into the jurors' minds. Better still, if he could have somehow implicated the Holleys; after all, they'd found the bodies (in such a remote area, too.). It was a long shot, but Elton Schwarz was accustomed to taking long shots. He knew the criminal elements, had defended them for years, and he knew the court system. He deftly maneuvered through both of them.

The next witness called was Patrick Duval of the St. Lucie County Sheriff's Office. In answer to Stone's questions he related how he'd been called away from his Fort Pierce home and to the scene of the discovered bodies. He related to the court the condition and position of the bodies, the names of the other investigators, and that Dr. Schofield (the medical examiner for the 19th Judicial Circuit) was called in. In particular, he described the grave (Schwarz continued to argue that it was "just a hole"), the jeans with the owl and the roadrunner patches, (Georgia Jessup's) and the many pieces of broken and chopped bones, and scattered teeth. He told of finding first one scalp, with reddish brown hair, then the second, blonde scalp, almost two weeks later. He also described a tree in the area that appeared to have been used in the execution of the girls.

DUVAL: In the area, about 9 or 10 feet north of the grave, at the east end there was a tree, a rubber tree as we call it. I think it is a banyan tree, whatever, and on this tree was scratched the initials "G. J." and it hadn't been there too long, not enough to heal good. And down at the bottom of the tree there was a root extending about two feet, approximately two feet from the bottom, and it was raised up about six inches from the ground, and in this tree there were chop marks, and in the chop marks, there was cloth in two of them that I could see, two cuts in the tree, in the bottom of it, and it looked like part of a dress. To me it looked like part of a dress that was found at the bottom of the grave or back of the grave.

Q: So actually in the cut marks on the root of the tree were what you would call clothing fiber in there?

A: Yes, sir.

Q: Was there anything else in the tree?

A: There was a limb with rope burns on it, that I took to be rope burns.

Q: Overhanging?

A: An overhanging limb from the same tree, and just about parallel with the cut marks at the root of the tree.

Q: You say parallel. You mean directly over?

A: Directly over I would say.

Q: Let me ask you this. When did you first notice the tree, Lieutenant Duval?

A: It was during the first day.

Q: And the first day is when you noticed the cut marks and the initials and the rope burns?

A: Yes, sir.

Q: All right, now, what if anything did you do with that tree?

A: Well, we cut the tree. We had one of the fellows who had a chain saw, and he cut the tree, he cut the bottom of the root off, which was sent to the laboratory, and the limb of the tree, that was sent to the laboratory.

Q: Did you cut the part out that had the initials?

A: Yes, sir, we also cut that out.

The question of who carved the initials into the tree was never answered, but there were two schools of thought. One: That Gerard John Schaefer had gone back to the area and gloatingly carved his initials into the tree (at which time he may have unearthed the bodies for whatever abhorrent reason, for which there is some evidence) and did not have time to finish his initials, or was interrupted, or was just too lazy to finish his handiwork. Two: That Georgia Jessup, possibly awaiting her "turn" to be murdered, frantically carved her initials into the tree, in an effort to one day tell the finders of her mutilated remains, who she was. Both theories warrant some thinking, and undoubtedly, one of them is true.

Duval also described the finding of two pillowcases. This discovery, again, alluded to Schaefer's personal writings, where in one of his "stories," he described the killer putting a pillowcase over the head of the victim, before hanging her.

Oddly, Schwarz again tried to suggest throughout his cross examination of Patrick Duval that it was more than just beer cans that brought the Holleys into this remote area. In fact, he wore out this questioning about beer cans, and it became apparent that no one was going to believe that the Holleys were anything other than what they truly were: a couple of men out in the woods, innocently searching for scrap metal and quite accidently uncovering the remains of two murdered teenagers.

Schwarz finally discontinued that line of pursuit and redirected his interest to the "hole" (not grave) at the scene. Duval maintained the "hole" was a grave and it had been dug into twice.

SCHWARTZ CROSS EXAMINED:

Q: That is a conclusion you arrived at, right? (The grave being dug into twice.)

A: That is a conclusion.

Q: What facts did you find at the scene that you based this conclusion on?

A: The fact that it had rained sometime around the early part of the year, earlier, and the grave appeared to have been dug, and then dug again, because of the erosion, there wasn't enough erosion there to satisfy me that it had not been dug into twice.

Q: Did it look like it was over two months old?

A: Well, it could have been. I am not sure about it.

Q: It could have been, or it might not have been?

A: Well, it could have been either way,

Q: Either way?

A: Yes.

Q: Either way, is that your answer?

A: Over two months?

Q: Over or under two months, it could have been over, and it could have been under two months, right?

A: Well, I couldn't pinpoint that.

MR. STONE: I object to that, anyway. I think it calls for some kind of expert opinion. I don't think Mr. Duval has been qualified. I don't know that an anthropologist could come in here and tell us how long a grave had been dug, and whether it had been two months over or less. That is rather a general question for a man who is an investigator or detective.

MR. SCHWARZ: He is a detective investigator; I think he can. I don't think it takes an expert to give an opinion as to how long a hole has been in the ground.

THE COURT: I will overrule the objection, but if you can answer it, answer it. If you can't, tell us you can't.

A: Well, I don't know just...I would say it had been dug less than two months, at least two months.

Q: At least two months?

A: That would be my opinion.

Q: As much as three months?

A: Well, let's just leave it there.

Q: You don't want to give an answer on that, do you?

MR. STONE: Now, I object to that being argumentative, and I move it be stricken, saying that he does not want to give an answer. The man said he doesn't know for sure, and he said at least two months and that is what he is going to stand on.

MR. SCHWARZ: I am not arguing.

MR. STONE: If Mr. Schwarz wants to testify, let him take the witness stand.

MR. SCHWARZ: Will you vouch for my veracity?

MR. STONE: No, I wouldn't.

THE COURT: All right, gentlemen. Let's move along. I will deny the motion.

Stone had redirected examination of Duval, showing him photographs taken at the scene and asking him to identify them. As Duval did so, Stone introduced them into evidence as Exhibits, then gave them to the jury for examination.

At one point, he sent Shailer and a few men out of the court, and when they returned, they dragged in the sections of the tree in question, for Duval's identification. Schwarz was visibly miffed but remained silent... for a while.

MR. SCHWARTZ:

Q: I am going to show you what has been marked as State Exhibit S (the photographs of the remains of Susan and Georgia) for identification and ask you, without telling me what is in that picture, can you identify it?

A: Yes, sir, I can.

Q: Did you see that or discover what was in that picture when you were at the scene?

A: Yes, sir, I did.

Q: Is that the condition it was in when you found it?

A: Yes, sir.

Q: All right, and who took that picture?

A: Sergeant George Miller.

MR. STONE: Okay. As I understand it everything the State has had marked for identification, with the exception of Exhibit S, is in evidence?

THE CLERK: Right.

MR. STONE: I don't have any further question. Oh, I will offer it in evidence at this time. (At this time, Stone handed the photographs of Susan's and Georgia's remains to the jury. Their initial shock was obvious.

Some quickly passed the photos, while other scrutinized them, trying to figure which part went to which body. The effect was immediate and devastating.)

MR. SCHWARZ: Your Honor, I object to this exhibit on the grounds that it is solely inflammatory, and it serves no useful purpose other than to inflame the minds of the jurors. He described what he found, and I think that is sufficiently adequate. We stipulated as to the identity of the victims that were found. I strenuously object to this exhibit.

MR. STONE: He didn't describe them the way the photograph...

MR. SCHWARZ: He described what he found. I don't see what useful purpose that shows, or what the relevancy is.

MR. STONE: It has quite a bit of relevancy.

THE COURT: The Court will overrule the objection and the exhibit will be admitted.

MR. STONE: That is all the questions I have.

George Miller was called next. He worked with Duval at the scene of the crime, photographing the scene and all the evidence discovered. His testimony was concise and logical, and even Elton Schwarz found it difficult to get Miller to say anything but exactly what he wanted to say. He was a good witness for the state, and his testimony of the facts was solid.

After George Miller's testimony, the court took a recess for lunch. Upon returning, the state called Lucille Place to the stand. She appeared small and drawn as if she hadn't slept in months. Nervous and emotional, she took the stand, gingerly sitting down, as if she expected the seat to be pulled away at the last moment; she tried to draw courage from the memory of her daughter. Slowly, and more assuredly, she was recapitulating her previous deposition, recoiling slightly, then continuing when Schwarz would object, which he did frequently. (He objected several times citing the hearsay rule, which prohibits witnesses telling what was said in a conversation outside of the trial or hearing. They can only tell what they, themselves, said and tell the result of the conversation, otherwise it is deemed "hearsay" and inadmissible in court.)

Part of Mrs. Place's testimony included having to identify the man who was at her home, and had left with her daughter, on September 27, 1972. She asked permission to stand at that point, in order that she might see the defendant better. She stared into the face of Gerald Schaefer for several moments, slowly raised her hand and in a voice that resonated with hatred said, "He's sitting right there. In the white sweater."

Schaefer clasped his hands together and placed them on the table in front of him. He glanced about the courtroom nervously, noting the reactions on the people's faces. Then he looked back to Mrs. Place and smiled widely, as if they were old friends. When Schwarz cross-examined Mrs. Place, he was brusque, repeatedly hammering at her to recall what she'd stated in previous depositions. When she remembered things differently or added new information, he quickly reminded her of what had already been recorded. His point, if any, was to lend doubt to her testimony and further question the integrity of her daughter. On this, he interrogated Mrs. Place about Susan's previous "run-aways" and drug use.

BY MR. SCHWARZ:

Q: You say Susan's health was good. Isn't it a fact that she was an epileptic?

A: Yes.

Q: Did she take her medicine with her?

A: No.

Q: Didn't this cause you any concern when she left without taking her medicine?

A: She has been without it before.

Q: For how long a time?

A: Oh, a week, two weeks, three weeks.

Q: How often is she supposed to take this medicine?

A: Once a day. (The medication in question is Dilantin.)

Q: Once a day.

A: Uh-huh.

Q: Has Susan every used any drugs to your knowledge?

MR. SHAILER: Objection, Your Honor. That is pretty far afield, not relevant at all.

THE COURT: I will overrule the objection. You may answer the question.

A: Of course she used drugs. Dilantin is a drug.

Q: How about marijuana and heroin and other drugs, illegal drugs?

A: Not to my knowledge. She may have had some pot or something at one time or other, I don't know.

Q: She never admitted to you that she had tried just about everything?

A: She probably would try it. I know she would like to be a friend to everybody.

Q: Isn't it a fact that she admitted that she had tried just about everything?

A: What do you mean, just tried everything?

Q: Drug?

A: Oh, drugs? I don't see why that should have any bearing on what happened to her.

THE COURT: Now, you just answer the question, please, madam. We will decide what has bearing.

Q: Did she, or didn't she?

A: She admitted taking some things, yes, but I wouldn't say everything.

Q: Including heroin?

A: Heroin?

Q: Yes

A: No.

Q: She didn't?

A: She didn't take heroin.

Q: Didn't you tell me that when we were taking your deposition?

A: She may have. She wasn't an addict.

Q: I didn't ask you if she was an addict. Isn't it a fact she admitted taking heroin, trying it?

A: It is a possibility. I did say that. (Later Mrs. Place would tell me, she felt she had to admit it was a possibility, that anything was possible. However, she never felt or had evidence to believe that Susan had ever used heroin. In fact, this would be a dangerous risk to mix the two drugs, Dilantin and heroin.)

Q: And you were telling me the truth when you did say that?

A: I imagine so.

Before ending his cross-examination, Schwarz asked Mrs. Place about the photograph she showed Sergeant Scott, when she and Mr. Place had gone to the Martin County Jail to see Schaefer. The date that had been written on the back was October 27, 1972. A: careless, albeit unintentional and innocent, mistake by Mrs. Place. She knew, as did all concerned, that her daughter had been missing since September 27, 1972. This is evident when one views a missing person's report filed with the Oakland Park Police Department on October 1, 1972. She had simply made a mistake in writing down the date; understandable considering her loss. The mistake would become a strong point for the defense.

Mrs. Place had been strong on the stand until the photograph was introduced. When she saw the picture of Susan, though, she wept. She regained her composure long enough to finish her testimony, but she'd been emotionally drained. She quickly exited the courtroom. Later when she returned, and throughout the rest of the trial, she sat, quietly staring

324 - American Ripper

into a void, perhaps remembering her daughter and the sounds of her delicate playing on the piano.

The state called Ira Place next. The testimony correlated with Mrs. Place's, confirming that it was, indeed, Schaefer who'd been at their house on the night in question. He confirmed Mrs. Place's description of Schaefers' shoes (moccasins), tan or khaki pants, and fisherman hat. He could not remember the color of his shirt, nor any odd mannerisms. (Schwarz continually asked witnesses if they noticed Schaefer fingering the soles of his feet, or any other nervous habits.) Of particular note within Mr. Place's testimony was that at one point Schwarz tried, once again, to implicate Jesse Joe Holley. He asked Mr. Place if he'd ever seen Mr. Holley before. Mr. Place said, "No."

Robert Stone said he and Phil Shailer could not conceal their amusement at this line of questioning. In fact, they began to chuckle and whisper amongst themselves, until finally annoyed, Judge Trowbridge warned them, "Let's not have these little asides at the tables, please."

Again, Ira Place's testimony echoed the deposition he'd previously given. If anyone thought his identification of Gerard Schaefer was unsure or unreliable, the following excerpt of his testimony removed any doubt.

By MR. SHAILER:

Q: Mr. Place, is your identification today of this defendant based upon your observation of him on September 27 in your house?

A: On the characteristics, yes.

Q: Is it based on what you saw and who you saw on September 27 or is it based on photographs shown you last month or a couple of months ago by a police officer?

A: It is not based on that. I have seen photos and telecasts.

Q: As you sit here and look at that man, can you say that –?

A: I can tell by the looks of his eyes and the shape of his nose and so forth. I saw enough of him that I know that is the man.

Q: That is the person that was in your house?

A: Definitely.

Q: On September 27?

A: Yes, sir. May my life depend on it.

Mr. Place stepped down from the witness stand. He and Mrs. Place had waited, perhaps a bit too long, until they were more financially secure, to start having children. They certainly would not be having any more, and if it were possible for them to do so, how could any child replace their fragile Susan? Mr. Place is a huge man, with shoulders so wide they barely fit through a door opening. Perhaps those shoulders were a bit rounded that day, the emotional weight on them was tremendous. But as he walked, slowly by the defendant's table, the shoulders, as well as the rest of the man seemed stout enough, indeed, even menacing. Mr. Place is a quiet, and gentle man, especially considering his size, but if one drop of the hate that glistened in his eyes could be used as a weapon, it would surely have burned a hole through Schaefer's soul.

The state called David Yurchuk next. He was the officer in charge of the evidence search in Ft. Lauderdale, at Doris Schaefer's house.

Lt. Yurchuk (now Captain) spoke with confidence, in his thick New York-New Jersey accent. His facts were clear, ascertained by a well-documented evidence search. Admitted as State Exhibits, as identified by Yurchuk, were photographs of the Schaefer home in Ft. Lauderdale, the blue-green Datsun (and the contents of its trunk: a thick rope, various knives and some discarded .22 bullets and casing) and various articles from inside the "north bedroom". Articles including several rifles and pistols of various calibers, boxes of men's magazines (with bullet holes and hangman's nooses drawn onto the pictures of nude or semi-nude women), the written manuscript of Gerard Schaefer, describing various methods of executing women, and several articles of jewelry, as well as various other articles described in the Evidence Lists (earlier in this book).

Of particular interest to the state was the identification of the .22 caliber weapons. It was believed that Susan Place had been shot at least once in the face, in the lower jaw by what appeared to have been a .22 caliber bullet. Later, the defense would argue that Dr. Souviron, the dental forensic expert, proved the caliber to be that of a .25 caliber weapon. But Dr. Souviron would admit he was not a weapons expert. He had merely placed an unfired .22 bullet in the hole in the jawbone of Susan Place and stated that it was "a sloppy fit," indicating a larger bullet may have made the hole but that he still believed it was made by a .22 caliber gun. Furthermore, the defense did not take into account the expansion of the bullet after firing, and this might possibly have caused a slightly larger diameter wound. At any rate, the defense pushed the point heavily; there were no .25 caliber weapons found and they believed that that was what made the hole.

The state maintained there was also one .22 caliber "Saturday-night-special," that Hank Dean had seen, that was never found either, and that that weapon quite probably was used on Susan Place.

However, none of the weapons admitted into evidence were found to have fired the spent .22 caliber casing found at the murder scene, and so, the jury was never shown the actual murder weapon that was used on Susan Place. It was an area for doubt, inasmuch as the jury and the topic of a gun-as-a-murder-weapon was concerned. (Knives and ropes were another matter.) It was an issue that permeated the entire trial and was never, finally resolved. However, Schwarz did bring up another discrepancy while cross-examining Yurchuk.

Just before Yurchuk was to leave the witness stand, Schwarz asked him if he had ascertained the ownership of the car in question, (the Datsun). The car was shown to be owned by Gerard J. Schaefer, 2716 S.W. 34th Avenue, Fort Lauderdale, Florida. That is what was typed on the title of ownership to the car. This negated Lucille Place's testimony that she had found the car to be owned by Schaefer at 333 Martin St., in Stuart, Florida.

Stone tried to object to this information, but the court allowed it, and the jury began to have doubts about previous testimony. Schwarz beamed. Schaefer continued to grin and behave as if the whole procedure: his arrest, the hearing, the trial, were all a big misunderstanding, or a hoax. He quietly cajoled with his defense attorneys while waiting for the next witness. A: low-level hum began to creep through the audience. This was not going to be an open and shut case.

Stone called Patricia Webber.

DIRECT EXAMINATION BY MR. STONE:

Q: State your name, please.

A: Patricia Webber.

Q: Your occupation?

A: Clerk-typist, county courthouse tag office.

Q: Tag office? In your capacity do you have access as custodian of the records of the registration of motor vehicles?

A: Yes, sir.

Q: Were you subpoenaed to bring with you the registration of the vehicle involving tag 42 D-7228?

A: Yes, sir, I was.

Q: And was that...

MR. SCHWARZ: 1728 or...

Q: 1728. Excuse me. Did you bring that registration with you?

A: Yes, sir.

MR. STONE: Will you mark this for identification? (Whereupon, said tag registration No. 42-D-1728 marked as State Exhibit S-1 for identification.)

Q: I show you what has been marked State Exhibit S-1 for identification and ask you if that is the record of 42-D-1728 for the year '73, tag number on file in your office?

A: Yes, sir, it is.

Q: And who is that tag registered to?

A: Gerard J. Schaefer, Jr.

Q: What address does it show?

A: 333 Martin Avenue, Stuart, Florida.

MR. STONE: We offer that in evidence at this time.

Schwarz was silent for several moments as he scrutinized the document. His mouth hung open, lips moving, as he silently mouthed the information he read on the car registration.

CROSS EXAMINATION BY MR. SCHWARZ:

Q: Ma'am, the original on here indicates Fort Lauderdale, Florida, but it has been X'd out, is that correct?

A: Yes, it is.

Q: Do you know when that change of address would have occurred?

A: It would have occurred on date of issue.

Q: When was this issued?

A: August 16, '72.

Q: Would that ordinarily have been reflected on the records in Tallahassee?

A: It would have previously been when they made the change. The copy, of course, is sent to Tallahassee.

Q: How often are they sent to Tallahassee?

A: Well, during tag time we make a report usually around once a week, but ordinarily it is every couple of days.

Q: This was issued August 16 of '72?

A: Right.

Q: Would that have gone in before the 1st of September?

A: I would say so, yes, sir.

MR. STONE: We offer it in evidence. We can't vouch for what Tallahassee does. That is her record. It is what she had when it was issued August 16 of '72, and we would like to offer it in evidence.

The court took a recess after Patricia Webber's testimony.

The state called Harold Nute next. After establishing his credentials as a microanalyst and determining he was an expert witness, Stone began the questioning:

Q: All right, were you given some exhibits from the St. Lucie County Sheriff's Department, in reference to your Case No. 73040974?

A: Yes, sir, I have.

Q: And did one of those consist of a piece of root?

A: Yes, sir.

Q: That you have marked as Exhibit 56?

A: Yes, sir.

Q: All right, I am going to show you what has been previously admitted into evidence as State Exhibit No. 2 (a piece of the tree taken from the murder scene) and ask you if you have ever had that in your possession before?

A: Yes, sir, I have.

Q: Were you asked to run any specific tests on that?

A: I was asked, to examine the cut areas in the root for anything that I could find unusual.

Q: All right. Did you find anything in it?

A: In the cut areas on the top portion of the root, in one of the cut areas I found a small fragment of white cloth.

Q: Were you also submitted some cloth and some items that were alleged to have been found near that tree?

A: Yes, sir.

Q: And did you make an examination and comparison with them?

A: Yes, sir, I did.

Q: I show you a bag contained in Exhibit No. 37 and ask you if you have seen this item?

A: Yes, sir, I have.

Q: Can you tell us what the results were of the test comparison of those two items?

A: The item in the bag is a piece of white cloth. I compared the piece of white cloth to the small piece which I removed from the root, State Exhibit 2. I found that the two pieces of cloth were similar and with respect to their color, the type of weave and the type of fiber which the cloth contains.

Q: Were you also submitted and given a tree or a piece of tree limb to examine for whether or not there were rope burns or rope marks or rope fibers?

A: Yes, sir, I was.

Q: Did you do that?

A: Yes, sir, I did.

Q: Now, first I want to show you State Exhibit 4 that is in evidence. I think you also were submitted this, if I am not mistaken, and asked to examine these, what appear to be obvious rope marks. Did you make an examination of that?

A: Yes, sir, I did.

Q: Were you able to make any definite determination as to those marks?

A: No, sir.

Q: Is that a different kind of tree than the other tree that you examined?

A: Yes, sir.

Q: And does that appear to be of different type of bark?

A: Yes, sir,

Q: And these marks were smooth, weren't they?

A: Right. The marks on the tree are smooth texture, they are smoother texture than the rest of the bark. They appear to be caused by some damage, but as to what could have caused the damage, I have...

Q: Would they be consistent with rope burns?

A: I have no basis to say that it would not be.

Q: All right, now, I am going to show you what has been marked as State Exhibit 3 in evidence, and ask you if you were asked to examine this?

A: Yes, sir, I was.

Q: Can you tell us what the results of that examination were?

A: Well, the results of this examination were that in one of the areas on the tree, a small damaged area, I was able to find some fibers which I identified as being hemp fibers.

Q: All right, now, hemp fibers, is rope made with hemp?

A: Yes, sir, some ropes are made with hemp.

Q: And those marks, of course, are as—could you point those out—come over here and show the jury those marks.

A: The type of mark made that I examined are these darkened areas, where these marks are. The mark that I examined with the darkened areas, which were smoother, the bark was noticeably smoother than the surrounding area.

Q: And that would be where you found hemp in it?

A: In at least one of the areas I was able to find hemp.

Q: If a rope were just wrapped around there and no weight on the end of the rope to pull it down, would you be able to find any hemp on there?

A: I have no basis to make that determination.

Q: But there is a slight impression in there, it has worn some, hasn't it?

A: Yes, there is.

MR. SCHWARZ: I object to him leading the witness.

MR. STONE: He is an expert witness. You can lead an expert witness.

A: There is a...

THE COURT: I will sustain the objection. I don't believe that. Let's skip the leading questions.

Q: Let me ask you a question. Are those marks...they are different from the other marks, aren't they, from the rest of the tree?

A: The darkened area, the surface of the darkened area is smoother than the surface of the rest of the tree.

Q: Would it require that some pressure be put on that rope?

A: If it were in fact a rope there would have to be some type of pressure to cause damage to the bark.

Q: And you did find hemp in those marks?

A: I did.

MR. STONE: Thank you.

Schwarz, obviously upset by Stone's leading questions wryly remarked about the tree section: " Do you want to leave it there, so you won't have to haul it back?"

Stone answered solemnly; "Examine him."

BY MR. SCHWARZ:

Q: While you are over here, will you point out the area in which you found the hemp?

A: No, sir, I don't remember the exact area. I looked at the entire tree, and the same two or three areas that are damaged, I looked at the damaged areas and took all the debris in the damaged areas and looked at this under a microscope and separated out the ones that resembled fiber and/or the portions that resembled fibers, then conducted the rest of my examination on those.

Q: But you don't recall the area?

A: The exact area, no, sir,

Q: There was only one area?

A: With the number of fibers I had, I had a small number of fibers, possibly one area, possibly it could have been more.

Q: And that was hemp, right?

A: Yes, sir.

Q: And on this other tree limb that you testified to, you found no fibers similar to either sisal or hemp or anything else, rope fibers at all?

A: There were no fibers which would be to my knowledge used for making rope.

Q: That would include nylon or anything else?

A: That is correct.

Q: It would be equally consistent with your testimony, those are not rope marks on there, is that correct?

A: That is correct.

Q: I understand you were submitted quite a few other items along with these, is that correct?

A: That is correct.

Q: Including what was listed on your report as Item 82, rope with a hook on it? (Found in the trunk of Schaefer's Datsun.)

A: That is correct.

Q: Did you examine that rope, also?

A: I did.

Q: What type of fiber was that rope?

A: Sisal, s-i-s-a-1.

Q: And it was hemp found on this tree limb?

A: That is correct.

Q: On this piece of cloth that you examined, that was in the tree root, where you checked it, did you examine that microscopically?

A: Yes, sir.

Q: Did you find any tracings of blood on it at all?

A: On which? On the cloth from the tree?

Q: Right.

A: No, sir, I did not find any blood on it.

Q: What about the other cloth that you compared it with?

A: I didn't find any blood on it, either.

Q: Approximately how many different items did you examine, do you recall? Do you have your notes with you?

A: Yes, sir.

Q: You can refer to them if you wish. As a matter of fact, if you have got your notes you might go down them one by one. You examined the root first, Exhibit 56, correct?

A: Yes, sir.

Q: Then we have gone over the five-foot limb with rope burn on it, right?

A: Yes, sir.

Q: And the white piece of cloth, piece of white cloth found near the grave, right?

A: Yes, sir.

Q: And the rope with a hook was mentioned there?

A: Yes.

Q: Sisal fiber. All right, No. 83, listed as a hammer. Did you examine this?

A: Yes, sir, I did.

Q: This rope you examined first, No. 82, I believe that as well as the hammer were examined for blood stains, correct?

A: Yes, sir. I did not examine them for blood stains.

Q: You did not perform that examination?

A: No, sir.

Q: What all did you examine on this list?

A: I examined the hammer and three pair of pliers.

Q: That would be Items 83, 84, 85 and 86, right?

A: Yes, sir.

Q: What were your findings from your examination on these items?

A: My findings were, I examined each of these items, with particular reference to the three sets of pliers, to see if there was any possibility that I believe it was requested to determine whether or not there was any possibility that they could have been used for pulling teeth.

Q: Did you conduct such an examination?

A: I conducted an examination of the surface of the working edges of the pliers for any material similar to teeth, and I did not find any.

Q: Did you perform any of the other examinations on any of these other items, the various knives and gloves and pillowcase and the belt and fishing knife and canvas bag and another knife?

A: No, sir, I did not.

Q: Do you know who did those?

A: Yes, sir.

Q: Who was it?

A: Mrs. Janet Clark.

Q: So as far as you are concerned, as far as any comparisons were concerned, your tests were negative, right?

A: (No response.)

Q: Well, you found there was some rope fibers on the tree, but it didn't compare with the rope you were sent to compare it with?

A: I did not have any comparisons, that is right.

Q: And the hammer and three pair of pliers were negative?

A: Yes, sir.

MR. SCHWARZ: Nothing further.

REDIRECT EXAMINATION BY MR STONE:

Q: Mr. Nute, one question, Mr. Schwarz asked you about the cloth, let me present it to you hypothetically. If, of course, you had a bone laying there and a cloth over it, and you cut through the cloth to the bone, there was no blood on the bone, there wouldn't be any on the cloth, either, would there?

MR. SCHWARZ: Your Honor, I object to the question. I don't think he is qualified as an expert in pathology or medicine.

MR. STONE: You asked him if there was any blood on it.

MR. SCHWARZ: He is a laboratory microanalyst.

THE COURT: I will sustain the objection.

MR. STONE: Okay, I will withdraw it. You can be excused.

When Nute stepped out of the witness stand, it was evident on Stone's face he was not satisfied with his testimony. Yes, it had been determined a rope was used on the tree, and the tree used as a cutting makeshift board, but the rope was the wrong kind and the cloth fibers in the tree proved nothing without blood stains. Stone shuffled his papers nervously and stuffed them into his briefcase. It became apparent to him at the close of that first day of the trial that he had a lot more work to do.

The defense had hit home some rather strong points with the jury. Unless Stone could convince them otherwise, the jury would have their reasonable doubt, and Gerard Schaefer would be back on the streets, "leaving a trail of dead bodies to cover the state of Florida."

Stone rubbed the back of his neck vigorously and wondered how much more he could put into this case. Since he began looking into it six months earlier, he'd lost sixty-five pounds, his salt-and-pepper hair was clearly getting more "salt" in it and, more often than not, he was substituting two martinis for a good lunch. His marriage was in trouble and sleep was brief, elusive moments, grabbed restlessly throughout the night. Still, as he shuffled doggedly out of the court that day, his briefcase weighing at least a ton, he believed he had a few more tricks up his sleeves.

* * *

The second day of the trial began, once again, promptly at 9:30 a.m. All were present and eager to start the day, including Gerard Schaefer was still the picture of banality, as he sat incessantly grinning; the Cheshire cat on trial for murder. In addition to the usual medley of reporters and curious onlookers in the audience, were two more interested persons; a tired security guard and his wife, the parents of Mary Alice Briscolinas. They came all the way up from Ft. Lauderdale to watch these proceedings, still hoping to find an answer, or at least some clues as to what may have caused their fourteen-year-old daughter to be senselessly murdered almost one year ago. They believed Gerard Schaefer could provide that answer.

The state called their first witness for the day, the eloquent Dr. Richard Souviron.

Dr. Souviron not only runs a private dental practice in Coral Gables, which utilizes the latest technological advances in that field, but his background in forensic dentistry is unparalleled anywhere. At that time, he was the only dentist in the country appointed to present forensic dentistry by the Justice Department of the United States. His credentials are voluminous. He has been qualified as an expert witness in a dozen states, as well as the US Federal Court. He is the chairman or president of dozens of dental or forensic science organizations, a teacher and lecturer of dental identification at the crime scene, as well as other related subjects. Additionally, he had opened a new area of investigation; bite-mark identification, about which he has published numerous articles. (Later, Dr. Souviron would be instrumental in the Ted Bundy murder trials, identifying that killer's teeth marks on the bodies of the slain Florida State University coeds.)

Despite his rather capacious background, Dr. Souviron is still speaks with almost boyish enthusiasm. He is handsome and tanned, undoubtedly a terror on the tennis courts, with a mouthful of perfect teeth, of course.

Stone took the time to establish Dr. Souviron's expertise, as any good state attorney would and much to the dismay of Mr. Schwarz (who sat annoyed crossing and recrossing his arms, eagerly awaiting his time for cross examination.) The following are excerpts of Dr. Souviron's testimony. Of note, is the testimony about Carmen (Candy Hallock) and the rather obvious animosity between Schwarz and Dr. Souviron.

BY MR. STONE:

Q: Dr. Souviron, I am going to show you State Exhibit T-1 for identification and U-1 for identification and ask you if you can please, to examine those, if you can identify them, and tell me what examination you performed.

A: These are four Polaroid pictures, close-up pictures of a series of teeth that were identified as those of Georgia Jessup. I have three x-rays of a jaw fragment that was identified as that of Georgia Jessup.

Q: The jaw fragment is broken there, it appears. Can you tell me, were you able to determine how that jaw fragment was broken?

A: No, sir. (Years later, Dr. Souviron would tell me that he believed the jaw was broken post-mortem (after death) by "a horrendous force," done by a strong man, and not unlike what one might expect to find in an airline crash victim.)

MR. STONE: At this time, we would like to introduce these into evidence, these two.

A: Try to keep them together.

MR. STONE: Yes, sir.

BY MR: SCHWARZ:

Q: Referring to U-1, Doctor, this one photograph of the one isolated tooth, what is that?

A: This was one of the major means of identifying these teeth. This is a molar, and it has an enameled – if you will notice that little deal there, which is an anomaly, it is an unusual finding. (Indicating an area on the tooth.)

Q: These are x-rays?

A: Of the fragments, right.

MR. SCHWARZ: I have no objection.

THE COURT: They will be admitted.

BY MR. SCHWARZ:

Q: Doctor, Exhibits V-1, W-1 and X-1, these are basically the same thing, only these are Susan Place's?

A: Correct.

Q: You took these photographs yourself?

A: I did.

MR. SCHWARZ: No objection.

THE COURT: All right, they will be admitted.

BY MR. STONE:

Q: Doctor, I show you what has been admitted in evidence as State Exhibit No. 40 and ask you if you would look at that and tell me what it depicts.

A: These are three Polaroid shots of a human mandible, which is the lower jaw. The shots are from the lining wall side in two instances, and one from the labial aspect in the other instance.

Q: Whose teeth were those?

A: These are Susan Place's.

Q: I show you 41 and 42 and ask you if you would identify those for me, also?

A: 41 is the mandible which we had two fragments and we were able to piece them together and these (pictures) show how they fit together. They were from, we took these pictures from the right side, from the occlusal of the top, and again from the occlusal lining wall on the right side, so we have the right, we show some fillings here on the left.

Q: When you are talking, would you please refer to the exhibit number here?

A: 41. The right mandible and showing the amalgam fillings and what-have-you. This shows the right and the left bicuspid, which were important, and the last one is the left bicuspid.

Q: All right, now, referring specifically to No. 40, I want to ask you a question about that. Did the picture in the middle – did you examine that microscopically or through x-rays?

A: Yes, we did.

Q: And did you find any foreign matter in there?

A: Yes, we did.

Q: What was the foreign matter you found?

A: Metal.

Q: Metal?

A: Right.

Q: All right, and what type metal was it, Doctor?

A: We didn't destroy the jaw in order to pull the bullet out, because it was within the jawbone. It was not visible or in any way detectible from outside. It was actually within the marrow space of the bone.

Q: Was it in around a hole that was in the jawbone?

A: It started from the hole and worked its way back, all the way back to the third molar.

Q: Doctor, based on your experience and your training, do you have an opinion with reasonable medical certainty as to what caused that hole and what put that metal fragment in there? MR. SCHWARZ: Your Honor, I object to that hypothetical question. There are no facts which he has stated in there other than just his theory, I mean, or his opinion. You have got to set forth the facts he is relying on an opinion in a hypothetical question of that type.

Q: All right, Doctor, assuming there were a .22 casing found at the scene of this, where these teeth were found, and assuming that there were—it was put to you that there was a spent .22 cartridge found at the scene, and you have examined this fragment and found foreign metal fragments in there, and you have examined this hole, and with your training and your experience,

Do you have an opinion as to the reasonable medical certainty as to whether or not that hole was caused by a bullet and if so, what caliber?

A: To answer your question, Mr. Stone, is without knowing a casing existed, I put that in my report the time back in April when I saw just the fragments, that it was a .22 bullet.

Q: And that is your opinion with reasonable medical certainty?

A: Without any question.

MR. STONE: Okay. Your witness.

CROSS EXAMINATION BY MR. SCHWARZ:

Q: Dr. Souviron, couldn't it equally have been a .25 caliber bullet that made that hole?

A: Mr. Schwarz, you are asking me to...I am a dentist and I am testifying as to the measurements that were made. The measurements were compatible with a .22.

Q: Would they also be compatible with a .25?

A: Well, I think the only way we would be able to do this would be to measure a .25 caliber shell, going through this particular mandible, what size hole it would make, in comparison with a .22, then we could say with certainty.

Q: Did you make a comparison? Did you measure that hole?

A: Yes, I did.

Q: What were the measurements of it?

A: It is in my report, it measures approximately five to six millimeters.

Q: Do you know the diameter of a .22 caliber bullet?

An In millimeters, no, not right offhand.

Q: How about a .25 caliber bullet?

A: No.

Q: How did you arrive at the opinion that it was a .22 caliber bullet as opposed to a .25?

A: That is a good question, because at the time I took a .22 bullet and placed it in the hole, and it measured out.

Q: Was there any leeway at all on it?

A: It was a good fit. Sure, it was a sloppy fit, but it fit.

Q: A: .25 might fit just perfectly?

A: No, I don't think so. A: .25 would have been too big.

Q: Did you compare it to see?

A: I compared it with a .38.

Q: A: .38 and .25 are quite a bit different?

A: Right. You have got the jaw fragments. You can do it yourself.

Q: I don't have it.

A: You should. The State has, Lieutenant Duval has it?

Q: Ask Mr. Stone. I don't have it.

A: Okay.

Q: Were you able to ascertain what the type of metal was?

A: I said we did not destroy or in any way dismember the fragments. We kept them as they were.

Q: You don't know whether it was lead a or steel-jacketed bullet that made the hole or copper-clad bullet or anything of that kind, they would all show up the same on the x-ray, wouldn't they?

A: No. If it were a steel bullet it would go through. A: metal armor-piercing bullet would have gone right through and would not have disintegrated like this did. This had to be a soft-nosed bullet of some type.

Q: Is there any way from your examination you can arrive at an opinion as to whether, or not, that bullet hole was caused before or after death?

A: We can say this. I can say this much about it, based on my experience, that there are no powder burns as such on the bone. This would indicate that either it was fired at a distance or that it was fired at the time of death. Whether it was before the death of this individual or immediately after, but there was tissue over this area.

Q: Or it was fired at a distance say of from as far as I am from you right now? (About 5-7 feet.)

A: Yes.

Q: Either one would be consistent with your findings, right?

A: Right.

Q: And it would also be consistent if it was fired from this distance (about 10-12 feet) it would have happened after death?

A: If that is...yes, it could have. It is possible.

Q: These teeth that were delivered to you, also I believe these photographs show where some were fitted back into the jawbone?

A: Yes.

Q: Would that be a normal occurrence in a body that had been dead for several months, for teeth to fall out?

A: Yes.

MR. SCHWARZ: I have no further questions.

MR. STONE: We would like to proffer something outside the presence of the jury.

THE COURT: Ladies and gentlemen of the jury, retire to the jury room for a few moments, please.

At this time, the jury withdrew to the jury room and the following proceedings were conducted in the absence of the jury:

BY MR. STONE:

Q: Dr. Souviron, were you also given a tooth identified to you as belonging to someone named Candy Hallock?

MR. SCHWARZ: Do you mean a tooth given to him identified...

A: That is what he asked me.

Q: Were you given a tooth and x-rays of Candy Hallock, and asked to compare them?

A: I was given a vial that contained a gold crown, a tooth that had a gold inlay in it, and two other teeth, and we were subsequently...I was subsequently furnished with some x-rays of an individual by the name of Candy Hallock, and the gold crown and the tooth with the gold inlay in it were those of Candy Hallock.

Q: Do you have that tooth with you this morning?

A: Yes, I do.

Q: May I have it please?

MR. STONE: We would like to mark this for identification.

BY MR. SCHWARZ:

Q: Doctor, I know the teeth are in a vial. Is that the same vial they were delivered to you in?

A: Yes, it is.

BY MR. STONE:

Q: Who delivered those to you, Dr. Souviron?

A: Dr. Joe Davis.

Q: That is the medical examiner of Dade County.

A: That is right,

Q: Where did you obtain the x-rays of Candy Hallock from?

A: They were delivered to me by a detective from Fort Lauderdale. I don't have his name right offhand.

Q: Did you compare this tooth with those x-rays?

A: Yes, I did.

Q: And what was your finding?

A: They were identical.

Q: And you say to reasonable medical certainty that that tooth that is in that vial we are marking now as State Exhibit Y-1 for identification, in your expert opinion, can you say to reasonable medical certainty that was a tooth of Candy Hallock?

A: Not only the tooth, but also the little gold crown in there definitely were Candy Hallock's. No question about it.

MR. STONE: Do you want to question him?

MR. SCHWARZ: No. I object to it, Your Honor, on the grounds it is totally irrelevant,

MR. STONE: I haven't offered it in evidence. I am just identifying it. Do you want to question him about the identification?

BY MR. SCHWARZ:

Q: Just one question, Doctor. Is the absence of these teeth from a body consistent with life or death?

A: I would say that the tooth that is in the vial, the absence of that from a body would be consistent with death.

Q: For what reason?

A: It is a vital tooth. There is no pathology involved with that tooth, and there would be no indication whatsoever for extraction.

Q: What about the tooth that goes with the other cap?

A: I don't have the tooth that goes with the other cap. It was by itself.

Q: You don't know what the condition of that tooth was?

A: Yes, I do.

Q: What was it?

A: I have the x-ray of the tooth.

Q: What was it?

A: It was a good, capped tooth. There was nothing wrong with that.

Q: When were those x-rays taken?

A: I will have to look at the x-rays to tell you that. Do you want me to look this up to answer that question?

Q: Sure.

A: I have, the most recent x-rays I have are 12-2-68. 12-2-68.

Q: And you don't know when these teeth were removed, do you? That is almost five years ago. You don't know when these teeth were removed?

A: I have absolutely no idea when they were removed.

Q: A: lot could have happened to this other tooth that is missing, couldn't it?

A: Of course.

Q: You say the absence of these teeth is consistent with death. Isn't it a fact that is only because you found nothing wrong with the teeth?

A: Based on these x-rays that I have of December of 1968, December 2nd, these teeth were in excellent condition. They were well.

Q: A: person could still be alive without them, couldn't they?

A: Yes, they could be alive without them.

Q: You are not saying because of these two teeth, the tooth and extra cap, that Candy Hallock is dead, are you?

A: No, what I am saying is there was no reason to remove these teeth, none whatsoever.

Q: Did you examine these microscopically to determine whether there were any indications of excessive force in removing them?

A: I looked at them with a magnifying glass. That would be considered microscopically.

Q: What did you find?

A: We found that there was no indication on these teeth, per se, in the crown, per se, of any abnormal marks other than marks that were caused by a dental burr, which was part of the means of identification.

Q: You were furnished a couple other teeth, also, weren't you?

A: Yes, I was.

Q: Have you compared those with anybody?

A: Mr. Schwarz, you told me in your own words that those teeth were those and these also were those of Mr. Schaefer. (Schwarz tried to trick Souviron by giving him Schaefer's teeth,)

Q: I never told you these were.

A: Yes, sir, you did. And the other ones were also, and I told you that all you had to do was furnish me with Mr. Schaefer's dental x-rays and I could tell you at that time whether, or not, those teeth in fact were his, or not.

Q: Did you ever receive those x-rays?

A: I never received anything from you. I would be delighted to examine Mr. Schaefer and tell you whether those are his teeth or not, or whether he still has those teeth.

MR. SCHWARZ: He is right here.

A: I don't have the teeth with me.

Dr. Souviron did not examine Schaefer, and Schwarz continued to assault him with questions about Schaefer's teeth. In the end, however, the astute dentist got the last word in.

Q: In your conclusion you state, is it not true, that it appears this tooth was removed before or shortly after death, because of the tissue attached, the chips on the medial root are suggestive of excessive force in removal and are probably not produced by a dentist, there are no forceps marks visible. In other words, forcibly removed by someone other than a dentist?

A: It was removed by, if it was removed by a dentist, he had a heavy hand.

Q: Some dentists do, don't they?

A: They sure do.

Sergeant Williams A. Scott of the Martin County Sheriff's Office, was put on the stand next. He was the officer in charge of the jail where Schaefer was incarcerated for the abduction of Paula Sue Wells and Nancy Trotter. When the Places came to the jail to inquire about Gerard Schaefer, Scott took a photograph of Susan Place that they had given to Schaefer to see if he could give them any information as to what may have happened to their daughter. Scott testified that Schaefer commented that Susan was "a nice-looking girl," but that he hadn't seen her and didn't know anything about it. Schaefer then turned the picture over, noticed the date (wrongly penned by Mrs. Place) and said, "I wasn't even in Ft. Lauderdale on October 27, of '72."

No one had mentioned Ft. Lauderdale, and the photograph did not indicate an address.

Upon cross-examination of Scott, Schwarz used a common legal tactic: discredit the witness, discredit the testimony. It was relatively successful. Within his testimony Scott admitted that Schaefer, working for the Martin County Sheriff Department, twice stopped Scott for excessive speeding on his motorcycle, and ticketed him. The implication was clear. Scott had reason to be prejudiced against Schaefer, and so might lie on the stand in order to seek a personal revenge. Schwarz was not missing a trick.

Stone called Cheryl Jessup to the stand. Cheryl (Georgia's little sister) was twelve years old, a bit small for her age, and nervous to be put in front of so many strange people. Despite all that, she would turn out to be one strong young lady, and an excellent witness for Stone. As she spoke in her diminutive voice (she had to sit up straight and speak right into the microphone, or not be heard) the jury's hearts went out to her. The sole reason she was there was to testify that the purse in question (the brown suede "hippie" purse) was indeed her sister's. When she was through testifying, no one had any doubt that it was.

Schwarz once again rained questions upon the witness, some totally irrelevant, i.e., "Did she carry marijuana in the purse?" and so on. When

Cheryl said the purse was a little dirtier than she remembered, Schwarz pounced on that. "In other words, that purse doesn't look now like it did when you saw it with your sister, right?" Cheryl firmly replied, "No, it does look like it."

"But you said this one is dirtier than you remember the one that your sister had."

"A: little bit," said Cheryl, almost coyly.

Stone interjected, "Of course, she doesn't know that purse has been out in the field."

George Jessup, Georgia's father, was called next. As he did in his previous deposition, Mr. Jessup testified that he'd met "Jerry Shepard" about one week before his daughter disappeared. When asked if he could recognize that man in court, he pointed to Schaefer. He told how Schaefer had come to his home looking for "Crystal" (Georgia's nickname). He had not allowed the man into his house but stepped out to talk to him. He described his approximate weight, height and general appearance, all matching Schaefer's description. He could not clearly remember the clothes, whether Schaefer had a mustache, or exactly what time in the evening it was.

Bruce Colton handled cross-examination. He questioned, heavily, about the mustache and the time Schaefer was reported to have been at the Jessup house. In his deposition, Mr. Jessup had stated that "Shepard . . . was clean shaven . . . but wore a mustache."

Now, he denied that he'd said that. Additionally, he had stated that it was getting dark and may have been close to 8:30 p.m. Colton inferred that Mr. Jessup could not see the person at his house clearly, because it was dark enough at that time, in an effort to now cloud his memory as to whether the man even had a mustache. Then, too, Mr. Jessup had testified that Schaefer "looked different . . . thinner, with darker hair than before." Even though Mr. Jessup would tell Stone there was no doubt in his mind that Schaefer was the man at his house, Colton's repeated insinuations of Mr. Jessup's unclear memory caused more doubt among the jurors.

Colton, like Schwarz, asked time and again about Georgia's drug use, whether there was marijuana in the house, did Mr. Jessup know what it looked like, smelled like, and so on. It is unclear what the significance of this line of questioning was. It has been surmised that the defense was trying to tie Georgia to drug traffickers, and so another possible, albeit unknown, murderer or group of murderers. If this was the reason for these questions, then perhaps they are justifiable. However, if the questions were intended to discredit the character of the victim, for whatever reason, then they were erroneous and uncalled for, and still skirt the problem: that despite anything she may have done, or been, Georgia Jessup had been murdered.

One of Georgia's closest friends, a young lady named Joyce Froggatt, was put on the stand next. Again, the subject of the purse was brought up, as was the subject of marijuana use. Joyce was adamant about the purse. Not only was she positive the purse was Georgia's, she testified she had seen Georgia with it "hundreds of times" and that she had borrowed it on several occasions and had asked Georgia if she could have it. To throw some doubt onto this testimony, Schwarz configured a different line of attack. Throughout Joyce's testimony, the purse was referred to, but not physically shown. As he cross-examined her, Schwarz produced three small brown suede purses.

He knew he could not have them admitted as evidence, but he could have the court mark them for identification. His intent was to cause doubt in Joyce's recollection, and possibly cause her to say that the purse looked like any one of the three substitute purses. It was a good play. Stone was not amused. As Schwarz had the purses marked for identification, Stone objected, the court allowed Schwarz to use them, and Joyce responded. The following is a record of that transaction.

MR. STONE: At this time, I object to any testimony whatsoever concerning these exhibits, because I asked Schwarz to provide me and tell me what documentary evidence he had, and he told me two items, and none of them were these.

MR. SCHWARZ: Other than impeachment... (the process of calling into question the credibility of a witness.)

MR. STONE: Just like the Court said a few minutes ago about impeachment. I asked you right here at this counsel table about ten minutes ago for you to show me any documentary evidence you had and you showed me a little old badge out of your pocket and the passport, and you said that is all you were going to use.

MR. SCHWARZ: I gave you a copy of the passport.

MR. STONE: And I object to it. I strenuously object to it.

THE COURT: I don't know what is going to be done yet. Anything can be marked for identification at this point, but where we go and what you intend to use it for...

MR. STONE: I think it is a definite attempt to deceive the State and to prevent them from properly preparing.

MR. SCHWARZ: I haven't attempted to deceive you about anything.

MR, STONE: We have given you anything you wanted, even copies...

THE COURT: All right, gentlemen, let's move along. Let's see what Mr. Schwarz is going to do with this.

BY MR. SCHWARZ:

Q: Joyce, I am going to show you three other purses and ask you if you can identify either one of these?

A: I have never seen none of them.

Q: You haven't?

A: No.

Q: Is there anything distinctive about them?

A: Like what?

Q: Other than, anything more distinctive about this one or any of these than the other one? (Referring to Georgia's).

A: I just know the other one, because I have used it. I haven't used none of those.

The ploy did not work.

* * *

When Shirley Jessup took the stand she was, in the words of one reporter there, "an emotional basket case." Mrs. Jessup and her daughter were very close despite their differences. They labored through the usual concerned parent-adolescent daughter squabbles, and to relieve some of that tension, Georgia had stayed part-time with her father, but mother and daughter were not so far apart in age, and so a loving bond always managed to sustain them.

Mrs. Jessup's eyeglasses were smeared with tears and served to amplify her puffy eyes and swollen red lids. She had to continually clear her throat to speak and did so with great difficulty. As with Mrs. Place, she seemed to have aged ten years in one year's time.

Once again, the little suede purse (State Exhibit 44) was identified. Once again, the marijuana questions came up.

Stone, finally, objected vehemently to the questions, stating, "In the first place, these victims are not on trial. They are not on trial for anything, and it is way beyond the scope of my direct examination."

In spite the passion displayed by the state attorney, the court allowed the questions. The defense continued to ask about marijuana, and marijuana seeds in the purse. Eventually, Mrs. Jessup said she may have recalled seeing some in the purse. The defense, (Colton) apparently satisfied with her answer, asked no further questions.

What is blatantly obvious here, though the defense must not have recognized the fact, is that by confirming that Georgia used the purse to carry marijuana, the implication confirms that the purse was hers This being the case, one must once again ask, "Why did Gerard Schaefer have the purse?"

After her testimony, Shirley Jessup was asked to leave the courtroom. Elton Schwarz made it quite clear that he would prefer that she not stay, probably because of the effect her emotional display would have on the jury.

Stone, who had asked that she be permitted to stay and was denied, told Schwarz, "Well, remember that when you ask for the same privilege, please."

Following Shirley Jessup, Ann Chapman was put on the stand. She was Georgia's grandmother. She testified that she gave Georgia a small jewelry box, for her earrings and such; it was old, faded green, with gold on it. Just like the one Lt. Yurchuk had found at Doris Schaefer's house, in the north bedroom.

Yurchuk was recalled. Phil Shailer directed the questions on this round, and he asked about the jewelry box at this time. (Later, he would ask about it when Yurchuk was called a third, and then a fourth time. Yurchuk, eventually was able to testify where he obtained the jewelry box—at Doris Schaefer's house where, at that time, she had not recognized the box as anyone's she might know.)

During this questioning, Yurchuk identified the purse as the one that Hank Dean had given him. He also identified the "murder manuscripts" and morbidly graffitied magazines found in the north bedroom. One other item was entered as evidence by the state: a manila envelope, also found in the north bedroom, addressed to Jerry Shepard, 2716 SW 34th Avenue, Fr. Lauderdale, Florida. The address, of course, of the Schaefer home.

What Yurchuk could not say on the stand was what he would tell me years later, in a taped interview. He said he remembered a time when Doris Schaefer had come into the Broward County Sheriff's Department complaining of finding "notes," that made threats against her life. She would find them in various places in her bedroom. She told police she thought possibly, her son might have been the author of those notes and came to ask their advice. Because Gerard was a juvenile at that time, and taking into account that there were marital problems existent in the family (with the father being away most of the time or suffering from alcoholism the rest of the time) the sheriff's department did nothing.

Teresa Schaefer was called to the stand. Her testimony recapped her previous deposition, with Stone hammering questions about her taking the purse to Ft. Lauderdale, upon Gerard's request. He repeatedly probed the issue of the missing "Saturday-night Special," the .22 caliber handgun that was missing. She held to her story that the purse had been a gift from Gerard, that he purchased it during his travels in Morocco.

Teresa maintained a calm facade as she testified. She'd faced Stone before and knew his questions would be personal and harsh. Though her testimony could not be considered helpful to Gerard's case, her appearance in court as the loving, devoted and dutiful wife, made the jury like her. If they could hold her in favorable light, could not that light shine just a bit on her ill-fated husband? During recesses, the young couple often exchanged light kisses and hugs, and almost constantly held hands. Teresa was an asset for Gerard, if not with her testimony, at least as a voucher for his character. She appeared attractive in her new mini-dress, but innocent, faithful and believable. She was the court darling, even the press liked her and represented her as the virtuous unfortunate wife, caught up amidst a macabre and tangled tale of law and murder.

Hank Dean was called next. He, too, recapped his original deposition. This time his testimony was even more damning to Schaefer. He told of Teresa calling him to help move some things from Stuart to Ft. Lauderdale, particularly those items Schaefer had asked her to move: the purse and the gun. The implication was obvious. Schaefer wanted them not to be seen. Dean, with his background in law enforcement and still maintaining an acquaintance with Lt. Yurchuk, made the decision to take the purse to the proper authorities. There had been no record of dissension between Dean and Schaefer, but now an undisguised resentment grew between the two men as Dean, more and more, became one of the state's key witnesses. Nothing he said, even on cross-examination from Schwarz, could throw any favorable light on Schaefer.

Dean described the "cheap-looking," small .22 caliber pistol that Schaefer always took on target shoots. This was the one pistol investigators could not locate, and Dean failed to recognize it among the guns he was shown. Additionally, he told of his conversation with Schaefer at the Martin County Jail, where Schaefer had asked him, "Do you want me to confess?" He also told Dean, with Teresa present, that there were no heads found within the remains of the two girls, and that without them a positive identification could not be made. Finally, Schaefer had asked Teresa, in

Dean's presence, if he should accept Time magazine's offer of money for his "true" story.

Also, of note, was that Dean commented on how much weight his brother-in-law had lost since one year ago. The comment merely echoed what the Places and Jessups had said.

After Hank Dean, a bank clerk was put on the stand. She testified that Gerard Schaefer had made a withdrawal (of $25.00) from the First Federal Savings and Loan of Plantation, where she was an employee, and Schaefer was an account holder. The date of the withdrawal was September 27, 1972. This proved that Schaefer was in the Ft. Lauderdale area on the day that the two girls became missing. (It also proved that Schaefer was at least a semi-regular visitor to the city of Plantation, where Mary Briscolina and Elsie Farmer had lived.) This branch of the bank was only about two miles from Oakland Park, where the Places lived.

Following the bank clerk, Robert Crowder took the stand. He had been the Sheriff of Martin County. Schaefer was an employee of his. He testified that Schaefer's duty would have been to patrol Hutchinson Island. He also said that when Schaefer applied for the job, he told him that he could leave a message (if he was hired) at a Ft. Lauderdale phone number, because he was going to Colorado for a vacation.

Detective Edward Spiher testified that he'd made out the original missing person's report on Susan Place. It was dated October 1, 1972. This proved that the date on the back of the photograph of Susan Place (shown to Schaefer in jail) was incorrectly written; that Susan had been reported missing before October 27, 1972.

The end of the second day of trial was a bit premature; the attorneys had run out of witnesses. Judge Trowbridge, only slightly annoyed, adjourned the court until Monday morning, once again warning the jurors not to discuss the case or read about it, or watch the television news coverage. He ended his warning with, "Let's give this case a fair trial for both sides."

* * *

Dr. Joseph Davis, the renowned Dade County Medical Examiner, was the first witness called on behalf of the State on September 29, 1973, promptly at 9:30 a.m.

The State spent about a half-hour just questioning Dr. Davis on his credentials that qualified him as an expert in forensic medicine. Considering the magnitude of his educational and professional background, they could easily have spent the whole morning. He is one of the foremost medical examiners in not only in the United States, but throughout the world. He was performing an autopsy in Africa at the time he was called back to Florida for this case.

Dr. Davis began his studies as an engineering student at Lehigh University, which were interrupted by World War II. While in the Army, he attended Virginia Polytechnic Institute and Princeton University. He graduated from the Long Island College of Medicine in 1949, and interned at the University of California, in San Francisco. Again, a war interrupted his formal training, this time it was in Korea. After two years of serving his time there, he returned to the States and worked as a resident in pathology at the United States Public Health Service in Seattle.

This public health service also had a branch in New Orleans, where he transferred for a year, before finally settling in Miami.

Since 1956, he was a professor at the University of Miami and a practicing medical examiner in that city. In 1973, at the time of the trial he had been the Chief Medical Examiner of Dade County (for several years) and kept that position for 40 years. He published over a hundred articles in various professional medical magazines, and performed tens of thousands of postmortem examinations (autopsies). He was the president, or vice president, or chairman of about a dozen associations, academies, or commissions that deal with forensic science. Yet for all his background, and despite his inhuman work schedule, he was an accessible, witty and humorous person to talk to. A: warm and brilliant conversationalist who would take the time to talk to a student who needed advice, or a colleague in need of an answer. His secretary honestly loved the man and tried not to schedule too many interviews or appointments for him, because she knew he would take the time to fulfill them, no doubt at the expense of his own leisure time. He was an excellent witness for the State.

(Shailer asked the questions in this excerpt of Dr. Davis' testimony.)

Q: All right, Doctor, in the course of your ordinary business as Dade County Medical Examiner did you have occasion to receive certain skeletal remains from St. Lucie County on April 7 of this year?

A: Yes.

Q: Will you describe for us, please, the state of deterioration of those remains?

A: On April 7th, in the morning, I received from Lieutenant Duval, I believe, of the St. Lucie Sheriff's Office, and Sergeant Browning, two black plastic bags. Each bag contained human remains. The remains were in pieces. They were not intact.

Q: When you speak of two bags, were you able to readily determine that each related to one, or separate individuals at that time?

A: No, I was not at that time, because the state of decomposition and skeletonization, plus the dismemberment, plus that it was difficult to immediately determine which part belonged to which.

Q: How do you process such remains? What do you look for?

A: There is a twofold approach to such remains. The first is to determine as far as possible from ancillary evidence, from information from police and other sources, the circumstances under which the skeletonized remains were found, and in Dade County if a skeletonized remains is found it is customary for myself or one of my associates, or two or three of us to go to the scene and actually participate in the recovery of the remains. We try to determine as much as we can about the circumstances under which the remains were found, the terrain, the weather conditions, and so forth. We also try to run down information pertaining to missing persons who might possibly fall in this category.

Q: Do you attempt to determine a specific cause or causes of death?

A: Yes.

Q: Is that normally the case regarding skeletal remains in this state of deterioration?

A: No, it is not, unless there happens to be a clear-cut injury pattern, say a gunshot wound to the head or something, with evidence of vital bleeding in the area. Once in a while we can determine with reasonable medical certainty a cause of death, a specific medical cause of death. More often than not it has to remain on an inferential basis, or on a basis of ruling out certain things, but not necessarily ruling in. As far as our investigation, to continue my answer to your previous question, the remains themselves are examined from the standpoint of the degree of deterioration. An estimate is made as to the sex of the individual, the approximate range of height or stature of the individual, the presence or absence of any identifiable injuries or patterns, old fractures, for example, or dental evidence, and so forth, and every effort is made to elicit such information, however skimpy it may be, from the remains.

Q: Did you attempt to determine the sex or age and height of these bodies?

A: Yes.

Q: Were your findings ultimately determined to be consistent with the identities that were ultimately made known to you?

A: Yes.

Q: Doctor, did you attempt to reconstruct these remains, that is, to realign these particular bodies?

A: Yes.

Q: Describe for us what you did and what you were able to accomplish in that regard?

A: The degree of deterioration was such that it was not readily apparent as to the relationship of these remains. The various bones had to be examined with care and over a period of time. I found by counting vertebrae that the remains had been mixed up, and in general the remains consisted of four major parts, not counting smaller looser fragments. I had two upper halves of a body and two lower halves. The bags, as I received them, I found had been mixed up in that the upper half of one body was with the lower half of the other, and the only way an intact or reasonably intact body or skeletal remains could be obtained was to match the upper half of one body from one bag with the lower half of the other body from the other bag.

Q: Were there any particular sections and/or limbs that were noticeably absent?

A: Yes.

Q: What were those?

A: Well, the heads in both cases were missing, and the upper vertebrae, what we call the cervical vertebrae, the neck bones were partially missing and in one of the cases, and I will have to refresh my memory as to which one, this was what we call or what I called the Body No, 1, which was consistent with a missing person called Susan Place. There was evidence of a cut through the fourth cervical vertebra.

Q: Would you show the jury where you are referring to, please?

A: Well, if you count from the base of the skull down four bones, of the neck bones, the fourth one down was cut through.

Q: When you say a cut, would you be more particular and describe what you mean by that?

A: It was apparent from the margin of the bone that some sharp instrument, not a blunt instrument like a dull ax, but a sharp instrument, like a heavy bladed knife, a sharp knife, had chopped through that particular vertebra and the upper portion was missing and was not recovered by me, but the lower portion containing the chop mark was still apparent,

Q: Did you determine the direction from which that chopping must have come, that is, could it have come either front, back, side, or otherwise, or could you make a specific determination?

A: In that one I could not make a specific determination. It appeared to be more consistent with a blow from the rear rather than from the front, but I could not be certain. (At this point, Shirley Jessup who had been allowed back in court got up, and looking rather faint, rushed from the court room.)

Q: All right, sir. Continue, please, regarding the dismemberment, I believe, that you just began telling us about.

A: In reference to Body No. 1, which was consistent with a missing female by the name of Place, there was a separation through the backbone, or the lower portion of the spine, between the third and fourth lumbar vertebrae, and the degree of cutting of this particular instance I could tell was from the—or the angle of cutting was from the rear. This also appeared to have been done with a sharp or heavy-bladed instrument. There was, through the left shoulder joint, another cut which partially separated the upper portion of the joint and completely separated the head of the humerus, which is the arm bone, into two portions, so that a portion of the head was still adherent to the socket of the shoulder joint, but the whole left upper extremity from that point down was completely separate from the body, but the cut edges could be matched together to show that that free left upper extremity was from that particular body, from the left shoulder joint.

Q: Continue on down, please.

A: In that particular body, there was also a complete cut through the mid portion of the right arm, the humerus or arm bone was cut through again by some sharp instrument that must have been with considerable force to cut the bone. Now, the right upper extremity from the mid-arm region down through the elbow, forearm and hand was missing. And this was never presented to me. I have not seen it and I do not know where it is. There were the injuries that I could determine. This particular body, Body No. 1, these were cutting type injuries. I found no obvious simple fractures or blunt type injuries. I x-rayed the body in a search for knife fragments, metal fragments, bullets, and I could find no evidence of these in the remains as submitted to me.

Q: All right, sir, would you switch your attention now to Body No. 2. Tell us, first of all, whether your findings as to sex, age and height were consistent with the ultimate identification?

A: Yes, sir, they were.

Q: With regard to Body No. 2, were your findings as to sex, age and height consistent with the ultimate identification of Georgia Jessup?

A: Yes, it was.

Q: Now, if you will continue by detailing your findings as to the evidence?

A: In this particular body, missing was the head and the upper portion of the cervical vertebrae. There was in the remaining vertebrae no evidence of a cut, so whether the head was actively dismembered or whether it had spontaneously fallen off or come loose from the cervical spine from decomposition or putrefaction, I could not tell.

Q: That is as opposed to your finding regarding Body No. 1 in that regard?

A: Yes, in Body No. 1 there was a very definite cut through the vertebrae showing there had been a mechanical interference with the integrity of the body, and in Body No. 2, it could very well have come loose by the natural processes of putrefaction and decomposition.

Q: Continue on with No. 2.

A: In Body No. 2 there was a cut or separation between the lumbar vertebrae as in the first body, but a little higher, between the first and second lumbar vertebrae, so that was, I should say that was also a cut rather than a natural deterioration. In this particular body, lower extremities were cut free from the torso. The cuts involved the femurs, which are the thigh bones. These are rather heavy bones. They have a diameter of approximately three-quarters to an inch in diameter, and these cuts had been inflicted with a sharp bladed instrument and it was consistent of a chop mark with a partial cut, and then a remaining break of the margins of the bone. These cuts were just above the knees, so the lower extremities in Body No. 2 were completely separate from the torso but could be matched up because of the cut ends.

Q: Doctor, based upon your pathological findings, do you have an opinion as to whether dismemberment could have been by animals in the area where the bodies were found?

A: Yes, I have an opinion.

Q: Would you state for us that opinion, please?

A: It would be impossible, because there were cut marks rather than biting or chewing marks.

Q: I would like you to assume as a hypothetical fact that the area where these bodies were found was searched extensively for the better part of three days, not only the immediate area where the bodies were found, but a substantial area surrounding this specific area, and that no skulls or heads were ever found. Do you have an opinion, to any degree of reasonable medical certainty, as to whether those skulls could have been taken off from the bodies and carried away by animals?

A: Yes.

Q: What is that opinion, Doctor?

A: In my opinion they would not. I might explain that. My experience with the recovery of skeletal remains indicates that it is not at all unusual for the skull to become loose from the cervical vertebrae in the process of natural decay, and small animals can roll these bones about, and it is not unusual to find them, say, within a space of twenty feet or thirty feet from the skeletal remains, but...

Q: That is based on approximately how many previous situations where you found that to be a fact? Just approximately?

A: I can think of, or I would estimate, I could think of several, but I would estimate considering the total number of skeletal remains that I have been associated with, I would estimate in about one quarter of the cases the skull has obviously been mechanically removed from the skeleton and scattered by animals.

Q: Doctor, in approximately how many cases have you made an ultimate determination that death was by natural causes?

A: You mean in all medical examiner cases?

Q: In all your experience as a medical examiner, or associate medical examiner, just approximately. Once again, I know you can't give us an exact figure.

A: It would be many, many thousands. I personally, myself, without, not working with other persons, but just by myself have performed over 8,000 autopsies. The majority of autopsies that I do are natural deaths, and I also, by review of medical records and terminal circumstances, certify a great number of cases as natural deaths, so I would estimate many thousands. I have records in my office of approximately forty to fifty thousand deaths, and the majority of these are naturals and I have played a significant role in certifying many of these.

Q: Doctor, with regard to the ultimate certifications of natural deaths, is it normal to find evidence of dismemberment by cutting?

A: No, never.

Q: Is it rather rare?

A: I have only heard of—no I have never heard of any case. I was thinking of an accidental death one time. I know of an accidental death, not in Dade County, where there was dismemberment afterwards, but I know of no natural death.

Q: That would be the rare exception rather than the rule, the one you just referred to?

A: Yes.

Q: Doctor, in reaching your opinions in your capacity as a forensic pathologist, and as a medical examiner, do you base your opinion as regards your ultimate findings solely upon your own pathological postmortem examination within the confines of the morgue, or your lab?

A: No, not necessarily. It depends on the question I am asked. My opinion depends upon the nature of the question and the amount of information and evidence that I must take into consideration to answer that question,

Q: As a forensic pathologist then are you saying that you draw upon matters and information other than just your own microscopic and personal evaluation of the remains?

A: Yes. The approach is very similar to a physician's diagnosis where the history, the laboratory, the physical examination aspects are all taken into consideration and we do the same thing.

Q: All right, sir. Doctor, let me now give you a hypothetical question and ask you to assume and consider the following hypothetical facts, if you will, please. One, that both girls were last seen alive together. Both were shortly thereafter reported to the police as being missing. Both were of reasonably good prior medical health. Nothing was heard from either of them from the time of their disappearance until their bodies were found in St. Lucie County on April 1. That both these bodies were found together. That those remains as found were in fact intermixed or interspersed. The limbs and body sections had been dismembered or were found dismembered. The bodies were found in a remote area inaccessible to regular traffic. That although there were several days of search, no skulls were ever found in the vicinity. That there was a bullet hole in what was found to be a part of a lower mandible. That the wrists of one body were bound together by some kind of rawhide, or leather. That the remains when received by you were in substantially the same condition as they were when they were found a week earlier in St. Lucie County. Now, Doctor, taking all those hypothetical facts, coupled with your own personal postmortem examination of the bodies, do you have an opinion to any degree of reasonable medical certainty whether death was by natural causes? Just tell us whether you do or don't have an opinion, please.

A: I have an opinion.

MR. SCHWARZ: Your Honor, I am going to object to the hypothetical as considering matters not at this point in evidence. Specifically, that the wrists were bound together. I don't believe there is any evidence whatsoever that the wrists were in fact bound together. There was a photograph showing a piece of cloth tied around one wrist, but I do not believe there is any evidence that they were bound together. Also, it is an incomplete hypothetical, because the doctor has testified that one portion of one arm, I believe, was in fact also missing, and it was not found in this search. Also, it considers in the hypothetical the fact that both girls were in good medical or physical condition, and I believe the evidence shows to the contrary. One of the girls was in fact an epileptic and that both girls had been known to use drugs. I feel that the hypothetical as posed would be incomplete and not in accord with the evidence that has been presented so far.

MR. SHAILER: Your Honor, I believe State's Exhibit No. 19 in evidence relates to the one element of the hypothetical Mr. Schwarz is talking about on the question of the hands being bound. I believe as to the other matters, the hypothetical is as complete as can be.

THE COURT: I think Mr. Schwarz's objection is well-taken. If you will modify your hypothetical to eliminate the statement about the wrists being bound, and you can refer to that picture, however, and include it and add to it the information that Mr. Schwarz has added.

BY MR. SHAILER:

Q: Doctor, deleting from this hypothetical the one particular hypothetical fact concerning the wrists being bound, let me show you what has been received in evidence as State Exhibit 19 and ask you to look at that, please.

MR. SCHWARZ: Your Honor, for purposes of the record, rather than deleting and adding and so forth, I would rather have him state one specific hypothetical, so we know what we are dealing with in the way of assumptions that he is asking the doctor to make.

Q: Doctor, deleting that...

MR SHAILER: Your Honor, shall we start over on that? Would you rather have it again?

MR. SCHWARZ: A: hypothetical question he is going to ask the doctor his opinion on, he should start it, so we know what we are talking about.

BY THE COURT:

Q: Well, Doctor, you have heard the original question, then you have heard Mr. Schwarz's comments which I have concurred in. Are you able to assimilate that and have an opinion about that on the matter?

A: Yes, it is my understanding the hypothetical as originally given has now been altered to omit the reference to the tying of the wrists.

BY MR. SHAILER:

Q: That is correct, sir. And to substitute therefore your examination of State Exhibit 19 in evidence.

THE COURT: And in addition to that, the other comment Mr. Schwarz made about the health of the girls.

MR. SCHWARZ: And the other missing limb.

THE COURT: And the missing limb.

BY MR SHAILER:

Q: Yes. Of course, well, I said...and these hypothetical facts coupled with your own pathological findings.

A: Yes.

Q: The fact that one of the girls was an epileptic but was considered by her family to be in good medical health.

MR. SCHWARZ: And, that they both had been known users of drugs.

MR. SHAILER: I am not putting that in my hypothetical, Mr. Schwarz. You can.

MR. SCHWARZ: It is in evidence.

THE COURT: I will sustain the objection if it doesn't go in then, but there is testimony to that effect.

MR. SHAILER: That they were known users of drugs, Your Honor, or that they have tried or experimented with drugs?

THE COURT: I am not going to get into . . .

BY MR. SHAILER:

Q: Doctor, I will add to the hypothetical that these girls were known to have experimented with or tried drugs of one sort or another.

A: And the final question of the hypothetical?

Q: Is based upon those hypothetical facts, coupled with your own personal postmortem autopsy examination; do you have an opinion to any reasonable degree of medical certainty as to whether the death of either, or both, of these two girls was by natural causes?

A: Yes, I have such an opinion.

Q: Would you state for us that opinion?

A: It would be my opinion that death was not by natural causes.

Q: Doctor, assuming these same hypothetical facts, coupled with your personal postmortem examination, do you have an opinion to any reasonable degree of medical certainty as to whether death was by accidental means or causes?

A: Yes.

Q: What is that opinion?

A: It would be my opinion that death was not due to accidental means.

Q: Again, based upon the same hypothetical factors, coupled with your own personal examination of the bodies, do you have an opinion to any degree of reasonable medical certainty as to whether death was self-inflicted?

A: Yes, I have an opinion.

Q: State for us that opinion.

A: It would be my opinion that it was not self-inflicted,

Q: Assuming again the same set of hypothetical facts, coupled with your own personal examination of these bodies, do you have an opinion to any degree of reasonable medical certainty as to whether death was by non-self-inflicted violence?

A: Yes.

Q: State for us that opinion, please,

A: It would be my opinion that death was by non-self-inflicted violence. In other words, by violence by another person or persons.

Upon cross-examination, Schwarz questioned Dr. Davis about the length of time the two girls could have been dead before his autopsy:

Q: Doctor Davis, it is my understanding from your testimony here that your opinion would be that the bodies were dead somewhere between four and six months?

A: Yes, taking into consideration the date of September 27 as given in this last question.

Q: Now, isn't it a fact that the actual determination of time of death once you exceed a period of a month or two is pretty much a guesstimate?

A: It becomes more and more inexact the longer the time duration.

Q: When you examined these bodies or the remains of these bodies, what was their general condition? Was it the term, "Skeletonized"?

A: They were mainly a combination of skeletonization and mummification. Some flesh, some skin was still present and mummified or dried. The odor of the bodies was not as offensive as a more freshly dead body.

Q: More of a musty odor?

A: It was a musty odor.

Q: In the course of your examination did you determine whether there was any soft tissue still in existence at all?

A: Yes, there was.

Q: There was some soft tissue still in existence?

A: Yes, this mummified dried flesh was originally soft tissue.

Q: There were certain ligaments and things that way that were still somewhat soft?

A: Well, they weren't...by soft tissue I mean tissue as opposed to bone or teeth. The tissue that remained was quite dry and had increased in its texture or in its firmness in drying, but it would still be classified as soft tissue.

Q: And there still was some of that present?

A: Yes.

Q: Doctor, isn't it a fact that among pathologists there is a general rule of thumb as to rate of deterioration of a body dependent upon whether it is exposed to the elements, whether it is buried in the ground or whether it is in water?

A: There is a general agreement, I think based upon people who are experienced in the field, that there are modifications of deterioration depending upon the place where the body has been buried and various characteristics of the body itself. Some bodies, and I think this is well documented in medical literature, I personally have not seen such a case, but some bodies have been preserved in a remarkable state as far as the soft tissues were concerned for thousands of years when buried, say in the peat bogs with high tannin contents, and I know just recently there was a report emanated from China where an embalmed body 2,000 years old was remarkably well-preserved due to the embalming process. So, there are factors which will modify the rate of deterioration of the soft tissues and even the bones.

Q: Isn't it a fact, Doctor, that amongst the profession of pathology that this rule of thumb that I refer to is that decomposition or putrefaction proceeds at approximately one week in the air equaling one week in the water or eight weeks in the soil?

A: I have never held particularly to that formula.

Q: Basically, would you say that is fairly accurate?

A: I wouldn't say it was accurate no, because you must take each case into its own and you have to consider it in the light of the particular geography, the particular area. A: body immersed in frigid water, water near freezing, can remain in a remarkable state of preservation for many, many months, whereas a body in water in a South Dade canal in a period of two weeks can be in an advanced decomposition. So, there is no real simple formula that can be applied to these.

Q: In addition to normal insect activity on a body exposed in the air, are there any other insect activity affecting the bones, the marrow of the bones, items such as that?

A: The marrow can be penetrated by larvae, maggots, and so forth.

Q: How about carrion beetles?

A: And beetles. The beetles usually come later. The first insects that attack the body are the common blowflies. Within a matter of hours, if they have access to the body, they can deposit their eggs and the eggs can start to hatch the larvae which are commonly called maggots which emit strong enzymes that melt away the flesh quite rapidly. I have seen a body become quite skeletonized in as little as ten days under the proper circumstances with maggot activity.

Q: Well, isn't it a fact that bodies will decompose or putrefy much more rapidly when exposed to the air than if they are buried in the ground?

A: Yes.

The implications of Schwarz's questions were that the girls were never buried, that the so-called grave was "just a hole." Later in the cross-examination Schwarz asked if it were possible the girls died of drug overdoses (again) and dismembered later.

Dr. Davis stated it was possible, but that there wasn't enough remains intact to make that determination, or not make that determination. Near the end of his questioning Schwarz asked

Dr. Davis about his trip to Africa, implying with his inquiries that perhaps Dr. Davis could have made it to court earlier, and perhaps, less prepared. The state maintained that these questions were irrelevant, the court was not pleased with the implication either and overlooked the questions.

* * *

Nancy Trotter and Paula Sue Wells were both put on the stand (separately of course). Their testimonies were similar and told of their abduction by Schaefer in July of 1972. The state used them to show that Schaefer was not only capable of abducting two girls against their will, but carried the implements used to contain them in his car, and that the location of their containment was Hutchinson Island.

Schwarz parried this damning testimony by asking: "Did he (Schaefer) hurt you?" "Couldn't he have tied you up better, where you wouldn't have gotten away?"

Schwarz was trying to make it look like Schaefer had been "easy" with the girls and was trying to teach them not to hitchhike. He inferred that the girls were habitual runaways, that Schaefer was simply over-zealous with his lesson, trying to make a lasting impression on them. Schwarz suggested that Schaefer would have done anything he wanted to the girls, and asked them, "Did he assault you in any way?"

Nancy replied, "Well, he pinched my ass." She also mentioned that Schaefer had told them he could "dig a hole and bury them and no one would find us."

Immediately after the testimonies of Trotter and Wells, the state offered into evidence the manuscript written by Gerard Schaefer that described how to "properly execute" young women, "in order to remain unapprehended." Schwarz objected strongly to the manuscript being admissible, citing that it was irrelevant. The court overruled his objection. The state then handed each of the jurors a copy of the manuscript. The jury was aghast. The correlations between the manuscript's "instructions" and the incident with Trotter and Wells, and finally the evidence found at the site of the murders of the Place and Jessup bodies, was overwhelming.

After collecting the copies of the manuscripts from the jury, and handing them to the court clerk, Stone announced that the state was resting its case.

The defense asked for an acquittal, stating that the state had not proven its case and that all evidence was circumstantial, that no one could tie the defendant to the crime scene. The court ruled against acquittal and said the state had done its job. This did not mean the trial was over. Far from it. The defense had to call all their witnesses yet. Then too, another surprise came up.

Schwarz asked for the entry of a mistrial and renewed his motion for change of venue. Additionally, he asked for the removal of one of the jurors, William Forbes. Schwarz then put himself on the stand and had Colton ask him some questions.

Schwarz testified that he received two phone calls, indicating that Forbes had preconceived ideas of Schaefer's guilt and that he'd related those ideas to several people before the trial began.

He had recorded one of the phone calls and the court allowed it to be played. (All of this, the accusation against Forbes, the tape, etc., were outside the presence of the jury.) Surprisingly, everything was handled courteously between the defense, the state, and the court.

The court said there was no way they were going to declare a mistrial. Stone said he wanted to get to the truth of the matter, and even Schwarz (with an apparent change of heart) said that it was not his intention to retry this case, but that in order to supply the best defense possible for his client, he had to bring up the new development. Judge Trowbridge stated everything was in order and all charges were made proper, but without the "anonymous cowardly phone caller," the accuser, then the accused, Mr. Forbes, would not be discharged from the jury. He added again, everyone was doing their job properly, but that "the real villain is this faceless, nameless, backboneless individual who would like to screw up American Justice by an anonymous phone call, and I would like to see him appear in court . . ." The matter was not over yet.

What happened next was one of the strangest aspects of the trial. A: videotape had been made; a reenactment of Schaefer's abduction of Nancy Trotter and Paula Sue Wells. The tape showed where the girls were taken, how they were tied and how they escaped. However, it was not Stone that admitted the tape into evidence. It was Schwarz. Oddly, he said, "I merely want to show this video tape in order to show an accurate portrayal of the scene."

Later, outside the courtroom, reporter Jayne Ellison approached Schwarz at a water fountain as he prepared to reenter court. She asked him what he had in mind when he elected to show that tape. He replied, "I wanted to show how easy it was for those girls to escape. That there was no real danger, no harm done." However, there was harm done—to Schaefer's case.

Ellison would later tell this writer that it was the viewing of that tape, (and having just read the Schaefer manuscripts) that changed the course of the trial and began to convince the jury that Schaefer was the true killer. As the court and its audience watched the tape, Ellison watched the faces of the jurors. Some shook their heads in disbelief while others frowned or stared open-mouthed as Sgt. George Miller (enacting the role of Schaefer) hog-tied the girls and placed them in precarious positions with hangmen's nooses about their necks. Schwarz had asked that the tape be shown silent, so that whatever was said during the reenactment would not influence the jury. But the silence added a macabre and dark presence to the film, "like scenes from a Hitchcock film," that it may have not exhibited otherwise. The jury watched entranced, and when the film was over, as their eyes adjusted to the bright flow of the relit courtroom, they stole furtive glances at Schaefer who, in keeping with character, continued to grin as if he'd enjoyed the film,

The girls again testified, saying that the film was an accurate depiction of the Hutchinson Island incident, except that Miller had not tied the ropes as tightly as had their captor. Nancy added that she had had longer hair too, and it had gotten caught up in the noose, and that she originally did not wear shoes, all of which had made the escape more difficult.

* * *

The defense called the sister of the defendant, Sara Jane Lane. She testified that Schaefer had brought home the little brown purse from Morocco (as would all the witnesses for the defense) and that he used it to carry bullets when he went target shooting. She went on to say that the north bedroom, where most of the evidence was taken, was at one time her room and now was used for storage by several friends in the neighborhood. It was during her testimony that the question of an emblem came up—that of the Fraternal Order of Police, that was supposedly affixed to Schaefer's car tag. Schwarz pressed this issue heavily, throughout the remaining defense witnesses' testimonies, implying that if the emblem was on Schaefer's car (as all his witnesses testified) why hadn't Mrs. Place reported it?

It was also during this testimony that the topic of "fever blisters" was presented by the defense attorneys. Several of the defense witnesses, Sara among them, reported that throughout the end of September, Schaefer had been afflicted with this strange virus that had manifested itself by producing transient fevers and weakness—at times forcing Schaefer into bed for days at a time—and raw oozing blisters "inside and outside, around his mouth." The implication again was clear; why hadn't Mrs. Place noticed and reported the blisters?

Sara went on to state that, indeed, her brother had had these blisters all around his mouth when he visited her home on September 31, 1972, that they were in a healing stage and would had to have been present and easily noticeable on the 27th of the same month.

Shailer, in cross-examination, asked rather shyly if Sara was positive of that date. She replied, "oh, most definitely," and gave a lengthy explanation as to why it would've had to have been that day. Her child was born six weeks earlier "to the day" and Gerard was coming to see the baby for the first time. She added that she'd taken pictures of Schaefer and the baby and, "you can see the blisters." (They are very faint in the photo, if present at all.) Shailer then asked if she remembered the old poem of the months, in which is the line that says, "Thirty days hath September . . . " Sara became very defensive after that, and when Shailer asked if she loved her brother and would like to help him, she answered, "Well, there are not many people here, I don't think, that would."

Schwarz tried to remedy her testimony by getting the date squared away. Shailer objected.

Q: All right, now, if Sunday of the last weekend was actually October 1, would that refresh your recollection at all as to what day it actually was, as opposed to Saturday or Sunday? As he pointed out, there are thirty days in September, and if the 30th was Saturday and the Sunday was October 1, would this refresh your memory as to this date?

MR. SHAILER: Your Honor, Mr. Schwarz is becoming a wonderful witness. I think we ought to get him on the stand. I object to his leading the witness.

Teresa Schaefer was put on the stand next. Mrs. Place had previously testified that Schaefer was wearing moccasins and had a blue cooler in the back seat of his Datsun. In defense, Teresa admitted that he did have a pair of moccasins, "but hadn't worn them for at least a year," and that the cooler had a green top as opposed to a blue one that Mrs. Place had seen. The point was moot, the, defense weakening. Inadvertently, Teresa's testimony only strengthened Mrs. Place's.

Schwarz desperately questioned the defense witnesses about several topics aimed at proving his client's innocence. The license plate emblem and its position on the tag, the brown suede purse, (He got in Morocco, right?) the ice cooler, (it had a green top, didn't it?) the moccasins (He never wore them, did he?). Additionally, the Places had testified that Schaefer wore a "flat, roll-up type fishing hat and a long-sleeve blue plaid shirt."

The Schaefer family testified that Gerard "didn't even own a long sleeve shirt," and never wore the described hat. He also asked about the length of Schaefer's hair. The Places said it was a little longer than it appeared in court. The defense witnesses swore he never wore it longer. The issues went back and forth, but ultimately, it became apparent that the defense's strategies were falling apart. The jury began to believe that the witnesses would say almost anything, in opposition to the Place and Jessup testimonies, in order to shed more favorable light on Schaefer.

Stone referred to one witnesses' time on the stand as "ridiculous testimony." Schwarz had put the man on the stand, as a member of the Fraternal Order of Police, to recognize and validate the type of emblem that was reported to have been on Schaefer's tag. They used a new one, the original was not on Schaefer's car and was never found. The testimony was valueless.

As the trial wore on, the defense witnesses' testimonies became less and less significant to the case, and it was obvious that they were grabbing at straws. James Holt, the Sheriff of Martin County was called to testify that Schaefer had turned himself in on time (like a good boy.) to begin his six-month sentence for the Trotter/Wells case. Harold Baker, the superintendent of the Fort Pierce City Water Plant, was called. As part of his job, he kept records of rainfall in the area. Schwarz was trying to convince the jury that, if Schaefer had dug the grave in the fall of '72, then it would have been filled in from the weather by the time of its discovery in April of '73.

Stone audibly moaned, "Oh, boy." He negated the whole testimony by asking Baker, "If it poured down rain where you measured it (several miles away from the crime scene) and it didn't rain over on the beach, this wouldn't accurately depict the rainfall on the beach, would it?"

Baker answered, "No, sir."

Stone whirled away from the witness stand smiling broadly, and said, "No further questions."

Schwarz continued. He called Schaefer's friend and barber, Ed Ferris, who testified Schaefer never had longer hair. Another friend, David Rogers, swore that he and Schaefer always carried purses (like the brown suede pouch) when they went target shooting, and he never saw Schaefer wear a long sleeve shirt or long hair.

Stone also questioned Rogers:

Q: Would you consider yourself to be a very close friend?
A: Yes.
Q: You have been hunting with him on occasions, haven't you?
A: Yes, I have.
Q: Would you consider you are the type person that John would confide in over this time?
A: Would I confide in John?
Q: Would he confide in you?
MR. SCHWARZ: Your Honor, I think he was referring only to his appearance. I don't know what he is talking about.
MR. STONE: Let me ask the questions. He is answering them. You have had your opportunity.
MR. SCHWARZ: I object to it.

Q: You say you are a close friend of his, right?

A: Yes.

Q: And you consider yourself to be the type person he would confide in?

A: Do I consider myself the type person he would confide in?

Q: Yes, would he confide in you? You went hunting together didn't you?

A: Yes.

Q: Did he tell you about his thoughts?

A: We would talk just like you and I.

Q: Well, I haven't known you for ten years. I have never been hunting with you.

A: That is true.

Q: Right. So, you would consider yourself the type person that you would talk to him about the way he felt and things he thought about, right?

A: That is right.

Q: Did he ever talk to you about the fact that he wrote a document called "How to Perpetrate the Perfect Murder and Remain Unapprehended?"

A: No.

MR. SCHWARZ: I object to this. I don't see any relevancy to this.

MR STONE: I see all the relevancy in the world. It is in evidence.

MR. SCHWARZ: He is referring to his appearance, not anything of this type.

BY MR. STONE:

Q: Did he ever talk to you about that document?

THE COURT: Just a moment now, Mr. Stone. There is an objection made. Don't ask the same question over again. Do you want to reply to that objection?

MR. STONE: Yes, sir. I think it is relevant, because he said he has known the man, he has been hunting with him, he has talked to him, he has confided in him. The only thing he is coming in here telling us is the self-serving part. I want to know if he ever talked to him about this document he wrote.

MR SCHWARZ: I do not think there is anything self-serving, Your Honor.

THE COURT: What is it in cross of?

MR. STONE: It is cross to the fact he said he was a clean-cut boy, he had known him ten years, and they confided in each other and hunted together,

MR. SCHWARZ: That was in response to concerning his appearance, that is all.

THE COURT: Sustain the objection.

BY MR. STONE:

Q: Did you ever know him to use the name Jerry Shepard?

A: No, sir.

Q: Have you ever heard that name?

A: No, sir.

Q: You haven't?

A: Not until this case. I have read it in the newspaper.

Q: All right. Do you know what address that is on State's Exhibit 46 in evidence? Whose address is it?

A: It is the address of the Schaefer home in Lauderdale.

Q: Whose name is on there?

A: Jerry Shepard.

Q: Jerry Shepard. You don't know how that got on there, do you?

A: No.

Q: Do you know how that got in the north bedroom of the Schaefer home?

A: No, I don't.

Q: All right, I am going to show you State's Exhibit 48 (The manuscript on how to murder.) Do you know how that got in the Schaefer bedroom?

A: No.

MR. SCHWARZ: Your Honor, I object to this. I don't believe this is in cross of anything brought out on direct. I didn't ask Mr. Rogers anything concerning that bedroom or that house.

THE COURT: I will sustain the objection.

MR. STONE:

Q: Have you spent as much time with him since he got married as you did before?

A: Well, when he got married he moved away, so obviously I wouldn't spend as much time with him.

Q: So a lot of his habits you don't really know about since he moved away, do you?

A: I wouldn't know, because...

Q: All right, because you are not around him as much, right?

A: I wasn't around him as much.

Q: And did you ever go target shooting with him over on Hutchinson Island?

A: No.

Q: In Martin County?

A: No.

Q: So if he was ever over there, you wouldn't have been with him, would you?

A: No.

Q: All right, now. Did you ever hear the name Susan Place before, or Georgia Jessup?

A: Not until this was all brought out in the papers.

Q: Okay. Now, you say that emblem that was on the back of John's car— did you specifically see one on the Mustang? (Teresa Schaefer's car, not the Datsun.)

A: Yes, I remember one on the Mustang.

Q: You remember seeing one on the Mustang?

A: Yes.

Q: Do you know where that is now?

A: The Mustang?

Q: Do you know where the emblem is?

A: No.

Q: All right, did you see this car on September 27, 1972? (Shows a picture of the Datsun.)

A: I wouldn't know. I don't remember September '72.

Q: So if that car was in Fort Lauderdale at the home of Susan Place you wouldn't know, would you?

A: No, I wouldn't.

Q: And if that emblem wasn't on there you wouldn't know that, either, would you?

A: No.

Q: And if he picked up Susan Place and Georgia Jessup and brought them to Stuart, Florida, you wouldn't know that either, would you?

A: No.

MR. STONE: That is all the questions I have.

One of the last, and most significant defense witnesses called was John Sojat. Sojat was a firearms consultant who'd examined the bullet shell casing found at the crime scene and compared it to Schaefer's guns. He testified that the casing had not come from Schaefer's guns, at least, the ones that had been turned in as evidence. His testimony was weakened somewhat though, by Stone cleverly asking, "Do you know where the casing did come from?"

Sojat replied, "No, sir."

Detective Peter Renje, of the Oakland Park Police Department, was called by the defense. He testified that Mrs. Place had not mentioned that last name of the man named "Jerry," in the missing person's report. His testimony, too, was shot down when Stone produced a copy of the original missing person report with the name "Jerry Shepherd" included within its pages. The court ruled the report inadmissible, because the officer who originally wrote the report was not present in court. The jury still knew it existed.

Finally, Lt. David Yurchuk was recalled by the defense and asked simply, "Did you ever look for a suspect named Jerry Shepherd"? Yurchuk answered, "No."

Schwarz, having called all his witnesses, now made a motion asking for acquittal because "the hypotheses of innocence outweighs the circumstantial evidence."

The court denied the motion.

By September 26, 1973, eight days after the trial had begun, all the witnesses had been heard. The court was beginning to get things wrapped up, preparing to give final instructions to the jury, when Elton Schwarz came up with one last surprise.

Once again, he called for the removal of the juror, William Forbes, Judge Trowbridge was not pleased. He had ruled on the matter once, and now it seemed to him that Schwarz was using this latest motion as a stall to buy time. What he hoped to accomplish in this last hour was unclear; the evidence was in and the next step would be the final arguments, then send the jury into chambers for the verdict decision. When Schwarz announced he had witnesses that would testify to Forbes' prejudice, Trowbridge knew that neither the jury, nor himself, were going anywhere soon.

Schwarz called Ernest Davis.

Q: Are you acquainted with William J. Forbes?
A: Yes, I am.
Q: How long have you known him?
A: I have known Joe about two years.
Q: He goes by the name of Joe Forbes?
A: Yes.
Q: Do you know where he was working at the time you met him?
A: He was working part time for Universal Ambulance Service. So was I.

Q: All right, since April 1, of 1973, have you had any occasion to talk with Mr. Forbes concerning the case of the State of Florida vs. Gerard John Schaefer, Jr.?

A: I talked with Joe one day. It was three of us, another friend of ours.

Q: Where did this conversation take place?

A: Behind the offices of the Universal Ambulance.

Q: Do you recall when this was?

A: Approximately a month ago, it was. He had gotten a subpoena to serve for jury duty one or two days prior to the date we talked.

Q: And who all else was present at that time besides yourself?

A: Since he wasn't subpoenaed, do I have to tell who he was?

Q: Yes.

A: James Waters. He was a full-time employee for Universal Ambulance.

Q: Was there anyone else present?

A: No.

Q: There was just you, Mr. Waters and Mr. Forbes?

A: True.

Q: Do you recall talking to me on the telephone last Friday?

A: Yes, I do.

Q: At that time did you tell me that there were two other people present?

A: I said two people with me. I meant Joe, Jim and myself.

Q: All right, do you know where Mr. Waters is?

A: Right now he is unemployed. He has resigned from Universal Ambulance. He is going to work next week for the Martin County Rescue Squad. He is on vacation. I have no idea where he is.

Q: Did Mr. Forbes at that time make any statements to you concerning the fact that he had been subpoenaed as a prospective juror?

A: Most of his conversation was more towards Jimmie than myself. He and Jimmie were closer friends than Joe and I were.

Q: What did he say? Mr. Forbes?

A: He said he had gotten a subpoena for jury duty, that someone had told him it was for the Schaefer trial, it didn't' state on the subpoena, I take for granted, and he said he hoped that was the trial he would get to sit on.

Q: Did he say why he hoped that would be the trial he would get to sit on?

A: He said that he had heard a lot about the case. I don't know whether he said he knew or knew of Schaefer—is that his name?

Q: Schaefer.

A: And that he didn't...he had ill feelings towards, you know, the case.

Q: Did he say that he had known Schaefer while he was a cop?

A: That I know of, Joe is—you mean while Schaefer was a cop?

Q: Right.

A: He mentioned something about "of all the bullshit" was his words, that Schaefer was a cop in Martin County, that he shouldn't be allowed to get away with things, you know, like that, because of the fact that he was a cop.

Q: Did he express any opinion to you as to, or make any statement expressing his opinion, as to the guilt or innocence of Mr. Schaefer?

A: He felt he was guilty.

Q: Did he make any statement to you or in your presence at that time concerning any preconceived opinions as to Mr. Schaefer's guilt?

· A: Well, he had a...he said a few words about what he would like to do to him.

Q: Will you tell the Court what he said he would like to do?

A: In the words he used?

Q: Yes, sir, the same as you told me on the telephone.

A: He said he would like to take the son-of-a bitch and hang him by his balls.

The state cross-examined Davis, but nothing new was learned and his testimony stood firm. Schwarz then called Clyde Hissong.

Q: Are you acquainted with William J. or Joe Forbes?

A: Mr. Joe Forbes, yes.

Q: And how long have you known him?

A: I have known him approximately a year and a half.

Q: Since April 1 of this year have you had occasion to be present at any time that Mr. Forbes may have discussed either to you, or in your presence, the case of the State of Florida vs. Gerard John Schaefer?

A: Yes, sir.

Q: When did this occur?

A: I am not positive of the date, but it was the second day of your jury selection.

Q: The second day we were selecting the jury?

A: Yes.

Q: Where did this take place?

A: Across the street from the Crystal Cafe.

Q: That was at lunch time?

A: Approximately 12:10 when it started.

Q: What did you hear Mr. Forbes state at that time?

A: Well, may I go into the start of the conversation?

Q: Just go ahead and tell us what occurred. You went over to have lunch. Were you eating lunch with Mr. Forbes?

A: Well, yes, my wife and I eat there, because a friend of ours works there and we seen Mr. Forbes across the street and we asked him to join us and he did. And I hadn't seen him since he got out of the hospital with his surgery and the conversation led to where he was working, what he was doing, et cetera, et cetera, and I asked him what he was doing there that day all dressed up and he said he was over here as a selective juror, and he said that it was on the Schaefer case and a few things were said, I don't know the exact words, but the thing that didn't even register in my mind at that time was he didn't want to be on the jury because it would interfere with his new job at first, but if he was selected for the jury he would like to be on the Schaefer jury because he needed to be hung.

Q: When he said that he was referring to Mr. Schaefer?

A: He was referring to Mr. Schaefer. When that was said I told... I am not sure what I told Joe, but I know just shortly after that the conversation ended along that line, because of the waitress and when it came back we were in an entirely new train of thought, and I want to go ahead and say one of the reasons I haven't come forward until this time, because it didn't register on me until the night I seen the newscast.

Q: Did you convey this same information to Judge Tye?

A: I didn't go to see Judge Tye. I went to see Deputy Sheriff Atkins who lives on Yachtview Lane, across from me, who is a friend of mine, to ask him what I should do, because if I may go ahead and say...

Q: Yes, certainly.

A: The part that disturbs me is that I don't know Mr. Schaefer and if the man is guilty then I believe he should be dealt with fairly. If he is not guilty then I believe the man should be released, but I have a daughter that I wouldn't want something to happen to in another fifteen years. I went to find out information from Mr. Atkins on whether if it was let go and this trial went to its finality, and this man was declared guilty, and later on it was thrown out of court because of a bad remark made by a juror, the man might go free? If the man is guilty, I don't want him to go free. If he is innocent, I want him to. I know Joe. Joe is a friend of mine. At least, I consider him a friend of mine. I am not doing this to put Joe down. I think it was a remark that was made without thinking and out of place, but it is something that could affect this jury or this trial.

Q: In other words, your interest is the same as the State's and mine, just making sure Mr. Schaefer gets a fair and impartial trial?

A: All I want to do is make sure that it is fair, and that later on something don't happen to reverse it, because of a remark a man made that I feel is out of place.

Hissong was cross-examined by the State and his testimony remained unchanged. Finally, Schwarz called his last witness, John L. Potts, who told a story very similar to Hissong's. He said that he knew Forbes, had worked with him at a previous construction-type job, and Forbes had mentioned Schaefer should be hung.

Schaefer, who'd been so quiet throughout the trial, now spoke up after each witness withdrew from the stand. He had also managed to stop smiling, and looked almost somber as he addressed first Davis, "You have got guts, Mr. Davis," he said.

Then, to Hissong and Potts, he said, "Thank you for your honesty." This was a different Schaefer, no longer dressed in his casual, V-neck white sweater and corduroy slacks; now he wore a well- pressed forest green suit and tie. In spite an occasional toothy grin, he was now the serious, wrongly-accused-police-officer-on- trial. It was a noticeable change, yet for whatever impact it was intended to make, it seemed to be too little, too late.

The State called another witness, too, Bryant Summerlin. Summerlin testified that he had discussed the case with Forbes and Forbes had told him that he was "going to have to listen to the facts and draw his own conclusions," before he could comment on Schaefer's guilt or innocence. This was intended by the State to show that Forbes was impartial, but in truth, it showed that Forbes had been discussing the case, and this too was a violation of the judicial system.

The Court ruled to remove Forbes. However, Trowbridge would not declare a mistrial. He simply moved one of the alternates (who had heard the entire trial from the beginning) into Forbes' spot on the jury. Joanne Harton, the 21-year-old nurse's aide, took Forbes' place on the jury.

There was some final business to take care of a legal requirement that is called the conference on charges. This is where the judge and attorneys for both sides discuss exactly what the jury will decide on. Though it sounds simple, it is a lengthy procedure, where "every 't' is crossed and every 'i' dotted." The conference took the rest of that day.

The following day, Wednesday, September 27, 1973, the attorneys began their final arguments. They were limited to two hours each. In that two hours, it was their job to convince the jury that Schaefer either was guilty, (in the state's case) or innocent. The state was allowed two arguments, Shailer giving the first, and Stone the last, with Elton Schwarz giving his defense argument between the two prosecutors.

As the day began, promptly at 9:30 A.M., the attorneys shuffled through their notes, presumably for the last time. The court was full, the press was in attendance eagerly awaiting what would have to be dramatic dissertations from both the state and defense attorneys. Others were there, too. The Places. The Jessups. The Briscolinas. The Schaefers. All were obviously nervous and fidgeted in their seats. Lucille Place looked most anxious as did Doris Schaefer. Shirley Jessup looked pale and unhealthy with her red-rimmed eyes. George Jessup was the picture of contained anger, while Ira Place seemed melancholy and stared unflinching straight ahead, hands folded together, almost prayer-like. The Briscolinas whispered silently amongst themselves and appeared curious.

Gerard Schaefer was led in wearing handcuffs, and he was back in his white V-neck sweater. His hair was mussed a bit as he entered the courtroom, and he brushed it to the side, pressing it down with his bound hands. He was smiling too, indeed, beaming. This was his day. He looked about the courtroom, at the Jessups and the Places, and nodded as if greeting old friends. The star had arrived.

Phil Shailer had the opening argument. Though Shailer was a brilliant legal tactician and inquisitor, he seemed uncomfortable, perhaps unsure of himself. But the jury liked him. They knew whatever he had to say was no nonsense, and straight from the hip. Though his monologue perhaps lacked the flavor, the Southern gentility of Robert Stone's, he was nonetheless, the young, striving, honest, open-faced, American-boy-lawyer that juries and court audiences seem to love.

By Mr. Shailer:

"I think it is rather fitting, perhaps in an ironic way, that today happens to be September 27th. I am going to ask that you go back with me right now to one year ago today, September 27, 1972, the last day that Susan Place and Georgia Jessup were ever seen alive. And the evidence has clearly and unequivocally shown you that they were last seen alive in the company of that man sitting right over there in that sweater, because they left the Place house sometime in the evening hours of September 27.

Now, what do we have in that regard? What has been proven to you regarding the Defendant Schaefer, as having been the person who left the

Place home with those two girls on that date? Let's just rattle it off, then we will come back to it.

The identification by Mr. and Mrs. Place, and Mrs. Place writing down the license tag, and the verification of that license tag was registered to that man, the Datsun automobile with that license tag on it. The comments by Mrs. Place reported to the police department regarding the name Shepard, regarding Colorado, her writing down of the license tag number. How many things do you need before identity is proven, not only beyond a reasonable doubt, but beyond any shadow of a doubt? And that is exactly what we have here, isn't it? That on September 27, there can be no doubt whatsoever that that was the man that left the Place house with both those girls.

Now, they have made quite an effort to try and show disparity in the length of the sleeves and the question of the hair, and I think you will probably hear a lot about this from the defense, and I am sure you are going to hear something about it from Mr. Stone in his rebuttal argument, so let's direct ourselves to all of these affirmative facts that we have.

This license plate taken from the vehicle of that defendant. The license plate that was copied down. The tag number copied down by Mrs. Place the night of September 27. Mr. Schwarz went through quite a rigmarole with this. This, of course, isn't even the one, but apparently one similar to it which was supposedly was bunched up in the upper left-had corner and purportedly obscuring the 42-D. It was so obscured Mrs. Place was able to report 42 D 1728 four days later to the Oakland Park Police Department. You heard that from Detective Spiher on the witness stand. Mr. Schwarz talks about all the rust marks, that apparently, I guess, he is trying to suggest they were created by this little emblem being so permanently up here in this corner.

The judge is going to tell you if any of you want any of this evidence back in the jury room with you for your deliberations you can ask for it and you can take it back and I urge you to do so. Take it back and look at this and see if you can determine that there is an impression up in this upper left-hand corner from this emblem, he is trying to suggest to you exists. Because you will find that no such marking exists on there. You can't find much difference with that corner than this corner.

Let's talk about Jerry Shepard just a minute. Do you recall this manuscript? Excuse me. This manila envelope? Jerry Shephard, S-h-e-p-a-r-d, 2716 Southwest 34th Avenue, Fort Lauderdale, Florida. And whose address is that? Doris Schaefer's, isn't it?

Now, apparently you will recall Mr. Schwarz offered into evidence, with no objection from the State, what must be a very telling piece of evidence, the Fort Lauderdale phone directory, which has, you can look at this, it has in it an address of a Gerard or Jerry Shepard, spelled with an e-r-d, on a Birch Road address, and I guess what we are going to be able to see, and I am very anxious to see it also, is that Mr. Schwarz is going to pull something like the rabbit-out-of-the-hat trick. I think he probably has a hat over there. He is going to pick it up and put that telephone book and this manila envelope into that hat, jumble them up, and when he pulls this envelope out Shepard is going to be spelled differently and will have a different address on it. I think it is going to be quite a performance. There is no doubt, is there? None whatsoever.

And what other items can we have besides the positive identification given by Mrs. Place as she sat on that stand and pointed to that fellow right there, the one grinning and smiling now, right there? And Mr. Place? And how about his own barber? His own barber, a fellow who was able to get up in the jail here and cut his hair last week. Remember what he said? And let's give him the benefit of the doubt about his remembering having been with this defendant on Wednesday, September 27, and what did he say? He was with him until 7:00 o'clock p.m. (in Ft. Lauderdale). It fits right in with everything, doesn't it?

Shepard, or rather Schaefer, he is down in Fort Lauderdale. He is with his barber until 7:00 o'clock. He goes to the Place house. Remember, he had Georgia with him when he got to the Places' home. So, he had to go pick up Georgia somewhere. What did that take? Fifteen, twenty, thirty minutes? He gets to the Place home. It can't be later than 7:30, a quarter to 8:00. He is there an hour, to hour and a half, according to Mrs. Place's testimony. It is rather interesting, isn't it? Because in an hour, an hour and a half, he wouldn't have left there until after 9:00 o'clock.

Where is Teresa? She is always with him after 9:00 o'clock. He is never out of her sight after 9:00. And, of course, she is up in Stuart about an hour or hour and a half away. He couldn't have gotten home until 11:00. But let's say that is the only rare occasion when he is not home after 9:00 o'clock at night. I love my wife, always home, never out at night after 10:00 o'clock, and I see her grinning back there right now when I say that. It is funny in a sense that it is ludicrous, isn't it? Ridiculous.

Now, let's change our focus for a moment. Let's come to these two items of evidence. What has been called at various times a hippie purse, a suede purse, a little purse? You know the one we are talking about. And the jewelry box, or jewelry case. Let's talk about this little purse here. You have Georgia's sister, Cheryl, and Georgia's girlfriend, Joyce Froggatt, who took this in her hand on that witness stand, who sat there, who looked at it carefully and who said that was Georgia Jessup's. And why did they say that and how could they know? Because Joyce said, "I have seen her with it hundreds of times. I have used it myself. I wanted it myself." And her sister, who lives with her, who sees her clothing, and her property and her items, who knows that purse and yet we hear some testimony that, well, that is apparently an ammo pouch and Schaefer brought it back from Morocco with him, back in 1970. Remember that? And his close buddies, they have been out hunting with him, and they always carry their shells in here. Not the shotgun shells, but the ones they go target shooting with, the .22 caliber shells and .22 caliber pistols.

And don't you wish we could know about all those pistols? We know about six guns. We still don't know anything about that missing Saturday night special that Hank Dean told you about,

do we? But this is the item that he carried on his hip for the .22 caliber shells. And strangely enough, it is the item that before November of last year his own wife had never seen before, had she? That he gave to her, according to her testimony, in November of last year. Remember that?

Now, why a fellow finally decides to give his wife an old smelly, musty ammo pouch, an ammo case, is rather bizarre, rather strange, isn't it? But that is apparently what they are trying to sell you on. Positively identified by three people, yet an ammo pouch that he carried around.

They say, well, as a matter of fact, all of them but one said, "Well, this looks something like an ammo pouch that he had been carrying." All right, let's move from that for a moment. We say well, it looks something like this.

Okay, let's come over to this item right here. That is a little old frayed, worn, distinctive jewelry case, isn't it? You have seen it. You will be able to take it back there with you. What do we know about this jewelry case? Well, first of all, of course, we know it has been positively identified as having belonged to Georgia Jessup.

And then we come to the defense side of it, don't we? Then we hear the Schaefer team again, don't we? First, we hear from the sister and you remember her, Mrs. Lane. A: very pleasant

lady, very nice, very sweet and very good until it got time for cross examination. Do you remember how hostile she was with me? Remember when I was asking her questions, standing right here facing her, and Mr. Schwarz right over here, right where Mr. Gaffney is now, and she sat on the stand and I asked her a question and she sat there and looked over at Schwarz as if to say, "Tell me how to answer that." She was pretty hostile, wasn't she? She had reason to be. And she told us that she had seen that jewelry box, because it had belonged to her father, or grandfather or some such thing. She had seen it in a dresser drawer or some chest in one of those rooms.

You remember finally, after pulling some teeth, she finally got to the last time she had seen it was five years ago, but of course, she recognized it. She recognized it so fast that when Mr. Schwarz put it up here, she didn't even have time to grab it, she said, "Oh, I recognize that," right away. She didn't pick it up, check the inside, check to see whether she remembered whether it was green inside or brown. She just picked it up and boom, "Oh, yes, that is the one I saw." But she saw it five years ago, didn't she?

And then we come to—and remember now—three witnesses for the defense, and this time the Schaefer team, contrary to as in the little purse, remember this is where they had the relatives and two old, long-time family friends, the barber and the hunting buddy. This time the Schaefer team limited their defense as to this box to just blood relatives. It was just sister, it was just mama, it was just brother Gary. And sister finally told us that, well, it was five years ago the last time I had seen this box. But, remember Mrs. Doris Schaefer? She sat here and she leaned up into that microphone, as the tears welled in her eyes, and she said, "Oh, yes, Grandpa Schaefer, yes, it was his and I gave it to my son."

I don't know whether Grandpa Schaefer is dead or alive, and I mean no disrespect to him, but if he is alive, he must have had a heart attack when he heard that testimony. If he was dead, he must have rolled over in his grave.

And Gary, Gary told you, yes, that is the case that was Grandpa's, or Papa's, it was in the house. It was in the desk or in the dresser, wherever. They weren't too sure about that.

Can you imagine, or can you understand that for the past six, eight, nine months, what an ordeal this has been for the Schaefer family? The news media swarming down, law enforcement agencies, prosecution, defense, family, friends, and whether the family was strong or not before, they must have become strong and close since, haven't they? Remember the old expression to circle the wagons when the Indians would come, and they circled them, didn't they? Mom said that was Grandpa's, I gave it to my son, just like it had been sitting out on the dining room table and she had seen it every day.

They circled so hard and they circled so fast they didn't see the forest for the trees, did they? They just flat forgot, and they got caught. Well, they got caught.

You all had an opportunity to read visually State's Exhibit No. 48, a two-page writing, positively identified as having been found in Doris Schaefer's house during the search on April 7th, positively identified as having been written by the defendant right over here, I don't want to dwell on it a long time, but I want to ask you when you get back there to perform a little test using this as your guide. I want you to go through this item by item and see if you can catalogue and inventory how many things you find in this little manuscript that coincide with what we have in this case right here against this defendant, and you are going to find, depending upon how you ultimately evaluate it, that there are anywhere from fifteen to seventeen specific items in this one and three-quarter page writing of the defendant's, that we have in our case right here: Execution style. Isolated area accessible by car. Short hike away from police patrol. Noose overhanging limb of tree. It is reasonable to assume rope fibers over that branch. The trunk of the tree. Grave prepared. Even two victims. Bind and gag. Torture. Pillowcase. We have got all this clothing and stuff from the scene. You can take that back there with you, too. Two pillowcases in there. Nylon stockings in there. Body should then be mutilated. I don't think we need to dwell on that at all. You heard Mr. Davis' testimony as to how these bodies were dismembered, which wasn't by normal deterioration. It wasn't through animals. It was through cutting. Through cutting, and that one cutting on one of those bodies, with a machete-like object.

Just one further factor, among many things found in that bedroom, Lieutenant Yurchuck's report; knives and machete.

All identification papers destroyed. Well, you didn't find any anywhere, did you? Place of execution dismantled. No ropes around there. After mutilation, bodies then carried to grave and buried.

Well, you go through it yourself. I am not going to dwell on it but itemize it. You will be amazed at how many of them you find that fit this case and this document has come from the mind and the thoughts and the pen of that defendant right there.

You remember that video tape. Remember that scene when Nancy Trotter, standing on that wood or stump, and the limb over there. Someone will carry those back for you. But you will recall the limbs and the stump and the tree right near that grave site. You will recall the similarity of the remoteness of the area, the foliage, the dense underbrush or overbrush.

The fact that both areas are out here only nine or ten miles apart from one another in the same general area of Hutchinson Island, an area reasonable to assume well-known by this defendant, who when he was a patrolman down there had his zone out in that area. He sure knows both those spots, doesn't he? You bet he knows them, because he was at both of them.

And I do have to concede there was one glaring dissimilarity between the Wells-Trotter incident and the Place-Jessup incident, thank God. That is, that Wells and Trotter escaped.

You get back there and you think about it and you write up the similarities, you compare them and it is going to lead you only to the conclusion that the fellow positively identified as the person in the Wells-Trotter incident is the person in the Place-Jessup murders.

Let me come now to Hank Dean, the brother-in-law, Teresa Schaefer's brother. I want you to recall Hank Dean's visit to the Martin County Jail on May 18th of this year. Remember he went there with his sister to talk to Schaefer, and he told you he went there because he was concerned for his sister's well-being, her mental stability and mental well-being, however, and they had a discussion with the defendant, Teresa and Hank Dean and the defendant, and you remember the substance of that conversation. There were several topics brought up, weren't there? One of the initial ones was, "Hank, do you want me to confess to you?" "Do you want me to confess to you?" We wish Hank had said yes, don't we? But what did he say? He wasn't up there as a cop. He wasn't there as a law enforcement officer. He said, "Jerry, I only want to get at the truth. I only want to get at the truth."

And you remember another little matter, the matter of the skulls. Go back if you will to Dr. Davis' testimony. I don't think any of you can forget him. He has been with Dade County, and I think Dade County and the State of Florida are extremely fortunate to have a man of his expertise as a medical examiner. And you heard him describe in detail his findings, and his findings in the postmortem examination of the bodies of these two girls, based on his accumulation of things concerning this scene and his investigation and you heard his conclusions and opinions, and you will recall one of the things I asked him was hypothetical concerning skulls and you will recall, of course, all the police departments up here conducted an exhaustive search of that scene in a wide area for almost a three-day period. No skulls were ever found. Do you remember that? And then do you remember my conversation, my questioning of Dr. Davis in that regard? Do you remember him saying in response to my question, "Well, Doctor, how about animals, could animals have carried away something like that and caused this destruction and made it impossible to find it?" Nothing is beyond the furthest iota of possibility, granted, but do you remember him saying based upon his experience and having been medical examiner for what, almost twenty years, thousands and thousands of cases, in situations where there had been animal moving, the skulls would usually be found somewhere in the general area; in other words, fifty or a hundred yards, somewhere in the outer perimeter of the death area. And there weren't any in this, were there? And then we come back to May 18th, in the jail, and Hank Dean. Hank's testimony, remember, he apparently had read something in the paper or was apparently led to understand one way or another that they found the bodies but not the skulls or heads, something to that effect. You will have to draw on your recollection of that testimony. But anyway, it is one of the things that he confronted Schaefer with, and asked him about it, and he said, "Yes, they found these bodies and apparently your name has come up and supposedly you are possibly involved in this. We want to get at the truth. They found some skulls out there." Schaefer said, "They didn't find any skulls. They didn't find any skulls."

Excuse me, am I interrupting you, sir? (Referring to an inaudible statement made by the defendant.) So, he slips a little sometimes, a little, but it helps, doesn't it? It helps paint this picture of a fellow, who from a premediated design, murdered those two girls.

I am not going to dwell further. I expected to go probably for a good hour or hour and a quarter. I am not going to. I am not going to just stand here and try to rehash for you the evidence and what it has shown and what is hasn't shown. I think you are the ones that can do that much better than I, and you are the ones that are going to have to do that, because your job is going to begin really in earnest tomorrow morning. Your job is going to begin in sifting this out, getting rid of the ridiculous testimony, and focusing on what has been proven and finding this defendant guilty of murder in the first degree on two counts.

Our system, I think, is unequal and unexcelled in the history of this world because it provides for you and me, everyone in this courtroom, and to this defendant, certain safeguards, certain protections, all of which come from our great Constitution. One of those is the presumption of innocence. The other is the burden of proof placed upon us representing the people of this State. Another is the right to have the benefit of effective counsel, which he has had. To have a jury of his peers sit here and deliberate and determine the question of guilt or innocence.

Susan and Georgia didn't have any such rights, did they? There was no presumption of innocence for them. There wasn't any burden of proof or any defense counsel there. There wasn't any independent, impartial jury at a public hearing. There was just the prosecutor, judge and executioner out there, all wrapped into one, carrying out all those functions at the same time.

We have carried our burden of proof, ladies and gentlemen. I am confident that you as jurors are going to find this defendant guilty as charged. I am going to sit down at this time, and it will be Mr. Schwarz's opportunity then to speak to you. Under our particular rules of procedure, the State, we have the burden of proof, we have the right to go forward with closing argument, and have the final say of closing argument. Consequently, Mr. Schwarz will follow me and then we will have an opportunity to speak again and we will be hearing from Mr. Stone. Now, this is the last time, therefore, that I have an opportunity to talk to you, either by way of questioning witnesses, or making objections, or giving jury speeches. It is always kind of sad for a lawyer to sit down and not be able to talk. Maybe that is something you have gathered. But that time has come, and I know you will give Mr. Schwarz and Mr. Stone the same great attention that I have noticed all of you giving me here. I want you to know I appreciate it and I am confident all of you are going to do your job as you see it, and I am further confident that you are going to see that we have proved this man's guilt beyond all reasonable doubt, and you will come back with a verdict of guilty of murder of first degree against that man sitting right there. Thank you."

When Shailer finished, he walked briskly back to the State's table. He had developed confidence as he spoke and now, he occasionally glanced back at his wife and nodded his head proudly. She smiled back as if to say, "good job." Then he turned his attention back to his notes, as if to see if he had left anything out.

Schwarz stood up slowly, the hush in the courtroom drawing more attention to him than if he were to shout out loud. Yet, the silence did not seem deliberate, it seemed as if he were searching for where to begin. He seemed to have realized that he was arguing from a precarious standpoint, like someone yelling at the thunder. There was a feeling of hopelessness, and it could be seen in the face of Elton Schwarz. Still, the jury seemed to want to hear what this man had to say.

BY MR. SCHWARZ:

"All right, sir. May it please the Court, ladies and gentlemen of the jury: I also want to thank you on my own behalf and on behalf of my client, Gerard John Schaefer, Jr., for the attention that you have paid throughout the past two weeks to the testimony that you have heard here in this courtroom. Contrary to what Mr. Shailer says, I don't have any hat over here that I am going to start pulling mysterious things out of. I don't believe that that is the function of a lawyer in a trial such as this. What I do intend to do is to try and go through the evidence that has been presented here during the last two weeks, and show you the fallacies in Mr. Shailer's argument, his argument to you that the State has proven beyond a reasonable doubt that Mr. Schaefer killed Georgia Jessup and Susan Place.

Now, I want to go over briefly some of the evidence that we have got. I might as well start first with the jewelry case. You remember how positive and definite and certain the testimony of the Jessups and Ann Chapman, Georgia Jessup' grandmother, was as to this purse, or not this purse, but this jewelry box. Over the years I have developed a little bit of a question in my mind when a person gets up and, even under oath, and makes such a positive and bold statement, "Yes, there is no question but this is mine," unless of course, it has got their name on it or their initials or some distinctive marking on it. There is absolutely nothing distinctive about this particular box. I venture to say that most of you, if you took all your identification out of your wallet, whatever it was, and set it aside somewhere for a couple of months, six months, and somebody was to walk up to you with that and say, "Is this your wallet," could you say positively without a question of a doubt that that is your wallet, assuming there is no identification in it? Of course not. I couldn't do it and I don't believe anybody could do it.

Then Mr. Shailer comes up with this circle of wagons, the Schaefer team. Be reasonable, ladies and gentlemen. Who else other than members of the family would know what would be in a dresser drawer or a desk drawer? You are not going to get the next-door neighbor to come over there and say, "Oh, yes, I used to go through their dresser drawer five years ago, that was there. I have been through it, I go through their dresser drawers once a week, and this has been there." That isn't reasonable.

When you weigh the testimony of these witnesses you have got to do it considering your own everyday common experience, your own feelings as to what is reasonable, what can you expect of a person.

They get to the little pouch. Joyce Froggatt, a close friend of Georgia Jessup's, and Georgia Jessup's sister, they are the ones that identified it as being Georgia's, but I venture to say I don't see anybody's initials on here. I don't see anybody's name on it. I don't see anything distinctive about this purse as opposed to probably hundreds of other ones, either identical, or similar to it throughout the country or the world.

The testimony was that from the defendant – that is, not from the defendant, but from his witnesses, members of the family, members who have hunted with him, that John brought this back from Morocco. And, ladies and gentlemen, you have got in evidence, and if you take the evidence back there, that will be included, you have got his passport, which substantiates the fact that he was in Europe in 1970.

They testified that he carried it various times in different ways; sometimes he had it on his belt, sometimes he had it over his arm, on his arm the way he was target shooting, and flip it open and reach in there and take bullets out. A: lot easier than reaching in your pocket and opening a box and pulling bullets out of a box and putting them in your gun.

Again, they say "the Schaefer team." Who else would have seen John with this pouch, out shooting with it, unless they were friends of his who were out shooting with him? Again, you have got to be reasonable.

Your heard Mrs. Place testify that the individual that she saw in the house was Jerry Shepard. Susan told her his name was Jerry Shepard. He had hair down to his collar, kind of curled up. Clean shaven. Long-sleeved sport shirt on with the sleeves rolled up. He had a hat on, a little brim around it. He sat there in Indian style moccasins, rubbing the inside of his foot. None of these are consistent with one bit of testimony presented on behalf of the defendant, in fact, you recall yesterday, I believe it was, we put into evidence the statement that Mrs. Place had made to, I believe it was Detective Renje of the Oakland Park Police Department in April of this year. She told him at that time that until she had talked to Mrs. Jessup, she didn't know what Jerry's last name was. That was the statement she made then. When she testified here, she said no, his name Susan had told me, it was Jerry Shepard.

I don't know when she talked with Mrs. Jessup. It could have been in any time within that four-day time lapse, between when her daughter left home supposedly to go to the beach, to play the guitar, and October 1, when she finally got concerned enough and called the police department and reported her missing. I have no idea what went on in that four days, but I will tell you one thing. If that was my daughter talking about running away, I would have found out a lot more than just the tag number. I would have found out the man's last name. I would have asked him, "Who are you? What time are you going to be back?" "We will be back around 12:30 or 1:00 o'clock." If that was a man I had never seen before and my daughter was going out to the beach with him, I would find out his last name, and if they weren't back, or she wasn't back by at least 2:00 or 3:00 o'clock in the morning, I would have called the police right then, and I think any concerned parents would, but no, four days elapsed.

She says she wrote down the license tag number and she produced a piece of paper, blue-green Datsun with license tag on it, and street address in Stuart. Very exact about that. But if she knew it was Jerry Shepard why didn't she write his name down there. And you will recall, the testimony, I believe, was that she went to the police department to obtain the address. You heard the testimony from the police officer, Detective Yurchuck, that the computer where law enforcement agencies punch these names in, then a few seconds later back comes the information. The name, address and identification on the car showed the Fort Lauderdale address. Not the Stuart address. True, the registration records in Martin County, in the Tax Collector's office in Martin County, showed the change. You have got the registration. You can see where the Fort Lauderdale address had been Xed out and the Stuart address put in.

You will also recall that Mr. Schaefer was in the Wilton Manor Police Department down here in Fort Lauderdale for a while, and when he got in some trouble in Stuart in July of last year, the Trotter and Wells incident, I am sure there was adequate news coverage of that throughout Broward County as well as up in Martin County.

I don't know how Mrs. Place got that license tag. I don't believe she got it off that car on the night of September 27. Did she recall the incident in July of '72? Did she go to Martin County in those four days? His picture was in the paper. It may have resembled the man who was there in her house. I don't know about that. She could have very easily have gotten that license tag number, the license tag number from Martin County, of John Schaefer. That didn't coincide with the name. Then she heard from Mrs. Jessup, "Jerry Shepherd."

Mr. Shailer tried to allude to a great extent as to the spelling of the name differently on the envelope that they put into evidence and the Gerald Shepherd that is listed in the Fort Lauderdale directory as living in Fort Lauderdale Beach, but no one has ever testified throughout this whole trial as to how the name Shepard was spelled by the man who identified himself as Jerry Shepard. Nobody said it is spelled S-h-e-p-a-r-d, or any other way. They merely wrote it down. It was a phonetic spelling. Nobody has testified there was any identification of Jerry Shepard.

And isn't it unique, assuming for a fact, for a moment, that it was John Schaefer who went to the Place's house on the night of September 27, that he went to such great extremes to wear clothing that he had never been seen wearing before, used a fictitious name, removed the emblem from his car, and still drive up there in his own car, with his own license tag on it, which is the clearest way of identifying a person there can be. It is not consistent. It isn't consistent with what a reasonable person would do if they were trying to conceal their identity.

Then there is one thing they didn't even bother to try and explain how he could have concealed it, and that is the mustache, ladies and gentlemen. Now, they tried to allude, apparently, that this has been some sort of conspiracy here of the Schaefer family to come to their son's defense, and I have asked all of these witnesses if I ever told them anything other than to tell the truth, and they all said no, I had not. Believe me, I didn't, and I am sure Mr. Shailer didn't mean to accuse me of that, and the Court, I believe, in its instructions will tell you that it is completely proper for an attorney to talk to witnesses. He would be a fool if he didn't. One of the oldest sayings I think in practicing law is never ask a question if you don't know what the answer is going to be. There is no way of finding out the answers unless you talk to the witnesses. It is something that is done in every single case.

So, how did the State assist Mr. Place in the identification? Mr. Jessup admitted that his identification was somewhat tainted because of the photograph and things he had seen of John Schaefer. He was very honest about that. He didn't see him for very long. He admitted these photographs affected his ability to identify him. But what did the State do for Mr. and Mrs. Place? When they went up there to the Martin County Jail and handed this picture to Sergeant Scott, who by the way I am sure has no love for John Schaefer, a fellow law enforcement office that he stopped twice for speeding. Of course, he admitted he was speeding. John was doing a job. He didn't care whether he was a fellow law enforcement officer or fellow deputy or not. Sergeant Scott, I am sure, had no love for John Schaefer. So, what did he do? Took the photograph of Susan Place up and showed it to John. John looked at it, said something about it was an attractive girl, looked at the back, saw the date October 27, 1972, and I don't recall which one testified to it, but I believe someone testified that he wasn't in Fort Lauderdale on that date, October 27, '72. You heard the testimony that he wasn't. He was probably en route back from South Dakota. They were there from October 13th to October 29th. What more logical thing would there be for a person to say?

So, at that point Sergeant Scott, being a good investigator, efficient law enforcement officer, goes to the files and found a negative, not a photograph, but a negative of John Schaefer and handed it to them and said, "Here, look at this. Is this him?" That is a real comparative identification. He didn't call the Sheriff or jailer or something and say, "Hey, we have got some people here concerned about their daughter. Let's set up a lineup, bring in five or six men, similar description and put them in a lineup room here and all equal, put Mr. Schaefer in No. 1 position, No. 5 position, wherever, and see if they can pick him out."

They didn't do that, ladies and gentlemen. What they did is they took this negative and said, "Here, this is the man, isn't it?" What would you expect him to say? Approximate height, general description. How many people do you know that would fit that same basic general description?

You were here Wednesday when we started taking testimony. I swear, I think Jesse Holley, who took the stand as the first witness, fit the description just as well as anybody else. Six-foot one, two hundred fifteen to twenty pounds. Wears his hair in practically the same style as John, a little bit longer. I noticed Mr. Holley's hair curled up. I am not saying or trying to infer to you Mr. Holley is the one who killed those girls. I am not inferring that at all. All I am doing is trying to question the identity or identification made of John Schaefer. I did ask one question of him that I wasn't certain of and that is was he in Fort Lauderdale and he said yes, he was born there. He lives in Stuart now, though.

Now, Mr. Holley testified here, Jesse Holley, he wasn't the one who found the bodies, it was his father, I believe he testified, actually found the bodies. Why they didn't call him I don't know, other than I asked Jesse Joe Holley if he was present when his father made a statement to the Sheriff's Office, and he said he was. And, "Do you remember your father stating that he was out looking for beer cans and dead bodies?" And he said he didn't remember him saying that. Maybe that is why they didn't want to put Mr. Holley on the stand. It is an odd thing to be looking for when he sure enough found them.

We have an open — it was described on this chart as being an open grave, five-foot-long; two foot, ten inches wide; and two foot, three inches deep. A: .22 shell casing eight feet from the grave. Numerous other items scattered around including portions of the bodies. It is described that the open grave was 212 feet from the center of the dirt road. People don't intentionally misconstrue things or misstate things generally when they are on the witness stand. When Pat Duval said that this grave was a thousand feet off the dirt road, I am sure he just wasn't recalling it, he didn't deliberately try to confuse anybody, to say it was a thousand feet off from there, because Sergeant Miller, who measured it, said it was 212 feet.

They found the shell casing. They found jewelry. They found the remains of a pair of blue jeans, indicated as apparently belonging to Georgia Jessup. On these blue jeans was a large owl patch on the right-hand side. The road runner patch and some smaller patches. It seems strange to me at least that if she was wearing this when she left on September 27th, if Georgia was wearing that September 27th when she left the Place residence, that Mrs. Place didn't recognize something as distinctive as this owl patch and road runner patch, which is on the right front of the jeans. It is strange also that she can remember so much about Mr. Schaefer or Mr. Shepard, or whoever was there, but she didn't even know Georgia Jessup's last name at that point.

And isn't it strange that Georgia Jessup would go off with someone that she apparently didn't know too well? You heard Joyce Froggatt testify that just wasn't Georgia. She wouldn't go anywhere with somebody she didn't know. She doesn't trust people. And yet whoever it was that she was with apparently took her to the Place residence, and then the three of them went off together somewhere, may have gone off together. The last time they were seen, the man was sitting on the porch and the girls were sitting on the porch. The car drove away, and they were all gone.

It is circumstantial. You can infer that the three of them were there and the three of them were gone and they left together, but that is merely inference. There is no proof. No one saw Georgia Jessup and Susan Place leave the Place residence with any man. The man may have left in a car himself, and the girls may have walked down the street. He said it was almost 9:30. It is almost too late to go out and play guitar. Maybe he said, "So long, girls, I'll see you tomorrow." Maybe Susan or Georgia said to the other one, "Well, let's go for a walk down to the corner or somewhere," and I am not trying to impeach the character of these two victims. I certainly would not intend to do so, but we do know from the admissions that have been made that they did experiment with marijuana or drugs, something of that type. It was shown that Georgia Jessup had at least on one or two occasions carried marijuana in her little pouch. Of course, when this pouch was turned in it was examined and there were no traces of any marijuana in it. Nothing to show that John Schaefer had at any time ever been involved in any drugs whatsoever; marijuana or anything, which would lend credence to the fact that there was marijuana in this pouch.

Again, going back out to the scene, the .22 casing, we had, or the Sheriff had, and produced here six .22 caliber firearms, four pistols and two rifles. Lieutenant Yurchuck testified that these guns were obtained either from Mr. Schaefer's residence in Martin County, or the residence of his mother in Broward County and they were the only six .22 caliber firearms found or obtained.

Yesterday Mr. Sojat of the Dade County Crime Lab, highly qualified firearms identification man, ballistics expert, testified here. His testimony is unimpeached, unrebutted, that the .22 short casing that was found eight feet from the grave on Hutchinson Island was not fired from any of the firearms obtained from Mr. Schaefer, his mother's residence or his wife's residence.

The State has attempted to make you believe, or let you believe or lead you to believe that there was another gun that John had, his favorite Saturday night special. Hank Dean said so. His brother-in-law. They can't find the gun that fired the casing, so they conjecture up one. I am sure maybe he has a hat here also that he is going to pull this mysterious gun out of. I am sure Mr. Dean testified as truthfully as he could. I don't infer any malice to Mr. Dean or any misrepresentation to him or anything else. But stop and think. What did he actually say? He was shown one gun and he said that isn't it.

They had these guns out here. Did they take all other five of these guns and lay them out like I did with these witnesses and say, "Did you ever see John with another pistol or another .22 caliber gun other than any one of these?" They didn't do that. From his recollection he said he thought it was one of these little Saturday night specials, it looked similar to a photograph I showed him, but he thought it had a longer barrel. They didn't bring that gun out and show it to him. They didn't bring the other pistols out with the longer barrels. Why didn't they do it? Could it be because Mr. Dean would say, "Yes, that is the other one that it was?" I don't know. You don't know, but I am sure the State is going to argue to you that it isn't any one of the guns that John had or that he had here. But they didn't even show Mr. Dean what guns they had. So how could he know whether it was one of the others? It is impossible. But in any event, the casing that was found at the scene was not fired from any of those .22 caliber pistols.

Again, at the scene we have got a piece of a root. The expert, I believe it was Mr. Nute from the Florida Department of Law Enforcement, the officer said there was a piece of cloth imbedded in one of these chop marks on it similar in characteristics to a piece of cloth found at the scene where the bodies were found.

Mr. Davis testified as to the dismemberment of the bodies. If those girls died at that scene on Hutchinson Island and were dismembered shortly after death, why weren't there any blood stains on any of the cloth? Why weren't there distinctive markings on the bone fragments or something of this type that would indicate blood remaining in the body? There isn't. They don't have the first bit of evidence that those two girls died on Hutchinson Island at that location.

They have got a writing in evidence, one and three-quarter pages. This admittedly was written by John. We stipulated to that along with many other things. I didn't want to bore you

for four to five weeks while we brought witness after witness saying I found this here and I gave it to so and so, and I bring him in here and he says, yes, I got it and took it here, and a handwriting expert to say this is John's handwriting, all that. We eliminated from this trial probably two-thirds of the time by getting rid of what you might call dead wood and getting right to the heart of the situation, the factual evidentiary testimony, to see what the State did have.

When you go back there and if you want to look at this you can. Again, when was it written? 1960? 1965? 1969? 1970? I don't know. You don't know. No testimony at all as to when this was written. We know that John Schaefer didn't live in that house of his mother's since September 11, of 1971, when he got married to his wife, Teresa. So, if you are going to start inferring things, the only reasonable inference that you can come up with from that is that it was written before September of 1971, over a year before any of this ever occurred, and in reading this, if you are going to condemn a man and convict him from a writing, even if they are his thoughts, on a mere writing of what he may have written years before, why is Alfred Hitchcock still walking around loose, or Erle Stanley Gardner? Any of the writers of the fiction murder mysteries and stories, you can pick up in any newsstand. Is that evidence of a crime? Is that evidence of a crime? If it is, ladies and gentlemen, I say we ought to take those people and put them behind bars. Maybe there are some unresolved crimes maybe their books will lead to the solution of. Maybe if we go over these, we can close the files on a number of missing persons or homicides. That is all that writing means, nothing more. (This infers that this writing *did* lead to a homicide case, * author's note.)

When they searched the house or the car in Fort Lauderdale, they got a rope with a hook on it. They grabbed it and said, "Ah ha, we have got the rope." They sent it up to the laboratory. What did they come back with? I may have them backward, but I think the tree limb showed either sisal or hemp, and this was found to be the other one. This rope had never been over that tree limb. The only other rope they found was this that they found in the mother's home in Fort Lauderdale. They examined it, checked it for any blood stains or wear marks or anything that way, and absolutely negative.

Dr. Davis testified that these victims were dismembered with a heavy sharp instrument. You sat here and you heard Lieutenant Yurchuck list off the items that were seized; knives and firearms, all of it, quite a bunch of hunting knives. Some may have belonged to John. Some may have belonged to his brother. Some may have belonged to friends of his that were storing their hunting and fishing gear there. To go hunting to kill some game, you have got to have a knife to clean it with. It is not uncommon for a person who hunts to have knives or a gun. But he read off quite an impressive list of knives. Where are they? There is not one of them in evidence. Not one of them that the State was able to show bore any reasonable relevancy to the issues of this case. They were all sent to the lab. They were all tested. Not one weapon has been introduced into evidence by the State.

They didn't even bring them out and show them to you, yet they want to say that Gerard John Schaefer on September 27th of 1972, with a sharp instrument, mutilated these two girls or killed them and mutilated them. What with? They have everything. They say, oh, he disposed of it. He disposed of his Saturday night special. Is that reasonable? For a man who spent supposedly an hour in the one girl's home, driving his own car, with his own license tag on it, assuming that was John, and assuming that was his car that was there? Certainly not. No reasonableness to that in any way whatsoever.

Ladies and gentlemen, they have got the wrong man, and I hate to think of that, because somebody did this, but I don't believe it was Gerard John Schaefer, Jr. Again, going back to a little bit more of the evidence, you remember we didn't, the defendant didn't even require the State to prove the identity of the bodies. That could have taken a long time. We are satisfied of that. I talked to the doctors. I talked to practically all the witnesses in this case. Very few of them I haven't talked to. I took the depositions of Dr. Souviron, and Dr. Davis. That probably saved another couple days of trial and a lot of boring testimony and eliminated certain elements of proof so that you could concentrate on the real issues that are to be tried. Who did it? Not that it was done. We do not deny that the girls are deceased. As to how it happened, when it happened, or why it happened, that we do not know.

They allude to, or infer that Gary, John's brother, and his mother changed their testimony as to this jewelry box. They haven't in any way said anything about the identification that Mrs. Lane, his sister, made five years ago in his father's dresser. A: lot has happened in five years. Five years ago, Sara Lane said that was in the dresser. That testimony is unimpeached. True, it is his sister, but again who else would you call but his sister to establish that. If I had called the next door neighbor and put him on the stand, as I said before, and got him to say, "Yes, I saw that in his father's dresser drawer, the upper dresser drawer in the corner over here many times, I always go through there," you wouldn't believe him. I wouldn't believe him. You just don't come up with that kind of witness.

One other thing I want to go into before we break for lunch, and that is this grave, the alleged grave. Here is a picture of that. Here is the hole in the ground that they have referred to as a grave. Now, I want you to stop and think carefully. These girls disappeared on September 27 of 1972. This hole was found April 1 of 1973, over six months later.

We have in evidence, and I will be the first to admit, these records weren't taken from Hutchinson Island, they were taken from the only official recording station in St. Lucie County that we know of, in close proximity, to show the rainfall during that period of time. Now, when you get back there you can add the figures up if you wish here. They are totaled at the bottom of each page. I did it myself, and I am not testifying myself, but you can add them up and check my figures if you want to, but from the evening of September 27th there was some rain recorded between 6:00 and 7:00 p.m. on September 27, but after that to January 15th when Gerard John Schaefer went to jail voluntarily, there were 12.76 inches of rain in St. Lucie County. From January 15th to April 1 of this year, during which time Mr. Schaefer was in St. Lucie County Jail, or Martin County Jail, there was an additional 6.33 inches of rain. Almost 7 inches of rain between January 15 and April 1.

Ladies and gentlemen, I just cannot believe that that hole was dug before January 15th, either the first, or if there was more than one time, the last time, you can observe the edges of it, the amount of erosion taking place, virtually none, yet almost seven inches of rain had fallen.

Then one other point. John Schaefer knew in December when he was sentenced that on January 15th, he was to commence serving a six-month sentence in the Martin County Jail. He knew at that time that there was no work release program or anything else in effect on which he could guarantee that he would be released for a period of at least five months. One month off for good behavior out of a six-month term. He knew this in December. Is it reasonable to believe that Gerard John Schaefer, Jr., the man sitting at counsel table, would go out to Hutchinson Island, dig that hole to bury the bodies and leave everything scattered around identifiable, leave the bodies unburied, and turn himself into jail for five months?

Stop and think. If Gerard John Schaefer, Jr. is the type of man who could do something like that, he certainly would have, as stated in the writing, "how to do the perfect crime," he would have completed it before he ever went to jail for five months. But he didn't do so, because he didn't do it. And I don't think he even knew it was there. I don't think he has ever even been to that area. There is no evidence of it.

One of the other essential elements is going to be the date of death. The date that these two girls died. The State has alleged this occurred between September 27 of 1972 and December 7 of 1972, and the State is bound to those dates.

If you find that on December 8 there is reason to believe these girls might have been alive, then in that event it would be your duty to find Mr. Schaefer not guilty, because they had not proved beyond and to the exclusion of every reasonable doubt that the two girls had died between September 27 and December 7 of 1972.

Now, on this point the only evidence that there is is that of Dr. Davis, the medical examiner, admittedly a very talented, skilled doctor, a specialist, been a medical examiner for many years, but you recall his testimony was that in his opinion these girls, or their remains, indicated that they had been deceased approximately four to twelve months. Ladies and gentlemen, that is a pretty long-time span, eight months. Eight months that they could have died within.

As was pointed out, it is apparent they were alive on September 27. Four months, admittedly, prior to the time the remains were found would bring us up to December 1. But you have got to find from this testimony of Dr. Davis beyond and to the exclusion of every reasonable doubt that these girls were not alive on December 8, or later.

On cross examination I asked Dr. Davis if it isn't a fact that determination of the date or time of death is pretty much a guesstimate, and he told you yes, it is not like on TV where a doctor comes in and says there is no question in my mind at all this individual died eight months, thirteen days ago, at 10:45 p.m. It isn't that way. Medical science has not progressed to that point. As a matter of fact, in older remains, I guess maybe they can tie it down to which century it was, within a thousand years' span on ancient remains, but in this case, he said between four and twelve months, and there is really not much to go on.

Basically, I think that pretty well covers the matters relating to the tangible items of evidence we have here before us today, and the testimony. You have heard my views and my versions of what weight should be given to it, what it means and what it showed.

For a couple brief minutes, I just want to sort of glance over some of the law that I think is going to be applicable to this case that I think the Court is going to give you in your instructions. Again, I want to caution you what I say is not an instruction on the law. The Court will read to you the law that you are to apply to the facts in this case. In addition to reading it to you, you will be given a copy of the law that you are to apply to the facts of this case and it is how you put these two together that determines whether or not your verdict should be guilty or not guilty.

I think the Court is going to charge you that by entering his plea of not guilty the defendant has placed a burden upon the State to prove beyond and to the exclusion of every reasonable doubt every material allegation of the Information, the charges that are set forth in the Information, and that this reasonable doubt has to be eliminated by the evidence presented, solely by the evidence and it is to this evidence that can look for the proof beyond a reasonable doubt, that Mr. Schaefer is guilty.

When we selected you people, ladies and gentlemen, to serve as jurors, I believe the majority of you admitted that you had read encounters involving this situation over a period of time, but you all agreed and you all promised that you had formed no opinion one way or the other as to the guilt or innocence of Mr. Schaefer.

You were asked specifically by Mr. Colton if you felt that after you had heard several weeks of testimony that you could put out of your mind or separate in your mind what you may have read in the newspapers, heard on the radio or TV, from what you heard and saw in this courtroom, and base your verdict solely and exclusively upon what you saw and heard in this courtroom in the way of admissible evidence and the instructions of the law that will be given to you by the Judge, and each of you promised that you would. You not only promised, you swore that you would.

You even entered into a binding three-party contract with Mr. Stone that you would require the State to prove beyond, and to the exclusion of every reasonable doubt, every material allegation of this charge, or these charges, and that you would do this based solely upon the evidence and the law as given you here as jurors. You each promised this and that is all that we are asking.

The charge in this case, as has been explained to you against Gerard John Schaefer, Jr., two counts of murder in the first degree. I think that the Court is going to give you a basic idea of what, or tell you what, the elements of this charge are. Three main things.

First is the death of the person alleged or persons alleged to have been killed. We have eliminated that, ladies and gentlemen. We have stipulated that the two individuals who were killed or are deceased are Georgia Jessup and Susan Place. We didn't require the State to produce proof of that.

Second, that such death was caused by the criminal act or agency of another. This, ladies and gentlemen, I don't know. You have heard the testimony of Dr. Davis and his opinions. There is no way that he can medically establish a cause of death. His opinion as to the cause of death is no greater than yours, based on inferences. No expert medical testimony whatsoever as to the cause of death.

Third, and most important, at least in this case, that the decedents were killed by Gerard John Schaefer, Jr. Here is where the big issue lies. Here is where you are going to have to weigh this evidence and the testimony that you have heard here. No one saw it happen. No one saw Mr. Schaefer in St. Lucie County. And, ladies and gentlemen, 1 don't believe anyone actually saw Gerard John Schaefer, Jr. with Susan Place or Georgia Jessup.

We have established, or tried to establish by the testimony, that at no time during this particular period of their lives, was Gerard John Schaefer, Jr. outside the presence of his wife, unless on a hunting trip or something like that, after 9:00 o'clock at night. That is what we call an alibi, for the simple reason that you have heard the testimony here as to the length of time that it takes to drive from Fort Lauderdale to their home in Martin County, is somewhere between an hour and an hour-and-a-half.

You also heard this testimony that whoever was at Susan Place's house just before they left or, before he left, or before anybody left, he said that it is almost 9:30. Ladies and gentlemen, that was a statement that was made by Mrs. Place, not by me. The statement that she said Jerry said, it was getting close to 9:30, it is almost too late to go to the beach to play the guitar.

If it takes from 9:30 until after 10:30 or 11:00 to get back to Stuart, there is no way that that could have been John Schaefer, if you believe the reasonable testimony of his wife, and there is no reason to disbelieve it. There is not one person who has taken this stand and said, "Hey, I saw him out at 11:00 o'clock over at Frankie and Johnnie's," or "down here at Big Daddy's" or something like that, "having a drink with the boys one night when his wife wasn't around." They didn't produce any witness that said they had ever seen John Schaefer out after 9:00 o'clock at night without his wife.

If you believe that there is a reasonable doubt that John Schaefer was with those girls and killed them at that time, then it is your duty to find him not guilty. If you believe Mr. Ferris at all, if you believe Teresa Schaefer at all, there couldn't help but be a reasonable doubt.

They have testified truthfully, nervously, maybe, I think anyone would be nervous in a situation like this. If you believe their testimony at all there cannot help but be a reasonable doubt, a reasonable doubt, as to whether this was John Schaefer at 9:30 at the Susan Place residence.

In eliminating this presumption of innocence, it must be done solely and exclusively from the evidence that has been presented by the State or the lack of evidence. Two things you can consider. Either the evidence, the tangible items that are here, the testimony you heard, or the lack of evidence.

The failure of the State to produce any weapon which they claim inflicted any of these injuries. The failure of the State to prove by any evidence that Mr. Schaefer was ever in St. Lucie County. The failure to prove that any of the items found at the scene either belonged to Mr. Schaefer, or to prove conclusively beyond a reasonable doubt, that any of the evidence, physical evidence, found in Mr. Schaefer's possession, belonged to these girls. You have got some testimony on the little pouch, and some testimony on the jewelry case, but I fail to believe it was theirs, and that is not proven beyond a reasonable doubt.

They have brought in, on the question of identify of Schaefer, as being the party who may have done this, or did this, Miss Trotter and Miss Wells, who testified here before you, alive, healthy, as to what occurred in July of 1972 when they were involved with Mr. Schaefer. At the conclusion of that, when the State rested and I opened my case, the first thing I put on was video tape of the re-enactment that was done at this scene this summer. You can see how they were tied. You saw how they were tied. And you heard those girls testify that yes, Mr. Schaefer had every opportunity to do anything he wanted to them, but he never physically or sexually harmed either of those girls in any way whatsoever other than, as Miss Trotter said, he pinched her on her butt. Hardly a physical or sexual assault.

Why he did it, I don't know. Foolish. Stupid. You saw how those girls were tied and you saw how long it took them to get loose. I believe it was Miss Trotter, the first one; it took her maybe twelve or thirteen minutes to get completely loose. She said she had a more difficult time getting loose when they did this re-enactment than she did back in July of 1972. Miss Wells, you saw it took her thirty seconds. Does that establish the identity of Mr. Schaefer as the individual who may have done this or who wrote about it?

In conclusion, I merely want to remind you of the reasonableness of what the State has proven. Has the State in your mind proved beyond and to the exclusion of every reasonable doubt that Gerard John Schaefer, Jr. is the man who perpetrated this crime? When you six were here, and our alternate, when you were sworn last Tuesday, a week ago this past Tuesday, you undertook an oath. The oath administered to you said you do solemnly swear you will well and truly try the issues between the State of Florida and the defendant, whom you shall have in charge, and a true verdict rendered, according to the law and the evidence, so help you God. We took you at your oath. Mr. Schaefer placed his trust, his life, his future, his dreams and his hopes in your hands, at the age of twenty-seven years.

Ladies and gentlemen, may God govern you in your deliberations."

* * *

Robert Stone began his argument immediately, before Schwarz had even sat down. He was extremely confident. He'd presented the State's case, the evidence was in, and he felt it would speak for itself. His able assistant, Phil Shailer, had given a strong opening argument. Now, as he had done in the beginning of the trial, he leaned against the rail that separated the jury from the rest of the Court, now he was tied in with them and into them. He made them feel as if they were working together toward a common goal. He did not smile, they had work to do. When he began speaking, his voice was so low that only the jurors could hear. This brought him closer to them, made them feel as if he were talking only to them. As he continued, his voice grew louder, his gestures became more animated, arms sweeping out, pointing to the Places, the Schaefers and to the defendant himself. He was a true dramatist and built his argument like a Southern evangelist delivering fire and brimstone, and liberating the truth. The jury was held, almost mesmerized by his speech.

BY MR. SYONE:

"The purpose of this argument, or of any rebuttal, is simply to point out to you what we think that the defense attorney in his closing arguments has said that we feel is just not what the evidence shows in this case, to point out to you the facts that we feel that the evidence has clearly shown beyond and to the exclusion of every reasonable doubt.

Now, when we picked you as jurors, as you have been reminded of at least three times, we talked to you about the presumption of innocence, and we told you that we wanted you to give that presumption of innocence to this defendant, and we told you that in every criminal trial the person was entitled to the presumption of innocence.

We also talked to you about the burden of proof. We told you that the State of Florida has the burden of proving his guilt beyond and to the exclusion of every reasonable doubt. We also told you that we welcomed that burden, that we welcomed it, we didn't shirk from it, we didn't back off from it. We welcomed it, and that during the course of this trial when you were sworn as jurors, we were going to put evidence on this witness stand to prove beyond and to the exclusion of a reasonable doubt that Gerard John Schaefer, Jr., is guilty of two counts of murder in the first degree. And we have done it.

We told you also it was going to be done by circumstantial evidence. We told you we can't bring somebody in here that can say they went out there and saw him hang those girls to that tree, that saw him hang them and let them die and dangle. We can't bring somebody in here that saw him mutilate their bodies.

Remember, he has written an article on how to go unapprehended in a crime like this. But we are going to prove it to you by clear, convincing circumstantial evidence,

Now, you listen to what the Court says circumstantial evidence is, and it can do it. Circumstantial evidence is legal evidence, and a crime can be proved by circumstantial evidence in a court of law. The Court will instruct you that if circumstantial evidence is susceptible to one or more reasonable constructions, listen to that word "reasonable," reasonable constructions, and any one or more of those constructions is consistent with innocence, then you are to adopt the one that is consistent with innocence, but it has got to be a reasonable construction. A: reasonable construction.

Now, I thought Mr. Schwarz was going to come up here during this two hours, and he took every minute of it, and gave us a reasonable construction of innocence with this circumstantial evidence, with the facts we have got, and they are not all circumstantial, by the way, some of it is real hard-core evidence. I thought sure he would come up here and give us some construction of reasonableness.

Now, I am going to go over what I think he said and what I think the evidence shows and we will go over it briefly.

I am not going to try to answer everything he said, because some of it is ridiculous, but that is his job, he must get up here and try and create some sort of reasonable doubt. I am not going to try to rebut the fact he says he gave it, the purse, to his wife. I am not going to try to rebut things like that. I am only going to talk about what is in evidence here, what you have got before you, what you can consider.

He tried to put Mrs. Place on trial. He tried to put her in issue. She just wasn't a good mother, because she didn't do what he would have done if it had been his teenage daughter. If his daughter left with somebody and he didn't know his name, he would have been out looking for her, but what did she do? Teenagers are not like they used to be. I have a sixteen-year-old girl, and I tell you, they are not like they used to be. We are living in a different society. You don't always interfere with their lives when they get that age. But what did she do? She tried to talk her out of it first. She didn't want her daughter in Colorado. She tried to talk her out of it. That was her first step, which is what a good mother should do. She saw she wasn't going to be able to talk her out of it, because of this smooth-talking guy here who had convinced her to go with him. So, she did the next best thing. She goes out and she checks the tag, which Mr. Schwarz got kind of confused on what he was trying to say. First, he said why didn't she notice these emblems on the car when she looked at it? Then he later came back and said if he was going to hide something why didn't he hide the tag? He was admitting the tag was the best means of identification and it is. You can't hide that registration slip that is on file. You can take it back there. That is on file in the Tax Collector's Office with his name, his address in Stuart, Florida. You can't hide that. That is the best means of identification. She got it and she did everything she could do. She turned it in. She turned the name in.

Incidentally, I feel that emblem might even have been on that Mustang, anyway. Not necessarily on the Datsun. But Mrs. Place did what a reasonable person would do and what a reasonable mother would do under the circumstances, under the facts she said she had problems with her daughter before.

Now, a lot has been said about her identification of this man and alluded to the hair, and talked about the length of the hair, and he showed you this picture and says this is a little fuzzy, but there is no evidence as to when it was taken. But I submit to you that it was taken sometime during the past fourteen years Mr. Ferris has been cutting his hair, and it sure is a little long and fuzzy right there at the back, but they are trying to tie you up on the fact that they are wrong about the shirt, maybe wrong about the mustache, maybe wrong about the hat, but you know they just can't get away from this. They just can't get away from this. They just can't do it. That is his tag on his car, positively identified. Plus, the fact that he himself was positively identified by Mrs. Place at her house.

Now, something very interesting about this picture. That is the one Mrs. Place took up to Sergeant Scott. She identified Schaefer or Shepard at the time, at first. He pulled out a photograph. Yes, that is the man. She first identified him. Right away he knew who it was. She got this photograph and she took it and showed it to him, and, you know a lot has been said about that October 27, 1972, on the back. I don't know why Mrs. Place put that on there. I don't have any idea. But you know what it did. It gave him away. He turned it over and he said at first, "'Oh, a pretty girl." He turned it over and said, "Oh, October 27. I have got an alibi, that date I wasn't in Fort Lauderdale, I couldn't have done it." He didn't say, "I don't know her." He turned it over first and saw the October 27 date, and right away, boy, it hit him, and "I have got an alibi. On October 27, I was in South Dakota." That was his first reaction. Not, "I don't know that girl. I have never seen her before. Who is she? A: pretty girl, huh?" He turned it over and "October 27th, I wasn't there that day."

All right, now the mustache, and I don't want to dwell too much on identity because, really, I think that is one thing you shouldn't have any question of or any doubt about. I mean the tag, the name. They say maybe Mrs. Place went out and got the tag number during that four-day period. Do you think Mrs. Place put that in his house or his mother's address on that? Do you think she took that loot up there and put it in his house, in with his belongings, in with these manuscripts, in with Georgia's jewelry box? Do you think Mrs. Place did that? Trying to make it look like she went out and just got a tag number because there had been two girls involved in an incident up here previously.

All right, now, a lot was said about Mr. Schwarz laid all these guns out about fifteen times, everybody said, "Well, have you ever seen Mr. Schaefer with a gun other than that? Can you identify those guns?" You know what is amazing to me? Mr. Ferris' gunsmith, the man he has known for years, his barber for all these years, who knows all his guns, who works on them, couldn't identify one of them. The Stuart gun. The gun that went from Hank Dean to Lieutenant Yurchuck. That is one that Mr. Ferris didn't know about. That is one that he laid out there and Mr. Ferris couldn't identify. It was up in Stuart after he moved. I submit to you that Mr. Ferris didn't know about that Saturday night special, either. And you will never find that Saturday night special, because it is in a canal with those skulls.

(Stone: Holding up Schaefer's manuscripts of how to murder.)

All right, they want to say he didn't write this. No proof of writing. I don't care whether he wrote it or not. He used the name Jerry Shepard. It has got his mother's address on it, and it was in a box with this, which he wrote. It is in his handwriting. So, are we going to say maybe these neighbors who walk in and out just put that envelope in there along with this handwritten manuscript, his handwritten plan, scheme and design, how to murder and kill? Do you want us to believe somebody just happened to drop that in there and it just happened to be the same name Mrs. Place was introduced to? Just happened to be the same name Mr. Jessup had met nine days earlier, just happened to be? And during that nine days when he snowed Georgia, it took him about eight days to convince her to go with him.

All right, the purse. We have got all kinds of talk about this purse. Well, it came from Morocco in 1970. Do you recognize it, Cheryl Jessup? She picks it up, looks at it. Yes, my sister's. I have held it. I know it. Okay. Do you recognize this, Mrs. Jessup? She picks it up, looks at it. Yes, my daughter's. Do you recognize it, Miss Froggatt? Yes, I have held it. I have used it. I wanted to buy it.

Then we start the charade. Lay it there. Do you recognize it? Yes, he brought it back from Morocco in 1970. How many of them picked it up and looked at it and examined it? The first thing they did was say, "Yes, I recognize it, he brought it back from Morocco in 1970."

He didn't ask Teresa that question. We put her on the stand and asked her about the purse. And they didn't ask Sandy Moses about the purse, because she is only dating one of them and is not going to get married for five years. She is not quite in the family circle yet. Because Sandy, who has been hunting with him, target shooting with him, the reason they didn't ask her, because she is going to say, "I have never seen it before." They just forgot to ask her.

Now, I want to tell you something else interesting about that purse. Teresa would tell you they were deeply in love, never apart, never out past darkness without her, has known him since 1970, since 1970, December; married to him September of 1971, has been on hunting trips with him, never saw that purse until November. Yet these other people say he always had that. They had seen it hundreds of times. But what about the one that he loves and is closest to, that he has known since December 1970? She hadn't seen it.

I tell you, Teresa is just mistaken about that 9:00 o'clock, because I don't think she lied about it. I think she is just mistaken. Teresa is a rose among the thorns here, because she told you she didn't see it until November. That is when he probably went back out to that site where he killed those girls and picked it up, when he was admiring his handiwork, and he brought it back and gave it to her in November 1972.

All right, you can't tie him to the scene, he says. Let me tell you something. As I told you, our case is based on circumstantial evidence. He was the last person seen with them alive. They are seen in his car with his license tag on it. He is found in possession of two items of their very personal property after their deaths, and their bodies are found just a little bit north of where Trotter and Wells were tied up, and just a little bit north of where he was living.

Oh, it is coincidence? It is coincidence? They just went off, walked to the beach and walked up to St. Lucie County? He brought them up here and killed them. That is what happened.

Before he killed the girls and made them watch him, he dug that grave. He did it before he killed the girls, made them watch him dig it.

Now, another smoke screen, the lab test on the knives, some of these things I don't feel like answering but I feel like I have got to show it. It is a smoke screen. This is the type guy who writes about how to commit the perfect crime. Do you think he is going to leave any blood on any of his knives? Take them home with him? Do you think he is going to take the gun home with him with a shell left out there?

A: lot about those lab tests. Do you think he is going to leave any blood on those knives? He knows. He is a police officer, been to the police academy, he knows the first thing they are going to do when they get ahold of those knives, they are going to send them to Tallahassee and examine them, find out if there is any blood on them.

Now, the date of death. Dr. Davis. I have practiced criminal law for ten years and I sat there, I was spellbound. This man is an expert. Truly an expert, and he knows exactly what he is talking about. In his expert medical opinion to a reasonable medical certainty, those bodies had been dead from four months to one year. I submit to you they weren't alive too much longer after September 27th, which is a year ago today and that is when this tragic event started and ended up with the deaths of those two girls.

Now, as Mr. Shailer said, I think it is so appropriate that we are arguing this case to you today. It really is. It is almost poetic justice, that it would happen.

All right, now, he (Schwarz) made some comment as to Trotter and Wells. I want to dwell on that, because I think it is only for the purpose of identity. You can take the similar facts and identify it. The tree is one of them. Just recall the tree Miss Trotter was on and look at this tree. Look at this tree. It is almost a duplicate, almost identical. But let me just talk about that a little bit.

Mr. Schwarz wanted you to see the video tape, without sound. We agreed to it. You know why? Because he didn't know I was going to ask Sergeant Miller the question I asked him. He said,

"Sergeant Miller, does this tape adequately reflect the reenactment of what happened in June of this year? Yes, sir, it does. I offer it in evidence. Well, can I ask one question before you offer it in evidence?" The Court: "Yes, sir, Mr. Stone, go ahead." "Weren't the nooses much looser than they were last July for the protection of the girls? Yes, they were looser. They weren't as tight."

So, he wants to get up here and say, look how they got out, and use that video tape. They were lucky. They were lucky. And then he talked about them again, and he said if he had wanted to, he could have tied them to a tree. Well, they don't hang too well if they are tied to a tree, if their hands are tied to a tree. But I can tell you whatever it took to see that they didn't get away, he made sure of that, after September 27th of 1972, when he picked up Georgia and Susan. He made sure that the next time they wouldn't get away.

And the Court will also instruct you there are other things that you can consider, but those are the important things I want to point out to you. Demeanor. Did Mrs. Place get antagonistic to Mr. Schwarz on cross examination? No. She was as nice as she could be. What about Mrs. Schaefer? Boy, when Mr. Shailer cross-examined her, she got defensive. She got downright adamant. I thought she was going to come out of that witness stand after him at one time. Sara Jane Lane did the same thing. Why do you do that? You are on the defensive. You know what you have been telling is not the truth and you are trying to cover you tracks. That is exactly what happened in this case.

Consider the police officers. What interest do they have? What interest do the Places and Jessups really have in this case? Do you think a verdict of guilty against that man is going to bring their daughters back? It is not going to do it. They are not here to hang anybody. They came here to tell their story, to submit to you the facts as they know them. They have no interest.

The circle of the wagons. The family has an interest. I don't blame them for having an interest, but that interest has tainted and fabricated and falsified the testimony that they have given to you here under oath, and the Court will say that you should resolve any conflicts you can without imputing untruthfulness, but if you can't do that, then you are to reject that testimony which is unbelievable and to believe that testimony you feel is believable. You don't have to believe it just because it is said up here under oath, I can tell you that.

All right, now, he said it was all circumstantial evidence. Mr. Schwarz did. I want to tell you some facts that are not circumstantial, that don't leave any reasonable construction of innocence. Susan and Georgia left with Shepard or Schaefer. We almost get them mixed up. Jerry Shepard, John Schaefer, it is hard to say one without saying the other, almost. They were in his car with his tag. They were found dead in St. Lucie County, just a little bit north of where Trotter and Wells were, and then the cover-up attempts after that, they lie about the jewelry box, they lie about the purse. They attempt to get the purse out of the home in Stuart. These are facts. These are facts.

They are not circumstantial. They are facts.

The Court is also going to tell you that you can bring back five different verdicts in each case. Murder in the first degree as charged, murder in the second degree, murder in the third degree, manslaughter, and not guilty. The Court will instruct you on what each one of them constitutes, the definition of it, but I submit to you on behalf of the State of Florida, the people of this county, there is only one verdict you can bring back. You can go back there, as far as the State is concerned, you can pull out second degree, third degree and manslaughter and lay them aside, because the only verdict you can bring back is murder in the first degree against that man right there, on two counts. That is the only verdict the State submits to you is reasonable in this case as based on the evidence presented here.

Mr. Shailer told you we were back here with a man who has had every possible opportunity of a fair trial. He has been afforded the right to face his witnesses. He has been afforded the opportunity of counsel. He has had all the Constitutional guarantees. As Mr. Shailer told you, one year ago the events started in motion. That wiped out all that for Georgia Jessup and Susan Place. They can't be here for a fair trial. The prosecutor, jury, executioner, and I submit to you one more, God, because he decided he was going to let them live or die. He became God! (Stone had worked up to an emotional shout as he stood pointing at Schaefer. He fell silent for a moment, then continued.)

Mr. Schwarz says, "I think they have got the wrong man." But the evidence doesn't point to that. That is a statement on his behalf. I wonder what Susan and Georgia would say if they were here. They would look at him and say, "Jerry Shepard, you hung me by a tree until I died, then you mutilated my body." That is what they would say, exactly what they would say if they were in this courtroom today and I want your verdict to say, "We are not going to let you get away with it!" Thank you.

*   *   *

There were a few moments of silence after Stone finished his argument. Then Judge Trowbridge explained the charges to the jury and gave them instructions on how to determine the difference between first, second, and third-degree murder, manslaughter, and so on. He went on at great length, telling them to judge only the evidence, not opinions or hearsay, or personal feeling. He conveyed upon them the importance of their roles in the judicial system. Finally, he excused the remaining alternate, Mildred Lovelglio, thanking her for her time and dismissing the jury to begin their deliberations. At 3:45 p.m., the jury left the courtroom to begin their deliberations. At 3:55 p.m., they requested all evidence used in the tria1.

A: bomb threat was called in at this time and, the jury was moved to another room. No bomb was found. The caller was presumed to have been a friend of Schaefer's.

They stopped at 7:08 p.m. for a dinner break, and resumed at 9:10 p.m. At 10:55 p.m., they informed the Bailiff that they had reached a verdict. At 11:05 p.m., the court reassembled.

Before the verdict was read, Judge Trowbridge warned against any outbreaks of emotion.

THE COURT:

"Now, this has been a long trial and it is an emotional situation, but this is still a courtroom, and everybody is going to have to restrain themselves. If it is a verdict it is going to be one way or the other. If anybody thinks they can't handle the emotional impact of the verdict you had better get out of this courtroom right now, because if we are going to have any demonstration of any kind as a response to this verdict there will be some of you that will be going from this courtroom directly to the jail that is adjacent to here without passing through the outside. So, if there is anybody in this courtroom that doesn't think they can take this verdict, whichever way it comes up, I suggest you leave the courtroom at this time.

All right, bring the jury out, please.

All right, ladies and gentlemen, have you reached your verdicts in this case? Don't read them, just say yes or no."

FOREWOMAN BETTY HAUGH: "Yes, Your Honor."

THE COURT: "All right, hand them to the Bailiff, please. All right, the Clerk will publish the verdict. You may omit the captions. Just read the body."

DEPUTY CLERK DOUGLAS DIXON: "As to count one, verdict: "We, the jury, find the defendant, Gerard J. Schaefer, Jr., guilty of murder in the first degree. So say we all. Dated this 27th day of September, A.D., 1973. Signed, Betty Haugh, Foreman.

As to count two, verdict: "We, the jury, find the defendant, Gerard J. Schaefer, Jr., guilty of murder in the first degree. So say we all. Dated this 27th day of September, A.D., 1973. Signed, Betty Haugh, Foreman."

Judge Trowbridge asked each juror if this verdict was theirs, and each answered, "Yes, sir." The verdict came, some have surmised, at approximately the same hour, exactly one year before, when Susan Place and Georgia Jessup were being murdered on Hutchinson Island.

As the court guards led Schaefer out of the courtroom, bombarded by flashbulbs and questions from the press; he smiled into the cameras.

Doris Schaefer appeared to be in shock, staring as her son was led, manacled, from the courtroom. A: tear escaped from her unblinking eyes.

Teresa Schaefer sobbed softly into her hands. She appeared frail and lost, and small. Elton Schwarz put his arm around her to comfort her.

* * *

On October 4th, 1973, the Court reassembled to sentence Gerard Schaefer. When asked if he had anything to say before sentencing, Schaefer said that he "did not know those girls and never killed anybody in my life." But he asked the mercy of the Court, to send him to a state mental hospital where, "the doctors in their wisdom, if they can find if I did it, then I will know it."

Judge Trowbridge sentenced him to two concurrent (served at the same time, rather than consecutive) life sentences. That day, had she lived would have been Susan Place's nineteenth birthday.

Three days later, on a perfect, sunny day, they lowered a bronze casket into the Florida soil, containing the remains of Susan Place. Surrounding the grave were floral tributes, signed "In Loving Memory"; most were delicate pink roses. One wreath was "To Susan, From Robert E. Stone."

Within the same week, Georgia Jessup's remains were cremated and thrown upon the Atlantic Ocean, along with some fresh-picked flowers.

* * *

On November 27, 1973, two months to the day after Gerard Schaefer was found guilty of two counts of murder, Elton Schwarz released the following press statement:

> "Teresa and I plan to be married –
> hopefully before the end of the year. We
> have not applied for the license as yet and
> have not announced a definite date or place.
> However, it will be a small private wedding.
> Her divorce was handled by Tom Cavel of the
> firm of Allsworth, Doumar, and Schuler of
> Ft. Lauderdale.
> Ordinarily the law provided a 20-day delay
> before entry of a Final Judgment. However,
> the Court has the right to enter it sooner if
> it finds that injustice would result from the
> delay. The Court agreed with her attorney,
> Mr. Cavel, that the continuing publicity for
> the next 20 days would create an injustice
> and entered the Final Judgment on Wednesday
> afternoon, about 45 minutes after the Petition
> was filed. My only participation in the hearing
> was to verify that she had been a Florida
> resident for more than 6 months and that John
> had signed the Answer and Waiver of Notice
> voluntarily and with full knowledge of all
> the circumstances and that he was competent
> at the time.
> I first met John in July of 1972 when he was
> arrested for the Trotter and Wells incident.
> I talked with him in the jail and the facts

related to me by him corresponded with the statement given by the girls. At the time of sentencing, in December of 1972, I pointed this out to the Court in mitigation of his sentence. I first saw Teresa in Court that day but did not meet her until April 9th of this year when my office was appointed to represent John. Because the circumstances surrounding the Jessup and Place girls seemed so out of character with the description of John given by his friends and family, I felt it necessary to find out everything possible about him in order to properly defend him against these charges. For this reason, I spent a great deal of time with his entire family: his mother, brother, sister and his wife, as well as many of his friends, strictly in a professional capacity. I visited with them in their homes and went out with them socially. I found that by doing this, I was able to gain a great deal more insight into John's character, than by talking to these people across a desk. Also, a lot faster.

It was difficult for Teresa to find anyone that she could talk with. For this reason, we developed a rather platonic relationship, more to keep her spirits up than anything else. I do want to point out that I was separated and had filed for divorce before I ever met Teresa. It was not until the trial was over that I started seeing her with any degree of regularity or that there was any real form of romantic attachment between us. As to why I plan to marry her, I feel that it is not uncommon for two people who are in love with each other to get married. It has nothing whatsoever to do with John's appeal or anything else. I love and respect her and she loves and respects me, period.

Although I do not believe that John received a fair trial, I do not in any way attribute this to my friendship with Teresa. Because of the widespread news coverage given to the case, I do not believe that he could have received a fair trial anywhere in South

Florida. I said this before the trial, and it
is in the record. I do not know of anything
that could have been done, that wasn't done to
furnish John with the best representation and
defense possible. The entire record will be
reviewed on appeal and I am willing to stand
on the record. There is no question whatsoever
in my mind which would indicate that my
personal feelings had any adverse effect on
John's trial. I discussed this with him at
Lake Butler, (where Schaefer was in prison)
and he agreed. I also talked informally with
one of the Judges from the District Court, and
with Richard Jorandby, the Public Defender
from the 15th Judicial Circuit in West Palm
Beach, who will be working with me on the
appeal. Both agreed that this should have
nothing whatsoever to do with the appeal,
and that I would be remiss in my professional
obligations if I were to withdraw from the
case unless John requested it, or I felt I
could not separate personal feelings from my
professional conduct. John has requested that
I continue representing him and I intend to
do so to the best of my ability. However, my
participation in the appeal will be limited
to arguing for the reversal of the conviction.
As to any matters which would result in John's
continued confinement, such as the involuntary
hospitalization or Mentally Disordered Sex
Offender proceedings, I would personally
prefer to leave this up to Mr. Jorandby or one
of his staff.

In Conclusion, I hope that the News Media
will not try to make a serial out of our
personal life".

At 11:00 a.m., December 21, 1973, less than two months after Gerard Schaefer's trial, Elton Schwarz and Teresa Schaefer were married at a private ceremony in Fort Lauderdale.

Chapter 10

Schaefer Speaks

*Evil thoughts became my sole intimates, the darkest and
most evil of thoughts. The moodiness of my usual temper
increased to hatred of all things and of all mankind.*
                    From 'The Black Cat, by Edgar Allan Poe

W hen I began this book, I fully intended to tell "both sides of
the story." However, the problem with such an endeavor is
how much of each side can one include? Certainly, there
are thousands of pages of accessible evidence against Schaefer, and so the
main body of this book is made up of that. Additionally, most of Schaefer's
defense argument was self-proclaimed, and in the words of Harry Crews,
(the author of "A Feast of Snakes" and several other books, and Schaefer's
former teacher) "Schaefer is so undeniably full of shit, that anything he
will tell you would be a lie anyway..." With that in mind, one must wonder
not what it is you want to believe, but how much can you believe?

I approached Schaefer with the unbiased view of a reporter. No
promises were made, or bargains drawn, although it was plain to see from
the start that Schaefer was desirous of a contractual agreement that would
render him some financial gain. None was given, but I did tell him that I
would include in the book anything which he wanted to offer in his defense.
This chapter is comprised of that information which, it should be pointed

out, does not clear Schaefer of the other murders and/or disappearances he is alleged to have taken part in.

What this information does accomplish is to bring up some very important questions about our judicial system, and the people who work within its closed society. Questions like: what the hell was going on in the state attorney's office, with its connection to drug smuggling and pay off? What was the secrecy surrounding David McCain, the former justice who became a fugitive from the law, wanted for conspiracy to traffic drugs? How did Schaefer's two concurrent life sentences suddenly become two consecutive life sentences? What evidence exists that supports the alleged escape attempt of Gerard Schaefer, and subsequent transfer from a minimum to a maximum-security prison? Who else was murdering people in the 19th Judicial Circuit? And finally, most importantly, why was Schaefer never prosecuted for the Briscolina/Farmer, or Goodenough/Wilcox murders, and if found guilty, sentenced to death?

The following letter is the first of literally dozens I received from Schaefer. I collected hundreds of pages of information from him, sometimes getting two or three letters a day, then nothing for a month, then a manuscript-length packet of information, then a deluge of letters explaining the contents of the packets. I still occasionally received letters from him, though they were less frequent, up until his death in December of 1995.

> Dear Mr. Kendrick:
>
> I must say that I was surprised to receive your letter; that you should be working on a book "in which my story is paramount" is quite intriguing to me. I find it difficult to believe that anyone would be interested in a "precise and factual" rendition of the story of my life and times. There has only been one other writer in the last ten years who wanted to hear the truth behind the bombastic blathering of Robert Stone and his band of racketeers masquerading as public officials. The last writer who interviewed me and left with the facts joined the Federal Bureau of Investigation (Barbara Madden).

Robert Stone has, thus far, failed in his attempts to have me killed although I must give him credit for exemplary efforts. Why would he do that? There will not be mystery about it when you come to know the truth. I am not altogether certain that you really want to know the truth; the facts of my case are certain to cause you much official unpleasantness. You are probably astute enough to realize that there is a great deal about my case that does not add up. You speak of newspaper "documentation," Mr. Kendrick. The newspapers, particularly the Palm Beach Post, were spoon fed by Mr. Lem Brumley and Mr. Robert Stone. Read those papers and you will discover only one side of the accusations---the State and police side.

Certainly, my letter is already taking a dramatic turn and that is bad. You want the facts, and I do have them; and after ten years I just may feel safe enough to turn loose of them under proper conditions and circumstances.

I would like to have the opportunity to meet with you in person; before I do so, I must contact the Justice Department and ask if it will be permissable or would it interfere with their investigation into the corrupt offices of Mr. Stone. I do not think that they would object to you interviewing me on the subject matter unrelated to narcotics traffiking and some of the activities engineered by Stone on which the statute of limitations has run out.

I am of mind to sit down with you and make a determination concerning the extent of my cooperation with you, assisting you with your endeavor so to speak. The interview must be set up in the following manner.

Write a letter to Mr. Jerry Wicker, Classification Officer, APCI (Avon Park Correctional Institute) on your official letterhead; requesting that I be asked to give my permission for an interview by your publication. Because you will be requesting the interview as a member of the working media, I will be asked if I will agree to see you. I will, at that time give my permission. You will be notified by Mr. Wicker that I have granted permission for an interview and then you will be able to come here any day between 9 AM and 5 PM, Monday through Sunday, present your credentials at the control room and be admitted into the prison. Penthouse Magazine interviewed me at length but decided that what I had to say might be a bit too hot, for even them to properly handle.

I will sit down with you and we can spend a little time getting to know each other as human beings. I would like to hear some background on you, and how you happened to become interested in me. I am a forthright and straightforward man. I tell it like it is and do appreciate reciprocal candor. The reluctance of both Mr. Bradford (head of DOC) and Mr. Fortner (Warden at APCI) to grant you permission to visit me in person is due to the fact that they do not have the authority to grant the interview and, also due to the fact that I am presently under special protective custody status pursuant to my cooperation with several ongoing Federal

Investigations and due to threats against me and attempts to have me killed. My cooperation with federal authorities has been extensive.

I spend my time in prison reading law; I am regarded as perhaps one of the finest post-conviction litigators in the Florida system. I have won relief for inmates in 26 different cases, some of which are written up in the law books. I make a passable living at it. I, like yourself, am a freelance writer; so, we should enjoy a certain professional rapport in that respect. I have been under contract to a literacy agency, been published in professional journals and sold in the neighborhood of 25-30 short stories during the past two years. My legal discertations on the Law of International Treaty has been used before Federal Justices in the litigation of International disputes. In short, I have used my time profitably and wisely during the past ten years.

My conviction was without foundation in Law and violative of the Declaration of Right of the Florida State Constitution; I will be delighted to point this legal position out to you later on. I have passed a number of lie detector tests during 1983 and have *written* verification that I am cleared in most of the crimes that Robert Stone continues to accuse me of.Remarkably, I even have a handwritten letter from the father of one of the girls I was accused of murdering stating that he believes me to be innocent. I was scheduled to appear on the national television program, Lie Detector, but that is another chapter of the story. The

polygrams that were to be used on the show
proved me to be innocent.

Unfortunately, frame-ups by public
police and prosecution officials, even when
they can be documented and proven are
better left alone.

I am afraid that I would never be able
to entertain you with any Bundyesque tales
of murder, sexual mayhem and torture of
young innocents. My position has been,
from the first, that I did not have
anything to do with mass murder except in
my capacity as a writer of bizarre fiction.
In the event that it is a criminal act
to attempt to publish bizarre stories of
murder (thought crime?) I should be in
stimulating company with the likes of
Stephen King, John D. MacDonald, Harry
Crews (who taught me how to do it well),
Flannery O'Connor and a host of lesser
known dabblers in the fascinating and
spine-tingling world of violence.

Recent comments of Robert Stone to the
contrary, I possess a clean bill of mental
and emotional health from the Department
of Corrections. There is no finer way to
destroy the credibility of a man than
to bandy about the rumour that he is a
psychopathic liar and killer; particularly
where vest-pocket state shrinks can be
hired to write reports to that effect.

Sir, you are lifting a very slimy rock
when you explore beneath the surface of
my case. There may be stinging poisonous
hurting beasties that lurk in wait,
indifferent to your probing so long as
you probe with a dull stick. Sharpen
your quest for truth so that the crawly
things begin to squirm in the light of

veracity, and you may find any number
of unpleasant things happening in your
life; non-cooperation by the established
authorities will likely be the least
disruptive for you. You could end your
days labeled mentally incompetant, if you
are fortunate; or you could be sent to
prison easily enough, and if you become
too annoying you could turn up dead. That
is how their game is played, don't believe
me? Let me ask you this:

What evidence was ever presented at my
trial that I murdered those two women to
the exclusion of every reasonable doubt?

What direct evidence ever linked me to
the scene of the crime?

The case is one of speculation,
inuendo, hypothesis and a public clamour
generated by newspaper horseshit. Tell
me about the evidence. That is what is
supposed to count; not the opinions of
a racketeer. Ok, Kendrick, you've been
warned, so watch out if you elect to
persue the truth.

Nice to hear from you. I'm interested;
hope you do not scare easily.

Best Wishes,
Gerard J. Schaefer

A few items in this letter should be clarified:

1. Penthouse denies ever having sent a writer to interview Schaefer.

2. Schaefer *was* involved in a Federal Investigation, in cooperation with the office of Senator Paula Hawkins, in connection with a child pornography ring that was being operated from within the prison walls of APCI. (More information on this will be presented later in this chapter.)

3. I have not seen the letter that he says was written "by the father of one of the girls I was accused of murdering." All the fathers I talked to were convinced of Schaefer's guilt.

4. The FBI did investigate Robert Stone's office, and his personal life after arresting a very wealthy drug smuggler by the name of Donald Raulerson who was quoted as saying, "I have the state attorney's office in my pocket" referring to Stone's administration. The result of that investigation was the arrest and conviction of Lem Brumley, Stone's chief investigator. Stone's name was cleared at that time. (Again, more information on this will be shown later in this chapter.)

Of primary importance within the abundance of Schaefer's information, and before we can look at his many claims of political corruption, we must look at his rebuttal of the Place/Jessup murders. He has maintained his innocence since the day of his conviction and did even when we met. That said, he enjoyed the title and infamy of being considered one of the most heinous killers in Florida history, while proclaiming his innocence. However, it is interesting to note that he did not uphold, or try to prove his innocence, by placing the body of his arguments against the incriminating evidence that convicted him. That is not to say he did not refute that evidence, he did vehemently, but the basis of his argument is not how innocent he was, but how guilty everyone else was. Now, it is up to the reader to weigh the evidence and determine how much, if any, favorable light may be thrown on the various people involved in this case. In truth, many of those persons do not "come out smelling like a rose" when all the facts are in. But in the interest of fairness and accuracy, all sides must be heard.

The following letter is a chronological following of events, written by Schaefer and sent to me. It is his plea for innocence, however brief... and inconsistent.

```
CHRONOLOGY #/1
March 25, 1973

    Mrs. Place goes to Martin County;
fingers Schaefer. Lies. April 1, 1973
    Big story on Schaefer connection;
bodies found same day. April 2, 1973
    Bodies sure to be Place Jessup; no
other theory even discussed.
    Parents say Schaefer drove off with
girls September 27, 1972.
    FACT 1. Parents later admit lying about
girls being in Schaefer car. Original date
```

of October 27, 1972 changed to September
27, 1972. Even though photo shown Schaefer
in evidence reflects October 27, 1972 date.
One body clad in blue denim dungarees
with patches. Knitted pullover shirt with
horizontal blue and white stripes and
patches struck familiar chord with *Shirley
Jessup*. One body nude.

FACT 2. It was the body of Susan Place
wearing dungarees, yet her mother, Lucille
Place, testified that when Susan left
home, she was wearing blue green hip-
huggers, white sleeveless banlon sweater
and two toned suede oxford shoes. There
was never any clothing of this description
found at scene or anywhere else. One body
was found nude,

FACT 3. Clothing consisting of
knitted pullover shirt, a light pink
short dress, size 9 spike heel shoe
and white underpants were found *by* a
hole near bones. Also, a *second* dress
was found near the hole. White, lace,
rhinestones at waist.

COMMENTARY:

The evidence found at the scene is not
consistent with the theory that the women
were killed on September 27, 1972; for the
following reasons:

1.The Jessup woman left a note saying
she was leaving and took clothing and
personal items with her. It is reasonable
to conclude she knew where she was going
before she left.

2. Friends and even relatives of Jessup
reportedly saw her as late as November
1972. (Deposition of Shirley Jessup) This

would not be inconsistent with the time of death estimate of four months as stated by Medical Examiner Schofield. Original range being four to six months,

3.Susan Place was a drug user (heroin) with arrest record for hard drugs. Her mother even knew she was an active confidential informant for the Ft. Lauderdale police. A girl who gets heroin has no trouble getting epilepsy medicine. Heroin is expensive. Susan was broke and very attractive. We know how good-looking female junkies pay their way,

4.Susan and her mother had a bitter fight and Susan was told to leave and not come back. (Deposition of Mrs. Place)

5.Clothing found on bodies and at scene do not match what girls were wearing when at Place home on September 27, 1972. Two bodies and two dresses at the scene; at Place residence both girls were in jeans or long pants. Susan took no clothing when she left home; neither parents recognized the dresses but recognized the jeans and shirt.

It is therefore reasonable to conclude that dresses were bought or borrowed after September 27, 1972.

6. Puzzle: Place was found in jeans. When or why would a girl wear a dress *and* long pants and maybe overblouse?

A. If there were many mosquitoes or sandflies about?

B. If it were particularly chilly or even cold?

C. If the underbrush were thick enough to scratch bare legs?

(Women who do farm labor *often* wear pants under a skirt)

Had the women died September 27, 1972
it would be reasonable to think that they
would have on them clothing they were last
seen alive in.

"CRIME SCENE" EVIDENCE NOT
LINKED TO SCHAEFER

Investigators report that a considerable
amount of material evidence was found at
scene; none of this material was found to
be connected to Schaefer in any way.

The very critical aspect of this fact
is that even though none of the evidence
is linked to Schaefer, the police name no
effort or attempt to learn to whom said
evidence was linkable to. With Brumley
coordinating the case, it was important to
him to make sure the spotlight remained
focused on Schaefer.

Examples:

1.Cigarette butts were found
at the scene.

   (Schaefer does not smoke)

2.The hole in the ground was described
as fairly fresh due to a lack of noticeable
erosion. Beach soil is sandy, and a hole
would collapse from water seepage in a
short time. Rainfall would also collapse
a sandy hole.

A. Schaefer was in jail from January
15, 1973 to April 1, 1973, a period of
75 days. This indicates the hole was dug
after Schaefer was in jail.

B. Empty Cartridge casing(s) found at
scene were *not* linked to any weapon owned
by Schaefer.

3. Evidence indicates that victims
were shot in face or head (testimony of
forensic dentist) due to jawbone being
shattered and lead particles found

422 - *American Ripper*

imbedded in bone. The empty cartridge casings were of a small calibre and the wound was consistent with that made by a small calibre gun. Fact: Small calibre guns are often prefered by asassins doing murder of informants: A. Easy concealment of gun, B. Deadly effectiveness at close range. C. Minimum messiness. D. Projectile is destroyed by impact. E. Minimal report from gun.

FACT: Shooting an informant in the mouth is an underworld "signature" crime.

CHRONOLOGY # 2

* Week of September 14, 1972

Place and Jessup were picked up by police in Palm Beach County either going toward Fort Pierce or returning from that area. Police hushed this fact up during investigation.

* September 27, 1972

Place and Jessup voluntarily drop out of sight into drug culture underworld. Mrs. Place acknowledges Susan is an informant for Ft. Lauderdale Police Department and is drug user.

* November 1972

Georgia Jessup is seen repeatedly in Lauderdale Beach area.

* January 15, 1973

Schaefer enters Martin County Jail.

* March 25, 1973

Mrs. Place makes trip to Fort Pierce, returns via Martin County; Fingers Schaefer, tells verifiable lies to police.

* April 1, 1973

Corpses of Place and Jessup found just south of Fort Pierce.

Police reports and depositions cite Mrs. Place as stating that when the girls left her home they were wearing:

A. Susan Place

1.Bluegreen hiphugger pants.

2.White sleeveless banlon sweater.

3.Two-toned suede oxford shoes.

B. Georgia Jessup

1.Jeans.

2.Blouse.

When found, the corpses were wearing or had near them:

A. Susan Place

1.Blue denim dungarees with patches (wearing).

(Pants that were identified as belonging to Jessup)

2.Patterned red sash tied around left hand.

B. Georgia Jessup - nude.

C. Found near bodies:

1. Light pink short dress.

2. White lace with rhinestones dress.

3. Black spike high heel shoe (size 9)

4. White underpants.

Black high heels are compatible with a pink or white dress. Who wore size 9 shoe?

PUZZLE: Lace and rhinestone dress appears more decorated that other clothing items.

ANSWER: Some fabrics deteriorate faster than other.

(Elementary chemistry)

QUESTION: What were Place and Jessup doing tricked out in spike heels and short glittery dresses?

POSSIBLE ANSWER: This type of attire is consistent with what a young hooker or drug pusher's "old lady" might wear. Place took heroin (strongly addictive) and any ''junkie'' girl will turn tricks to score her needed "fix''.

REASONABLE THEORY: Place and Jessup were living with "underground" types after September 27, 1972. Someone found out that Place was collecting information for police. Both women were shot. Bodies, clothing, property dumped 100 miles away. Dismemberment probably occurred so bodies could be carried from house or apartment to transport vehicle without attracting attention, a simple act of carry-out garbage in a sack.

1.No conclusive evidence that women were killed at site where bodies were found.

A. Finding empty cartridge(s) at scene supports death at scene.

B. Lack of footwear.

C. Dismemberment.

D. Fancy type of attire – supports death elsewhere.

2.Sex killer theory of Brumley and Stone inconsistent with factual evidence.

From the beginning Brumley and Stone advanced the theory that the two women were victims of a "sex killer''; yet there is not a shred of evidence to support the "sex murder" theory. On the contrary, the evidence shows: it was not a "sex crime".

While it is true that the bodies were dismembered, a careful reading of the medical examiner's reports will show that neither body was subject to genital mutilation common to sex murder by knife; when the crime was sexually motivated, (Jack-the-Ripper; Peter Kurten; H.H. Holmes; and while Albert DeSalvo-Boston Strangler-strangled the women he first

raped, he also mutilated their genitals
in various ways such as forcing an object
up the vagina or rectums such as a
broom handle.)

The bodies were not randomly slashed,
rather purposefully cut up into manageable
parts of 5 portions each. As I recall the
reports, it went:

1.Place: Decapitated, arms severed,
cut in half at waist. Each part could
be carried in a bag. The genital area of
Place was not even exposed, the lower half
was wearing the dungarees. The torso and
bosom was nude but *not* mutilated.

2.Jessup: Decapitated, legs severed
at area of knees, severed at waist.
Arms apparently not cut off. No
apparent slashing or mutilation of
genitals or bosom.

I *think* that is now correct, the M.E.
report has it all stated very explicitly
and correctly. The cutting, it is said,
was done with a heavy blade. Stone and
Brumley were also fond of expressing the
theory that the women were killed by
hanging them. Factual evidence does not
support that theory. It is beyond reason
to allege that the women were hanged, shot
and then cut up; yet Stone did say that.
(Trial record)

Brumley and Stone deliberately misled
the press and Public completely with-
holding evidence of Place and Jessup's
connection with the drug trade.

* * *

There are several items in this letter that beg for comment.

First, allowing for a bit of "dime store psychology," the various reference
to the girls as hookers or drug pushers shows an obvious animosity toward
the girls on Schaefer's part. There has never been any evidence presented

that would substantiate that either of the girls were prostitutes, and other than the admission of both girls' parents that the girls may have "smoked a little pot," it can be safely said that neither were heavy drug users, let alone drug pushers. This animosity only serves to echo what psychiatrists have noted earlier in this book; that Schaefer saw himself as an "eliminator of wicked people = immoral women = all women."

Other discrepancies include: In the Chronology #1 section:

ITEM – "FACT" #1 – Neither parent ever admitted not appeared to be lying about anything.

ITEM – "FACT" #2 and #3 – The rather detailed description of clothing and its placement about the scene of the murders, I feel, serves to incriminate Schaefer, rather that acquit him. The descriptions are more detailed than either the law enforcement investigators' or the medical examiners' descriptions. In truth, due to the mutilation of the bodies, even the medical examiner had a difficult time trying to determine which body wore which clothes. It is interesting that Schaefer knew exactly which girl wore which clothes.

In the "Commentary" section:

ITEM - #2 - No one to my knowledge saw Georgia still alive as of November of 1972.The deposition of Shirley Jessup does not say that either.

ITEM - #3 – Mrs. Place told me Susan was never "an active confidential informant" for any policy agency.

ITEM – #4 – Susan and Mrs. Place did not have a "bitter fight." There was an argument between mother and daughter, because Mrs. Place did not want Susan to leave home, particularly with a stranger. It could hardly be described as bitter.

In the "Crime Scene Evidence *Not* Linked to Schaefer" section:

ITEM #3 - States "that victims were shot in face or head." This would indicate that both girls were shot; but most of Georgia's head was never found, and that section that was found did not contain bullet fragments. Again, it would seem that Schaefer knew more than he should if he were innocent.

In the "Chronology #2" section:

ITEM - September 14, 1972 – Susan and Georgia were picked up in Palm Beach, their proposed destination unknown. However, if the girls were going to, or returning from Martin County, then it should be pointed out that is where Schaefer lived.

ITEMS - September 27, 1972 and November 1972 - References to Susan and Georgia being alive in the "drug culture underworld" have both been acknowledged as being totally false.

In the "Reasonable Theory" section:

ITEM - "#1" and "#1-A"– These two items totally contradict each other: The first says there is no evidence that the girls were killed at the site; the second says bullet cartridges support the fact that the girls were killed at the scene. Overall, this entire letter shows that Schaefer had very little in defense of himself, and what he did offer was all repeated twice within a six-page letter. Now, there were other arguments that Schaefer offered in his defense over the next two years as we discussed his case. However, they were mostly rehashed versions of the previous letter. He could offer no new evidence that would substantiate his claims, nor an alibi for his whereabouts on September 27, 1972, later in that evening. It is known he was in Ft. Lauderdale on that day and in fact, in another letter he wrote to me he said:

"But, for the sake of argument, suppose I say yes, I was there at the house as Mrs. Place said. I then got into my car and drove home and the girls parted with me at their front doorstep. *Now that I admit I was there*, let us get on with the question of proving that I had something to do with killing them."

So, it would seem, as it did to a jury in September 1973, that Schaefer is without an adequate defense. But is that the end of this case? No, it is not. For while Schaefer may have "been caught red-handed," as one investigator noted, he was eligible according to the law for an appeal, and possibly for parole. We will not get into the moral right or wrong of this issue right now, but instead look at the legalities involved.

In order to understand these legalities, one must realize that the State of Florida prosecuted Schaefer by "Information." That is, rather than by "Indictment." An "indictment" requires the use of a grand jury and prosecution by "information" does not. However, the Florida State Constitution clearly states, in Article I, section 15(a)-"No person shall be tried for a capital crime without presentment or indictment of a grand jury..."

Robert Stone, in defense of his decision to prosecute by information rather than indictment, has stated that he was not trying to obtain a death sentence against Schaefer, and in so doing, did not have to use a grand jury and an indictment.

In filing for an appeal for Schaefer, Michael Tarkoff, an attorney in Miami who took over the case, cited at least sixteen cases, similar to Schaefer's, ruled with the constitution: The court held to the Article that required an indictment with a capital offense charge and in so doing ruled in favor of the defendants' in those sixteen cases. Out of those sixteen cases, three bear close scrutiny.

Those cases are:

State ex rel Manucy v. Wadsworth, 293 So.2d 345 (Fla 1974), Manucy was charged via information on October 17, 1972 with first degree murder allegedly committed in 1968. In reversing Manucy's conviction, the Florida Supreme Court found that:

Subsequent to (October 1, 1972) . . . the requirement of Fla. Const., Art. I, Sl5, which commands that capital cases "shall only be by indictment by a grand jury, was once again controlling."

* * *

To charge Manucy (by information) was clearly violative of the constitutionally guaranteed procedure for commencement of trials in "capital crimes."

Thus, the *Manucy* court held that if the crime in question was a "capital crime" at the time of its alleged commission, any prosecution therefor must be via grand jury indictment.

Smith v. State, 315 So2d 224 (Fla.1st DCA 1975), the appellant had been informed against on December 29, 1972 for first-degree murder. In reversing Smith's conviction, the Court found that in order to be *tried* for first-degree murder, Smith "had to be indicted and tried by a jury of twelve citizens." The District Court mentioned neither the date of the alleged crime, nor the date of Smith's arrest, instead basing its decision upon the date of the information. Reading the Smith case together with the Manucy rule, a person must be indicted if the crime in question was a "capital crime" either at the time of its commission *or* at the time of trial.

Hunter v. State, 358 So.2d 557 (Fla. 4th DCA 1978), the defendant allegedly committed first-degree murder on July 6, 1972, but was not informed against until August 27, 1973.In reversing Hunter's conviction and life sentence, the Court held that:

Although the (failure to charge the defendant via indictment) was not altogether unreasonable at the time the information was filed, the Florida Supreme Court has since resolved the question (citing Manucy). The operative facts are indistinguishable from the present case; *the crucial factor of both is that the charging document was filed after the effective date of the new death penalty statute.* On authority of Manucy we reverse . . . 358 So. 2d at 559.

Schaefer was also informed against after the effective date of the new death penalty statue of October 1, 1972. Under the rationale of Manucy, Smith, and Hunter, his conviction is patently void.

If this is true, then not only was Schaefer entitled to an appeal, his previous conviction could very well be overturned. Conversely, if he had been put on trial again, and found guilty for either the Place/Jessup murders, or for any of the other murders he has been accused of, he could very well be sentenced to death, Schaefer knew this and still wanted another trial.

* * *

In addition to a possible appeal on grounds of the above-mentioned precedents, Schaefer pointed out that his "presumptive parole release date" (PPRD) has been wrongly calculated. That even without another trial, he should be eligible for parole, if not now, then very soon. Again, Schaefer had the paperwork that, at least in part, substantiated his claim.

It is general knowledge in the Florida judicial system, that if a prisoner is convicted of first- degree murder and is sentenced to "1ife" in prison, that life term is usually only ten years. It is possible that a "lifer" can be paroled in seven years, sometimes less, with good behavior. Schaefer was given two life terms, which even if they were to be served consecutively would've meant he would be eligible for parole in about twenty years, or roughly in 1993. However, Schaefer was given two life terms, to be served *concurrently*, that is, at the same time. This means, all semantics aside, having served over fourteen years as of this writing, he was eligible for parole in 1987.

This is true, if we accept the general norm for most Florida prisoners. However, if we look closer at how the Department of Corrections (DOC) figures presumptive parole release dates (PPRD) we can arrive at a different date still, for Schaefer's possible parole. The DOC has a list of "matrix time ranges," which are predesignated lengths of time a prisoner must serve according to the offense he has been convicted of. These range from "Low-Least Serious" to "Greatest-Most Serious II." The "Low" includes gambling, desertion and non-support, misdemeanors, property offense, etc. Then there are five other categories in between: Low Moderate, Moderate, High, Very High, and Greatest- Most Serious I, and finally Greatest-Most Serious II. These incorporate a variety of crimes from: alcohol law violation and statutory rape (Low Moderate) to explosives and fondling (Moderate) to incest (High) to armed robbery (Very High) to murder II (Greatest- Most Serious I). All crimes fit into these five categories, some seem incorrectly placed (for instance "Murder III" is in the "High" category, while "Armed Robbery without injury to victim" and ''possession of marijuana, 2000 lbs. or more" are in the "Very High" category) while others are more logical. Each category has with it a minimum to maximum "matrix range" that is equal to months. That is, a matrix range of 18-33 would mean the prisoner will serve 18-33 months. The exact time he served would be determined by his behavior at the correctional institute he was placed in, and all of them in Florida abide by these same matrix scores.

Gerard Schaefer was given a matrix range score of 168-226 (roughly fourteen to nineteen years) with a recommended presumptive parole release date for 4/14/92. This would have equaled about nineteen years in prison for Schaefer. Then in May of 1979, six years after Schaefer's incarceration, someone for unknown reasons took the maximum number he already had (226) and added the maximum from another category, 288, giving him a total score of 514. The new PPRD now, as it stands, is August 4, 2016, which would've given Schaefer a total of almost forty-three years in prison.

The decision to maintain this new score is not that of any one man. It is the result, prison officials have explained, of years of annual reviews of Schaefer by various interviewers and officers within the prison system. However, in reading over these annual reports, one finds most of them do not list any actions on Schaefer's part that could warrant the additional 288 months he was given. Now, there are some complaints listed in these annuals by the interviewers, such as:

"Although defendant had a pleasant attitude at the time of interview, he exhibited very little emotion and seemed to be somewhat weird and had a very fixed stare." (l974)

"Subject has a real high opinion of himself . . . I think that before this man is released on parole that we should take a very hard look at him, as I feel he could be extremely dangerous." (This 1977 report also lists Schaefer as being in disciplinary confinement for mail violation.)

"Schaefer is having considerable difficulties now with various mail violations and has been kiting out letters while working in the library. Some of these letters were extremely vulgar. It is of particular interest to note that he has written various unknowing individuals, describing himself as a female locked up on Death Row with children, and has in fact, gotten two couples to agree to adopt his infant children. On other occasions, he has had various people send him female undergarments which of course were found before he actually received them . . ."

So, while Schaefer may not have been the model prisoner, it is questionable as to how the prison authorities arrived at the decision to increase his matrix score. Schaefer said that it was the result of his accusations against Robert Stone that increased his score. He maintains that Stone "and his cronies" altered the score so that he would not be released, " to tell the truth . . . about the goings on in the 19th Judicial Circuit."

For whatever reasons, as it stood, Schaefer's earliest parole date was to be in 2016. He would've been about seventy-one years old.

In one of his earliest letters to me, Schaefer sent additional information that he felt would help clear his name. In one of these "packets," he included a 78-page transcript of a conversation with Captain Ben Butler of the Plantation Police Department, and detectives Brian Flynn and Frank Carbone of the Pompano Police Department who were interested in Schaefer's possible involvement with the still unsolved Briscolina/Farmer murders (Plantation) and the disappearances of the Rahn/Stephenson girls (Pompano). The results of these officers' inquiries, and their polygraph tests were as follows:

In respect to the Rahn/Stephenson disappearances, Schaefer was given a letter from the Pompano Police Department that "cleared" him of any involvement with those two girls. In that case, he is no longer a suspect.

In respect to the Briscolina/Farmer murders; the polygraph test deemed "inconclusive."

Additionally, it should be pointed out that he was asked just a few repetitive questions about that case, questions that he'd had several days to review, and before testing was asked repeatedly. Exactly why this polygraph test was given in this fashion is unclear, but the point is, some experts feel he may have had plenty of time to "get comfortable" with the questions, and his body may not have exhibited the stress indicators that determine which answers are true and which are false on such a test. Additionally, Captain Ben Butler in a taped interview with me, said that he still felt that Schaefer was guilty of the Briscolina/Farmer murders.

The following letter is part of that same information "packet" that Schaefer sent to me. In it, he reemphasizes some points he'd made previously, and adds a few more items of note. The letter shows him to be even more aggressive with his accusations about the "corrupt police officials" he so often writes about, and once again, somewhat evasive as to his actual involvement with the Place/Jessup murders. It should also be kept in mind that Schaefer was diagnosed as a *paranoid* schizophrenic, and the paranoia becomes increasingly more evident in his letters, Also, he often speaks of himself in third person, saying "Schaefer did this" and "Schaefer did that," rather than "I did this," an affectation that is common among schizophrenics.

    Dear Mr. Kendrick:
    In this packet I am going to send you
    a transcript (that has never been made
    public; so, the newspapers do not have
    this material) and a very exhaustive
    newspaper story printed by the

Palm Beach Post on May 13, 1973 which
is the basis for many of the stories that
have arisen about me since that time.
I will also send a few other newspaper
stories that point up certain things and a
letter written to Elton Schwarz concerning
those cases recently turned up in St.
Lucie County.

You will be interested to know that I
never saw the Palm Beach Post story of
May 13, 1973 until two years ago. I was
lamenting to my father a remark made to me
by a parole interviewer to the effect that
I would never get out of prison because
I am a suspect in so many murders. I was
honestly puzzled about that and he sent
me the Post story and it was at that time
that I embarked on the saga of attempting
to clear my name. When I read that story,
I understood many of the things said to
me that I never understood before. The
story outrages me, I am so angry when I
read it that I hardly can contain my sense
of perspective. How could those people
be permitted to print such a story about
me? Consider that I was not charged with
anything until the end of May 1973 and the
information was not amended until July 2,
1973. Stone never even tried to go before a
grand jury, he had nothing.

This letter will probably be the first
in several thousand pages of letter
narrative that I will be sending to you
in the future.

We begin with the accusation that "It
may be the greatest crime in the history
of the United States." There are definitely
six dead and twenty-eight may be. The 28
figure is in South Florida alone. And from

the beginning it is important to keep
in mind that we are supposedly dealing
with a SINGLE, depraved cultist who fucks
corpses. You are going to see where that
word SINGLE comes into play much later
and I am prepared to prove that in at
least one case there had to be a number
of people involved, and how the police
(Robert Stone) has gone to great measures
to avoid addressing the reality that I am
innocent and that HE could prove it.. . if
he was inclined to do so.

Moving on, we read that the police say
that Schaefer may be the "most heinous
killer of all time" I have often wondered
how they ever reached such an immediate
conclusion without evidence. When you read
the chronology of events, you see that
it was Brumley and Stone who called the
meeting of all the various jurisdictions
and in the words of Robert Stone:

"At that meeting we advised the
authorities of what WE thought."

Their combined advice, Brumley and
Stone, was that Schaefer was a mass killer
of young girls. More than 30 they said.
Isn't it peculiar to you that those 34
persons were never at any time named?
Oh, some were, but for the most part
the alleged victims of Schaefer are a
figment of the imagination of Brumley and
Stone. The next time I send a packet of
information I will send a copy of the
Rules of the Court 1984 page 550-551
dealing with the permitted statements
by public prosecutors during trials and
investigations. I was able to get it
xeroxed and it is enclosed) Please note
DR 7 107. Trial Publicity. As you can

plainly see, Mr. Stone has in his official capacity violated the Code of Professional Responsibility in every serious manner. Is he going to say that he never realized that there was such a code? Hardly. But why should he go to such extraordinary lengths to violate the code and risk censure? The answer to that mystery is that he had more to fear about what he suspected Schaefer could have revealed about corruption in the Martin County area, a network of corruption that led to the doorstep of the state attorney's office, than he was about a mere bar censure. It was vital for Stone to destroy, irretrievably, the credibility of Schaefer once he learned that Schaefer had been made party to certain highly illegal activities that were going on and had refused to become a part of them. At the time, Lem Brumley and Robert Stone were men above suspicion but on down the road in time it was revealed that at least Brumley, by his own admission in Federal Court, was a major narcotics racketeer. In light of that information, a few things might now be clearer. Returning once again to the statements of Stone:

"There was quite a bit of evidence gathered at the Place and Jessup murder scene."

You see that Stone admits that he was in possession of crime scene EVIDENCE. Not a little evidence, not sketchy evidence, but QUITE A BIT OF EVIDENCE. This is no small matter when you consider that of all that evidence gathered at the crime scene, NOT ONE PIECE OF THAT EVIDENCE WAS LINKED IN ANY WAY TO SCHAEFER. Now that is

pretty heady stuff, is it not? The question
that must arise is, naturally, if the
evidence was not linkable to Schaefer, who
was it linked to?? Well, sir, obviously to
the person who did the crime. But while
that is a solid truth, that the evidence
found at the crime scene was not in any
way connected to Schaefer, why did the
investigator (Brumley) and the state
attorney (Stone), who have a responsibility
to both convict the guilty and vindicate
the innocent, fail to forthrightly come
right out and tell the media that the
evidence was NOT LINKED to Schaefer???Who
were they protecting, and why? But what
is even more important, why was it so
necessary to make Schaefer out to be a
madman? Schaefer knew too much and he
might talk, in fact he did talk, but that
is another story.

Continuing on; Stone said:

"We had some spent cartridges, which we
wanted examined."

It is an undeniable fact, but not a
publicized one, that the two women were
shot in the mouth. This decision was
reached by the findings of the forensic
dentist, Dr. Souviron, and the medical
examiner, Dr. Davis. Their findings are in
their reports. It is also a fact that the
bodies were cut up. But it is very much
in doubt as to when the murders occurred.
Now about these spent cartridges that were
found. Later it was revealed that they
were found at the "scene of the crime",
and we use that term loosely because there
is no evidence to confirm that where the
bodies were located is the actual scene
of the crime. That is a supposition.

Well, Schaefer did have a lot of guns.
He had a gun collection. He was a hunter
and a fisherman and a swamp guide. Guns
were not out of the ordinary for such a
man to possess. All of Schaefer's guns
were confiscated by the police. The spent
cartridges (casings) were tested to see if
they have been fired by a gun in Schaefer's
possession. It was decided by the forensic
scientists who tested the shell casings
against Schaefer's weapons that NONE of
those casings found at the scene of the
crime came from a gun owned by Schaefer.
This hard and undisputable scientific fact
supports the statement of Schaefer that
he did not shoot the women. Who can deny
that? Certainly not Stone.

Stone continues on and says:

"We chopped down a tree at the murder
site with knife marks on it."

Any forensic scientist can tell you that
when a knife cuts wood it leaves indelible
marks as unique as a fingerprint. The cops
cut down the tree and the cops took every
knife they could find out of Schaefer's
house and they tried to match the marks
on the tree with the metallic blades of
the knives. It is significant to know the
FACT that not one of the confiscated knives
matched the marks made in the tree. This
factual evidence substantiates the story
of Schaefer who says that he did not cut
up the women or make the marks on the tree
that was cut down by the police.

Thus far, here is what we have:

1."Quite a bit of Evidence" gathered at
the Place- Jessup murder scene; NOT LINKED
TO SCHAEFER.

2.Cartridge casings recovered at the crime scene, NOT LINKED TO SCHAEFER, after testing all his weapons.

3.A tree with cut marks in it, tested against all knives owned by Schaefer and found to be, NOT LINKED TO SCHAEFER.

Now in any normal police investigation, all of that evidence showing that a man was *not involved* in a crime would be sufficient to send the police looking in different direction because with all of that evidence available, it was damn sure linked to SOMEBODY. But in spite of the evidence of INNOCENCE, Stone and Brumley came hard on at Schaefer with a relentless pursuit. Now let us back up and take a look at the chain of events that brought Stone and Brumley into the picture to begin with.

April 1, 1973:Two bodies are found. (Both Jane Doe)

"After the bodies were found, I followed the case closely, but did not want to interfere with St. Lucie County Sheriff, Lanie Norvell."

April 2, 1973:Stone:"I called the next day to volunteer help."

April 4, 1973:Stone:"Wednesday of that week, it was April 4, I was called by the sheriff's department about the legality of obtaining search warrants."

April 5, 1973:Stone: "Thursday, we met with the St, Lucie County sheriff and requested all authorities with interest in the case to attend."

April 6, 1973:Stone: "Friday we met with Broward, St. Lucie and Martin counties sheriffs' investigators and my chief investigator, Lem Brumley."

April 6, 1973:Stone: "I assigned Mr.
Brumley to coordinate the case. He has a
tremendous amount of experience and he
could assist and advise."

Let's take a look at the jurisdiction
of this thing. The two unidentified bodies
were found in the jurisdiction of the
county sheriff, Lanie Norvell. Under normal
circumstances, it would not be unusual
for a representative of the sheriff's
department to call on a representative
from the office of the state attorney to
stand in on the investigation of the crime
scene. Apparently, this normal course
of events was not followed. The Sheriff
did not invite Stone to come in on the
investigation, Stone called the Sheriff and
invited himself to come in on it. Not by
any means a normal procedure.

By April 6, 1973 Robert Stone and
Lem Brumley had placed themselves into
a position where they would, in the
words of Robert Stone, "coordinate the
case". At this point in time the search
warrants had not been issued and served
and the searches conducted, nor had, I
believe, the bodies of Place and Jessup
been identified. Stone was, at the time
he invited himself and Brumley into the
position of coordinators of the case, not
in a position to know who the dead persons
found on April 1, 1973 actually were.

What reason did Stone have for calling
in the Sheriff department of Martin County?
The alleged murders had taken place in
St. Lucie County and there was no reason
at all to even confer with Martin County
police, particularly when at the time it
was not known who those bodies were. It

would certainly appear from the sequence
of time and events that Robert Stone
and Lem Brumley knew just a little bit
more than everyone else. But then, it
is important to remember that Robert
Stone and Lem Brumley were, at that time,
persons above reproach in the community.
They were also the persons holding the
vastest amount of prosecutorial power and,
naturally, the sheriffs and other police
departments deferred to them when they
made "suggestions".

On April 6, 1973, Robert Stone made
the statements: "Based on my knowledge
and intuition; I feel that this may be
the biggest crime in history of the
United States."

Robert Stone's most prophetic words
were uttered later: "I may be proven
wrong later."

Schaefer has been in the process of
proving himself innocent for several
years; the past three in deadly earnest.

Moving right along, we come to the
famous "list" of victims that was
published by the Palm Beach Post and it is
interesting to note that no other listing
of "Schaefer victims" has been published
until that list published by the Stuart
News in 1981. That list, revised as it was,
was considerably different than the one
published in the Post.

Another oddity that crops up is the
fact that nowhere does anyone come out
and say that Schaefer was "hostile"
toward females in general or any female
in particular. On the contrary, just the
opposite seems to be the case. Schaefer
had many good relationships with various

women; none of who could say anything bad about him or his conduct. Schaefer does not fit the stereotypical "mass killer" in that many of the common traits of "serial murders" are not attributable to him. Schaefer certainly could not be described as a "loner" or in any unusual way different from his peers. It is noteworthy that Schaefer possessed the skill and dedication while in high school to become a golfer of such high standards that he was granted an athletic scholarship for golf to Broward Community College. Any person who has ever tried his or her hand at golf will concede that one does not become a player of excellence without thousands of hours of hard work and extreme dedication.

Another most outstanding thing, when all things are considered, is that Schaefer PASSED a polygraph test administered by Carl Lord of the Broward county sheriff's department to determine pre-employment misbehavior. This test was administered in 1971. Had Schaefer been killing all of these women, and many were alleged to have been murdered before 1971, there would have been some significant indication of that hidden criminal activity on the polygrams of Carl Lord. It is vitally significant that no such indication of major untruthfulness occurred. Schaefer PASSED the Broward county exam and the FACT that he did is largely hushed up by the police. It is also significant that Schaefer passed a Wackenhut Corporation polygraph examination when he applied and worked for that security agency in 1969. Had Schaefer been having a crime spree, something would have shown up in an obvious way on that test. Yet nothing was indicated as being amiss and Schaefer was hired and had a good employment record.

One of the most bizarre twists in the case comes when Schaefer, after being accused of being involved in the deaths of Leigh Hainline and Carmen Hallock, told investigators that he indeed did have knowledge of those two crimes. Schaefer pointed the finger at Vietnam veteran and small-time drug dealer, John "Jack" Dolan who had admitted to Schaefer on several different occasions that he had killed both Leigh Hainline and Carmen Hallock. This admission was so bizarre that he was given a polygraph-voice stress analysis test by the Public Defender, Elton Schwarz, in 1973. Schaefer passed that test. Schwarz then went and found John Dolan and taped a conversation with Jack Dolan asking him if he had made such admissions to Schaefer. Analysis of the tape made showed that Dolan was lying when he denied making those admissions. Dolan was the lover of Carmen Hallock and, at one time, the roommate of Schaefer. The gold crowns that were found in the desk, that reportedly had been in Dolan's portion of the house, were supposedly stolen from the home of Carmen Hallock by Dolan. While this evidence was turned over to coordinator Brumley, no action was ever taken to question Dolan....

There are many other areas that we must get into, but time is short today.

1. You will learn that the name "Jerry Sheppard" was invented by the mother of

Susan Place. It comes out, when the woman is under an oath, that *she* was the one to come up with the name Jerry Sheppard.

2. You will also learn that the original license number reported to the police by Mrs. Place, from the car she saw in her driveway, was NOT Schaefer's license number. It was the license number of a car in Pinellas County.

3. It will be revealed that Susan Place was working as a confidential informant for the Fort Lauderdale police and HER MOTHER KNEW IT. This information was completely suppressed at the trial and in the press.

4. Likewise it was suppressed that Susan Place and Georgia Jessup had been picked up in West Palm Beach only a week before they were last seen on September 27, 1972.It was never revealed by the police what they were doing in that area, but it can be reasoned that they were up there gathering intelligence on incoming shipments of drugs along the southern coast of Martin County. It is an underworld "signature" to shoot a confidential informant in the mouth.

5. Leigh Hainline, Carmen Hallock were both admittedly into some type of drug informant activity. They both made some type of statements to friends that they were doing this. Both were associated with Dolan, a known drug pusher, and both 'disappeared' after associations with him. In fact, Leigh Hainline approached Schaefer in August 1969 and asked him to drive her to the Miami airport. Hainline told Schaefer that she had to leave the area because she was in fear for her life.

Lastly, we see an article carried by the Palm Beach Post where Stone revises his estimation that the number of "Schaefer victims" is now nine or ten. That story was printed in 1977.

In one swoop his accusations drop from 34 to 10. But for a period from 1973 until 1977 that man knowingly allowed the entire nation to believe his earlier reports that Schaefer was responsible for the deaths of up to 34 persons. To me, and to any reasonable and decent person, the fact that a government agent would place such a monstrous lie on a citizen is enough to evoke tremendous anger and contempt. Yet the public seems not to care. It's sad. What must a man do to prove that he was framed? Worse, once the proof is in, what must a man do to sever the accusation of "mad killer" and secure his release from a prison where he had no business being in the first place?

Out of time today. Library closing. More tomorrow

NEXT DAY:

The library is going to be closed most of this coming week, so I will not have much time to work in here with a typing machine.

Jumping ahead for a moment I will ask you to look at the attached clipping from the Saint Petersburg Times run on May 15, 1973 that claims, "EX DEPUTY Is Linked to 7 Murders." We can discuss other parts in detail later but at this time I want you to direct your attention to the underscored portion that says:

"He said (Stone) formal charges to be presented to a grand jury awaited final reports from two laboratories investigating evidence."

This critical portion of this statement is twofold:

1. It shows that Stone recognized the necessity to proceed before a grand jury and,

2. It shows that evidence that was being forensically tested by an outside agencie(s) FBI & FDLE came back showing that Schaefer had nothing to do with the crime scene.

It is a fact that is undisputable that the submitted evidence did NOT implicate Schaefer. The upshot of that fact is that Stone was left with absolutely NOTHING tangible that he could present to a grand jury, and in order to overcome this lack of evidence Stone filed the information using the incorrect rationalization that if he did not ask for the death penalty that he did not need to proceed by grand jury indictment. Of course, every court in Florida has held that theory to be legally invalid, and I can send you proof of that letter.

The important thing to know here is that Stone KNEW that he had to present his case to the grand jury but when evidence cleared Schaefer of any implication in the crimes, he had nothing to proceed with. This is the fact. That is the truth.

Returning to the article on May 13, 1973, I want to comment about the alleged "grave". The fact is that nothing having anything to do with those two women were found in that hole. Look at that little

chart. There is a "tree girls tied to"
marked and that is next to the grave. The
fact is that there is no evidence that
ANYONE was ever tied to that tree, much
less those two girls. There was a TREE
AND A HOLE IN THE GROUND and, to the best
of my recollection and belief, there were
never any SKULLS found anywhere. That
the skulls were missing was one of the
major flaps surrounding the whole affair.
What I am trying to tell you is that what
was printed, released by Lem Brumley and
Robert Stone concerning the crime scene,
was *completely* without basis in FACT. Now,
of course, you would ask what was the
motive in making such a completely false
representation to the public???

Brumley and Stone used the incident
with Trotter and Wells, that did occur in
July of 1972, as a springboard to accuse
Schaefer of the murders of Place and
Jessup. That the two incidents were in
truth factually dissimilar, completely,
did not stop Stone/ Brumley from making
much use of it. I will get into the
Trotter/ Wells thing on another day and
when you get the story you will see that
it is plausible and rational and sensible—
though wrong on my part to have done it—
but understandable. They used the first
incident, that Schaefer admitted to, to
accuse him of the murders, which Schaefer
denied complicity in.

I will stop here due to lack of time;
this ending my commentary on the May 13,
1973 article. There is a lot more to go
into, but I will wait and get your letter,
I am sure you have questions, before I go
off into other areas.

In February of 1983 I learned that there was a new TV show to go on the air called LIE DETECTOR. I was told of this show by a person who thought that I could prove my innocence by appearing on the show. I called the producers of the show and after some discussion they made a decision to give me the test and put me on the show; everything was set up for this to happen. I suggested that they also interview Stone so he could tell the nation what a murderous rotten killer I was because that would look real good when I passed the test. They agreed that this was a good idea and they called him and asked him to appear on the show and denounce me in front of the nation. Stone flatly refused to go on the program despite the assurances of the program directors that he would have more than equal time to tell the nation his side of the controversy. The producers called Stone on a number of different occasions and finally told him that I, Schaefer, would appear on the show whether he would or not.

A week later permission from the D.O.C. needed for Mr. Ed Gelb to come into the prison to give me the polygraph test was denied without comment. Schaefer and the producers of the show were undeterred because both were determined to reveal to the nation this obvious, and increasingly more and more obvious, lack of justice in Florida. Schaefer made an agreement with a polygraph examiner and police authorities from Plantation Police Department who

came to take a polygraph test concerning
the Briscolina/Farmer case, a murder
the police were convinced Schaefer
committed. When the men arrived to give
the test, they had absolutely no difficulty
in getting in to administer the test,
because they were a police agency making
the application. The following transcript
was made, and that transcript contained
the agreement that the POLYGRAMS from
the tests given, whether detrimental to
Schaefer or to his benefit, would be sent
to the producers of

LIE DETECTOR for their use and
examination. Another part of the agreement
was to be that the test would be given,
and determination made as to whether
the truth was being told or whether the
polygrams indicated deception. If the test
was deemed to be "inconclusive" then it
would be given again until some conclusive
results could be made.

As you can read in the transcript, this
was the understood agreement. Particularly
pertinent parts are marked.

What happened is this: The test was
given. Schaefer passed the test. The test
showed that Schaefer was not responsible
for the deaths of Briscolina and Farmer.
The police refused, after the test
came in favorable to Schaefer, to send
the polygrams out to Ed Gelb or to the
producers of Lie Detector. A letter was
sent to Schaefer stating that the test was
"inconclusive" but that was not truthful.
The test did indicate that Schaefer was
innocent of those murders that he had
been repeatedly accused of. The police
never came back to either interview or

re-test Schaefer as was provided for in
the agreement should the test be deemed
inconclusive.

You may have ample proof before you
that the police cannot be trusted to keep
their agreements; just one more thing that
shows that they have framed me in the
truest sense of the word.

As soon as I am able to get some more
money, I will have more copies run off of
other articles and things of interest
to you. Try to come up here as soon
as possible, and while you may think
this a laughable request, I would like
your written assurance that you are not
intending to give any of this material
to the police, nor are you acting as
their agents, nor will you discuss our
correspondence with them. Police trickery
is not unheard of with me and I am nervous
about it. So, please, do assure me that
you are not going to be giving all of this
information to them.

Thank you,
Gerard J. Schaefer, Jr.

Within this letter, there are several items that should be clarified.

Schaefer has pointed out that Robert Stone "violated the code of Professional Responsibility in every serious manner." This may, in fact, be partially true. The book of codes for attorneys, that includes strict guidelines for professional responsibility, does state in section DR 7 107, under "Trial Publicity," certain criteria which a lawyer, for defense or prosecution must follow. In particular the code says: "A lawyer . . . from the time of the filing of a complaint, information, indictment (etc.)... shall not make or participate in making an extrajudicial statement that a reasonable person would expect to be disseminated by means of public communication and that relates to (in order of possible violation):

1. The character (reputation, etc.) of the accused . . .

2. Any opinion as to the guilt or innocence of the accused . . .

3. The performance or results of any examinations . . .

4. The existence or contents of any confession, admission, or statement by the accused . . . (Schaefer's manuscripts might be construed as a confession.)

There are other items which, with a subjective interpretation of the code might also be said to have been violated. To what degree, or if they are in violation at all, would be for a judge to determine, which in this case, has not happened.

Another item is the connection between the state attorney's office (Stone's) and' "major narcotics racketeering." While it is true that Lem Brumley was found to be involved in drug trafficking in 1980, along with racketeer Donald Raulerson, Stone himself was cleared by the FBI. The FBI investigated Stone for almost a year, looking into his past, (going back about ten years) and giving him a "clean slate." However, Schaefer never came forth with any information implicating wrongdoing by Lem Brumley, or any other official in the 19th Judicial Circuit, until years later, after it received mass media attention. Schaefer once earlier mentioned "having knowledge about illegal" activities, in a letter written in 1975, to Virginia Snyder. Ms. Snyder was then a reporter interested in Schaefer's story for a possible book; she now runs a private investigator company.

Schaefer had asked Snyder: "What would an editor pay for these stories:

1. Inside information on white slavery in this county?

2. International drug smuggling?" (But he did not mention any reference to the authorities of the 19th Judicial Circuit.)

He also mentions a "satanic cult and human sacrifice in South Florida," and that he knew who killed Leigh Hainline and Carmen Hallock. Ms. Snyder did not pursue the project.

So, his earliest accusation against Stone and the authorities in his jurisdiction would have to be around 1980. But what is interesting, is that several people involved in the illegal drug trade in that same area were murdered, including Donald Raulerson's brother. Some of those murders were mutilation-type murders similar to the Place/Jessup killings, and after Schaefer's incarceration.

Further in the letter, Schaefer questions why Stone called in another sheriff's department from another county. The fact is, he did not. Calvin Wiggins, upon being told about the discovery of the bodies by Jesse and Henderson Holley, wrongly called in the Martin County Sheriff's Department, thinking it was in their jurisdiction.

Another item in the letter, is Schaefer's accusations concerning John Dolan. Now, Schwarz, being Schaefer's attorney, did question Dolan, but did not obtain any evidence of Dolan's involvement. Stone did not question Dolan, nor did any other authority involved with this case. So, we only have Schaefer's accusation, with nothing on record to back it up. I did question Schaefer, and in a taped interview asked, "Why would a man with aspirations of becoming a police officer or a schoolteacher (Schaefer) not go to the authorities and tell them his roommate (Dolan) had admitted to murdering two girls, one of which had been a close friend?"

After some hesitation, Schaefer said that he was afraid Dolan would kill him. Once again, the accusation is unsubstantiated, and its believability I leave to the reader of this book's discretion.

Finally, Schaefer also brings up the license tag number reported by Mrs. Place. The fact is, Mrs. Place wrote down the correct number, but the police wrongly traced it to a car that was not Schaefer's, either by a "computer foul-up," or a mistake in copying down the information. The number that Mrs. Place wrote down was the same as Schaefer's tag number. Also, Schaefer says that Mrs. Place knew Susan was "a confidential informant for the Ft. Lauderdale police." Mrs. Place still denies this vehemently.

As with most of Schaefer's information, it seemed that he persistently tried to direct guilt away from himself by putting guilt, however unrelated, on others involved with his case. In all his letters, he never showed me any concrete information that would help substantiate his alibi on September 27, 1972. When we finally met in person at Florida State Prison, he told me what he could remember of what happened that night.

After leaving his mother's house, he drove up the interstate and got off at the Pompano exit and stopped to see a friend that worked at Lerner's, a women's fashion shop. His friend was not there. He talked to a manager but does not remember her name. He said he then drove up A1A, until he pulled into an Italian restaurant that was under renovation and only served pizza. This was in Deerfield. He did not remember the name of the restaurant, either. He said a "cop show was on, probably Mannix." He thought this was around 9:00 p.m. He bought a pizza and went next door to a convenience store for a Pepsi. He then drove home to Stuart.

In the course of my investigation, I could not find this "Italian restaurant" in Deerfield on A1A. I could not find anybody that could remember the events of September 27, 1973, much less anyone that looked like Gerard

Schaefer, along that same route. Of course, many years had passed, which did not help, but in any case, his alibi still cannot be validated. Finally, he inasmuch, admitted to being at the Place house, though he does not confess to killing the girls.

* * *

In keeping with his manner of defending himself, Schaefer often expounds upon his virtues, again unrelated to his murder charges. These "virtues" include his cooperation with several governmental agencies, that helped to convict, (or at least bring to trial) a few various offenders of felony crimes.

One such case involved a fellow jail mate, whom Schaefer overheard bragging about killing a woman during a robbery. When offered better accommodations at a more comfortable correctional institute, Schaefer agreed to testify for the state against this prisoner, a man named Darren. Schaefer says the state was not satisfied with his testimony; "it was not incriminating enough," and he was sent back to Florida State Prison. While there, Darren's homosexual lover made an attempt on Schaefer's life. It was in February, and cold, so Schaefer was wearing a thick jacket. Darren's lover leaped out of the shadows and stabbed him, but the jacket prevented the knife from inflicting any lethal wounds. He did sustain a laceration on his abdomen; and was then sent to a different correctional institute.

Schaefer "helped out" with another case that is particularly interesting because it was investigated by Jay Howell, who worked with United States Senator Paula Hawkins. It is a bizarre case, not only because the offense is that of child pornography, but because of the complicated machinery that allowed Mervyn Eric Cross to operate this "kiddie porn" ring from within the walls of Avon Park Correctional Institute (APCI).

Schaefer had gotten his wish, he had been transferred to a comfortable, minimum security prison (APCI) and was allowed the use of a rather extensive library, copy machines, typewriters, and most importantly, a phone. While at APCI, Schaefer met and befriended Eric Cross, a fellow inmate who had been convicted of molesting children in at least four countries. His prison report listed him as a "multinational sex offender," and he was known among inmates and throughout Europe as the "King of Porn." What drew the two men together is unclear. Schaefer says that he deliberately went out of his way to befriend Cross, so that a Senate Subcommittee on Labor and Human Resources could "nail" Cross, using Schaefer to get information on him. Schaefer's opponents argue that Schaefer knew Cross first, that their common bond was the sexual exploitation of children, and that Schaefer, realizing a way to possibly get a parole deal, contacted Paula Hawkins and agreed to work with her subcommittee, only when he thought it would be beneficial to him. Whichever the case, Schaefer did help the subcommittee's investigation, and did not receive any parole deal. The following letter, written by an investigator for the Senate Subcommittee, Jay Howell, confirms Schaefer's working relationship with that office . . .

In the spring of 1983, I was serving as investigations counsel for the Senate Committee on Labor and Human Resources in Washington, D.C. Prior to that time, the Labor Committee's Subcommittee on Investigations and General Oversight had conducted a series of inquiries concerning child victimization and child pornography nationwide. The Subcommittee had been asked to investigate the status of Eric Mervyn Cross, an inmate at the Avon Park Correctional Institute.

In the course of our inquiry, we were contacted by Gerard J. Schaefer who was himself an inmate at the Avon Park Correctional Institute. Mr. Schaefer offered his assistance in developing information about the activities of Mr. Cross and an alleged child pornography operation which was being conducted from inside the institution. As the following description indicates, Mr. Schaefer provided the Committee information which initiated several investigations by law enforcement agencies in different parts of the United States. At the time of our initial contact with Mr. Schaefer, only one promise was made to him. We indicated that we would accurately and fully disclose the nature of Mr. Schaefer's assistance to the Committee

to any individuals or institutions that
he requested. In accordance with that
promise, I am now forwarding you this
information because Mr. Schaefer has
requested that we share a description of
these events with your office and the office
of Mr. G. S. Fortner, the Superintendent of
the Avon Park Correctional Institution.

Mr. Schaefer provided critical
information to the investigation conducted
by the United States Senate Subcommittee
on Labor and Human Resources. In the late
spring of 1983 this information was turned
over to a host of law enforcement agencies
from Florida as well as Seattle, and
Los Angeles, California. The information
relayed by our office to the authorities
in Los Angeles and Seattle initiated an
investigation which resulted in the arrest
and conviction of at least two individuals
and which also resulted in the seizure
of thousands of pictures of children in
nude or pornographic poses. Eventually,
the information from this investigation
led to the seizure of sexually explicit
material in four states. The initial
information which Mr. Schaefer had given
to the Committee was verified by subsequent
investigations.

Mr. Schaefer had indicated to the
Committee that certain specific photographs
of school children from the State of
Florida would be found in the possession
of a particular individual in Seattle,
Washington. Subsequent arrest and search
warrants served in Seattle, indicated
that this information was in fact true.
As a result of the information provided
by Mr. Schaefer, Seattle authorities were

able to seize and take out of circulation
several nude pictures of Florida school
children. A detailed description of
searches conducted, or arrests made would
show that, as this investigation grew
and expanded to different parts of the
United States, at least four individuals
have been charged or convicted of
activities related to these transactions.
In addition, thousands of pictures and
videotapes involving children were seized
in such locations as Seattle, Albuquerque,
Alexandria, Virginia and Florida. In
the course of our extensive dealings
with Mr. Schaefer, we did not receive
any information from him that we later
determined to be false or misleading.

The Committee at no time undertook an
inquiry into the circumstances surrounding
Mr. Schaefer's convictions which resulted
in his incarceration at the Avon Park
Correctional Institute. Of course, we can
make no comment upon those facts. As I
indicated at the start of this letter, we
did promise Mr. Schaefer that we would
at any future date, represent honestly
and accurately the extent and nature of
his participation in the investigations
concerning child pornography and mail
fraud allegations. If there are any
additional questions regarding the nature
of Mr. Schaefer's assistance to the
Committee on Labor and Human Resources,
please contact me at (202) 634-9827.

Sincerely,
Jay Howell

To get the whole story, one must look at Schaefer's involvement in the case, and his relationship with Cross.

When Cross came to Avon Park Correctional Institute (where Schaefer, finally, took up residence) he arrived with a long history of child molesting. His records included a memo from a former prison counselor that read, "Subject has proven himself to be a super con man, very intelligent, with an ongoing mental problem concerning young females. In my estimation, this makes him a very dangerous person indeed, for the potential harm he has already done and for the amount he could inflict in the future on young females."

Apparently, this warning was not taken very seriously. Almost immediately Cross began his "operations." Under the name of Viewfinders, Inc., a corporation he'd set up as a would-be talent search agency, Cross began to solicit, by mail, would-be models or actresses for "legitimate" TV or ad work. All of his "clients" were children. The system worked like this: Cross convinced a real talent agency, the Dott Burns Talent Agency in Tampa, that he was a British movie producer. He was making a film, to be titled "Susan's Magic Carpet", and he needed many new faces to star in the movies. Specifically, he needed girls, 8 to 12 years old to try out for the lead role. However, Cross could only contact Burns through the mail. He needed an outside phone through which he could conduct his business. This is when he met Schaefer.

Cross told Schaefer about "Viewfinders, Inc." He told him there was money to be made, photographing children for "an educational series. "But first, they needed a phone. At that time Schaefer's father, a St. Petersburg, Florida, resident, was visiting Schaefer regularly. Schaefer introduced Cross to his father and told them of their "business" plans. Mr. Schaefer, Sr., was asked to put in a conference line, so that he could accept collect calls, then redial any number Cross wanted, including the prison, and Cross could call him and accomplish the reverse. Mr. Schaefer, Sr. would not have to sit by the phone all day, because Cross would have his own secretary. The "secretary" was Rutskana Diwan, a pen pal of Gerard Schaefer's from Tanzania, who needed a job and a place to stay in the United States. She obtained both at the home of Mr. Schaefer, Sr., who let her stay in the vacant room downstairs at his house.

Cross would call Diwan collect, she would redial a number of his choice, then say, "Wait a minute, I have Mr. Cross on the line," and forward his call to whomever he needed to talk to. He often told people he was on the run at an airport and couldn't be called back right away. People accepted this or could call his office number (Diwan) and leave a message. It was ingenious, though simple, and it worked. Cross began conversations with Dott Burns. He slowly gained her confidence and she began sending him photo composites of the potential "stars." Finally, Cross told Burns, that he'd selected 20 semi-finalists for the movie. However, there was one drawback, he explained. Because it was to be a "European film with an international appeal", there would be some nudity scenes shot. "Swedish sauna baths, Japanese girls diving for pearls, and Brazilian Indian fertility rites," were some of the scenes, and he needed young girls who could pose nude, naturally and comfortably in front of the camera. Could he get some test shots? Surprisingly, he could.

It seemed, where many parents were concerned, if a legitimate talent agency wanted their children to pose nude for an international movie, it was perfectly okay.

Cross did not stop with the Tampa business. He began writing to several countries, Greece, Australia; and in the Philippines he contacted an old friend, a woman who could procure photos of many young Filipino girls, nude. From these photos, he selected girls he wanted hard-core photos taken of and he directed his wishes by code. If he wrote saying he wanted a girl "dancing in the fountain," it really meant nude. If he wrote "irrigation ditch," it meant he wanted photos of a girl urinating.

Schaefer's father swore that he knew nothing of the true nature of Cross' business. However, when phone bills began to roll in, in the amount of $200.00, then $400.00, he began to get suspicious. Finally, a bill came from the long-distance phone company, MCI, for over $2,000, and Cross would not pay it. Mr. Schaefer, Sr., had the conference line removed. It was about this time that someone phoned Jay Howell in Senator Paula Hawkins' office and "suggested" Cross was up to something at APCI. Jay Howell would not tell the identity of the caller, but it can be surmised that it was either Gerard Schaefer, protecting his father's financial interests, or his father himself. It is doubtful that Rutskana Diwan would have called, she needed the job, and no one else knew of the scheme.

The results of the intervention of Mr. Howell produced arrests in Seattle, Washington and Alexandria, Virginia, where just two of Cross' accomplices lived and distributed photographs of child pornography. It is easy to speculate that given more time, Cross could have set up an even larger international "kiddie porn" ring, exploiting hundreds, if not thousands, of unfortunate children.

The question that remains is, was Schaefer legitimately working with Cross in an attempt to set him up for a bust, to put a feather in his own cap? Or did he just bail out of the child exploitation deal with Cross, because his father had been taken advantage of? Only Schaefer knew for sure.

* * *

In yet another attempt to put himself in a more favorable light, Gerard Schaefer offers the David McCain story.

McCain was a former Florida Supreme Court Justice who was indicted for drug smuggling charges in 1983. After arranging to be set free on federal and state bonds totaling more than one million dollars, McCain skipped out. The authorities interested in his recovery believed McCain to be hiding out in the Bahamas, Schaefer maintained that he knew where McCain was, from having met some of McCain's associates in prison. Schaefer wanted a deal: for the delivery of McCain and two other unnamed fugitives, Schaefer would be given Federal Witness protection and a release from prison. No one accepted his offer, and in November 1986, McCain died of cancer; not in the Bahamas, but in Jacksonville, Florida where he'd been living with relatives since 1983. McCain had originally come from Ft. Pierce, Florida, and practiced law in the 19th Judicial Circuit, as did Robert Stone.

McCain had been appointed to the State Supreme Court by Governor Claude Kirk in 1970. In 1975 he resigned to avoid impeachment from allegations that he'd helped friends in court cases by exerting pressure on lower court judges and for mishandling campaign funds. In 1978, the same court he had formerly presided over, ruled to disbar him. At that time, he was practicing law in Miami. The disbarment was quite a shock to the former Florida Supreme Court Justice, and to the local news media. McCain was scandalized.

A few years passed and then in October of 1982, McCain was arrested for conspiracy to smuggle marijuana from Colombia to Cameron Parish, Louisiana. In his years away from the judicial system, McCain had found a new line of work. In 1983, the indictment came down, charging McCain and forty-three other people with scheming to smuggle drugs into Everglades City, Florida. Authorities investigating McCain said he'd been involved in the drug business since 1980.

Schaefer maintains that the reason McCain was able to successfully traffic drugs for three years, and then escape prosecution for another three years, is because he was another crony of Robert Stone's. He says that he had approached Stone's office with information about McCain's whereabouts and that Stone turned a deaf ear to his claims. He added that he managed to interest the Assistant State Attorney Rick MacIlwain with that same information, but MacIlwain was told by Robert Stone to "lay off" and convinced him that Schaefer was a mad man.

Schaefer tried to convince the public of the sincerity of his knowledge through media attention he was provided in the comfortable, minimum security prison in Avon Park, Florida. Schaefer had always been able to get media attention since his incarceration in 1973, but in 1985 he was getting even more. While in Avon Park Correctional Institute, Schaefer had access to a phone (from which he often called this author to give me information), to a copier and unlimited mailing rights. In addition to numerous articles about Schaefer's case appearing in various publications throughout the state, Schaefer began a letter writing campaign that claimed he was framed by Stone, accused of the Place/Jessup murders in order to protect Stone and his "cronies" (McCain and Raulerson) drug operations. He added that Elton Schwarz was guilty, too, of inadequate defense, because he planned to marry Teresa Schaefer before the trial was over. In short, he was disparaging everyone associated with his case, and the newspapers were listening.

In his defense, Stone denied all charges and said: "He's a madman, and if he claims I'm trying to keep him in prison, he's right. But it has nothing to do with conspiracies. If he got out, it'd be like signing people's death warrants.

"He has nothing better to do than sit in that prison all day and read through trial transcripts and the newspaper articles, trying to punch holes in them. And he's smart. He knows what's going on out here and what will sound good. But he's a murderer and if he were let loose, he would kill again."

Schwarz gave a rebuttal, too, saying:

"If he thinks I didn't do everything I could to protect him, he should seek legal relief by saying I gave ineffective counsel. He's never done that. Instead, he's going to the media, where Bob (Stone) and I can respond but we can't cross-examine him. And where we can't use much of the evidence we have."

Schwarz was particularly angered by Schaefer's accusations that claimed that he and Teresa Schaefer were "romantically involved" during the trial. Schaefer sent letters that stated those accusations (along with accusations about Stone) to dozens of private lawyers, state attorneys, and newspapers throughout Florida. Finally, on August 15th, 1985, Schaefer sent a letter to the Florida Supreme Court claiming Schwarz was guilty of misconduct because:

1. He had an illicit sexual affair with my wife during his representation of me.

2. He violated the attorney-client privilege by opening his files to the media.

3. He revealed Schaefer's cooperation with law enforcement agencies in tracking down fugitive narcotics traffickers.

Schwarz rebutted this by saying:

"I think all this is more of an attempt to provide embarrassment to me, my wife, and the public defender's office . . ."

Suddenly, in late August of 1985, after months of bombarding the media with his accusing letters, Schaefer was sent back to the maximum-security prison (Florida State Prison) in Stark, Florida. The reason? Richard Hamm, the superintendent at APCI, said Schaefer was transferred for "general security reasons." Then, the Florida Department of Law Enforcement (FDLE) said that "Schaefer was planning to escape with another prisoner from Avon Park . . . and Schaefer was going to kill (some) people." Tom Roper, the FDLE agent who handled the investigation said that Schaefer had "plotted to kill Public Defender Elton Schwarz and his wife Teresa, State Attorney Robert Stone, and Chief Circuit Judge C. Pfeiffer Trowbridge.

Trowbridge commented:

"I'm not panicky. I've always said that judges fear people in divorce cases more than they do criminals."

The Florida Department of Law Enforcement provided no further information and would not show this writer any information that substantiated their allegations of Schaefer's "escape plot." Tom Roper was "not in" and never returned my phone calls.

In September of 1985, after trying for almost two years to obtain permission to interview Schaefer in person, I was finally allowed to meet with him. I was told I could only have about one hour, but there was a mix-up when I arrived at the prison, and they believed me to be his attorney. I did not clarify their mistake and in the end, I was able to obtain several hours' worth of taped interviews with the infamous "killer cop."

Admittedly, I was intimidated, though we'd been corresponding through the mail for about two years. I was no more comfortable meeting with this accused murderer, than if I were meeting Jack the Ripper, himself. My fears were alleviated though when they brought the man into the cramped, pale, citrus-colored room, where we'd be locked in, alone and without guards for the next several hours.

Schaefer was an overweight, doughy-looking fellow with nerd-like black horn-rimmed glasses, slumped shoulders, and an expression that looked as though he would jump ten feet high if I were to suddenly clap my hands together. He was slovenly-attired, more so than one would expect even a prisoner to be, and he spoke in a boyish voice that belied his thirty-nine years. We'd spoken on the phone before, but I still was not prepared for this anachronism, this man accused of horrific mutilation-type murders who now stood grinning and blushing like a schoolboy who'd been caught stealing cookies.

As we spoke, I observed his facial expressions go through a variety of changes, sometimes complete mood swings, where one moment he'd be expressing his anger and frustration at being

"wrongly accused," and the next he'd be giggling about the absurdity of it all. It was as if his face was made of putty and could practically transform his appearance, something I later read Ted Bundy was able to do as well. I began to get a feel for Schaefer, if you will, and I tried to put myself into the position of a young, confused, teenage girl—and that is when I scared myself.

I almost understand, knowing how gullible some young girls are, where this emotional chameleon could gain the confidence of a troubled person who was looking for a listener, a problem solver, perhaps in the form of an older more experienced person. But knowing what I knew, I could also imagine him allowing me that confidence in him, as we drove off onto a bumpy dirt road, drinking beer, laughing as he got out of the car and opened the trunk. Then he would not be laughing anymore. He'd still be grinning, incessantly, as he 'd force me to put the noose around my neck at gun point and hang me for a while, not letting me die yet, but playing with me, as a cat would with a near-dead mouse. Then, when the play was almost all gone, he would take out his heavy-bladed hunting knife and with the sound a steak makes when dropped on a tile floor, the blade would dig into my spinal cord. When I screamed, he would shoot me in the mouth, aiming madly for where the irritating sound was coming from, and blow the lower jaw away from my face.

And, if by some perverse rule of nature my brain and heart still kept me alive and struggling, then the blade would flash again, perhaps severing my arm, or my legs below the knees, so that if I were, somehow, still living, I would be reduced to a quivering, bleeding torso with eyes, and I could watch him do the same to my friend, who would be by now staring, catatonic, at the writhing mass of flesh that used to be her friend. Dark thoughts can emerge when one immerses oneself into the study of such a monster and, admittedly, they have stuck in my mind since.

I interviewed Schaefer as professionally, as competently as I could while these visions flashed sporadically in my mind. I was attentive. I wanted the truth if it was at all possible for him to tell even one small part of it, but I was also wary and on guard. They'd locked the two of us in a tiny, soundproof room (so no one could hear our attorney-client privileged conversation), and though he was handcuffed and appeared as menacing as Fred Flintstone, I realized others had mistaken his harmlessness, too. Knowing his propensity for publicity, was it too much to imagine he might make a move on my life? Wouldn't that get him the limelight he sought so fervently? Sure, he would deny he killed me, another prisoner snuck in and strangled me, knocking him unconscious first and . . . I let my imagination run wild thinking about the stories Schaefer had the potential to fabricate and I knew stranger things could happen and I was prepared. I had already picked out a soft spot on the side of his head, on the temple, where if I were put in a life-or-death situation, I might, with some difficulty in an attempt to save myself, force a sharpened No. 2 pencil into his brain.

I also knew at that point I'd been working on this project too long.

I conducted our interview and tried to glean as much hard evidence and truth out of it that I could. The words of Harry Crews echoed in my mind, "He's so decidedly full of shit, anything he tells you will be a lie . . ." But I tried to maintain the reporter's non-biased view as I had done throughout my entire investigation of the case. I listened intently for anything new he might tell me that he had not told me in our letters and phone conversations for the past two years. Nothing much was new.

He repeatedly went over the incident with the Trotter and Wells girls. It was a mistake, he maintained. A case of bad judgement. He still maintained that that event did not make him a killer, any more than did his bizarre, "fictional" writings, or having a "few" pieces of girl's jewelry. Robert Stone and his "cronies" had killed all these girls, he said, because he was going to blow the whistle on them. But he could not give me any hard evidence; prison officials had raided his room and stolen it. He said he had never been connected to the crime scene, his defense attorney would have played that up more, if he wasn't romancing his wife. He knew who was smuggling drugs in and out of Ft. Pierce, who paid off Stone to look the other way. He knew where to find fugitive Justice David McCain. He believed John

Dolan killed Carmen Hallock and Leigh Hainline, but no one would listen to him. He said he knew of white slavery rings being operated in the US and of course, he was a friend to Senator Paula Hawkins—after all he'd spearheaded the investigations that broke up an international "kiddie porn" ring at APCI.

He was the innocent victim, he said, of the biggest conspiracy of all time.

Schaefer did convince me of one thing, though. He had not tried to escape. One look at the man could reveal that simple truth to anyone. At one time, he may have been the big, hearty, outdoorsman, but after thirteen years in prison, most of them spent in solitary confinement, he'd become a weak, pathetic creature who could not run a fifty-yard dash if his life depended on it. Direct sunlight would probably shrivel him up, kill him as sure as it would a leech sprinkled with salt. It became apparent to me why he'd chosen young women (and if he killed Leonard Massar, a partially crippled man) as victims. They were all weaker, smaller than him, and in his mind, inferior. They were also, in his mind, indecent, tainted people, criminals that needed to be exterminated from the earth.

I was glad to be out of that prison with its tangerine-colored walls and echoes of steel-barred doors clanging shut. I'd managed to get away without signing any contract with Schaefer. I'd told him his best bet would be to tell me the whole story, the truth, if that were ever possible, and I would put whatever he had to say in this book, as I have. I told him if he could give me some hard evidence that would help shine some favorable light on his story, then the readers would determine if he was in fact innocent. I have included his defense, such as it is, in this book.

He did ask me to try to find out what evidence the Florida Department of Law Enforcement had concerning his "escape plot." I have tried and as yet no one has shown me anything that proves he was planning an escape and I sincerely believe he was not. Tom Roper at FDLE did not return my calls and if he had, I don't believe he could show me anything that would convince me of Schaefer's escape plans. I think Schaefer was, in truth, getting too much media attention and that by sending him back to Florida State Prison, they were able to keep him quiet. That is not to say I've believed any of his "theories."

He did mention a few more names of people supposedly in league with Robert Stone's alleged drug ring. These men were cell mates of Schaefer at one time and were alleged (by Schaefer) to have seen Robert Stone take payoff money to "look the other way" during a drug smuggling operation. Their names were Charles Long and George Traber.

Mr. Stone had been patient in my earliest interview with him, but grew more impatient and embittered with every new accusation Schaefer threw at him at that time, for over thirteen years. Stone would not let me tape our last interview, and at that time, he was obviously livid about the whole situation, saying that he was "sick and tired of all these damned accusations from this madman. Why was it the press would even listen to this deranged killer?"

When I called again to question him about some accusations that Schaefer had mentioned in our interview, he was not in his office, but Rick MacIlwain, the Assistant State Attorney, was. I asked MacIlwain what evidence was available about Schaefer's escape plot, and could he lend any credibility to Schaefer's allegations about Stone and McCain being "chummy" in the drug trade, and did he know anything about two men, Mr. Long and Mr. Traber, who Schaefer said had witnessed Stone accepting payoff money to "look the other way" during a drug smuggling operation. He said Schaefer had repeatedly tried to incriminate Mr. Stone with the drug trade, but Stone had been investigated by the FBI and had "come out clean." He said he would not talk to me anymore on the phone and perhaps I should talk to Mr. Stone personally, concerning any other matters. MacIlwain refused to comment any further.

I called back a few weeks later and was told that Robert Stone had resigned.

AFTERWORD

ONE LAST VICTIM

As the reader may have noticed, I began each chapter with quotes from some of Edgar Allan Poe's works. I did this for two reasons. One: Schaefer was a diehard fan of Poe's work. If Schaefer and I shared any likes at all, I will admit I, too, admire Poe's work. Two: Poe often wrote stories where the primary character was a mentally deranged killer who tried to convince the reader that he was perfectly sane; that there was a rational reason for him to murder or mutilate an acquaintance (i.e. "The Tell-Tale Heart" or "The Black Cat").The correlation with Poe's work and Schaefer's activities is, at least, fascinating.

Some readers may wonder why I did not use photographs of the killer, or victims, or crime scenes; there are many and I have access to them. The reason I chose not to include them was because I didn't want to cause the victim's families any more pain then they have already experienced. Additionally, I chose not to aggrandize Schaefer, to make him more important than he was, or would have liked to be. Killers like him to not deserve to be remembered for anything than that which they were: inexplicable, deranged criminals with fundamental deficiencies. I documented a case as factually as possible but do not wish to exploit the crimes any more than they have been over the years.

Before his death, Schaefer would continue to try to prove his innocence by accusing others of their "guilt." He would say that I am another of Robert Stone's "cronies." I am not. In fact, I am sure Mr. Stone will not be pleased with some of the details in this book, as many people will not be. No one, it seems, has come out untarnished in light of Schaefer's accusations, because even if those accusations were all the product of a devious, psychotic mind, they have been heard by the people, and people have a way of believing what they want to believe.

I would, like to apologize to all those people whose lives I've disrupted over the past many years I've taken to write this book, and to those whose lives will continue to be disrupted as a result of this book's information. I have tried to seek out the truth and write about it. That is all. I recorded information as it revealed itself to me and can only hope I've done the best job possible.

I would like to say it is over for me, but I know it is not. It seems it may never be, even after Schaefer's death. My own life has been disrupted and I hope one day it will return to some normalcy. I've spent many nights tossing in my bed, tortured by the nightmare images of mutilated bodies, some laying in cold brackish water, abandoned, decomposing and calling out my name with lipless mouths.

After all the research, I still wonder, what in hell makes someone like Gerard Schaefer, a seemingly normal young man, suddenly begin to see the dark images, or hear the ethereal voices that summon the beast within? Why haven't I, or any of us, gone into the night, hunting lonely people and slaying them with knife and gun, wreaking this blood law? If I could kill someone, what could provoke it? A deed? An expression? A scent of a certain perfume? What would trigger the demonic urge within me to first kill someone, then ghoulishly dismember them and deposit their body into a shallow grave? When you begin to think like that, you can scare yourself. For a while, I quit cooking. I did not like handling knives. I tried to comfort myself with the knowledge that that is the price writers must pay for their obsessive desire to write, whether it be fiction, or documentation of an event that may have otherwise been a passing newspaper story, overlooked by the more prominent headlines about—at that time—Watergate, or the decaying orbit of the Skylab in the early 1970's.

Many will wonder why I chose to spend these many years pursuing an otherwise obscure murder case. I can only answer this: It was important to me.I was the same age as Susan Place when this story broke into the news. I lived in Palm Beach County at that time and followed the case, from its beginning to its end. My initial attention to the story was a photo of Susan Place shown in the newspaper; a beautiful blonde girl in her white, satin graduation gown, the picture of hope and innocence. I was immediately interested in her story, then horrified as I read the details of her murder. She looked very much like a girl I was dating at that time, and I remember thinking how easily it might have been my girlfriend who'd been murdered, and how terrible the loss would be for me, as it must have been for the Place family. I prayed for Susan Place and Georgia Jessup, and my own girlfriend that night.

I had, at seventeen, been exposed to something so terrifying and unreal, I could only wonder why God, or evolution, put people like Gerard Schaefer on earth, and it would forever alter my perceptions of humanity thereafter. If you could not trust a policeman, who then could you trust? I went on to college and finished my schooling, but the memory of that case lingered in my mind, and schools do not teach you to deal with such atrocities; experience does, but only sometimes.

I've had many terrifying experiences as a fire fighter. Life and death decisions that had to be made in seconds. Witnessing atrocities of cruelty from domestic and criminal offenders: a two-year old girl, raped and beaten to death with a baseball bat by her ten-year brother and a man doused in gasoline and set afire during a pawn shop robbery by a fifteen-year old boy. There were too many of these unspeakable events in my career and they haunt me, too.

But as a youth, I'd been relatively shielded from the terror of humanity's worse hatchlings. I'd had only three other experiences that horrified me almost as much as a boy. The assassinations of first President Kennedy and then his brother Bobby a few years later. I was unfortunate enough to be watching the television, and to have witnessed those news films that so clearly depicted their murders and as a child, it bothered me greatly to see that even people in important positions were not immune to violence.

The third experience was on my last candy-seeking Halloween, a night associated with dark elements. I was thirteen and knowing I was getting too big to shove through the horde of little witches and vampires, I resolved that it would be the last year I went trick-or-treating. I headed for home that night, carrying a pillowcase filled halfway with assorted candies. I'd stayed out late to reap as much tooth-decaying treats as I could, and I'd done so well I carried the heavy sack wrapped three times around my fist and slung over my shoulder.

I never saw what hit me, but as I was being dragged down the street by the thing that now had my candy sack under its arm and me in tow, I remember thinking of how totally helpless I was. Finally, after most of my body, and particularly my knees and tops of my feet, were covered with painful, bleeding "road rash" (abrasions and cuts), I released the sack. I watched the Sasquatch-like creature disappear into one of the nearby houses, then I hobbled home and called the police. They took me to the house, and I found the perpetrator was a huge, illiterate, unemployed woman with a half-dozen kids, now assembled in a semicircle, eating the fruits of my labors. Their faces were smeared with dirt and candy coloring, and they looked frightened, probably by the police. The woman denied having been out of the house. I looked at her one last time, saw the desperation in her eyes, and told the police I must've picked the wrong home. The ogre-woman smiled at me, revealing a toothless grin, and the police put me in their car and took me home.

But by seventeen, when I already thought I'd seen it all, the Place/Jessup murders occurred and it was all too close to home. I knew how helpless they must have felt just before they were murdered; as helpless as I felt as I was pulled effortlessly down the road by the candy glutton. I knew then that we all are mortal and could die at any time; a tough concept for a seventeen-year-old to grasp and underscored years later, when I became a fire fighter and witnessed the many other horrible things people do to each other.

Many people have asked what it is that I believe, since I've seen and heard all of what has been said by both sides of this case. I believe that Gerard Schaefer did kill Susan Place and Georgia Jessup, and at least nine other people I've pointed out in "The Victims" chapter of this book. I don't believe he killed all the others on the "List of 28," but that it is possible he killed many more of which we have no knowledge. I also believe his trial was in error; he should have been indicted by a grand jury before his trial, and if found guilty, then sentenced to death. I believe he should have been re-tried, then also tried for the Briscolina/Farmer murders, and the Goodenough-Wilcox murders. There is overwhelming evidence against him in both of those cases, and it is truly a crime that our judicial system in its self-appointed wisdom has chosen not to pursue the prosecution of those cases.

Additionally, I believe the federal government should keep its vigilant eye on the Florida

Keys and the Miami area for incoming drugs, but they ought to let that eye roam up the coast, to the Martin and St. Lucie County area, too. This is not to imply that I believe the authorities in the 19th Judicial Circuit of Florida were, or are, crooked, but that possibly they could use a hand from federal agents in patrolling a huge area that is largely, and mistakenly, overlooked as a popular incoming drug drop-off spot. In my investigation in that area, I heard too many stories about what goes on up there in the night.

I also believe that this project has made me more than a little paranoid. While the yellow Corvette that I believed followed me around town for months, was probably just coincidence, the many phone calls that simply hung up when I answered, or the bullet I found stuck in the bed-liner of my pickup truck led me to be at least a little wary of where I traveled and with whom I talked. Coming home and finding my office trashed one day didn't help, either.

I also believe that if you have nothing to hide, then you shouldn't act like you do. I say this because the prison officials made it extremely difficult for me to see Gerard Schaefer and wasted almost two years of my time with bullshit, red tape, and rhetoric before letting me in to see him.

Finally, I regret the relationships that have been ruined, and I'll try to rejoice the many that have been formed with people, either directly or indirectly, involved with this project. Also, I regret that the truth will be painful, perhaps again, perhaps for the first time, to people connected with this case. It is an inescapable fact that when dealing with law and murder, the truth will always hurt someone.

* * *

This is where this book should have ended when I first wrote it many years ago. At that time, in the late 80's, I'd found a publisher who wanted to publish the Schaefer book. But it took a long time for me to get the manuscript close to what I thought was finished. That publisher went out of business and while I sold some articles about the Schaefer case, I did not find another publisher interested in a story that was, by then, over a decade old. But I kept at it when I could. I felt I still had to find some truth to the story that hadn't been told and, moreover, try to solve some of the murders that law enforcement failed to solve, primarily because the suspect was already jailed and there was little to no pressure to continue to investigate cases. The articles that were published served to irritate Schaefer and solidify I was still writing a book on factually investigative information and not on his conjectures or fantastical versions of his case.

There were many additional pieces of information to include and, to this day, I still receive information about unsolved murders, or queries from law enforcement departments or people who want more information about someone they used to know, who is still missing. Along the way, I continued to write and publish some stories for newspapers as well as fictional short stories for various publications. The Schaefer manuscript was placed in a desk drawer and I no longer corresponded with Schaefer, which also irritated him. I ignored his taunts and focused on other projects and my fire fighter career.

Then there was the lawsuit. In 1993, I was contacted by a "student journalist" who said he was writing a story about Gerard Schaefer. He'd "heard" I was a person who could be a resource for him. Since then, I've learned this "college student" was a ruse by Schaefer to get me to say something in writing so he could sue me. The "student" said he wanted to meet with him, needed to know how I was able to get into prison to interview him, but was also intimidated by a killer "who was deadliest killer ever and believed to be worse than Ted Bundy..." Weary of the story, and Schaefer, I wrote back and said, "There's no reason to be intimidated. Schaefer is now a middle-aged, pale and doughy wimp, who prayed on victims that were physically and psychologically weaker than him...."

Within weeks, I was served a summons to appear in court for a lawsuit for libel that was launched by Schaefer. He was seeking a $500,000 judgement. Initially, I thought it was a joke. I knew a lot of fire fighters and cops and it was not above many of them to pull a prank like this. I was still a newlywed, had guests at my house who were there when I received the summons. I even asked the deputy who served the summons if it was a joke. He assured me it was not. My guests and I laughed about it, but my wife did not. She'd been working as a paralegal with a law firm and after I announced I would just ignore it because, "a serial killer who'd been imprisoned for a decade couldn't really sue me, right?" My wife assured me he could. At her urging, I hired an attorney.

The attorney I hired had no experience with libel lawsuits or literary works. No one in the area did. But that did not keep him from charging me for services as he learned how to defend a libel suit. Within two months, I had paid him over $6000, then more. When I asked why so much, he said he had "to learn how to defend a libel suit." I fired him and hired another attorney, who was married to a fire fighter I knew. She agreed to a set price no matter how long the lawsuit case might take. She was good to her word and defended me adequately. In all, I paid over $12,000 for the combined attorney fees, money that my wife and I were going to use to buy a new house. That wasn't a great way to start a married life.

I reached out to every politician in Florida to see how we could change laws that would prevent a deranged killer from being such a nuisance to working, tax-paying citizens. I also asked if there was a way in which Schaefer could be retried, this time properly, by indictment, and with a grand jury wherein the death penalty—now reinstated in Florida—could be sought. Governor Lawton Chiles, and Senator Bob Graham as well as many others answered my letters and were sympathetic to my pleas, but in the end stated the law allowed everyone to have the right to sue another person, even if it were frivolous, even if they were a convicted serial killer.

The case was settled, without me having to pay Schaefer anything. He wanted my manuscript. We settled for the one chapter that revealed exactly who the victims were, which ones showed evidence that he most likely killed them, and which ones my investigation revealed he did not, could not, have killed. That was what he was really after. In the end I had no reason to conceal that information as I still intended to publish the book and it would be public knowledge.

Despite the case being settled "with prejudice," which meant that Schaefer could no longer sue me, he sued me again. And again. If he were a civilian, I could've counter-sued him and won the suit, but as a prisoner, what could I gain from a man who had no money or assets? It would only cost me more attorney fees. The subsequent lawsuits were thrown out due to the findings of the first lawsuit but the entire ordeal of dealing with his lawsuits and the courts went on for about two years. When Schaefer began sending threatening letters to my home saying, "I know you are married now and I'd hate to see anything happen to your wife and family...I have many followers who are willing to do my bidding...," my wife had had enough. She asked me to stop working on the book and to never publish it. I complied.

Within months of this promise, Schaefer was murdered in jail. Evidently, his cell door was left ajar and he was murdered in a fashion that befitted his crimes by a prisoner named Vincent Rivera, who was serving a life sentence. He was stabbed multiple times, his eyes gouged out. Even people skeptical of karma would have to admit, the killer had gotten his just due. The motive was unclear and Rivera did not confess to the crime but it was well known in prison that Schaefer was a snitch. He often offered to give information to prison authorities in exchange for time off from his sentence—which never happened—or a better cell, conditions, writing supplies, even food. Serial killers do not blend into general prison populations, nor do former police officers, nor child murderers, and Schaefer was a morbid mix of all of these. It might have been a badge of honor, if you will, for Rivera to kill such a prisoner as Schaefer. In the end, Rivera had fifty-three years added to his sentence for Schaefer's murder.

For many years, I held to my promise not to finish nor publish this book, but as I became successful as a novelist, the information I'd learned from the Schaefer case invariably made its way into my fiction work. People would ask, "How can you think of the things you write, it's so demented." I would tell them, "Most of what I write about is based on true crimes, the names are changed and sometimes locations, but they are not made up." I think that confession probably scares people more than my fictional books.

Additionally, I still hear from people who ask if I have discovered any new information on one victim or another. I typically tell them what I know, as well as inform them that no matter what we find, Schaefer is dead and other than some police departments trying to clear cold cases from their files, there are no present investigations.

That said, going through some of the letters Schaefer sent me, I found a part where he argued with me about the numbers of murders he was accused of, which numbered anywhere from the original number of 28, formulated by State Attorney Robert Stone, to estimates that seemed to keep climbing, often initiated by Schaefer, to a number in excess of 80 killed.

He wrote, "...let's not forget about the Jenkins sisters...." As they were not on Stone's original list of 28, I did not research their murders when I initially wrote this book. But, as I went back in to finish the manuscript, I came across the letter and, once again, could not sleep wondering about why he'd mentioned them and who they were.

With a tool I had not possessed when I began the research for this book in the 1980's—the internet—I found a newspaper article from 2012 about the murdered Jenkins sisters, Mary, 16, and Maggie,18 who were found in Monroe County, Florida. Both had been sexually assaulted and murdered and left in the woods. They'd been hitchhiking back to their home in New Jersey from Key West in 1973. The article stated that police had the killer's DNA and though it was somewhat deteriorated, it was possible they might be able to use it to help identify the killer. I contacted the Monroe County Sheriff's office to tell them I had Schaefer's DNA on the letters he licked and sent to me, but the detective who handled cold cases had retired and I did not hear back right away. After a couple of weeks though, I got a call from Lieutenant James Norman, a Monroe County Sheriff Deputy who had taken over the cold cases. He told me I had kept him busy for the past couple of weeks.

Lt. Norman told me they did not need my letters or DNA samples. The Florida Department of Law Enforcement began the practice of keeping serial killer's DNA as far back as the 1970's though it's practical use in crime scene analysis was still not as refined as today. They compared Schaefer's DNA and it did not match. But new DNA had been submitted to the state and as he investigated further, he found it might belong to another serial killer, and now he was going to meet him at a prison in Texas for an interview and to ask about the Jenkins sisters. It seems this killer drew pictures of his victims and some of the pictures held likenesses to the murdered sisters.

I ask myself: will it ever end? Then, I answer my own question-will it ever end for the families who lost their loved ones to Schaefer or some other monster, one we may not have identified yet? No, it will not. Even as I submitted my manuscript to my publisher, I was contacted by the sister of another one of Schaefer's proposed victims, one that was never found but whose family Schaefer once worked for. I'm looking into that one now.

I've paid dues for working on this book beyond financial ones. In addition to the sheer physical work of a once young man tracking down details at a time when it was very difficult and uncomfortable to do, I've become part of the drama I'd just as soon have not played. It has cost me greatly and, along with my other traumatic work in the fire service, has plagued me with things seen that will never leave my mind. Going through this manuscript, even these many years later, has not eased that, and I have to ask why did I write it, and why has it stuck with me, existential questions that may never be answered.

I always come back to believing I wanted to say something for those poor girls who were killed by a monster who was as evil as anything that ever lived. Most times, to be honest, I've hated doing this book because there is no happy ending. But after reading it again, I still find it as horrendous—and compelling—as when I first heard of the case. Simply, it is a story that needs to be told if for no other reason than to caution people that this type of killer does exist. We must always be wary, vigilant, and keep our loved ones close.

Parents should always know where their children are, whatever their age. They should know their schedule and what they wore going out the door. It is often a recognizable piece of clothing that helps locate the children, hopefully while they're still alive. When my children were young, I used to insist they wear recognizable, often similar, clothes when we went to public events. Superhero shirts, or something one could easily describe to the police. There are location apps readily available for phones and your child should have his or her own phone that shows exactly where they are.

I recall I got lost at the county fair when I was four years old, and a man found me alone some distance away. He returned me safely to the fair, but I could not spell my last name at that age. A public announcement went over the fair's speakers describing a lost boy wearing a bright red shirt, named Pat. My mother, soaked in tears, retrieved me from the lost and found booth but this event could have gone very differently if another type of man had found me.

I think, too, about the time I sat with Susan Place's parents those many years ago, the quiet between questions asked as palpable as a pressure chamber as I awaited their answers, and I still feel that pain as if it were yesterday. I feel I know their terror, especially after having my own kids, and maybe this is a way I can exorcise that horror, for all of us, of this enigma, this monster in the closet.

END

We hope you enjoyed Patrick Kendrick's *American Ripper: The Enigma Of America's Killer Cop,* Gold winner of Published Book-Length Nonfiction, Published Biography, in the Royal Palm Literary Awards. May we also suggest his other books as featured at the beginning of this book. For his titles published through BluewaterPress LLC, as well as our other offerings, please visit us online at www.bluewaterpress.com.

Lightning Source UK Ltd.
Milton Keynes UK
UKHW040623310822
408116UK00001B/4